LOUIS COMFORT TIFFANY
AND LAURELTON HALL

LOUIS COMFORT TIFFANY AND LAURELTON HALL

AN ARTIST'S COUNTRY ESTATE

Alice Cooney Frelinghuysen

With contributions by Elizabeth Hutchinson, Julia Meech, Jennifer Perry Thalheimer, Barbara Veith, and Richard Guy Wilson

The Metropolitan Museum of Art, New York

Yale University Press, New Haven and London

This publication accompanies the exhibition "Louis Comfort Tiffany and Laurelton Hall—
An Artist's Country Estate," held at The Metropolitan Museum of Art, New York,
November 21, 2006–May 20, 2007.

The exhibition is made possible by The Tiffany & Co. Foundation.

Additional support is provided by the Gail and Parker Gilbert Fund.

The exhibition was organized by The Metropolitan Museum of Art, New York, in collaboration with
The Charles Hosmer Morse Museum of American Art, Winter Park, Florida.

Published by The Metropolitan Museum of Art, New York

John P. O'Neill, Editor in Chief
Gwen Roginsky, Associate General Manager of Publications
Margaret Rennolds Chace, Managing Editor
Margaret Aspinwall, Jane Bobko, Sue Potter, Editors
Bruce Campbell, Designer
Gwen Roginsky and Paula Torres, Production Managers
Robert Weisberg, Assistant Managing Editor
Kathryn Ansite, Desktop Publishing Specialist
Philomena Mariani, Bibliographic Editor

New photography of works in the Metropolitan Museum and Morse Museum collections, in other
public as well as private collections, and of the Laurelton Hall site by Joseph Coscia, Jr., Chief
Photographer, the Photograph Studio, The Metropolitan Museum of Art. A complete list of photograph credits is printed at the back of this volume.

Typeset in Adobe Fournier MT and Letraset Carlton
Printed on 130 gsm R-400
Separations by Professional Graphics, Inc., Rockford, Illinois
Printed and bound by Mondadori Printing S.p.A., Verona, Italy

Jacket/cover illustration: Louis Comfort Tiffany, Tiffany Studios, *Wisteria* panel (detail),
ca. 1910–20 (fig. 150)

Frontispiece: Joaquín Sorolla y Bastida, *Louis Comfort Tiffany*, 1911 (fig. 129)

Library of Congress Cataloging-in-Publication Data

Frelinghuysen, Alice Cooney.
   Louis Comfort Tiffany and Laurelton Hall : an artist's country estate / Alice Cooney
Frelinghuysen ; with contributions by Elizabeth Hutchinson . . . [et al.].
      p.   cm.
   Catalog to an exhibition at the Metropolitan Museum of Art, New York, held Nov. 21, 2006–
May 20, 2007.
   Includes bibliographical references and index.
   ISBN 1-58839-201-5 (Metropolitan Museum of Art : hardcover)—ISBN 1-58839-202-3
(Metropolitan Museum of Art : pbk.)—ISBN 0-300-11787-6 (Yale University Press : hardcover)
   1. Tiffany, Louis Comfort, 1848–1933—Homes and haunts—New York (State)—Oyster Bay—
Exhibitions. 2. Tiffany, Louis Comfort, 1848–1933—Art collections—Exhibitions. 3. Laurelton
Hall (Oyster Bay, N.Y.)—Exhibitions. I. Hutchinson, Elizabeth. II. Metropolitan Museum of Art
(New York, N.Y.) III. Title.
   N6537.T5F74 2006
   709.2—dc22   2006026597

Contents

Sponsor's Statement

The Tiffany & Co. Foundation is honored to sponsor the exhibition "Louis Comfort Tiffany and Laurelton Hall—An Artist's Country Estate." The Foundation thanks The Metropolitan Museum of Art for conceiving an exhibition that illuminates Louis Comfort Tiffany's multifaceted talent through the designs and furnishings he created for his extraordinary final country home and its gardens.

Louis Comfort Tiffany (1848–1933) was the son of Charles Lewis Tiffany, a founder of Tiffany & Co., the New York City jewelry and fancy-goods store, and one of America's most successful luxury-goods merchants. The younger Tiffany pursued an artistic career. While still in his twenties he developed his talent as a painter, and he eventually turned his creative energies to the design and manufacture of jewelry and decorative art objects as well as to interior design. His renowned work in stained glass later informed and inspired the palette of vividly colored and unusual gems with which he produced some of the most imaginative jewels and objects of the twentieth century. Many of these designs were created during his tenure as design director of Tiffany & Co.

The key themes of Tiffany's art—nature, in its intrinsically beautiful state, and the exoticism of ancient Egypt, Byzantium, and the Islamic world—are represented in the unique studios and residences he designed for himself, beginning in the late 1860s.

Tiffany believed that his designs and luminous masterworks, specifically his work in glass and his vibrant gemstone and enamel jewelry depicting myriad natural forms, restored the human spirit and sustained the soul. The exhibition admirably supports this belief. The works on view, some of the twentieth century's most powerful artistic expressions, move and uplift us still.

Since its inception in 1837, Tiffany & Co. has been guided by the belief that a successful corporation has a responsibility to the greater community. Through The Tiffany & Co. Foundation, established in 2000, the company has broadened the scope of its corporate giving efforts with grants to nonprofit organizations dedicated to arts education, the preservation of the arts, and environmental conservation.

Fernanda M. Kellogg
President
The Tiffany & Co. Foundation

Director's Foreword

The Metropolitan Museum is fortunate to have an extraordinarily comprehensive collection of the work of Louis Comfort Tiffany (1848–1933), one of the most celebrated American artists of the late nineteenth and early twentieth centuries. The Museum's first acquisitions of Tiffany's work date from 1896, when Henry Osborne Havemeyer (who with his wife, Louisine, was an enthusiastic patron both of Tiffany and of the Metropolitan Museum), donated fifty-six vases and roundels—the first examples of American glass of any kind to enter the Museum's collection. Another significant early gift originated with Tiffany himself. In 1925, to enhance the Havemeyer gift, the artist lent the Museum examples, from his personal collection, of his blown glass, enamelwork, and pottery; after his death, these works were donated to the Museum by the Louis Comfort Tiffany Foundation, which the artist had founded in 1918. Today, the Museum's holdings represent almost every medium of the many in which Tiffany worked—windows, mosaics, lamps, blown-glass vases, enamels, ceramics, jewelry, paintings, and drawings. In 2003 the Museum installed a generous selection from the collection in the Deedee Wigmore Gallery of the Arts of Louis C. Tiffany, putting the full range of Tiffany's work on view in a single space.

The loggia from Laurelton Hall, Tiffany's grand country estate in Oyster Bay, Long Island, has been among the glories of The American Wing's Charles Engelhard Court since its opening in 1980. Its faceted limestone columns and glass-and-pottery floral capitals support corbels faced with vibrant mosaics in blue and yellow. When Laurelton Hall was destroyed by a fire in 1957, the twenty-one-foot-high loggia was among the architectural elements and furnishings salvaged from the ruins by Hugh F. McKean, a former artist-in-residence at Laurelton Hall, and his wife, Jeannette Genius McKean. In 1978, after the Metropolitan had begun construction of a new American Wing, with a dramatic garden court, the McKeans generously donated the loggia to the Museum, in memory of Jeannette's grandfather Charles Hosmer Morse. Everything else the McKeans had saved was given to the Charles Hosmer Morse Museum of American Art, in Winter Park, Florida, which Jeannette McKean had founded in 1942.

It can be argued that Laurelton Hall, completed in 1905, was Tiffany's greatest achievement. He designed every aspect of the immense residence, as well as the grounds into which the house was consciously integrated; he filled the house with vast collections of his own work and of Islamic, Asian, and Native American art; he established a program that allowed young artists to be in residence at Laurelton. This exhibition and its accompanying publication examine these facets of Laurelton Hall and its evolution, offering insight into Tiffany's interior designs, architectural achievements, passionate collecting, and artistic vision. They also announce noteworthy discoveries. Many of the artworks from Laurelton Hall were auctioned in 1946, and for the most part their whereabouts since has been unknown. Several works thought lost have recently been located, however. We hope that, spurred by this exhibition, more will come to light.

The exhibition was conceived and developed by Alice Cooney Frelinghuysen, Anthony W. and Lulu C. Wang Curator of American Decorative Arts at the Metropolitan Museum, and organized by the Metropolitan in collaboration with the Morse Museum. Approximately half the objects and architectural elements in the exhibition have been lent by the Morse Museum, which expressly for this exhibition embarked on the ambitious and costly project of conserving and reconstructing two significant works in its care. We express our profound gratitude to the trustees of the Morse Museum and its director, Laurence J. Ruggiero. Without their contribution, the exhibition would not have been possible.

The Metropolitan Museum is indebted as well to the private collectors and other institutions that have lent their prized works to the exhibition. We offer special thanks for their participation and support.

Enormous gratitude is owed to the distinguished scholars who have contributed to this publication: Alice Cooney Frelinghuysen, Elizabeth Hutchinson, Julia Meech, Jennifer Perry Thalheimer, Barbara Veith, and Richard Guy Wilson. We also recognize Joseph Coscia, Jr., Chief Photographer at the Metropolitan Museum. His magnificent color photographs of objects from the Metropolitan and Morse museums, as well as other collections both public and private, and of the Laurelton Hall site today are an invaluable contribution to this publication.

We extend our deep appreciation to The Tiffany & Co. Foundation for its generosity in making this complex exhibition a reality. Tiffany & Co. is a longstanding supporter of the Museum, and we gratefully acknowledge its contributions to this project. Thanks for support of the exhibition are also owed to the Gail and Parker Gilbert Fund. Critical support for this publication was provided by the William Cullen Bryant Fellows of The American Wing.

Philippe de Montebello
Director
The Metropolitan Museum of Art

Acknowledgments

In the summer of 1982 I made my first visit to the site of Laurelton Hall, at the instigation of Lillian Nassau, a pioneer dealer in the work of Louis Comfort Tiffany. The visit was arranged by Joseph Ryan, the son of Tiffany's chauffeur. That trip, at the beginning of my career and in the company of the eminence grise in the field, kindled in me an interest in Tiffany's extraordinary country estate that continues to this day. I am grateful to them for that memorable introduction. I also had the good fortune to know Hugh F. McKean, a former artist-in-residence at Laurelton Hall and, later, president of Rollins College, and his wife, Jeannette Genius McKean, of Winter Park, Florida. When Laurelton Hall burned down in 1957, they took action to save whatever could be salvaged. Without their foresight and devotion to Tiffany's work, we would not have been able to mount the exhibition this publication accompanies. Their passion for Tiffany was infectious, and their warm hospitality to me on numerous visits to Winter Park was genuine and heartfelt. I wish they were alive today to witness this celebration of Laurelton Hall. In more recent years Robert B. MacKay, Director, Society for the Preservation of Long Island Antiquities, continued to bring aspects of Laurelton Hall to my attention and guided me on my visits through the labyrinthine roads of Oyster Bay. I have benefited from conversations with him and with Richard Guy Wilson, Professor of Architectural History at the University of Virginia, about publishing a volume devoted to Laurelton Hall.

A book and exhibition of this scope can be achieved only with the help of a wide range of supporters. Countless individuals offered their expertise, cooperation, assistance, and good wishes, and I give heartfelt thanks to everyone who has taken part. At the Metropolitan Museum, Philippe de Montebello, Director, recognized immediately the importance of pursuing this project, and he has supported it throughout. I am grateful to him and to the Trustees of the Metropolitan for backing this undertaking. Marukh Tarapor, Associate Director for Exhibitions, Doralynn Pines, Associate Director for Administration, and Martha Deese, Senior Administrator for Exhibitions and International Affairs, have also shown enthusiasm for the exhibition and have helped in many ways. Emily Kernan Rafferty, President, with Nina McN. Diefenbach, Vice President for Development and Membership, and Andrea Kann, Deputy Chief Development Officer for Corporate Programs, helped to secure critical sponsorship from The Tiffany & Co. Foundation. Other members of the development staff have been an essential part of the planning of opening events, particularly Claire E. Gylphé. In addition, Sharon Cott, Senior Vice President, Secretary and General Counsel, Rebecca L. Murray, Associate

Counsel, and Jeffrey N. Blair, Assistant Counsel; Missy McHugh, Chief Advisor to the President; Suzanne Rubin Schein, Amanda Maloney, and Heather Woodworth in the Director's office; Christina Black, Chief Planning and Budget Officer; Suzanne L. Shenton, General Manager, and her predecessor, Kathleen Arffman, in Visitor Services; Sean Simpson, Security; and Amsi Tadesse, Controller, all provided assistance in their areas of expertise.

I am especially grateful for the considerable assistance of my four coauthors from outside the Metropolitan: Elizabeth Hutchinson, Julia Meech, Jennifer Perry Thalheimer, and Richard Guy Wilson. They not only contributed important new insights into Tiffany's designs, collecting, and educational foundation; they also generously shared their knowledge and gave advice regarding the selection of works for the exhibition.

I would like to give special thanks to the lenders to the exhibition. Although institutional lenders are listed separately elsewhere, I wish to acknowledge the various contributions by their staffs, who agreed to part with works of art that in some cases have been prominently displayed. They have graciously agreed to disrupt the installation of their collections in order to send their pieces to the Metropolitan for more than six months. Their staffs have been especially helpful in shepherding loans, dealing with travel arrangements, and accommodating special photography. For their time and effort on behalf of this project I thank Peter Whiteley, Curator of North American Ethnology, and Kristen Mable, Registrar, Archives and Loans, Collections Management, at the American Museum of Natural History, New York; Peter F. Blume, Director, and Ruta Saliklis, Associate Director, Ball State University Museum of Art; Doreen Bolger, Director, Jay Fisher, Deputy Director for Curatorial Affairs, David Park Curry, Curator of American Art, Sona Johnston, Senior Curator, Painting and Sculpture, Melanie Harwood, Senior Registrar, Anthony Boening, Installations, Sarah Sellers, Associate Registrar, and Michael Scott, Coordinator of Rights and Reproductions, at The Baltimore Museum of Art; Arnold Lehman, Director, Susan Kennedy Zeller, Assistant Curator, Arts of the Americas, Kevin Stayton, Chief Curator and Vice Director for Curatorial Affairs, Barry R. Harwood, Curator, Decorative Arts, Nancy Rosoff, Andrew W. Mellon Curator and Chair, Arts of the Americas, Charles Desmarais, Deputy Director for Art, and Elisa Flynn, Assistant Registrar for Domestic Loans, at the Brooklyn Museum; Walt Tressler, Corporate Services Manager, and Ellen Denker, Archivist, for Lenox, Incorporated, a Division of Brown-Forman Corporation; Kristin C. Law, Curator of Collections, The Hermitage Foundation Museum and Gardens, Norfolk, Virginia;

Mitchell A. Codding, Director, Marcus B. Burke, Curator, Paintings, Drawings, and Metalwork, and Lisa A. Banner, Curatorial Associate, The Hispanic Society of America, New York; John Murdoch, Director, Art Collections, Jessica Todd Smith, Curator of American Art, Jacqueline Dugas, Registrar, and Joyce Liu, Assistant to the Director of Art Collections, The Huntington Art Collections, San Marino, California; Michael Govan, Director and Chief Executive Officer, Andrea Rich, former President and Director, Wendy Kaplan, Department Head and Curator, Decorative Arts, Nancy Thomas, Deputy Director, Art Administration and Collections, Michele Ahern, Assistant Registrar–Outgoing Loans, and Cheryle Robertson, Rights and Reproductions Department, Los Angeles County Museum of Art; John Vincent Boyer, formerly Executive Director, Debra Petke, Deputy Director, Beatrice Fox Auerbach, Chief Curator, Patti Philippon, Collections Manager, and Margaret O. Moore, formerly Archivist, The Mark Twain House and Museum, Hartford, Connecticut; Malcolm Rogers, Director, Elliot Bostwick Davis, John Moors Cabot Chair, Art of the Americas, Nonie Gadsden, Carolyn and Peter Lynch Assistant Curator of American Decorative Arts and Sculpture, Art of the Americas, and Kim Pashko, Registrar for Loans from the Collections, Museum of Fine Arts, Boston; Susan Henshaw Jones, President and Director, and Phyllis Magidson, Curator of Costume and Textiles, Museum of the City of New York; Eric Satrum, Assistant Registrar, and Kristine McGee, Archivist, National Museum of the American Indian; Stephan Jost, Director, Jean Burks, Senior Curator, and Barbara Rathburn, Associate Registrar, Shelburne Museum; Robert MacKay, Director, Society for the Preservation of Long Island Antiquities; Annamarie V. Sandecki, Director, Louisa Bann, Manager, Research Services, and Meghan Magee, Manager of Collections/Registrar, Tiffany & Co. Archives; Jock Reynolds, Director, Helen Cooper, Curator of American Painting, Patricia Kane, Friends of American Arts Curator of American Decorative Arts, Robin Jaffee Frank, Associate Curator, American Paintings and Sculpture, Vicki Cain, Senior Administrative Assistant II, Registrar's Office, and Suzanne Warner, Rights and Reproductions, at the Yale University Art Gallery.

An exceptional debt is owed to those private collectors who care for and cherish their works of art and yet are willing to part with them for a period of time in order to share them with the public. For their sacrifices and confidence I thank Mr. and Mrs. Werner Baehler, Mr. and Mrs. Walter H. Buck, as well as David Parker and Beth Perkins, who facilitated the loan, Ralph T. Coe, David Gilder, Joshua Gilder, Mrs. Rodman Gilder, Julia Hartman, Nadia Hartman, Steven Hartman, Florence and Herbert Irving, Mr. and Mrs. Hans König, A. Amasa Miller, Dr. Rodman Miller, Virginia Ann Miller, Mrs. Timothy Schmiderer, Mr. and Mrs. Kenneth Siebel, Roy Stillman, Eric Streiner, Mr. and Mrs. Anthony Terranova, Mr. and Mrs. Erving Wolf, and Mrs. T. Eugene Worrell and the late Eugene Worrell, with James Godfrey and Judy Coleman.

A special thanks goes to the staff and Trustees of The Charles Hosmer Morse Museum of American Art, in Winter Park, Florida, for their embrace of this ambitious undertaking. They endured numerous visits that disrupted the normal flow of their days. Laurence J. Ruggiero, Director, was especially encouraging, recognizing that a major exhibition on Laurelton Hall would be an enduring contribution to the study of Tiffany's oeuvre. The Trustees of the Morse Museum and Foundation wholeheartedly endorsed the project. I thank especially Harold A. Ward III, President, Ann Morgan Saurman, and Leila E. Trismen. Jennifer Perry Thalheimer, Collections Manager, who has lived and breathed Tiffany for much of her career and for whom no question was too big or small, has been an invaluable partner. I also thank April Brown, Catherine Hinman, Dave McDaniels, Grace Mazanek, and Bonnie Jackson, all of whom have contributed to the exhibition in innumerable ways.

At the Metropolitan, countless colleagues have contributed to both the exhibition and the production of the book. I am grateful to Morrison H. Heckscher, Lawrence A. Fleischman Chairman of The American Wing, for his encouragement and understanding during the years in which this exhibition has taken shape. Many thanks are due to my curatorial colleagues in The American Wing. H. Barbara Weinberg, Peter M. Kenny, Amelia Peck, and Beth Carver Wees offered their own wealth of experience and were always available to discuss and weigh ideas. Kevin J. Avery, Carrie Rebora Barratt, Frances Gruber Safford, and Thayer Tolles gave sympathetic encouragement along the way. Elaine Bradson, Associate for Administration, and Administrative Assistants, past and present, Karen Zimmerman, Nathan Vincent, Jeanne Ko, and especially Nadia Hartman performed essential tasks of all kinds. Our departmental technicians, Don E. Templeton, Sean Farrell, Rob Davis, Dennis Kaiser, and the late Gary Burnett, provided their usual exceptional assistance during both the exhibition's installation and a long period of preparation when many of the objects included in the show were being conserved, studied, and photographed. I am grateful as well to staff members Frances F. Bretter, Shauna Doyle, Medill Higgins Harvey, Ellin Rosenzweig, Cynthia Schaffner, Barbara Whalen, and Lori Zabar for their interest in the project. The Laurelton Hall exhibition proved to be a training ground for numerous interns in the Department of American Decorative Arts during the five years from its inception until its opening. I was immeasurably helped by their intelligence, hard work, and good nature. I thank Daniel Ackerman, Kristin Bayans, Alexandra Bowes-Lyon, Mary Catelet, John Gordon, Michele Kahn, Leslie Sykes-O'Neill, Jennie Tarr, and Lisa Wang. Many are now pursuing their own professional careers and I take pleasure in the knowledge that this project gave them a foothold.

Because Tiffany had wide-ranging collecting interests, a number of curators from other departments at the Metropolitan offered their expertise and made available for the exhibition loans of works that related to Tiffany's own. I thank especially, in the Department of Asian Art, James C. Y. Watt, Brooke Russell Astor Chairman, Denise P. Leidy, Barbara Ford, Joyce Denney, Hwailing Yeh-Lewis, and Kendal Parker; in the Department of Arms and Armor, Stuart W. Pyhrr, Arthur Ochs Sulzberger Curator in Charge, Morihiro Ogawa, Donald J. LaRocca, and Hermes Knauer; in the Costume Institute, Harold Koda, Curator in Charge, and Jessica Krick, former Collections Assistant; in the Department of Islamic Art, Stefano Carboni, Navina Haidar Haykel, and Paola Chadwick; in the Department of the Arts of Africa, Oceania, and the Americas, Julie Jones, Curator in Charge, and Hillit Zwick; in the Department of Drawings and Prints, Constance McPhee; and in the Department of Photographs, Jeff L. Rosenheim.

Since the fire at Laurelton Hall damaged many of the architectural elements and other works that were salvaged, this exhibition has provided innumerable conservation challenges. Without the insights, observations, and technical expertise of the Metropolitan's superb conservators, many of the pieces in the exhibition would not look the way they do today. I am especially thankful to Marijn Manuels, Yale Kneeland, Nancy Britton, Linda Borsch, Lisa Pilosi, and Drew Anderson, in the Department of Objects Conservation, who joined me in making initial assessments of the condition of the pieces at the Morse Museum. Marijn Manuels was instrumental in the examination of the dining-room furniture from the Seventy-second Street house and Laurelton Hall, which aided in the identification of original paint colors and finishes. Nancy Britton took the lead in the project to replicate the original upholstery for the dining-room furniture at Laurelton. Lisa Pilosi and Drew Anderson each performed critical work on individual glass items, Lisa on the tall vase from the Fountain Court, and Drew on the *Magnolia* panels and the Metropolitan's window from the Bella apartment. Ann Baldwin in Paper Conservation sensitively treated the drawings of the flowers from the capitals of the loggia at Laurelton Hall. Christine Paulocik, with Jessica Regan of the Costume Institute, adroitly stabilized the feathered peacock headdress. Elena Phipps in Textile Conservation was instrumental in mounting the Native American materials for the exhibition. I also wish to thank Dorothy Mahon in Paintings Conservation for her careful examination of the paintings in the exhibition and for her advice on the conservation of the stenciled wall panel from the Fountain Court. Alexandra Walcott and the other conservation preparators created the often intricate and unobtrusive mounts for many of the objects on display. The Museum's conservators were also instrumental in advising on and overseeing the work performed outside the Museum. I would like to acknowledge for their labors John Griswold and his staff at Griswold Conservation Associates, LLC, and Mark Rabinowitz and the staff at Conservation Solutions, Inc., who teamed up for the enormously complicated restoration and installation of the Daffodil Terrace and the marble-and-mosaic mantelpiece from the dining room; Kevin O'Brien and his staff, for replicating the silk velvet upholstery on the dining-room chairs; Olaf Unsoeld and the staff at Fine Wood Conservation, Ltd., for working on the finish of the dining-room chairs; Joseph Stegmeyer, Timothy Warner, and the staff at Passementerie, for producing the dining-room chairs' trimmings; and Luca Bonetti, paintings conservator, for his work on the original stenciled wall painting.

This publication has proved a major undertaking for the Museum and, through the considerable efforts of many colleagues, has been completed with professionalism and aplomb. John P. O'Neill, Editor in Chief and General Manager of Publications, believed that the book would find a wide audience and offered many astute suggestions. Editors Margaret Aspinwall and Sue Potter, and especially Jane Bobko, deserve special thanks for their enduring patience and gift of language in preparing the text for publication. Production was managed by Paula Torres, who brought a critical eye to the selection and reproduction of the myriad images. Gwen Roginsky, Associate General Manager of Publications, oversaw color correction and printing. The efforts of Margaret Rennolds Chace, Managing Editor, and Robert Weisberg, Assistant Managing Editor, were essential to the timely completion of the book. With Kathryn Ansite, Robert Weisberg also handled the desktop publishing. Bruce Campbell conceived the handsome design. His obvious love of the objects in the exhibition and his cheerful disposition made the process of laying out the book enjoyable. Important editorial work was also carried out by Margaret Donovan, Emily Walter, Joan K. Holt, Cynthia Clark, and Ruth Lurie Kozodoy. Philomena Mariani was the bibliographical editor.

The book's beauty derives in large part from the breathtaking new photography that Joseph Coscia, Jr., Chief Photographer in the Museum's Photograph Studio, produced for the majority of the objects in the exhibition. He gave up weeks away from his family to travel to Florida to shoot the works at the Morse Museum. Assistance was offered by other members of the Photograph Studio, notably Barbara Bridgers, General Manager for Imaging and Photography, Susan Melick Bresnan, Wallace Lewis III, Teresa Christiansen, Nora Kennedy, Bob Goldman, and Thomas Ling.

An exhibition of this size and scope involves concerted efforts on the part of the Registrar's office to organize the packing and travel arrangements of works borrowed for the show. For their careful attention to detail in this effort, I particularly thank Herbert M. Moskowitz, Chief Registrar, and Antonia Moser and her predecessors Lisa Cain and Jeanette D'Onofrio, all of whom conscientiously attended to the exhibition.

The Museum is always mindful of the public it serves and how best to reach it. Harold Holzer, Senior Vice President for External Affairs, Elyse Topalian, Chief Communications Officer, Egle Žygas, Senior Press Officer, and Diana Pitt, Editor of the Museum's *Calendar*, have worked tirelessly to publicize this exhibition to a wide constituency. Electronic means of communication are increasingly important, and I am grateful for the efforts of the staff of the Museum's Website, particularly Terri Constant, Senior Advisor to the Website for Strategic Planning, and Jonathan Munar, Production Manager. Many people in the Education Department have helped develop programs for visitors of all ages, from an extensive Teacher Workshop to gallery talks, lectures, and films. Kent Lydecker, Frederick P. and Sandra P. Rose Associate Director for Education, and Elizabeth Hammer-Munemura, Deborah Howes, Christopher Noey, Naomi Niles, Stella Paul, and Alice Schwarz have been especially helpful. Michael Belkin and Douglas C. Hegley in Information Systems and Technology provided thoughtful advice.

Much time and creativity were expended on a wide range of retail products developed in conjunction with the exhibition. For their patience and sensitivity I thank members of the Merchandise and Product Development departments, especially Valerie Troyansky, General Manager, Product Development, Joanne Lyman, Massiel Oyanguren, Robie Rogge, William Lach, Anna Raff, Deborah Katus, Sarah Kirtland, Sheila Bernstein, Marlene Reiss, Kirsten Rendina, Azhar Ali, Debra Jackson, and Steve Zane. I also acknowledge Marilyn Jensen, Book Buyer, and Stefanie Levinson in Wholesale Sales for their roles in this endeavor.

The Thomas J. Watson Library was consulted continually by the authors, research assistants, and editors of this book, and I extend thanks to Kenneth Soehner, Arthur K. Watson Chief Librarian, and Lisa Beidel, Robyn Fleming, and Linda Seckelson. I am also grateful to Jeanie M. James, Archivist, and to Carol Lekarew and Julie Zeftel, of the Photograph and Slide Library.

Michael Batista, Senior Exhibition Designer, is responsible for the exhibition's handsome installation. Sophia Geronimus designed the exhibition graphics. Clint Ross Coller and Richard Lichte worked magic with the lighting. The process of design and installation was overseen by Linda M. Sylling, Manager for Special Exhibitions and Gallery Installations. Tom Scally, Manager, and Taylor Miller, Associate Building Manager, consulted often and facilitated the more difficult aspects of the installation. Contributions were also made by Beth Kovalsky, in Design; Patricia A. Gilkison and Jennifer D. Hinckley, in the Office of the Vice President for Facilities Management; and Lena Smajlaj, in the Buildings Department.

Many museum colleagues, independent scholars, and individuals outside the Metropolitan have provided invaluable assistance with research for the exhibition and catalogue on Tiffany and his various homes. I would like to recognize the following for their help in myriad ways and for sharing their time and knowledge: James Alexandre; Bruce Bernstein, Department of Anthropology, National Museum of American History; Paul Crist; Dennis Doros, Milestone Film and Video; Robert Ellsworth; Eric Erickson, Tiffany & Co.; Wilson Faude, formerly Executive Director, Old State House, Hartford, Connecticut; Gretchen Fenston and Phyllis Rifield, *Vogue;* Michael Franses; Lou Gartner; Peggy Gilges; Nina Rutenburgh Gray; Nick Grindley; Marilynn Johnson; Thomas Kuehhas, Director, Oyster Bay Historical Society; Ben Macklowe, Macklowe Galleries; Nancy McClelland; Roberta Mayer; Christine I. Oaklander, Director of Collections and Exhibitions, Allentown Art Museum; Laura Pereira, Assistant Librarian, New Bedford Whaling Museum; Mr. and Mrs J. Perenchio; David Petrovsky; Dorrie Rosen and the Plant Information Staff, LuEsther T. Mertz Library, The New York Botanical Garden, Bronx, New York; Marco Polo Stufano; Arlie Sulka, Lillian Nassau Ltd.; Judith and Irwin Tantleff; Colleen Weiss; Joseph Weissinger; Deedee Wigmore; Margaret Wolejsza, Steinway and Sons; Kathy Woodrell, Decorative Arts Specialist, Library of Congress; and Doreen Hosking Wright and her daughter Sarah Shaw. I also thank William J. Stahl Jr. and his assistant, Catherine Torrey Stroud, Holly Congdon, David Roche, and Polly Sartori, Sotheby's, for their help. For assistance with photography I acknowledge Eva Greguski, Curator, and Christa Zaros, Collections Manager, The Long Island Museum of Art; Jill Thomas-Clark, Rights and Reproductions Manager, Corning Museum of Glass; Marcia Stein, Photographic Services Manager, Museum of Fine Arts, Houston; and Evelyn Trebilcock, Curator, The Olana Partnership. In addition, the following archives were invaluable during the course of our research: the Mitchell-Tiffany family papers, Yale University; the archives of the New-York Historical Society; the Rakow Library at the Corning Museum of Glass; and the Archives of American Art.

Bruce and Adelle Randall, for whom Tiffany's work has been a lifelong interest, welcomed me to their home on Long Island and shared with me their knowledge of Laurelton Hall. Martin Eidelberg, whose work on Tiffany continues to provide new insights, answered a variety of queries during the course of the project and was always willing to discuss one or another aspect of Tiffany's work and career. He also graciously read my essays for this book in draft form and offered valuable commentary.

Many members of the now extended Tiffany family have welcomed the exhibition, and I extend sincere gratitude to all who have willingly given their time and shared their collections, documents, and photographs with me. I thank particularly Nini and George Gilder, Mrs. Rodman Gilder, Julia Hartman, A. Amasa Miller, Rodman Miller, Virginia Ann Miller, Mr. and Mrs. Charles Platt, Mr. and Mrs. Graham Platt, Mr. Harry Platt, and the Hon. and Mrs. Thomas C. Platt.

Through its generous sponsorship of the exhibition, The Tiffany & Co. Foundation has demonstrated its continuing support of decorative arts at The Metropolitan Museum of Art. I am especially grateful to Fernanda Kellogg, President of the Foundation, and to Michael J. Kowalski, Chairman and CEO of Tiffany & Co., for helping to make the exhibition possible. Additional thanks go to John Jorg, Jacqueline Blandi, Anisa Costa, Linda Buckley, Maggie Wei, and Sara Dallaine.

I extend my appreciation to the Gail and Parker Gilbert Fund for its support of the exhibition. For support of this publication I thank the William Cullen Bryant Fellows of The American Wing.

I cannot adequately express my gratitude to Barbara Veith, Research Associate in American Decorative Arts and the author of the chronology in this volume, and to Monica Obniski, Research Assistant. They contributed extraordinary dedication, unfailing assistance, meticulous attention to detail, and good humor to this project, and the exhibition and catalogue could not have been realized without them. It has been a privilege to work with such fine professionals. Finally, I thank my husband, George, and sons, Henry and Russell, for generously allowing Louis Comfort Tiffany into our family during the past years.

Alice Cooney Frelinghuysen
Anthony W. and Lulu C. Wang Curator of
American Decorative Arts

Lenders to the Exhibition

American Museum of Natural History, New York 234

Associated Artists, LCC, Southport, Connecticut 70

Ball State University Museum of Art, Muncie, Indiana 138, 139

The Baltimore Museum of Art, Maryland 46

Brooklyn Museum of Art, New York 214, 215, 216, 217, 218, 219, 220, 231

The Hermitage Foundation Museum and Gardens, Norfolk, Virginia 180, 181, 182, 183, 184, 186, 187, 188, 189, 190, 191, 192

The Hispanic Society of America, New York 7

The Huntington Library, Art Collections, and Botanical Gardens, San Marino, California 90

Los Angeles County Museum of Art, California 154

The Mark Twain House and Museum, Hartford, Connecticut 34, 36, 38, 39, 40

The Metropolitan Museum of Art, New York 6, 11, 44, 86, 87, 89, 92, 93, 98, 99, 100, 101, 103, 104, 106, 108, 109, 110, 111, 112, 113, 114, 115, 116, 117, 118, 141, 142, 143, 144, 145, 146, 147, 148, 149, 150, 156, 159, 169, 170, 171, 172, 173, 193, 194, 195, 196, 197, 198, 199, 201, 202, 203, 204, 205, 206, 207, 209, 235, 238

Museum of the City of New York, New York 165

Museum of Fine Arts, Boston 73

The Charles Hosmer Morse Museum of American Art, Winter Park, Florida 2, 3, 4, 5, 8, 12, 13, 14, 15, 16, 17, 18, 19, 20, 21, 22, 23, 24, 25, 26, 27, 28, 29, 30, 32, 33, 35, 41, 42, 43, 45, 47, 48, 49, 50, 51, 52, 53, 54, 55, 56, 57, 58, 59, 60, 61, 62, 63, 64, 65, 66, 67, 68, 69, 71, 72, 74, 75, 76, 82, 83, 88, 96, 102, 107, 120, 121, 122, 123, 124, 125, 126, 127, 131, 132, 133, 134, 136, 140, 152, 153, 157, 160, 161, 162, 163, 164, 166, 167, 168, 174, 175, 176, 177, 208

National Museum of the American Indian, Smithsonian Institution, Washington, D.C. 229, 230, 233

Shelburne Museum, Vermont 210, 211, 212, 213, 221, 222, 223, 224, 225, 226, 227, 228

Society for the Preservation of Long Island Antiquities, Cold Spring Harbor, New York 31

Tiffany and Company Archives, Parsippany, New Jersey 185

Yale University Art Gallery, New Haven, Connecticut 1

Ralph T. Coe 236, 237

Florence and Herbert Irving 200

Mr. and Mrs. Ken Siebel 232

Eric Streiner 10, 77, 78, 79, 84, 85, 91, 94, 95, 97, 119, 128, 129, 130, 135, 137, 155, 158

Mr. and Mrs. Tony Terranova 80, 81

Mr. and Mrs. Erving Wolf 151

The Worrell Collection 9

Anonymous lenders 37, 105, 178, 179

Contributors to the Catalogue

Alice Cooney Frelinghuysen
Anthony W. and Lulu C. Wang Curator of American
Decorative Arts
The Metropolitan Museum of Art, New York

Elizabeth Hutchinson
Assistant Professor of American Art History
Barnard College/Columbia University, New York

Julia Meech
Independent scholar and Consultant to the Department of
Japanese Art
Christie's, New York

Jennifer Perry Thalheimer
Collections Manager
The Charles Hosmer Morse Museum of American Art, Winter
Park, Florida

Barbara Veith
Research Associate, American Decorative Arts
The Metropolitan Museum of Art, New York

Richard Guy Wilson
Commonwealth Professor of Architectural History
University of Virginia, Charlottesville

LOUIS COMFORT TIFFANY
AND LAURELTON HALL

Introduction

Alice Cooney Frelinghuysen

Louis Comfort Tiffany (1848–1933; fig. 1), one of America's leading artists of the late nineteenth century, worked in virtually every decorative medium and garnered an international reputation for his innovative leaded-glass windows and blown Favrile-glass vases. One might argue, however, that the most important—and, today, the least understood—aspect of his oeuvre was his quest to integrate all the arts in a single complete work of art. Tiffany achieved this aesthetic unity in the environments that he designed for himself—in his first painting studio, two New York City homes, his first Long Island summer residence, and, especially, Laurelton Hall (figs. 2, 6). Indeed, Laurelton, Tiffany's extraordinary estate in Oyster Bay, Long Island, represents the height of his artistic endeavor.

Tiffany built Laurelton Hall, located on nearly six hundred acres, between 1902 and 1905, with the help of the generous inheritance he had received upon his father's death. He controlled every aspect of the estate's execution, from the architectural and interior design of the eighty-four room, eight-level main house to the creation of gardens, terraces, fountains and pools, and numerous outbuildings. After the house was completed, Tiffany continued to make modifications to the interiors and to add architectural embellishments, so that Laurelton was ever evolving. He integrated decorative elements from his earlier homes, achieving new effects. On the grounds, he extended the gardens, experimented with new fountains, and built several structures, including buildings to house a chapel and an art gallery. Inside, Tiffany created a veritable museum. He filled museum-style cases with hundreds of the best examples of his own glass vases (see fig. 4), pottery, and enamelware (see fig. 5), juxtaposed with Roman and Syrian glass, Egyptian jewelry, and Near Eastern ceramics and tiles. A magnificent pair of Chinese ceramic lions that stood guard at the loggia evinced his passion for Asian art, as did myriad works on a smaller scale, from Japanese prints to delicate Chinese kingfisher-feather headdresses. Like many of his contemporaries, Tiffany also amassed a collection of Native American handcrafted objects, notably baskets.

Opposite: Fig. 1. Portrait of Louis Comfort Tiffany, ca. 1900–1910. Photograph by Rochlitz Studio. Courtesy of Phillips-Hosking Collection

Right: Fig. 2. View of Laurelton Hall. From Stanley Lothrop, "Louis Comfort Tiffany Foundation," *American Magazine of Art* 11 (November 1919), p. 49

Fig. 3. Louis Comfort Tiffany, *The Alhambra*, 1911. Watercolor, 14⅜ x 20½ in. (36.5 x 52.1 cm). Signed at lower left: *Louis C. Tiffany*. Collection of Eric Streiner

In 1918 Tiffany established the Louis Comfort Tiffany Foundation, to which he deeded Laurelton Hall, more than sixty-two acres, all of his personal art collections, and a sizable endowment with the aim of establishing a program to nurture artistic talent in young men and women. As Laurelton's function shifted from that of a grand American country house to that of an educational enterprise for artists, Tiffany explored new uses for traditional spaces. He converted the estate's stables, for example, into artists' housing, and a bowling alley into a gallery for Native American art. The house served not as a place for technical instruction but as a haven for fostering creative freedom, the kind of atmosphere in which Tiffany himself had flourished. For thirteen summers, until his death in 1933, Tiffany enjoyed watching over and giving advice to the next generation of artists and seeing that his unconventional creation in Oyster Bay gave them inspiration. A little more than a decade after Tiffany's death, the foundation deemed Laurelton Hall too expensive to maintain and determined that it, in fact, weakened the foundation's ability to support artistic talent. The trustees approved the sale of its contents at auction in 1946, dispersing Tiffany's carefully preserved legacy. In 1949 they sold the house and the land for a fraction of their original cost. In 1957 the house was destroyed in a devastating fire. However, the artist Hugh F. McKean, who had studied at Laurelton Hall, and his wife, Jeannette Genius McKean, salvaged many of the original Tiffany windows and architectural decorations. They subsequently donated these to the Charles Hosmer Morse Museum of American Art, in Winter Park, Florida (which Jeannette McKean had founded). Today, the Morse Museum holds the largest collection of surviving materials from Laurelton Hall. The McKeans also made a notable gift to The Metropolitan Museum of Art, the four-column loggia from Laurelton, which stands in the Museum's Charles Engelhard Court in The American Wing.

Tiffany was born into a prosperous merchant household in New York City in 1848. His father was Charles Lewis Tiffany, founder of Tiffany and Company, the fancy-goods store that soon became the country's most renowned jewelry and silver emporium, and his mother was Harriet Young, the sister of her husband's first business partner. Tiffany's formal schooling was limited to various pre-preparatory institutions and a three-year tenure at Eagleswood Military Academy, a boarding school in Perth Amboy, New Jersey.[1] It was there that he began his artistic career, as a painter, working with George Inness (1825–1894). His travels to Europe and North Africa and throughout America, in the company of family members and fellow artists, also offered him a visual education. Tiffany's first trip abroad, a seven-month sojourn in the winter and spring of 1865–66 with his older sister Annie (1844–1937) and his aunt, Lydia Ballon Young (d. 1894), took him to coastal England, Ireland, Paris and the South of France, Italy, and Sicily. A sketchbook from his trip contains more than fifty pencil and watercolor sketches of landscapes and architecture.[2] A few years later, in 1868–69, he traveled to Europe again; in Paris he visited the studio of the painter Léon Charles Adrien Bailly (b. 1826) and that of Léon-Adolphe-Auguste Belly (1827–1877), whose Orientalist paintings he found appealing. On a trip to the Mediterranean and North Africa in 1870 with fellow painter R. Swain Gifford (1840–1905), Tiffany experienced the architecture and culture of the East for himself.[3] His travels there made a lasting impression on him. Later, in the designs of his homes, including Laurelton Hall, he was to incorporate architectural details and other elements, such as fountains and patterned walls and tilework, borrowed from the exotic Eastern locales he had visited.

Orientalist paintings and watercolors executed by Tiffany on that 1870 sojourn, and after his return to New York, evince his interest in Islamic architecture (fig. 3). In February 1873, for example, he

Fig. 4. Louis Comfort Tiffany, Tiffany Furnaces, Vase, ca. 1910. Favrile glass, 6⅛ in. (15.6 cm). The Metropolitan Museum of Art, New York, Gift of Louis Comfort Tiffany Foundation, 1951 (51.121.10)

of a Moorish soldier standing guard at a prison door in Tangier, the figure was in shadow, but there was enough light on the scene, wrote the same critic, "to show the tracery of the Mooresque architecture of the structure"; furthermore, "every detail of the old doorway, in the form of carving and weather stains, is conscientiously shown."[8] Paintings such as *Snake Charmer at Tangier, Africa* (1872; fig. 115) also demonstrate Tiffany's interest in Islamic architecture. The broad white columns in that canvas, as well as details of the roofline, were among the architectural elements that were to reappear in buildings that Tiffany designed in subsequent decades. In the decoration of his own studios he was to replicate the shadowy and mysterious atmosphere that he captured in *Snake Charmer*.

Tiffany was an advocate of innovation in the arts. In 1877 he was a founding member and the first treasurer of the Society of American Artists, whose membership also included Inness, Samuel Colman (1832–1920), Augustus Saint-Gaudens (1848–1907), and Francis Lathrop (1849–1909)—to name a few of the artists with whom Tiffany had a close association.[9] In the same year he joined the Committee on Design of the Society of Decorative Art, with Colman, the textile designer Candace T. Wheeler (1827–1923), and Lockwood de Forest (1850–1932). In addition, he was an early member and ardent proponent of the Watercolor Society (then the American Society of Painters in Water Colors), promoting that undervalued medium. He began his business designing interiors in 1878, and it was to remain an integral part of his studios' work for his entire career.

Tiffany's interest in the commingling of the arts in a complete and unified interior stemmed from his absorption of the principles of the Aesthetic movement, as expressed in the influential work of the 1860s of British designers such as Charles Locke Eastlake, Christopher Dresser, Bruce J. Talbert, E. W. Godwin, and William Morris. The movement promoted art in the production of furniture, metalwork, ceramics, stained glass, textiles, wallpapers, and books. Its mission—to beautify the home—resonated with Tiffany, as did its focus on interiors as integrated designs. The work of the British designers was well known in America through articles published in the proliferating art and decorative-art journals of

exhibited such works as *The Sub Treasury at Tangier*, *The Mosque of Said Pacha at Alexandria*, *The Bazaar at Cairo*, and *The Old and New Mosque Lamp*.[4] Although he had no training as an architect, Tiffany's keen observations and draftsmanlike depictions of Eastern buildings—doorways, balconies, and windows—in the early 1870s trained his eye and pencil in that art.[5] After his visits to Tangier and other cities in North Africa, his portfolios were full of studies of "bits of architectural remains."[6] A critic commented that in the painting *Burning East*, as in several earlier pictures, Tiffany took great care "in the architectural drawing."[7] In a watercolor

Fig. 5. Louis Comfort Tiffany, Tiffany Glass and Decorating Company, Three bowls, 1898–1902. Enamel on copper, left to right: 1½ x 2 x 2 in. (3.8 x 5.1 x 5.1 cm); 2¼ x 3¹¹⁄₁₆ x 3¹¹⁄₁₆ in. (5.7 x 9.4 x 9.4 cm); 1⅝ x 2⅜ x 2⅜ in. (4.1 x 6 x 6 cm). The Metropolitan Museum of Art, New York, Gift of Louis Comfort Tiffany Foundation, 1951 (51.121.43, .34, .40)

Fig. 6. Aerial view of Laurelton Hall. Photograph by McCory, from *New York Daily News*, January 26, 1934, p. 14

the day and through books such as Owen Jones's *Grammar of Ornament* (London, 1865), a copy of which was in Tiffany's library at Laurelton Hall.[10] (Other publications were undoubtedly part of the extensive design library at Tiffany's studios.) Many of these designers adapted natural forms as ornament, as did French designers, whose published studies, such as Maurice Pillard Verneuil's *Encyclopédie artistique et documentaire de la plante*, were also important for Tiffany.[11]

Tiffany also mined various non-Western sources, particularly Japan, China, and the Islamic world, for artistic inspiration. Here, too, his extensive library on these subjects, including such notable titles as Jules Bourgoin's *Les arts arabes* (1873), James Fergusson and James Burgess's illustrated *Cave Temples of India* (1880), and *Lewis's Sketches and Drawings of the Alhambra* (n.d.), proved invaluable.[12] In the many interiors Tiffany designed from the late 1870s to the early 1890s, such as those for George Kemp's (1879) or Louisine and Henry Osborne Havemeyer's (1891–92) Fifth Avenue houses, the extraordinary public interior rooms of the Boston townhouse of Ellen and Frederick Ayer (1899–1900), the White House under President Chester A. Arthur (1883), or his own homes (the Bella apartment in 1878 and, in 1885, his family's house at Seventy-second Street and Madison Avenue), he melded decorative-art elements of West and East into a harmonious whole.

In addition to domestic commissions, Tiffany maintained a steady business in the decoration of public buildings—theaters (notably the Lyceum in New York), churches, hotels, department stores, and museum galleries. Perhaps the first commission he received was for decorations for walls, curtains, portieres, architectural treatment, and carpets for the upper floors of the Union League Club, working in collaboration with John La Farge (1835–1910). By most accounts, the result, though notable for the novel use of glass and the Japanesque designs, was less than satisfactory.[13] Just a few years later, Tiffany took the commission for the Veterans Room of the Seventh Regiment Armory, in New York.

Tiffany, like other interior designers of his time, focused on surfaces—walls, ceilings, and floors—incorporating complex geometric patterns based on Japanese, Chinese, Islamic, and even Native American design, as well as patterns derived from nature. Each design motif was related purposefully to the others, but no single motif dominated. Tiffany introduced unusual and untried materials into his interiors, and experimented with new uses for familiar ones. He covered walls with painted grass cloth or Japanese papers flecked with mica. (Tiffany owned several Japanese wallpaper books; the sample sheets, all with designs in reflective white mica in geometric and stylized foliate patterns, served as inspiration for his designs.)[14]

Tiffany summed up his philosophy of the harmonious interior in 1913 in a pamphlet on decoration published by his firm and entitled *Character and Individuality in Decorations and Furnishings*. Tiffany proposed that "Every really great structure is simple in its lines—as in Nature,—every great scheme of decoration thrusts no one note upon the eye. No plan of lighting makes its source predominant, and the charm of homes of refinement is in the artistic blending that is revealed when everything has its place and purpose, and when every detail unites to form one perfect and complete whole."[15] His workshops, beginning with the Tiffany Glass Company, one of his earliest incorporated entities (later Tiffany Glass and Decorating Company and Tiffany Studios), were loosely modeled on the art workshops of William Morris and Company in London. As early as 1887 the firm had facilities for an astonishingly wide range of decorative work, which included every variant of wall treatment (paint, wallpaper, fresco) as well as interior plaster work and woodwork, leather, fabrics, metalwork, stained- and leaded-glass, glass tiles and mosaic, and mosaic flooring.[16] Twenty-five years later, in 1913, the firm declared proficiency in "distinctive Furniture, imported Fabrics, choice Rugs, appropriate Woodwork, harmonious Decorations, special Lighting Fixtures, Ornamental Bronze, Wrought Iron, Leaded Glass, and Tiffany Favrile Glass Mosaic Work."[17] That period also saw Tiffany's development of new art objects, first in glass, as seen in the myriad different color and surface effects his scientists and gaffers accomplished. During the 1890s, Tiffany directed his staff of designers, craftsmen, and craftswomen in the development of innovative leaded-glass lampshades and other lighting fixtures, as well as successive experiments in enamelwork, jewelry, and pottery. In all of these undertakings, Tiffany seemed to have been preparing for the creation of Laurelton Hall. These interiors were a laboratory for experimenting with inventive materials and fresh ideas.

When Tiffany broke ground at Laurelton, in 1902, the *New York Herald* reported that "Country homes, with their mile long driveways are continuous for a hundred miles. Long Island is rapidly being divided up into estates of immense acreage . . . beyond all precedent of American country life."[18] Compared to these country homes, however, Laurelton Hall defies stylistic categorization. In the houses or mansions contemporary with Laurelton, historicizing styles prevailed: witness the palatial home, in the form of a French château, designed by McKim, Mead and White for Clarence Mackay in Roslyn, Long Island (1899–1902), or John S. Phipps's grand Georgian mansion, designed by English architect George A. Crawley, in Old Westbury (1906). Laurelton cannot be defined by a single style, though it was assuredly singular. It was an amalgam of different styles merged so skillfully that it is difficult to isolate individual sources.

To contemporary visitors, Laurelton Hall, on first impression, must have seemed exotic, with its emerald green molded copper roof and fanciful floral capitals. However contradictory, Laurelton also appeared modern. Its walls were of creamy stucco, smooth in some areas and pebble-encrusted in others. Continuous curved surfaces, obscuring all hard edges and corners, were to be seen, for example, in the large living hall (Tiffany had already introduced these in his Seventy-second Street home); no moldings appeared around windows or doors. Tiffany's integration of interior and exterior spaces relates his work to that of other progressive architects of the day, notably Frank Lloyd Wright (1867–1959). Other details—the floor-to-ceiling walls of glass, the horizontal ribbons of fenestration, and the severe asymmetrical facade combined with a lack of applied decoration—might also be said to anticipate the modern styles of subsequent decades.

Few artists' houses—even in comparison with Frederic Church's Olana, overlooking the Hudson River, or Frank Lloyd Wright's early house in Oak Park, Illinois—more fully express a single artistic vision than does Tiffany's Laurelton Hall. Today, a century after Laurelton Hall's completion, the essays in this volume offer a critical reassessment of Tiffany's estate. By examination of the extensive contemporary press commentary on Laurelton, period photographs, and recently discovered artworks displayed at Laurelton, the authors shed new light on Tiffany's estate—its design, architecture and grounds, interiors, and collections of artwork. The volume is a biography of sorts—not of a person but of a house.

1. Burke 1987.
2. Tiffany's sketchbook is in the collection of the Charles Hosmer Morse Museum of American Art, Winter Park, Florida (hereafter Morse Museum). The sketches in it were made between November 1865 and March 1866.
3. R. Swain Gifford Letters, MSS 12, subgroup 1, series A, subseries 2, folders 11–16, New Bedford Whaling Museum, Massachusetts.
4. Undated, unidentified newspaper clipping from Tiffany scrapbook, Morse Museum.
5. Undated, unidentified newspaper clipping from Tiffany scrapbook, Morse Museum.
6. Undated, unidentified newspaper clipping from Tiffany scrapbook, Morse Museum.
7. Undated, unidentified newspaper clipping from Tiffany scrapbook, Morse Museum.
8. Ibid.
9. New York 1979, p. 53.
10. Parke-Bernet 1946, lot 675.
11. Ibid., lot 681. See also Martin Eidelberg, "Nature Is Always Beautiful," in Eidelberg et al. 2005, pp. 36–65.
12. Parke-Bernet 1946, lots 585, 649, 654.
13. Oakey 1882, p. 736.
14. The Brooklyn Museum owns four Japanese wallpaper books, ca. 1880, with Tiffany's name on the outside cover and his signature on the inside cover. See also Parke-Bernet 1946, lot 711.
15. Tiffany Studios 1913.
16. *Decorator and Furnisher* 10, no. 5 (August 1887), p. 164.
17. Tiffany Studios 1913.
18. MacKay et al. 1997, p. 19.

A Marriage of East and West: Tiffany's Earliest Interiors

Alice Cooney Frelinghuysen

The opulently adorned artist's studio was a new phenom-
enon in late-nineteenth-century America.[1] Artists traveled
widely, not just to Europe but also to more distant coun-
tries whose cultures were new and tantalizing to them.
They brought back art objects, artifacts, and curios, acquired for
their artistic interest and, often, for use as props in their own
works of art. The studio of the American painter William Merritt
Chase (1849–1916; fig. 8), for example, in the Tenth Street Studios
building, in New York City, held a "dazzling array of beautiful,
exotic and curious things, decontextualized and massed for visual
effect."[2] Such profusely decorated studios, or "aesthetic bou-
tiques" (as the scholar Sarah Burns has called them),[3] functioned
as a kind of stage set against which the artist could perform, and
they created seductive environments for potential clients.[4] Tiffany
followed this trend by decorating his first painting studio with an
eclectic assemblage of textiles of diverse origins draped on the
furniture and hung on the walls, Oriental carpets, Chinese and
Japanese vases, and colonial furniture (fig. 9). The exotic flavor of
his studio's decoration—his very first interior—was to charac-
terize the interiors he designed for his own use over the next
several decades.

In the late 1860s, when Tiffany embarked on his painting career,
there were few artists' studios available in New York besides
the Tenth Street Studios, and vacancies there were few and far
between.[5] In that artists' building, which had opened in 1857, there
were only twenty-five studios, and rents were quite reasonable.
In 1869, the twenty-one-year-old Tiffany secured a studio for
himself in the newly built five-story headquarters of the New
York City chapter of the Young Men's Christian Association. The
fourth and fifth floors of the building, located at 52 East Twenty-
third Street, at Fourth Avenue (now Park Avenue South), were
set aside for forty artists' studios. Such was the desirability of the
studios in the YMCA Building, usually referred to as the Association Building, that all of them were rented almost immediately.[6]
Besides Tiffany, the first tenants included Arthur Fitzwilliam
Tait, William M. Hart, Alexander Wyant, and Charles Warren.

Opposite: Fig. 7. Detail of fig. 22

(Among later residents were the artists William Merritt Chase,
John F. Kensett, Edwin Austin Abby, Alfred Bricher, and—
for a time—John La Farge, who, like Tiffany, was to invent a new
kind of glass for making windows.) Given his privileged background and his father's willingness to provide financial support,
Tiffany could afford the rents of the Association Building, which,
at up to $250 per quarter, were higher than those at the Tenth
Street Studios.

As he was to do throughout his career, at the Association
Building Tiffany selected for his studio a space on the top floor, at
the end of a long corridor, where he could take advantage of a
skylight. Tiffany's studio included a stairway, an unusual feature,
leading to the roof, where he "pose[d] his models in the sunlight."[7] The visitor knew immediately that Tiffany's studio was
not the typical sort, for at the door "a queer brass manikin
squats out from a panel doing duty as a knocker."[8] Each of the
Association Building's studios had a separate bedroom, and Tiffany
lived there prior to his first marriage, in 1872.

The building offered more than a suitable space in which to
work. It was located in the burgeoning artistic center of the city,
directly across the street from the National Academy of Design
(today the National Academy), which had been founded in 1825
and to which Tiffany was to be elected a full member in 1881. It
fostered a sense of community among the artists, with common
spaces available for lectures as well as a reception room on the
fifth floor that served as a picture gallery where the artists could
exhibit their work, and from which doors opened into the adjoining studios.[9] In January 1872 Tiffany and the painter R. Swain
Gifford (1840–1905), who had traveled together extensively in
the Mediterranean and North Africa in 1870 and who had
adjoining studios, used the reception room for an exhibition of
their recently completed Orientalist canvases. On two consecutive
afternoons and evenings they hosted large receptions, attended
by some five hundred people. It was a gratifying experience,
Gifford commented: "We had such new and strange things to
show our friends that they expressed a great deal of pleasure at
the entertainment."[10]

In an unsigned and undated newspaper clipping, probably
from 1873, a journalist singled out Tiffany's studio in the

Fig. 8. William Merritt Chase (1849–1916), *Tenth Street Studio*, ca. 1880–81 and ca. 1910. Oil on canvas, 46⅞ x 66 in. (119.1 x 167.6 cm). Carnegie Museum of Art, Pittsburgh, Purchase

Fig. 9. Louis Comfort Tiffany's first studio, Association Building, New York. Engraving from John Moran, "New York Studios III," *The Art Journal (Appleton's)* 66 (January 1880), p. 2

Association Building, along with those of Gifford and Samuel Colman (1832–1920).[11] The studios of the three artists, the reporter said, were redolent of the East, with "strange and lovely walls . . . whose garnishing brings us the very aroma of the lands of the sun."[12] According to another unsigned account, "Turkish cloaks and Bedouin shawls are draped in graceful confusion over trophies of arms or carved furniture, while a great fireplace of sandstone rears its ruddy height on one side of the room."[13] A few years later the art critic John Moran described Tiffany's studio as one of "Oriental splendour."[14]

Tiffany kept his studio at the Association Building for nearly a decade, until 1878. By that time he had been married for six years and had a five-year-old daughter, Mary, and a newborn baby boy, Charles Lewis Tiffany II. The growth of his family prompted Tiffany to look for quarters larger than those the family had been occupying in the home of Tiffany's father at 255 Madison Avenue, between Thirty-eighth and Thirty-ninth Streets. He settled on the newly constructed Bella Apartments (fig. 10), at 48 East Twenty-sixth Street, a block from Madison Square, on the southwest corner of Fourth Avenue—three blocks north of the Association Building. The area was still considered an attractive one for residences, although the most fashionable area of New York City was now farther uptown, between Forty-second and Fifty-ninth Streets. The developer, Oswald Ottendorfer, christened the building "Bella," after his daughter.[15] Designed by the architect William Schickel (1850–1907), the Bella apartment building housed eighteen individual suites of rooms, two per floor in each of two five-story sections, one facing Twenty-sixth Street and the other facing Fourth Avenue, and two commercial spaces on the ground floor. Shortly after its opening the elegant building was described as one "exclusively devoted to domestic life and comfort."[16] It incorporated a number of lavish features, such as polished granite columns and marble floors in the entranceway, with ceilings and walls covered in ornamental fresco, as well as many innovations, including a hydraulic elevator and a heating system of direct radiation from steam pipes.[17] It was especially noteworthy for the abundant light in the rooms, a feature that must certainly have appealed to Tiffany. Indeed, Tiffany selected a suite on the top floor in order to profit from the additional light afforded by skylights. This large, grand apartment meant a slight increase in rent for Tiffany, as the suites ranged from $750 to $2,000 per year.[18]

The Bella apartment was Tiffany's second interior design for himself, after his studio in the Association Building. He designed the rooms and furnishings of the apartment from start to finish. From 1878 to 1880 he used the suite as a testing ground for various ideas that had been germinating since the previous decade. A departure from the prevailing, conservative standards of decoration, Tiffany's apartment revealed the influence of the Aesthetic movement, then reigning in America and much favored in Europe, as well as the stirrings of the Arts and Crafts movement. Tiffany introduced novel materials and forms (glass in many guises, as well as mica, antique textiles, antique woodwork, and

Fig. 10. The Bella Apartments. From *Marc Eidlitz & Son, 1854–1914* (New York, 1914), n.p. Collection of Princeton University Library, New Jersey

barn-style sliding doors) and freely combined decorative elements drawn from a variety of cultures, including Japanese, Moorish, and Indian. This amalgam of materials and homage to Eastern cultures would blossom into full flower at Tiffany's residential masterpiece, Laurelton Hall. The Bella apartment was Tiffany's first success in achieving a unified interior-as-work-of-art.

The apartment was the subject of much coverage in contemporary journals, some of it likely engineered by Tiffany himself, as a marketing strategy to attract clients for Louis C. Tiffany, Associated Artists, the interior-design firm established in 1881. Nonetheless, the detailed descriptions of Tiffany's apartment and the series of photographs taken shortly after its completion provide a virtual tour of these innovative spaces. The first notice came in 1882, in a series of eleven articles published by Donald G. Mitchell (1822–1908) in a new illustrated magazine covering history, literature, science, and art and entitled *Our Continent*. (Mitchell was a close friend of Tiffany's as well as a relative by marriage.)[19] Although nowhere in the articles does Mitchell identify the apartment under discussion as Tiffany's, his meticulous descriptions of the rooms and their decorative treatment, as well as some twenty-four accompanying engravings, confirm its identity.[20] The engravings are exceedingly important as records of small decorative details that might have been overlooked in an overall depiction of one or another room (see figs. 12, 18, 19, 52). Tiffany provided some of the early sketches, but most of the engravings were after drawings by the stained-glass artist D. Maitland Armstrong (1836–1918); others were from sketches by John L. du Fais (1855–1935), Frederic Church (1826–1900), and Elihu Vedder (1836–1923).[21] The four principal public rooms in Tiffany's Bella apartment were further documented in the lavish, profusely illustrated four-volume *Artistic Houses: Being a Series of Interior Views of a Number of the Most Beautiful and Celebrated Homes in the United States,* published in 1883–84. All the premier decorators of the day were represented in this publication. Tiffany's rooms were the first entry in the first volume and were unstintingly praised by the anonymous author, presumed to be George William Sheldon.[22]

Visitors to Tiffany's apartment exited an elevator, a modern convenience only recently introduced into buildings like the Bella, into a lobby with a steeply peaked ceiling with exposed wood beams that had been gouged and studded with bronze (fig. 11). Here, Tiffany made unconventional use of glass. For the transom and the windows flanking the entrance door he did not employ transparent glass, as was typical; rather, he selected milkier cathedral glass in small rectangular panes, which he utilized as well in twin casement windows on the sides of a door leading from the lobby to a small dressing room. Mitchell described "grooved olive-green glass tiles, looking for all the world as if they may have been the halves of Bordeaux bottles" set between the rafters of the peaked roof, providing, in a traditionally windowless space, a soft light from above.[23] Glass disks of the same color, which Mitchell said resembled "bottoms of those same Bordeaux bottles"

but which are reminiscent of windows depicted in Northern Renaissance paintings and prints, filled windows on two sides of the lobby. Combined with the rich brown of the wood rafters and the deep Indian red of the walls, the glass disks contributed to the room's warmth and gave it a decidedly nonurban mood.[24] These circular panes were probably not bottle bottoms, as they appeared to be; they were more likely molded circles of glass with centers thicker than the sides, of a shape, that is, that would cause light to filter through them unevenly. Such panes were used in some of Tiffany's earliest windows, including the first ecclesiastical window of his career, executed in 1878 for St. Mark's Episcopal Church in Islip, Long Island.[25]

A large exposed wood wheel and weight on a chain (fig. 12) facilitated raising and lowering the glazed upper half of the door opening onto the stairway.[26] Tiffany did not hesitate to show openly the mechanical devices necessary to his designs. Rather than install sliding folding doors or casement doors between the library and the drawing room of the Bella apartment—such doors consume space—Tiffany devised a rolling glass screen. The screen functioned as a decorative panel against the wall of one side of the passageway, allowing movement between the rooms; when privacy was desired, it could be rolled on large spinning wheel–shaped

Fig. 11. *Mr. Louis C. Tiffany's Hall,* ca. 1883. From [George William Sheldon], *Artistic Houses: Being a Series of Interior Views of a Number of the Most Beautiful and Celebrated Homes in the United States,* 1883–84, vol. 1, pt. 1. The Metropolitan Museum of Art, New York, Thomas J. Watson Library, Rogers Fund

No. 5.

Fig. 12. Corner of lobby, Bella apartment. Engraving by D. Maitland Armstrong, from Donald G. Mitchell, "From Lobby to Peak: A Lobby," *Our Continent* 1 (February 22, 1882), p. 21. Collection of Brown University Library, Providence, Rhode Island

Fig. 13. Louis Comfort Tiffany, Bella apartment window, ca. 1880. Leaded glass, 24¼ x 29½ x 1 in. (61.5 x 74.9 x 2.5 cm). The Metropolitan Museum of Art, New York, Gift of Robert Koch, 2002 (2002.474)

wheels to block the passage, and an attached Japanese silk curtain was drawn over it. As Mitchell pointed out, the spindled wheels complemented the decorative Japanesque swirls and circles on the wall treatment along the frieze, and the translucent glass panels of the screen were marked by a subtle pattern of weblike vines, which, when the screen was open, overlaid and intensified an identical pattern on the wall behind.[27]

Weapons of various kinds, from a Moorish gun and Caucasian dagger to a European or American flintlock rifle, hung on the walls of the lobby and were stacked near it in a haphazard way (fig. 11). Around the corner was a leaded-glass window of abstract design and bold splashes of color (fig. 13), the earliest domestic window by Tiffany known to survive. Like the lobby window, it could be raised and lowered. Both the nonrepresentational composition and the unusual glass would have been startling to Tiffany's contemporaries. The glass is in hues of deep amber, brilliant purple, dark emerald green, and varied shades of blue and

opal. Some of the glass included was at the time largely experimental: opalescent, marbleized, and an early confetti-type glass, as well as large colored crown glass and sizable, thick, rough-cut glass "jewels."[28] Tiffany utilized the properties of the medium to attain the maximum artistic effect. He achieved a sense of movement in the window, for example, by incorporating into the composition the striations that result, in the fabrication of crown glass, from the swirling of the glass on the end of a blowpipe.

It has been claimed by Robert Schmutzler and Robert Koch that the window is one of Tiffany's first expressions of high Art Nouveau.[29] It can more convincingly be interpreted as protomodern in its bold abstraction and in the highly textured glass that protrudes from the surface. The window's design, in light-filled saturated colors, seems to have been created by the broad strokes of a painter's brush. Indeed, in 1880 John Moran suggested that oil pigments inspired this piece, that Tiffany's design resulted from daubing "the scrapings of his palette with a view to the achieve-

Fig. 14. *Mr. Louis C. Tiffany's Drawing Room*, ca. 1883. From [George William Sheldon], *Artistic Houses: Being a Series of Interior Views of a Number of the Most Beautiful and Celebrated Homes in the United States*, 1883–84, vol. 1, pt. 1. The Metropolitan Museum of Art, New York, Thomas J. Watson Library, Rogers Fund

ment of accidental effects."[30] The palette of the finished window, thought Moran, suggested the "sea-depths with their rocks and parti-coloured growths" as well as "the sky, blending into all tints from delicate greys and blues, through rich purples and reds, into somber black."[31]

The experimental nature of the lobby window may have been matched by that of another window, which divided the library and the dining room of the Bella apartment. The panel is not known to survive, but Donald Mitchell's contemporary description suggests the novelty of the glass that was used as well as the panel's duality, as a window and as a mosaic. Mitchell wrote: "The qualities of the new opalescent glass are such that it is hardly less beautiful to look upon against the darkness, when it has good light from within, than under transmitted light. It offers to the eye under these conditions a great, glowing, sparkling field of mosaic, set off with wavy lines of golden leadings."[32] Like the lobby window, this panel was noteworthy for its textural qualities. It was made from heavy, chunky colored glass rather than from the traditional thin, even glass. Mitchell describes the window as hav-

ing "thick, irregular, broken masses; not large, but each maybe with a half dozen facets, flashing and refracting light—a series of jewels of red, or golden yellow, of blue, of topaz, inserted into perforations of the wood," giving it the appearance of "a blaze of gems."[33]

The entry space gave the visitor "an impression of mystery and indefiniteness," created in part through the unusual lighting effects from a circular burner overhead that was perforated "in such a manner that the gas comes through it flickering like the light of a torch," or like that of early American perforated tin lanterns.[34] The room continued to be discussed by critics nearly a decade after Tiffany had moved out of the Bella apartment and into the Tiffany house at Seventy-second Street and Madison Avenue.[35]

The decoration of the drawing room combined a variety of styles (fig. 14). Tiffany's collections of Chinese and Japanese pottery and porcelains were displayed there, and a mosaic of Oriental carpets of varying sizes covered the floor. Antique Japanese textiles hung between slender Moorish columns, separating the drawing room from the hall. The dominant piece of furniture was a cherry table in the center of the room. Its rectangular top was supported by slabs at each end, on shoe feet, with a long flat stretcher in between. Each end was made from a textile printing block imported from India, with roughly carved patterning (figs. 15 and 16 are among several found at Laurelton); long narrow blocks used for printing borders composed the shoe feet and the stretcher.[36] The tabletop, too, featured Indian printing blocks, with delicate patterning in brass inset into the carved wood decoration; the areas around the brass were filled in with a composition material, to yield a smooth surface. Tiffany thought to adapt for decorative use objects created for other, nondecorative purposes—a novel idea for the time. (In 1880 he used printing rollers as the legs of the monumental table that he designed and fabricated for the Veterans Room of the Seventh Regiment Armory, in New York City, and narrow rectangular printing blocks as ornamentation on the crest rails of the chairs; this project was concurrent with his work on the Bella apartment.)[37] Some contemporary photographs of the apartment show the table covered with an Oriental carpet, a touch that would have heightened the exotic flavor of the room. Surrounding the table, aligned near the walls or by the fireplace, were various side chairs, most simple in form and varying from a slender-membered chair, with a plain crest rail, to slightly more elaborate examples, with carved backs. Tiffany was to move the chairs from one home to another.

Some contemporary observers praised Tiffany's fusion of styles in the drawing room. "Extreme East and the extreme West," wrote Donald Mitchell, "may be married together, and wisely, in the offices of decorative art."[38] In *Artistic Houses* (1883–84; see above), Sheldon countenanced the mode, writing, "The Moorish feeling has received

a dash of East Indian, and the wall-papers and ceiling-papers are Japanese, but there is a unity that binds everything into an *ensemble*, and the spirit of that unity is delicacy."[39] Tiffany achieved lightness in part through the use of pink walls flecked with metallic patterns, ceiling papers with pieces of reflective mica, and mirrors.

Praise for the Bella drawing room was not universal, however. Nearly a decade later, in the popular periodical *Decorator and Furnisher*, an unnamed critic decried Tiffany's intermixing of styles, suggesting that the room would have been more successful "if all the appurtenances were carried out in the same style as the Moorish screen at the entrance."[40] The writer took issue with the Japanese wallpapers and with the "Japanesque feeling in the spider web design on the mica panel on the fireplace."[41] Although diminutive, the spiderweb of panels of mica directly over the fireplace opening created a focal point, especially when the mica glistened from the light of the fire. Tiffany utilized the spiderweb motif in subsequent designs, notably for the wallpapers he designed in 1880 for Warren and Company, described as of "filmy spider webs and feathery blossoms in silver."[42]

The fireplace in the adjoining library (fig. 17) did not have symmetrical shelving, as would have been expected. In an era preoccupied with the display of objects of all kinds, the étagère-like fireplace surround was intended to hold both books and curios. Tiffany arranged the shelves irregularly, following Japanese practice and that of other Western furniture designers working in the Japanese mode. (A similar arrangement could be found in the modest library of Tiffany's friend, collaborator, and sometime mentor Samuel Colman, who was as interested in the creation of artistic environments as was Tiffany, although primarily for his

Fig. 15. Textile printing block. Probably India, probably 19th century. Wood, 19 x 18¼ x 1½ in. (48.3 x 46.4 x 3.8 cm). The Charles Hosmer Morse Museum of American Art, Winter Park, Florida

Fig. 16. Textile printing block. Probably India, probably 19th century. Wood, 19⅜ x 19⅜ x 1½ in. (49.2 x 49.2 x 3.8 cm). The Charles Hosmer Morse Museum of American Art, Winter Park, Florida

Fig. 17. *Mr. Louis C. Tiffany's Library*, ca. 1883. From [George William Sheldon], *Artistic Houses: Being a Series of Interior Views of a Number of the Most Beautiful and Celebrated Homes in the United States*, 1883–84, vol. 1, pt. 1. The Metropolitan Museum of Art, New York, Thomas J. Watson Library, Rogers Fund

Fig. 18. Corner of the library, with horse chestnut leaf–pattern wall covering, Bella apartment. Engraving by D. Maitland Armstrong, from Donald G. Mitchell, "From Lobby to Peak: In the Library," *Our Continent* 1 (April, 12, 1882), p. 132. Collection of Brown University Library, Providence, Rhode Island

Fig. 19. Corner of the library, Bella apartment. Engraving probably by D. Maitland Armstrong, from Donald G. Mitchell, "From Lobby to Peak: A Library Corner," *Our Continent* 1 (May 3, 1882), p. 185. Collection of Brown University Library, Providence, Rhode Island

personal use.)[43] The light structural members supporting the various shelves were also a deliberate reference to Japanese design. One can deduce from Mitchell's account that the mixed-metal doors to the cupboard flanking the fireplace may have been actual Japanese metalwork. Mitchell described one of the panels as having a background of iron rust, "with the flower forms picked out with black lead and touches of silver and bronze," whereas the other panel depicted a "spray of bloom and leaves of iron rust, touched here and there with silver and gold, but this time on a lacquer-like ground of black lead."[44]

The asymmetrical rectangles created by the shelving were echoed in the wall treatment throughout the room. Chinese yellow straw matting was set into panels of various dimensions, framed by simple thin strips of wood. Painted over the matting was a subtle design in transparent pigment, in rich greens and browns, of a five-lobed leaf motif—perhaps Virginia creeper but more likely horse chestnut (fig. 18), a motif Tiffany was to reinterpret both at the Seventy-second Street house and at Laurelton Hall. The leaf pattern could be seen in other guises elsewhere in the room: for example, it was carved as a pierced design in the brown wood of the door frame between the library and the adjoining dining room; the piercing allowed those in the dining room to glimpse the golden straw matting of the library walls and thus harmonized the two

rooms. The bold carved horse chestnut leaves at the sides of the door merged, at the top of the door frame, into a more delicate motif of the pendulous foliage and blossoms of the Asian wisteria vine—Tiffany's first use of the flowering vine that was to feature prominently in all his future domestic designs, albeit in leaded glass (see figs. 119, 149–154).

In the library of the Bella apartment Tiffany initiated a new and unusual method of displaying paintings, integrating the canvases into the interior scheme. He dispensed with the heavily carved and gilded frames that, from the 1870s, were de rigueur for both the reigning American Hudson River School painters and the European salons. In the Bella library a Hudson River painting by Samuel Colman (see fig. 170) and a floral still life by an unidentified artist, perhaps Tiffany himself, were placed on the walls and framed in the same thin strips of wood that broke up the wall expanse into rectangular sections (fig. 19). The result, in the case of the Hudson River view, was to give the impression of a window opening on the landscape beyond.

Mitchell provided a glimpse of the color scheme and texture of the adjoining dining room (fig. 20), beginning with the fretwork above the fireplace opening, carved in a leafy pattern and "tinted uniformly with dark Prussian blue, so dark that to some eyes it might pass for black. Add to this the flashing fire-blaze, the gleaming

Fig. 20. *Mr. Louis C. Tiffany's Dining-Room*, ca. 1883. From [George William Sheldon], *Artistic Houses: Being a Series of Interior Views of a Number of the Most Beautiful and Celebrated Homes in the United States*, 1883–84, vol. 1, pt. 1. The Metropolitan Museum of Art, New York, Thomas J. Watson Library, Rogers Fund

Fig. 21. Louis Comfort Tiffany, Tiles from Bella apartment fireplace, ca. 1880. Glazed earthenware, each 4 x 8⅛ in. (10.2 x 20.6 cm). The Charles Hosmer Morse Museum of American Art, Winter Park, Florida

Fig. 22. Louis Comfort Tiffany, Louis C. Tiffany and Company, *Eggplant* window, ca. 1879. Leaded Favrile glass, 32¼ x 42¼ in. (81.9 x 107.3 cm). The Charles Hosmer Morse Museum of American Art, Winter Park, Florida

bolt-heads of the frame work, the sheen of the crystalline plates, the scarlet and purple and drabs and gold of the book-backs, the grays and reds and browns and whites and greens of the Japanese vases, and last, the folded richness of the embroidery at the top."[45] Mitchell deemed Tiffany's stylistic consistency here successful and artistic.[46]

The dining room incorporated shelving and cupboards for all manner of ceramics and glass of the sort typically collected by proponents of the Aesthetic movement. Asian pottery and porcelain vessels, Venetian glassware, Hispano-Moresque pottery, and other exotic vessels were an added visual stimulus in the room. Their varied shapes and surface designs added luster and sparkle to rooms throughout the apartment. The chair rail served as a shelf for "plaques, quaint old platters, half blue and white, or a Japanese array of dishes," held in place by a protective brass rod.[47] Ceramic teacups and tankards hung from brass hooks suspended above. The mantel shelf held a selection of five plates or chargers of varying sizes, patterns, and, presumably, origins.

The walls of the dining room, like those of the library, were compartmentalized into rectilinear sections, with different yet harmonious wall treatments of applied decorative paper or fabric. The coloration of the walls lightened toward the ceiling. A band of stamped leather or leatherlike paper in a rich bronze extended above the dado and served as a decorative backdrop for the bric-a-brac displayed on the walls. Other sections of the walls were in shades of blue, sheathed in what was described by George Sheldon as "Japanese mushroom wall-paper."[48] Japanese textiles covered the frieze and lower band of the wall; the uppermost consisted of a fabric in a pale sky blue, embroidered with birds and cloud symbols.

The late-eighteenth-century American mantel was a somewhat incongruous note in the room, but it also presented another opportunity for exploring a mix of different styles. The mantel was a reference to the American past, consistent with the prevailing post-Centennial interest in reviving colonial styles, and it injected a touch of familiarity, even nostalgia. The old-fashioned mantelpiece in the brand-new Bella apartment house was said by Mitchell to take "off the edge of raw New-Yorkism, and in any house at all carrying the traditional sweets of homishness."[49]

The design of the tile fireplace facing epitomizes the Aesthetic movement. Presumably decorated by Tiffany himself, it features an overall decoration that is asymmetrical in its composition. Its hand-painted quality is reminiscent of the work of members of the Tile Club with whom Tiffany was well acquainted.[50] Tiffany may have had access to their supplies and firing sources, but he would also have had recourse to several china-decorating establishments that had opened as part of the china-painting craze that was beginning to overtake the country.[51] It is more likely that Tiffany worked on the tiles at the New York Society of Decorative Art, where he had taught a class in pottery decoration as early as 1878. (During that same year Tiffany's sister Annie and his first wife, May, also took up pottery decorating.)[52] Mitchell wrote that Tiffany's fireplace tiles carried "a little fantasy of their own," with painterly swirls embodying "reeling clouds of smoke."[53] The wreaths of smoke framed picturesque passages of stylized flowers or circular reserves of simple seascapes. Still other areas depicted Japanese vessels, red pottery tea kettles suspended from iron cranes, or decorative blue-and-white chargers arranged on shelves (fig. 21).

Above the mantelpiece hung an enormous painting, as wide as the chimneybreast. Tiffany left it unframed, to create the appearance of a wall painting. The canvas, which is not known to survive, offered a close-up view of pumpkins and corn, with a plump feathered turkey in the center—an homage to a traditional New England Thanksgiving (see fig. 20). Game and vegetables had long been considered subjects appropriate for a room devoted to dining. Mitchell admirably conveyed the effect of the canvas, with its "flashing iridescence upon the breast of the bird, his scarlet wattles, and the brown gold of the corn and the red, gold of the pumpkin," all bathed in golden sunlight.[54]

The painting was complemented by a "window screen" of eggplants growing on a trellis (figs. 7, 22). Along with the abstract panel in the apartment's lobby, it is one of the earliest extant windows by Tiffany.[55] As Mitchell pointed out, the window had an important practical function. It was connected to visible pulleys and weights so that it could be raised or lowered as a shield against the sun. Although the idea of such a moveable screen was noteworthy, the window was far more remarkable for the novel qualities of the glass, for, in Mitchell's words, "its rich hues, its striated texture, its opalescence, and its adaptation to a multitude of decorative uses."[56] The thick vines and dark vegetal forms contrast with the delicate Japanesque bamboo trellis.

In designing his Bella apartment Tiffany navigated a new discipline, experimenting with novel materials and embracing exotic cultures, and, like his artist-contemporaries, demonstrating a belief that art should permeate all aspects of life. Other painters who pursued work in various decorative media, however, remained painters at heart. Tiffany, by contrast, altered the direction of his career. He did not turn his back on easel painting, but decorative work became his priority, his enduring passion, his lifelong work. In the years to come he was to continue his synthesis of eclectic design elements, from East and West, in the creation of singular residences for himself.

1. There has been extensive scholarship on the artist's studio in the late nineteenth century. See, especially, Blaugrund 1997; Burns 1993; Burns 1996; and Zukowski 1999.
2. Burns 1993, p. 211.
3. Ibid., p. 209.
4. Burns 1996, pp. 160–86.
5. For more information on the Tenth Street Studios, see Blaugrund 1987.
6. Oaklander 1992, p. 18.
7. "Studio" 1882.
8. "In the Studios," undated, unidentified newspaper clipping from Tiffany scrapbook, Charles Hosmer Morse Museum of American Art, Winter Park, Florida (hereafter Morse Museum).
9. Oaklander 1992, pp. 15–16.
10. R. Swain Gifford to Lydia Swain, January 21, 1872, Gifford letters, MSS 12, subgroup 1, series A, subseries 2, folder 19, New Bedford Whaling Museum, Massachusetts.
11. Like Tiffany and Gifford, Colman had traveled in 1870 to Italy and North Africa (in his case, to Egypt, Algeria, and Morocco).
12. Undated, unidentified newspaper clipping from Tiffany scrapbook, Morse Museum.
13. "In the Studios," undated, unidentified newspaper clipping from Tiffany scrapbook, Morse Museum.
14. "Studio" 1882.
15. "Bella" 1878, p. 243.
16. Ibid., p. 244.
17. Ibid., pp. 243–44.
18. Ibid.
19. Mitchell's brother Alfred was married to Tiffany's older sister. In addition, Mitchell was chairman of the judges for the decorative arts section of the 1876 Centennial International Exhibition in Philadelphia. In 1885 his son William Pringle Mitchell joined Tiffany's firm as a junior partner.
20. In the magazine's table of contents, moreover, Tiffany and Company is listed with Mitchell's name.
21. Armstrong had collaborated with Tiffany on the decorations for the Veterans Room of the Seventh Regiment Armory, in New York City. By 1880 he was assisting Tiffany in the design and fabrication of windows. He remained with Tiffany until 1886, when he went out on his own; he enjoyed a successful career as a stained-glass artist in New York. See R. Jones 1999, pp. 68–69. Church and Vedder both provided cartoons for stained-glass windows for Tiffany, some of which were included in the exhibition of windows, cartoons, and studies held at Tiffany's studios in February 1897. See "Stained Glass" 1897. John du Fais was in Tiffany's employ as director of the firm's architectural department. When the Tiffany Glass Company incorporated in 1885, he was named secretary of the company, a position he held until at least 1892, when the firm was reincorporated as Tiffany Glass and Decorating Company.
22. *Artistic Houses* 1883–84, vol. 1, pt. 1, p. 1–6.
23. Mitchell 1882b.
24. Ibid.
25. The window that Tiffany fabricated for St. Mark's was destroyed by a fire at the church and was replaced in the 1880s by a later Tiffany window, which was also destroyed, in a fire at the church in 1989. For an illustration of the original window, see De Kay 1914, opp. p. 15.
26. Mitchell 1882b.
27. Mitchell 1882k.
28. During conservation of this window, Drew Anderson, Associate Conservator at the Metropolitan Museum, observed that individual pieces of glass varied greatly in thickness, and some of the edges were nearly paper-thin—features that would challenge the skills of the glazier in connecting the pieces of glass with channeled lead cane.
29. Schmutzler 1962, p. 230; Koch 1974.
30. Moran 1880b, p. 3.
31. Ibid.
32. Mitchell 1882i.
33. Ibid.
34. "Tiffany's Hall" 1894.
35. Ibid.
36. For an illustration of the table, see Christie's 2005, lot 329. The original finish has been lost; the table was subjected to severe stripping and then coated with a thick polyurethane.

37. For illustrations of the room with its original furniture, see Burke et al. 1986, pp. 126–27.
38. Mitchell 1882g, p. 118.
39. *Artistic Houses* 1883–84, vol. 1, pt. 1, p. 1.
40. "Artistic Homes" 1894, p. 129.
41. Ibid.
42. Undated, unidentified newspaper clipping in Tiffany scrapbook, Morse Museum.
43. See Oakey 1882, p. 734.
44. Mitchell 1882h.
45. Ibid.
46. Ibid.
47. Mitchell 1882e.
48. *Artistic Houses* 1883–84, vol. 1, pt. 1, p. 4.
49. Mitchell 1882f.
50. For information on the Tile Club, see Pisano 1999.
51. See Alice Cooney Frelinghuysen, "Aesthetic Forms in Ceramics and Glass," in Burke et al. 1986, pp. 220–21. For an in-depth discussion of the china-painting craze in America, see Brandimarte 1988.
52. In the early spring of 1878, Tiffany's sister Annie wrote in her memorandum book of 1878 of several visits to "the pottery," presumably at the Society of Decorative Art. The first entry is dated March 6, 1878: "I went to the pottery. Decorated a plate." On March 27, she said she went to the pottery and made something there with May. See Memorandum Book [Annie Tiffany Mitchell] 1878, Mitchell-Tiffany Family Papers, Manuscripts and Archives, Yale University Library, group 701, series III, box 16, folder 12.
53. Mitchell 1882f.
54. Mitchell 1882g, p. 117.
55. Two trellis-and-eggplant windows were made. Today, one is in the Morse Museum, the other in the Louis C. Tiffany Garden Museum, Matsue, Japan, as part of the collection of Takeo Horiuchi and his son Takashi Horiuchi. See Duncan 2004, pp. 138–39. There are slight differences between the two. It is likely that the window in the Morse Museum's collection is the one made for the Bella apartment, whereas the window in the Horiuchi collection may be the one Tiffany had made, at about the same time, for the interior of the George Kemp house, on Fifth Avenue in New York City.
56. Mitchell 1882f.

"The Most Artistic House in New York City": The Tiffany House at Seventy-second Street and Madison Avenue

Alice Cooney Frelinghuysen

In 1882 Louis Comfort Tiffany's father, Charles, embarked on an ambitious architectural project when he commissioned a large multifamily house on the northwest corner of Seventy-second Street and Madison Avenue in New York City (fig. 24). Following the trend for commercial establishments, Tiffany and Company among them, to locate near Union and Madison Squares (at Fourteenth and Twenty-third Streets), the fashionable and well-to-do had begun to move farther uptown in Manhattan by the early 1870s. William H. Vanderbilt's grand mansion was completed in 1882 at Fifty-first Street and Fifth Avenue, and at about the same time Tiffany's clients Ogden Goelet and George Kemp built houses on Fifth Avenue at Forty-ninth and Fifty-sixth Streets, respectively.

By February 1883 the foundation for the new Tiffany house had been dug and the subcellar and basement were visible to passersby.[1] The location at Seventy-second Street had offered Charles Tiffany an opportunity to procure a large footprint of land on a wide cross street, ensuring not only extra light but also ample southern exposure. Along with the land, he acquired the adjacent single-family house on Madison, which was eventually incorporated into the main building. As he was to do on subsequent architectural projects, Charles Tiffany's eldest son, Louis, provided the inspiration for the design and plans of the new house at 27 East Seventy-second Street (or 898 Madison Avenue). Although hastily drawn, Tiffany's small pencil sketch (see fig. 93) conveys the overall concept of the building and shows the house's principal facades. The noted

Opposite: Fig. 23. Detail of fig. 49

Right: Fig. 24. Exterior of the Tiffany house. From "The Tiffany House," *Architectural Record* 10 (October 1900), p. 191

Fig. 25. Vignettes of the Tiffany and Marquand houses, drawn by Hughson Hawley. From "New York Architecture: The Tiffany and Marquand Houses," *Harper's Weekly* 30 (May 22, 1886), p. 324. Courtesy of Amon Carter Museum Library, Fort Worth, Texas

Fig. 26. Entrance to the Tiffany house. From "Entrance to House of C. L. Tiffany, Esq., New York, N.Y. Messrs. McKim, Mead & White, Architects, New York, N.Y.," *American Architect and Building News* 25 (January 19, 1889). Private collection

Fig. 27. Dining room, Tiffany house. From "The Tiffany House," *Architectural Record* 10 (October 1900), p. 202

Fig. 28. Wall with lunette in dining room, Tiffany house. From "Illustrations," *American Architect and Building News* 22 (December 10, 1887), p. 278

architectural firm of McKim, Mead and White, with which Tiffany collaborated on a number of projects, implemented the design of the four-lot, fifty-seven-room structure.[2] Then one of the largest private dwellings in New York, with a ground plan of 110 feet by 125 feet and walls rising 90 feet above the sidewalk, the house retained a picturesque charm, with its broad gables, clustered chimneys, recessed and projecting balconies, and round turrets (fig. 25). The size and the novel color scheme prompted one critic to call it "the most conspicuous dwelling house in the city."[3] Another complained that it was "an attempt not so much to make a picture out of a building as to make a building out of a picture."[4]

The attention to detail on the facade, the ornament, and the materials for what the *Ladies' Home Journal* headlined "the most artistic house in New York City"[5] suggests that Tiffany contributed far more than just the initial design. The entrance was an enormous stone arch giving onto a central courtyard (fig. 26). The ornamental metal grillwork on the innovative porte cochere, actually more a portcullis, could be lowered as a security gate, but when it was open it hung from the top of the arch like a delicate fringe of compressed C-scrolls, a motif that Tiffany was to resurrect decades later for a series of jewelry designs.[6] The house's exterior was eye-catching for its unusual palette and varied textures. In lieu of the

Fig. 29. Louis Comfort Tiffany. Panel from dining-room lunette, ca. 1885. Plaster, glass, paint, 23¾ x 23⅛ in. (60.3 x 58.7 cm). The Charles Hosmer Morse Museum of American Art, Winter Park, Florida. This panel can be seen on the lower right side of the lunette (fig. 28).

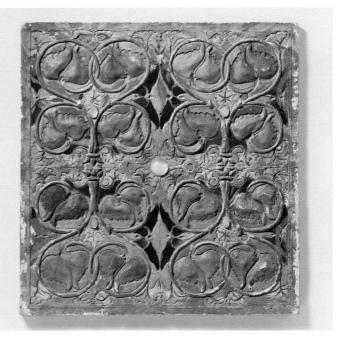

Fig. 30. Louis Comfort Tiffany. Panel from dining-room lunette, ca. 1885. Plaster, glass, paint, 23 x 22 in. (58.4 x 55.9 cm). The Charles Hosmer Morse Museum of American Art, Winter Park, Florida. This type of panel can be seen on the upper portion of the lunette (fig. 28).

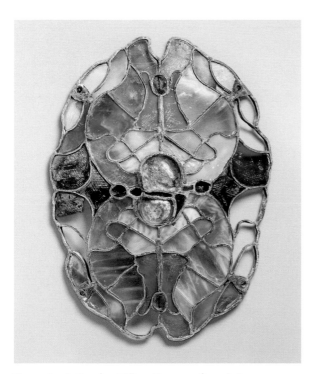

Fig. 31. Louis Comfort Tiffany. Fragment from dining-room lunette, ca. 1885. Leaded glass, 15 x 11 in. (38.1 x 27.9 cm). The Charles Hosmer Morse Museum of American Art, Winter Park, Florida. This fragment is one of eight that surround the central clock in the lunette (fig. 28).

Fig. 32. Louis Comfort Tiffany. Fragment from dining-room lunette, ca. 1885. Leaded glass, 19¼ x 19½ in. (48.9 x 49.5 cm). The Charles Hosmer Morse Museum of American Art, Winter Park, Florida. This fragment is one of four that surround the central clock in the lunette (fig. 28).

common and somber brownstone of earlier decades, the ground floor was faced with large chunks of rough blue stone and the walls above with bricks or modeled terracotta of yellowish brown clay mottled with black speckles, set off by a glazed black terracotta roof.[7] Not surprisingly, the brick was a completely new type formed of a semivitrified clay that could be made in multiple shades. Because it was first used on the Tiffany house, it was soon called "Tiffany brick." Although the bricks alone cost between $55 and $60 per thousand,[8] the total estimated cost of the house was a relatively modest $200,000,[9] only a fraction of the approximately $1.75 million William H. Vanderbilt spent on his palatial residence twenty blocks south.[10]

Embracing another innovative concept for the time, the building was a multifamily dwelling, with three apartments that were

Fig. 33. Breakfast room, Tiffany house. From "The Tiffany House," *Architectural Record* 10 (October 1900), p. 195

Fig. 34. Louis Comfort Tiffany, designer, J. Matthew Meier and Ernest Hagen, cabinetmakers, Table and side chair from Tiffany house, 1882–85. Maple, white enamel paint, table: 28 x 60 x 48 in. (71.1 x 152.4 x 121.9 cm); chair: 40¼ x 19½ x 18 in. (102.2 x 49.5 x 45.7 cm). The Mark Twain House and Museum, Hartford, Connecticut

Fig. 35. Entry for breakfast-room tables and chairs designed by Louis Comfort Tiffany, 1882. From J. Matthew Meier and Ernest Hagen Order Book, 1880–86. N-YHS Manuscripts Collection, Collection of The New-York Historical Society, Gift of *The Magazine Antiques*

Fig. 36. Designing room, Tiffany Studios. From *Character and Individuality in Decorations and Furnishings* (New York: Tiffany Studios, 1913), n.p.

among the largest and most generous ever built.[11] Charles was intended to occupy the first two floors (although he never moved from his house at 255 Madison Avenue) and Louis's sister Annie Olivia Tiffany Mitchell and her family the third floor, but in the end Louis was the only member of the family to reside in the building full time. He and his children (his first wife, May, having died in January 1884) moved into their apartment on the fourth and fifth floors in 1885. The other two apartments were leased, one of the first tenants being financier Henry Villard, who suffered financial reversals and was forced to sell his own sumptuous dwelling and the other houses he had hired McKim, Mead and White to design on Madison Avenue between Fiftieth and Fifty-first Streets (now part of the New York Palace Hotel).[12]

The building of the Seventy-second Street house coincided with a period of success in Tiffany's own career. His decorating business was thriving. His partnerships with textile designer Candace T. Wheeler (1827–1923) and fellow painter and decorator Lockwood de Forest (1850–1932) dissolved in the spring of 1883, although he maintained close ties with both of them.[13] Louis C. Tiffany and Company, Artistic Decorations, as his firm was now called, employed designers and highly skilled craftsmen on an unprecedented scale to create special-order decorations of all kinds for his interiors, among them three principal rooms in the White House for President Chester A. Arthur. While only a few years before, all Tiffany's work was carried out in a single nine-hundred-square-foot room, his workshops at 333 and 335 Fourth Avenue now encompassed three floors of a large building. These more extensive quarters had facilities for "designing and executing interior decorative works" in a variety of media and techniques, including "painting and papering, fresco and fabrics, relief ornament, leather and metal and interior woodwork," as well as "stained and leaded glass, glass tiles, and mosaic facings and mosaic floorings."[14]

With comprehensive workrooms at his disposal, it was therefore entirely appropriate that Louis should have a hand in the decoration not only of his own apartment in the new house but of the two others as well. The first room the visitor saw was the spacious and sparsely furnished entrance hall, where the walls, steps, and trim were sheathed in marble, with mosaic panels inset into squares decorating the walls. Four large hanging light fixtures anchored each corner.[15] The grand staircase from the first to the second floor was "all finished in marble and mosaic" with "water-green glass tiles," and the walls were stenciled in silver on a brown ground, materials Tiffany was especially fond of at the time.[16] (Tiffany had made lavish use of silver stenciling in the Veterans Room of the Seventh Regiment Armory in New York, completed in 1880, and also in the Mark Twain house, in 1881.) Indeed, stenciling was a decorative theme throughout the Seventy-second Street house: a stenciled pattern of palm leaves in many colors adorned the main hall, and in the bedrooms were friezes stenciled "in successive bands, to which a slightly waving effect is given, almost deluding the eye with the impression of . . . some printed textile fabric."[17]

Tiffany's concern for light predicated that, as in the Bella apartment, he and his family would have the top floors and that his enormous studio would occupy most of the upper floor, with its abundance of windows and dormers. This new house offered Tiffany another opportunity to mold raw space into something wholly his own. The house may have been Tiffany's most exotic creation, incorporating decorative ideas and the kinds of objects he was to return to again and again for the rest of his professional life. Although he transferred not only his ideas but also architectural elements, furnishings, and his growing collections from the Bella apartment to the newly designed residence, these rooms were to look exceedingly different, not just because they were

Fig. 37. Library fireplace, Tiffany house. From Cecilia Waern, "The Industrial Arts of America: The Tiffany Glass and Decorative Co.," *International Studio* (September 1897), p. 159

larger in scale but also because they reflected Tiffany's evolution as a decorator. The unusual house elicited considerable attention from the press, which described it variously as "artistic," "unique," and "an aesthetic warehouse."[18] It was bursting with objects of art from China, Japan, Persia, and India. Indeed, each highly individualistic room in the large Romanesque Revival structure gave one the impression of entering a different Eastern country. Irregularities abounded, not only in the decoration but in the floor levels and even the ceilings, which were variously curved, vaulted, or composed of curious angles. Tiffany was later to incorporate many of these furnishings and architectural elements into his designs for Laurelton Hall.

The room in Tiffany's apartment that most closely resembled the interiors in his contemporaries' newly built city mansions was one of the two cavernous dining rooms (fig. 27). With its exposed-beam ceiling, it evoked European baronial halls of centuries past. The furniture itself was surprisingly *retardataire*. A set of Chippendale-style chairs surrounded a pedestal dining table that harked back to the Greek Revival style of the early nineteenth century. Although it is difficult to tell from photographs alone, the furniture was probably American, dating at least as late as 1876, or after the Centennial celebration. It was remarkably close to the furniture in historical styles that Tiffany's own workrooms fabricated for a public that was not yet willing to embrace his more unusual designs. An artful arrangement of plates and chargers from his extensive collection of old pottery, including fourteenth-century Persian and seventeenth-century Hispano-Moresque lusterwares, was displayed on the walls, with vessels of varying shapes densely packed on the mantel shelf. Thin stalactite-shaped shades of blown Favrile glass hung delicately from the ceiling

Fig. 38. Bay window in library, Tiffany house. From Charles de Kay, "A Western Setting for the Beauty of the Orient," *Arts and Decoration* 1 (October 1911), opp. p. 470

beams. On two of the walls Tiffany mounted a pair of his own paintings, the large friezelike allegories *Spring* (fig. 173) and *Autumn*, which were later relocated to the upstairs balcony of Laurelton Hall. (*Autumn* was presumably destroyed by the fire there in 1957.) As was the custom, Tiffany deemed a vegetal theme appropriate for the dining room. He thus brought the *Eggplant* window (figs. 7, 22) from the dining room of the Bella apartment to display at one end of the new dining room and mounted it in a broad, flat frame held by a stand that recalled Chinese freestanding screens. In the photograph of the room what appears to be another window screen, possibly the *Squash* window, sits in front of the fireplace.[19]

An enormous lunette with intricate designs of glass and plaster panels with relief and painted decoration dominated one wall of the second large dining room (fig. 28). A number of the panels

from the lunette were later transferred to Laurelton Hall and survived the fire. The designs of arabesques and stylized leaves have an air of the Near East about them. The relief-molded and painted plaster panels are also decorated with glass insets, some opaque red, others flat and rippled in shades of blue (figs. 29, 30). Several leaded-glass panels in a related palette of peacock blue and gold were also part of the original lunette (figs. 31, 32). These panels feature mosaiclike designs of abstract insects or butterflies that incorporate tiny broken pieces of ancient iridescent glass along with Tiffany's own experimental glass.

That Tiffany was fully aware of the initial stirrings of the Arts and Crafts movement in England and the precepts of William Morris (1834–1896) was revealed in the breakfast room of the Seventy-second Street house (fig. 33), where quaint mottoes such as "Always Ready" and "Gude Folks are Scarce—Take Care

Fig. 39. Louis Comfort Tiffany, Tiffany Glass Company, Three *Magnolia* panels, ca. 1885. Leaded glass, 52⅞ x 18½ in. (134.3 x 47 cm), 52⅞ x 19½ in. (134.3 x 48.6 cm), 52⅞ x 19 in. (134.3 x 48.3 cm). The Charles Hosmer Morse Museum of American Art, Winter Park, Florida. These panels, three of five initially installed at the Tiffany house (fig. 38), were later moved to Laurelton Hall (fig. 157). Presumably, the other two were destroyed in the 1957 fire.

Opposite: Fig. 40. Detail of fig. 39

o'Me" were burned into the surfaces of the exposed beams. Likewise, the furniture Tiffany designed for the room conformed to Arts and Crafts ideals. Perhaps because in 1882 Tiffany's workshops were not yet making great quantities of furniture, Tiffany commissioned the small New York cabinetmaking partnership of J. Matthew Meier and Ernest Hagen to fabricate furniture from designs supplied by him for the breakfast room and other interiors in the house. Meier and Hagen were located at 213 East Twenty-sixth Street, near the buildings Tiffany's firm occupied at Twenty-fifth Street and Fourth Avenue (now Park Avenue South).

If the furnishings in the dining rooms were conservative, in the breakfast room they were avant-garde; their simplicity and functionality were a definite step forward from earlier historicizing styles. The table that sat in the center of the room (fig. 34), which Tiffany ordered from Meier and Hagen in 1882 (fig. 35), is little more than a smooth unadorned panel five feet long and four feet wide connected to legs that resemble traditional sawhorses. It is virtually a duplicate of the workbenches the designers and workmen used in Tiffany's studios (fig. 36). Two additional tables, identical except that they were not as long, could either be placed along the walls for service or joined with the large one to accommodate more guests.[20] In his 1882 order for the chairs Tiffany asked

Fig. 41. Corner of ballroom, Tiffany house. From Charles de Kay, "A Western Setting for the Beauty of the Orient," *Arts and Decoration* 1 (October 1911), p. 470

for one "Barnes straight back splint seat Chair for sample to experiment."[21] The experiment produced twelve tall-backed rectilinear chairs, two with arms, whose form recalled the vernacular American slat-backed chairs that appeared in the late 1600s and became ubiquitous during the eighteenth and early nineteenth centuries. The chairs were originally upholstered in "natural colour bridle leather with large iron hollow nails."[22] The plain cream-colored enamel finish on the suite presaged the white furniture other progressive designers such as William Morris, Charles Rennie Mackintosh (1868–1928), and James Abbott McNeill Whistler (1834–1903) were to produce at the turn of the century. Tiffany used the same finish on the woodwork in the breakfast room and on the built-in furnishings, including an inviting seat under the eyebrow window at one end of the room.[23] The window seat was amply cushioned with patterned and tufted upholstery and even had a floor cushion. (Such foot cushions appeared throughout the Seventy-second Street house interiors, even under the breakfast room table, to provide additional comfort, perhaps especially for Tiffany himself, given his short stature.)[24]

In decorating the new house Tiffany often used found or utilitarian objects in nontraditional ways to achieve unusual compositions. In the breakfast room, for instance, two large wrought-iron yokes fitted with large, nearly cylindrical pale opalescent glass globes served as light fixtures (see fig. 33). And set into the walls to provide extra storage space were large wine casks made of East Indian carved teak inlaid with ivory (see fig. 275). In 1882 Tiffany purchased some 2,500 Japanese *tsuba*, or sword guards, from Lockwood de Forest (see figs. 274, 277).[25] Made primarily of iron and ornamented with various metals and mother-of-pearl, *tsuba* were highly collectable at the time. (Both Edward C. Moore, chief designer at Tiffany and Company, and Henry Osborne Havemeyer, Tiffany's most important patron, were ardent collectors. See the essay by Julia Meech in this volume.) They were often decorative and featured motifs such as chrysanthemums and dragonflies that inspired the artists of the day. Tiffany used *tsuba* to face the wine casks in the breakfast room. In the library, the openings in the metal disks created

Fig. 42. Ballroom fireplace, Tiffany house. From Cecilia Waern, "The Industrial Arts of America: The Tiffany Glass and Decorative Co.," *International Studio* 2 (September 1897), p. 158

Fig. 43. Louis Comfort Tiffany, Tiffany Glass Company, *Butterfly* window, ca. 1885–92. Leaded glass, 63 x 61⅛ in. (160 x 156.5 cm). The Charles Hosmer Morse Museum of American Art, Winter Park, Florida

distinctive, almost stencil-like patterning on the chimney breast, as well as on the walls of the firebox, the fireplace hood, and the fender (fig. 37), where the disks' metallic and iridescent surfaces undoubtedly shimmered in the light of the fire. Repeated pairings of sword guards also embellished the vertical divisions between the five leaded-glass *Magnolia* panels that formed the enormous bay window in the library (fig. 38), and the two hanging lamps in the room, chains and all, were composed of sword guards.

The Japanese-style fireplace (later moved to Laurelton Hall) protruded into the library. The iron hearth hood could be raised and lowered using spherical weights like the ones Tiffany had devised for moving the stained-glass panels at the Bella apartment. Above the fireplace was a three-part painting by Tiffany. Borrowing an idea from the Bella apartment library (see figs. 17, 18), he covered the central panel with a dense pattern of horsechestnut leaves; the birds on the two flanking panels could be peacocks, another of his favorite motifs. Colored-glass panels set into

Fig. 44. Vestibule to studio, Tiffany house. From "The Tiffany House," *Architectural Record* 10 (October 1900), p. 197

the wall to the right of the fireplace, blue-stained walls, Spanish tiles, and a ceiling with blue crossbeams stenciled in gold added to the decorative scheme. The library was furnished with generously proportioned plush upholstered armchairs, as well as a deep, cozy window seat in the bay (see fig. 38) with enormous puffy cushions covered in soft velvet. Decoration was Tiffany's first priority, but he was also concerned with creating a comfortable environment.

The stained-glass panels in the bay window served as a transition between indoors and outdoors, mitigating the urban environment by bringing inside two of the plants Tiffany loved most: flowering magnolias and wisteria vines (fig. 39). By the time these panels were installed on Seventy-second Street, Tiffany had developed his ingenious Favrile glass, with its subtle variations of color and texture, enabling his glassworkers to re-create the mag-

nolia and wisteria with extraordinary verisimilitude. The pendulous blossoms of the wisteria entwined on a continuous trellis across the five transoms were rendered in rich hues of deep purple, blue, and pink. To fabricate the lifelike magnolias in the tall panels below, with their branches of cast lead to simulate the irregularities of bark and soft, cream-colored blossoms delicately tinged with pink (fig. 40), the glassworkers actually manipulated the glass, folding and creasing it while it was still in a semimolten state. The generous amounts of colorless transparent glass in both the tall windows and the nearly square transoms allowed a view of the outdoors and let in light.

The rounded dome of the oriel was "inlaid with deep blue glass mosaics studded with jewels which sparkle in the dull light of day, and which at night must be resplendent above the pendant

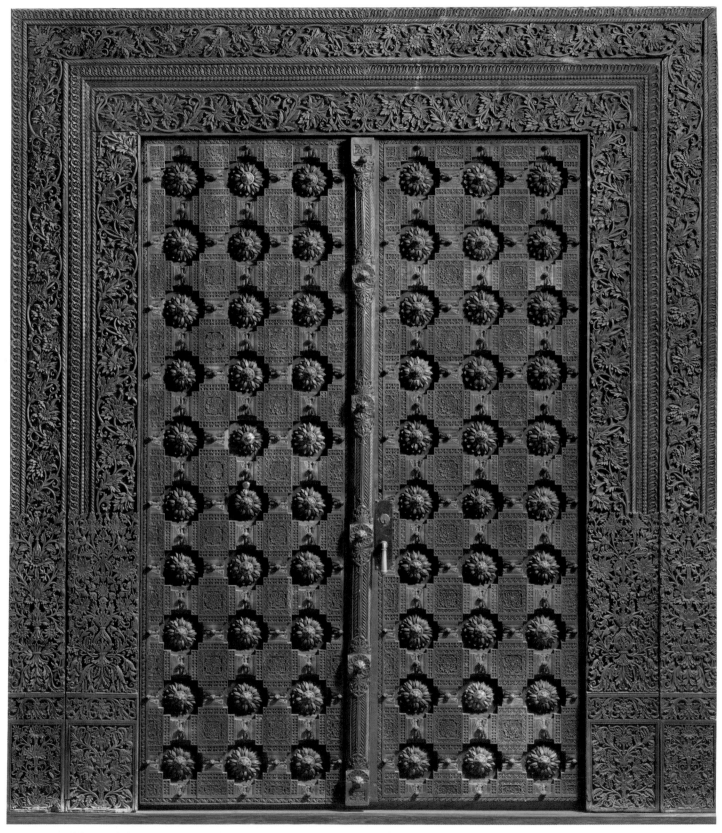

Fig. 45. Pair of doors with frame, originally from vestibule to studio, Tiffany house. Ahmadabad, India, 1882. Teakwood, 95 x 107½ x 5 in. (241.3 x 273.1 x 12.7 cm), with frame. The Charles Hosmer Morse Museum of American Art, Winter Park, Florida. The doors are visible at the entrance in fig. 46.

gas-light."[26] Tiffany had introduced mosaics into his decorations for the Union League Club in New York, which opened in early 1881, but he used them in a domestic interior for the first time in the Seventy-second Street house.[27] In fact, Tiffany paid a great deal of attention to surfaces, variously covering them with glass mosaic, wallpapers, stenciled patterns, or innovative painted finishes. The walls of the large ballroom (also known as the reception room or music room), for example, were given a stuccolike effect when they were stenciled with an East Indian design and then finished with sand that had been stained pink.[28] The narrow vertical ribbing on the deep coved frieze (fig. 41) suggested the bamboo patterning in such interiors as William H. Vanderbilt's

Fig. 46. Entrance to studio,
Tiffany house. From "The
Tiffany House," *Architectural
Record* 10 (October 1900), p. 198

Japanese parlor.[29] The "pink and gold ribbed cloth" on the furniture complemented the wall decoration.[30] To enhance the East Indian flavor of the room, Tiffany installed the wall hangings and slender carved twin columns he had brought from the living room of his Bella apartment (see fig. 14). He was later to incorporate them into the decor of the art gallery at Laurelton Hall.[31] (See the essay by Richard Guy Wilson in this volume.)

No surface in the ballroom, also called the reception room or the music room, was left unadorned. Tiffany's own paintings were double-, even triple-hung on the walls. Oriental carpets of various sizes and patterns created a mosaiclike effect on the floor, and glass mosaic itself was incorporated into the ornamentation. The unusually long chimney breast (fig. 42) was completely faced with glass tesserae, the rectangular overmantel in a seemingly abstract floral pattern, according to the only surviving period

description of it, "of pale sea-green glass, opaque, clear, clouded, or iridescent, on a platina foil."[32] The mantel shelf displayed an array of vessels, after the early 1890s many of them experimental lustrous blown glass vases from Tiffany's own furnaces. The collection of iridescent ancient glass that inspired many of Tiffany's Favrile-glass vases was kept in the shallow display case set into a glass mosaic framework to the right of the fireplace.

Fragments of ancient iridescent glass and abalone shell are set among the tiny pieces of opalescent glass in the window that was originally installed in an alcove framed by Indian woodwork and Islamic tiles in a corner of the ballroom in the Seventy-second Street house (see figs. 41, 42). Leading of varying thicknesses creates a mosaic effect in the large, nearly square window (fig. 43), which was eventually transferred to Laurelton Hall and is now in the Charles Hosmer Morse Museum, Winter Park, Florida.

Fig. 47. Detail of fig. 45

Fig. 48. Four tiles. Iznik, Turkey, 1575–1650. Glazed earthenware, each 7¾ x 7¾ x ¾ in. (19.7 x 19.7 x 1.9 cm). Ball State University Museum of Art, Muncie, Indiana, Gift of David T. Owsley

The two circular motifs just above center at either side are true mosaic, made of glass pieces joined together and then set into a composition backing that prevents light from coming through; the rest of the window is translucent. Stylized flowers and swarms of butterflies in an almost monochromatic palette of yellows, golds, creams, and pinks surround the large Japanese lantern in the center of the symmetrical composition. Tiffany may have been inspired by William H. Edwards's newly published *Butterflies of North America*, a copy of which he had in his library.[33] As in the *Magnolia* panels, the leads were cast to give them specific textures and shapes, here in order to fashion the butterflies' bodies and the twisted vines. The very fragility and translucence of a crinkled white paper lantern has been uncannily replicated in textured glass. The lantern, and the round motifs at the sides, may bring Japan to mind, but the rigid symmetry of the composition and its dense allover patterning, and especially the tightly wound vines at the bottom, recall stone tracery windows from India, which Tiffany would also have seen illustrated in books in his library.[34]

Tiffany's taste for the exotic also found expression on the fifth floor of the house, where visitors to his studio passed through a vestibule lavishly decorated with carved Hindustan teakwood said to have been taken from an "East Indian palace over two thousand years old" (fig. 44).[35] Lockwood de Forest may have supplied the woodwork; in 1882 he made a buying trip to Calcutta, Madras, Hyderabad, and Ahmadabad, where he purchased an entire house that had been slated for destruction. He sold the facade of the house to the Victoria and Albert Museum in London and supplied the rest to Tiffany for his "new house."[36] The workshop de Forest had set up in Ahmadabad in 1881 also provided the pair of immense teak doors that led into the studio (fig. 45).[37] The

doors, carved in stylized foliate patterns whose depth and crispness yield a highly decorative effect as light plays over the surface (fig. 47), were set into an equally ornate frame on the vestibule side. Some of the linear patterns in the frame reappeared in other furniture and woodwork Tiffany ordered from de Forest's Ahmadabad workshop. Tiffany mounted individual Persian tiles above the doorway and along the frieze in both the vestibule and the studio (fig. 46). These were among the many tiles of diverse origins, including a group of Iznik tiles (fig. 48), that were displayed in a number of rooms at Seventy-second Street and later transferred to Laurelton Hall.

The exotic flavor of the vestibule was further accentuated by the collection of antique weapons massed in one corner, which Tiffany had moved from the foyer of the Bella apartment (see fig. 11). Set into an alcove (see fig. 44) was a chest of dark wood inlaid with stylized mother-of-pearl cypress trees and roses that is virtually identical to a nineteenth-century chest from Damascus (fig. 50) that The Metropolitan Museum of Art purchased in 1918 as part of a large group of decorative objects once owned by de Forest.[38] Although the chest from the vestibule is not known to survive, the piece it inspired Tiffany to design for this house, the case for an upright Steinway piano, remains with Tiffany descendants (fig. 49).[39] The motifs on the piano's side panels as well as the stylized cypress trees and roses, six-pointed stars, and crescents are purely Ottoman and virtually duplicate designs from the chest. The ornament was skillfully carved and incised in Tiffany's own workrooms, with the "inlaid" sections not mother-of-pearl but instead painted in dull silver and outlined with a thin gold line (see fig. 23). The piano, which does not appear in any of the period photographs of the Tiffany house, presumably stood either

Fig. 49. Louis Comfort Tiffany (case), Steinway and Sons, New York, Piano, 1888. Cherry (?), 58 x 61¼ x 28¼ in. (147.3 x 155.6 x 71.8 cm). Private collection

in the vestibule or in the studio itself. It retains its original sounding board and felts and has a melodious sound to this day. Tiffany loved music; there were several keyboard instruments in his house, and he even hosted concerts from time to time.

Tiffany looked farther east for inspiration for the unusual leaded-glass pendant that hung above the chest in the vestibule (fig. 51). The pendant, composed of green and red varicolored opalescent glass and thick coiled lead came, owes its form to a Chinese jade hanging chime (fig. 53) that had been in Tiffany's personal collection from at least the early 1880s. In his Bella apartment he had suspended the carved and pierced jade musical chime from the ceiling of a curio cabinet in the library and fitted it with a socket for a candle or a lamp to illuminate the translucent jade (fig. 52).[40]

To at least one journalist, the vestibule looked like a "a bit from the palace of the Indian Rajah."[41] Yet it was but a prelude to Tiffany's studio, at once his most personal and most publicly heralded interior (fig. 54). The room was a true studio, where Tiffany painted and where people came to see his work. In certain of the period views, drawings and canvases, some framed, some not, are

Fig. 50. Chest. Damascus, Syria, 19th century. Wood, mother-of-pearl, 33⅛ x 56⅛ x 22¼ in. (85.4 x 143.8 x 56.5 cm). The Metropolitan Museum of Art, New York, Purchase, 1918 (18.45.1). A similar chest can be seen in the vestibule of Tiffany's studio (fig. 44). The Museum's chest was purchased from Lockwood de Forest, Inc.

Fig. 51. Louis Comfort Tiffany, Pendant, ca. 1885. Leaded glass, 21¾ x 25¼ in. (55.2 x 64.1 cm). Associated Artists, LLC. The pendant hung in the alcove of the vestibule to Tiffany's studio (fig. 44)

Fig. 52. Curio cabinet in library, Bella apartment. Engraving by D. Maitland Armstrong, from Donald G. Mitchell, "From Lobby to Peak: Between Rooms," *Our Continent* 1 (April 19, 1882), p. 148. Collection of Brown University Library, Providence, Rhode Island

Fig. 53. Musical chime. China, 17–18th century. Jade, H. 14½ in. (36.8 cm). Photo courtesy of The Hermitage Foundation Museum and Gardens, Norfolk, Virginia

Fig. 54. Studio, Tiffany house. From "The Tiffany House," *Architectural Record* 10 (October 1900), p. 200

Fig. 55. Fireplace in studio, Tiffany house. From "The Most Artistic House in New York City: A Series of Views of the Home of Mr. Louis C. Tiffany," *Ladies' Home Journal*, November 1900, p. 12

stacked on the floor. But the enormous loftlike space, with its forty-five-foot ceilings, also lent itself to entertaining and fêtes. The large four-sided fireplace in the center, of brick covered with stone-colored Portland cement, resembled the trunk of a giant tree (fig. 55). Tiffany depicted a smoldering fire in one of its openings in a painting of 1896 (fig. 56). He might have been describing the effect of this great fireplace when he later he spoke about the noble eighty-foot trees on his property at Laurelton Hall: "I came to these wondrous woods that I might live with the trees. I wanted to bring them into my house—to the very fireside."[42]

Large, antique, scrolled wrought-iron brackets that Tiffany purchased on one of his trips to Europe were attached to the fireplace. Some of the virtual forest of glass lanterns suspended at different heights on chains attached to the ceiling (figs. 54, 55) were also surely acquired during his frequent travels abroad. But they were joined eventually by globes of mouth-blown glass with combed and threaded decoration that represented some of Tiffany's earliest work in the medium, from the early 1890s. The wrought-metal chains, some purchased from de Forest in India, the others of varied origins, were themselves exceedingly decorative. A few appear to have been hung for decorative purposes alone, for no lamp was suspended from them. On the four chains that supported the weight of a hanging chaise (figs. 57, 59), birds and elephants alternate with decorative ornaments, some with a fringe of beads that tinkled when the chaise moved. The hanging bench itself, made in Tiffany's workrooms, featured turned spindles and a cushioned cover. A shimmering canopy of what looks like either metallic or beaded cloth hung like an awning above the swing.

Fig. 56. Louis Comfort Tiffany, *A Corner of the 72nd Street Studio*, 1896. Oil on canvas, 30¼ x 12⅛ in. (76.8 x 30.8 cm). Yale University Art Gallery, New Haven, Gift of Louise Tiffany Lusk, B.A. 1929 (1955.13.1)

Fig. 57. Corner of studio, with hanging chaise, Tiffany house. From Charles de Kay, "A Western Setting for the Beauty of the Orient," *Arts and Decoration* 1 (October 1911), p. 469

Fig. 58. Louis Comfort Tiffany, Tiffany Glass and Decorating Company, Detail of entrance-hall door to the H. O. Havemeyer House, New York (one of a pair), 1890–91. Wood, copper, beach stones, Favrile glass, 100 x 36 in. (254 x 91.44 cm). University of Michigan School of Art and College of Architecture and Urban Planning, on extended loan to the University of Michigan Museum of Art, Ann Arbor. Similar leaded-glass panels were installed behind the hanging chaise in the corner of Tiffany's studio (fig. 57).

Fig. 59. Four hanging chains from the Tiffany house. India, ca. 1882. Bronze, left to right: 52 x 3 in. (132.1 x 7.6 cm); 78¾ x 3 in. (200 x 7.6 cm); 39¾ x 5 in. (101 x 12.7 cm); 76¾ x 5 in. (194.9 x 12.7 cm). The Charles Hosmer Morse Museum of American Art, Winter Park, Florida

Fig. 60. Louis Comfort Tiffany, *Louise Tiffany, Reading*, 1888. Pastel on buff-colored wove paper, 20½ x 30¼ in. (52.1 x 76.8 cm). The Metropolitan Museum of Art, New York, Partial and Promised Gift of the family of Dorothy Tiffany Burlingham, 2003 (2003.606)

Fig. 61. Entrance to photographic studio, Tiffany house. From "The Most Artistic House in New York City: A Series of Views of the Home of Mr. Louis C. Tiffany," *Ladies' Home Journal*, November 1900, p. 13

Fig. 62. Louis Comfort Tiffany, *Taming the Flamingo*, 1888. Watercolor on paper, 23 x 28½ in. (58.4 x 72.4 cm). Signed and dated at lower left: *Louis C. Tiffany 88*. The Charles Hosmer Morse Museum of American Art, Winter Park, Florida

Fig. 63. Louis Comfort Tiffany, *Inside Studio on 72nd Street with Flamingos*, 1888. Oil on canvas, 23¼ x 29 in. (59.1 x 73.7 cm). Signed at lower right: *Louis C. Tiffany*. The Charles Hosmer Morse Museum of American Art, Winter Park, Florida

Behind the swing was an ornamental screen of glass and metal that was either a duplicate of or a prototype for the ornament Tiffany used, in 1891–92, in the entrance hall doors of the Fifth Avenue house of Louisine and Henry Osborne Havemeyer (fig. 58).[43] By embedding large, beach-worn stones into the intricate lead came scrollwork that frames square panels of marbleized glass, Tiffany found a novel use for common natural materials. The trompe l'oeil leaded-glass columns that framed the panels echoed the thick rounded columns throughout the studio.

At one end of the studio a series of arches topped a row of these unadorned columns, which were made of a polished composite material.[44] Shelves and terraced platforms along the western end of the large room held tropical plants and Oriental art in many media. The furniture, most of it light, spare, and easily moved, was in a variety of styles: Some of the chairs were in the split spindle-back style of the early eighteenth century, still others were of a Windsor type, and several wicker armchairs were spread about the room. A chaise upholstered in tufted green velvet provided a place for repose. In 1888 Tiffany depicted his second wife, Louise, reading on the chaise in the studio, with the cluster of three thick columns and a grand piano in the background (fig. 60).

A seat positioned between the two columns at one end of the studio (fig. 61) provided the setting for numerous family photographs. The seat was covered with a heavy Russian plush that had the appearance of thick fur, and connected to one of the columns was an unusual fountain, shaped somewhat like the fireplace, surrounded by plantings and with a goldfish bowl suspended above it. Not long after the house was completed Tiffany used this corner of the studio as the backdrop in a watercolor of a model feeding a flamingo (fig. 62), which he later translated into stained glass (see figs. 245, 246).

Glass became an even greater component of the interior decoration in this house than it had been in any of Tiffany's earlier residences. A large stained-glass window graced one end of the studio. In another corner was a lunette composed of a combination of glass, mosaic, and wirework in a color scheme the *Ladies' Home Journal* described as starting "at the top with a dark amber, gradually melting down into an old gold tone, which produces a mysterious effect and also results in enhancing the great height of this exceedingly delightful studio."[45] The succession of decorative projecting arches framing the lunette may have inspired the dramatic reredos Tiffany created for the famous chapel that he exhibited to great acclaim at the World's Columbian Exposition in Chicago in 1893 (fig. 112) and that, in 1916, he installed on the grounds of Laurelton Hall.[46] (See the essay by Richard Guy Wilson in this volume.)

The magic of this dramatically evocative room is perhaps best conveyed in Tiffany's own paintings (figs. 56, 63). For the studio was in fact far more than a studio. With its divans and mosque lamps and smoke emanating from the open hearths, one would be transported into some "dim seraglio." Despite his rumored shyness, Tiffany often hosted theatrical parties and musicales in this enchanted space. Anna Mahler (later Werfel) remembered attending one of these soirées in 1909 with her husband, Gustav Mahler, and Louisine Havemeyer:

> We entered a room so enormous it seemed to us immeasurable. Coloured lustres shed a soft, flowerlike light through the gloom. The prelude to *Parsifal* was being played on an organ. . . . A black fireplace in the middle of the room had four colossal hearths, in each of which a fire of a different colour was blazing. We stood stock-still in amazement. . . . The chimney went up and up for ever, no roof was visible, but high up in the walls panels of stained glass, designed by Tiffany, were let in, and lighted from without. We spoke in whispers and felt that these panels of flowerlike light might be the gates of Paradise. The music stopped and it was now apparent from the murmur of voices that a large company was assembled. Silent footmen perambulated with costly glasses, filled with champagne, which although on trays never clinked. Palms and sofas, beautiful

Fig. 64. Passage leading from studio, Tiffany house. From "The Most Artistic House in New York City: A Series of Views of the Home of Mr. Louis C. Tiffany," *Ladies' Home Journal*, November 1900, p. 12

women in odd shimmering robes—or did we dream? It was the thousand and one nights—in New York.[48]

An entirely different mood pervaded the passageway that led from the studio to the family's bedrooms (fig. 64). Here and in his designs for some of the bedrooms Tiffany revealed a contemporary sensibility. The white enameled woodwork and the cool gray walls gave the space an aura of simplicity, calm, and repose.[49] There were no hard corners; even the transition from walls to ceilings were "not square, but strongly rounded off," which gives the impression of space where "the opening recedes and has the appearance of being skillfully hollowed out—an appearance which adds materially to the artistic effect."[50]

Tiffany's interiors for the Seventy-second Street house, and in particular for his studio, left an indelible impression on all who visited. It transported one to dream, awakening "the senses to the imagination by means of skillfully crafted allusions."[51] The studio was a transforming environment, situated in a vibrant indus-trial city that was culturally coming of age but a world apart, a sanctuary from the daily bustle. Elements of Tiffany's artistic creations at his Seventy-second Street house as well as his earlier Bella apartment found a new life on Long Island, where Tiffany incorporated them into his ultimate country home, Laurelton Hall.

Well after his children had grown and moved into homes of their own, the house on Seventy-second Street continued to serve as Tiffany's city residence. That he transported many of the interior decorative elements to Laurelton Hall suggests that he reduced his quarters to suit the needs of a single widower, but how the interiors in the city house evolved can only be speculated. Tiffany died at home in his apartment in the Seventy-second Street house in 1933. Three years later the building was demolished to make way for 19 East Seventy-second Street, a seventeen-story limestone-clad luxury apartment building that was urban architect Rosario Candela's last major project.

1. "New Houses" 1883, p. 66.
2. "Artistic House" 1900, p. 12. Tiffany provided small pressed-glass tiles in varying opalescent shades for two residences McKim, Mead and White designed in the 1880s, the dining room at Kingscote in Newport, Rhode Island, and the Ross Revillon Winans House in Baltimore, Maryland, for which he also provided brilliant blue glass tiles for the facing of the fireplace in the entrance hall. For the tiles at Kingscote, see Frelinghuysen 1995, pp. 575–76. For the Winans House, see White 1998, pp. 57–61. Tiffany and McKim, Mead and White continued to collaborate on both public and private projects during the next two decades.
3. "Madison Avenue" 1884.
4. "Tiffany House" 1884, p. 786.
5. "Artistic House" 1900.
6. See Frelinghuysen in Phillips 2006, pp. 79–80.
7. "Tiffany House" 1884, p. 785.
8. Real Estate 1898, p. 403.
9. "Building Items" 1882.
10. Garrett 1999.
11. Janes 1912, p. 161.
12. See White 1998, pp. 78–83.
13. On Tiffany's work in partnership with Candace Wheeler, see Peck and Irish 2001, especially pp. 38–57. On de Forest's relationship with Tiffany, see R. Mayer and Lane 2001.
14. *Decorator and Furnisher* 10, no. 5 (August 1887), p. 164.
15. These fixtures, like many other elements from this house, were later moved to Laurelton Hall.
16. Janes 1912, p. 161; Humphreys 1887, p. 38.
17. Humphreys 1887, p. 42.
18. Ibid., p. 40; "Artistic House" 1900, p. 12.
19. See McKean 1980a, fig. 43, for a comparable window.
20. Louise Tiffany Lusk, Norwalk, Connecticut, to Hugh F. McKean, Winter Park, Florida, July 3, 1969, Archives, Charles Hosmer Morse Museum of American Art, Winter Park, Florida. According to the same letter, the tables were eventually moved to Tiffany's first Long Island country house, the Briars. They are owned today by the Mark Twain House and Museum, Hartford, Connecticut.
21. J. Matthew Meier and Ernest Hagen order book, entry for breakfast-room table and chairs, 1882, N-YHS Manuscripts Collection, Collection of the New-York Historical Society, Gift of *The Magazine Antiques.*
22. J. Matthew Meier and Ernest Hagen order book, invoice for breakfast-room furniture designed by Louis Comfort Tiffany, June 5, 1885, N-YHS Manuscripts Collection, Collection of the New-York Historical Society, Gift of *The Magazine Antiques;* see also "Artistic House" 1900, p. 13. On the breakfast-room furniture, see Naeve 1996.
23. See "Breakfast Room" 1900.
24. Louis C. Tiffany, Passport application, December 27, 1907. National Archives and Records Administration.
25. See R. Mayer and Lane 2001, pp. 25, 30. De Forest had purchased these sword guards in Paris in June 1882, on the account of Tiffany and de Forest.
26. Humphreys 1887, p. 42.
27. See Frelinghuysen 2002, pp. 44–45.
28. "Artistic House" 1900, p. 12.
29. For an illustration of the Vanderbilt parlor, see New York 1994–95, p. 232.
30. "Artistic House" 1900, p. 12.
31. I am grateful to Bruce Randall, a collector passionate about Tiffany's work, whose careful study of the art gallery interiors brought this to my attention.
32. Waern 1897, p. 161.
33. Among the books from Tiffany's extensive personal library that were auctioned off in 1946 (Parke-Bernet 1946, lot 598) was William H. Edwards, *The Butterflies of North America* (Philadelphia: American Entomological Society, 1879).
34. See, for example, Theodore C. Hope and James Fergusson, *Architecture at Ahmedabad, the Capital of Goozerat* (London: John Murray, 1866), pl. 37, reproduced in R. Mayer 1996, p. 8.
35. "Artistic House" 1900, p. 12.
36. Lockwood de Forest to Louis C. Tiffany, March 17, 1882, transcription by Meta Kemble de Forest, Lockwood de Forest Papers, Archives of American Art, Smithsonian Institution, microfilm 2731.
37. These were probably the doors de Forest ordered from his Ahmadabad workshops on December 12, 1882. He also ordered a large mantelpiece, which was installed in the house's upper-hall fireplace. See R. Mayer and Lane 2001, pp. 28–30.
38. These were probably among the many goods de Forest purchased in Damascus in the spring of 1882. See R. Mayer and Lane 2001, p. 25. I thank Navina Haidar Haykel, Associate Curator in the Department of Islamic Art at The Metropolitan Museum of Art, for her insights on the chest.
39. According to the Steinway and Sons archives, the piano was manufactured on June 6, 1888, and was delivered to "C. L. Tiffany" on November 13, 1888. There was an additional notation: "design by L. C. Tiffany." Letter from Margaret Wolejsza, Customer Service, Steinway and Sons, New York, to Alice Cooney Frelinghuysen, December 20, 2004.
40. Mitchell 1882i. Figure 51 was later moved to Laurelton Hall and ultimately to the parlor in Sarah Hanley's house on the property. See Phillips 1985, lot. 710. Figure 53, which hung in the library of the Bella apartment, was ultimately part of the Asian collection sold at the Louis Comfort Tiffany Foundation sale. It and nine other lots were purchased by Mrs. Florence Sloane, founder of the Hermitage Foundation in Norfolk, Virginia. The current whereabouts of this object is not known.
41. De Kay 1914, p. 58.
42. L. Tiffany 1917b, p. 43.
43. See Alice Cooney Frelinghuysen, "The Havemeyer House," in Frelinghuysen et al. 1993, p. 175.
44. "Artistic House" 1900, p. 13.
45. Ibid., p. 12.
46. For a full discussion of the chapel, see Frelinghuysen 2002.
47. John Moran, quoted in Burns 1993, p. 271.
48. Mahler 1969, pp. 160–61.
49. "Artistic House" 1900, p. 12.
50. Ibid.
51. Burns 1993, p. 218.

1807 *Lotus*

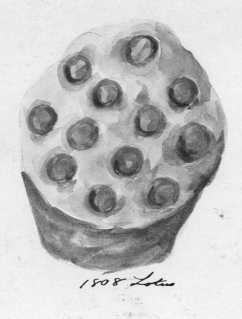

1808 *Lotus*

1812 *Poppy.*

1809 *Peony.*

1810 *Peony*

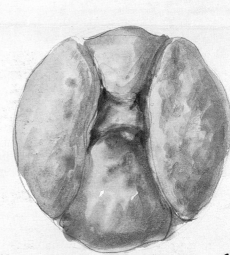

1811 *Magnolia*

1813 – *Poppy*

Louis Comfort Tiffany's Country Residences

Alice Cooney Frelinghuysen

L ouis Comfort Tiffany's love of the country was instilled during childhood summers from the late 1850s through the mid-1860s, when his parents sent him and his sister Annie (1844–1937) for extended visits to their Connecticut cousins. The benefits of country living were widely recognized, and it was considered highly desirable to escape the noise and commotion of city life, which were magnified as temperatures rose in July and August. Family correspondence during Tiffany's summer visits with his aunt Lydia in Norwich and New London, near Long Island Sound, conveys an image of carefree months spent "rowing, fishing, bathing and riding."[1] This early exposure to a pastoral life outside the city was to have a lasting impact on Tiffany as an artist and designer.

THE HOUSE AT IRVINGTON

When Tiffany was about seventeen, his father, Charles Lewis Tiffany, purchased property and a house in Irvington, New York, some twenty-five miles north of the city, overlooking the Hudson River. The younger Tiffany developed a boundless enthusiasm for the place and made his way there as soon as boarding school was finished for the year, and though the summer was a favorite season for European travel, he frequented the Irvington home for extended stays. His father facilitated these visits by securing the adjacent property and house for his young married children's use. Annie, who had married Alfred Mitchell in 1871, and Louis, who married Mary (May) Woodbridge Goddard (1846–1884), Mitchell's cousin, the following year, took full advantage of the fresh country air. For Louis, the estate also provided opportunities for making sketches and paintings of the flowers and scenery, as well as of his wife and children, and it was perhaps here that his interest in plant subjects evolved, forms that were later the basis of his designs in the decorative arts.

In his paintings of these early days, Tiffany would further idealize the country, evoking the nostalgia of the colonial period by portraying members of his family in costumes of the eighteenth century. This whimsical interest was one he would continue to pursue, collecting flamboyant costumes that served not only to clothe his models (often family members) but to outfit his guests at elaborate entertainments and parties that he staged throughout his life (see the essay "The Art of Magnificent Living" in this volume).

THE BRIARS

Irvington remained in the family until Charles Tiffany's death in 1902, when it was sold out of the family.[2] But already by the 1880s Louis was exploring the North Shore of Long Island as a possible site for a summer residence. Artists had long been drawn to the area, finding desirable subject matter in the windblown dunes, marshes, and waterways of the eastern end, in Southampton and East Hampton. On an 1884 visit with his friends Robert W. de Forest and his father, Henry G. de Forest, at Henry's recently completed Shingle-style cottage in Montauk, Tiffany spent long, pleasurable hours walking, driving, painting, observing nature, and collecting pebbles on the beach. For one of his earliest domestic windows he used an assemblage of smooth, translucent stones, integrating them into an underwater design.[3]

In the fall of 1888 Tiffany acquired land on the North Shore on which to build his first country house,[4] and the Briars, as it was called, was ready for occupancy in early September 1889.[5] Unfortunately, the only documentation on the house that has survived are a few photographs and newspaper descriptions. It was 144 feet in length and 48 feet in depth, quite modest when compared to Laurelton Hall. Reflecting the Shingle style of the de Forest house, a style in vogue for country houses of the 1880s, it was surrounded by expansive porches for family gatherings (fig. 66), but going beyond traditional weathered shingles, it incorporated stucco porch walls and benches (see fig. 94). The most distinctive feature was an immense clock tower that overlooked a circular court. A testament to Tiffany's abiding interest in technology, the clock had a four-bell chime on the quarter hour (as a courtesy to neighbors and guests, the chime had a 10:00 P.M. to 7:00 A.M. shutoff).[6] The Laurelton Hall tower was to surpass this with its great clock connected to the chimes of four bells, the largest of which was said to weigh eight thousand pounds.[7] Although Tiffany and Company sold clock workings, this impressive model

Opposite: Fig. 65. Design drawing of flower buds and seedpods, ca. 1900–1915. Watercolor, graphite, and ink on paper, 18⅜ x 14 in. (46.7 x 35.6 cm). The Metropolitan Museum of Art, New York, Gift of Lenox, Inc.

Fig. 66. View of porch and pergola, The Briars. From Samuel Howe, "One Source of Color Values—Illustrating Mr. Louis C. Tiffany's Significant Handling of Things Greater than Architecture and One Source of His Strength in Color," *House and Garden* 10 (September 1906), p. 112

was fabricated by B. Howard and Company of Boston. The clock face at the Briars, almost obscured by the ivy that ultimately covered the tower (see fig. 95), was of stucco, inlaid with Tiffany-glass segments.[8] Plantings, carefully arranged, mark the beginning of Tiffany's affinity for landscape design.

The only known contemporary description of the interiors of the Briars, in a 1901 *New York Times* article, confirms Tiffany's quest to design all the decorative elements to create a harmonious whole:

> One of these rooms, which is perhaps ideal, is that of Louis C. Tiffany in his Summer home, Cold Spring Harbor, L.I. This should be everything that could be desired, for the furniture represents the idea and design of Mr. Tiffany himself, and the room was decorated under his direction. The soft gray of the furniture is put into a soft old rose setting, with rose colored damask covering the walls and forming the hangings. The ceiling is tinted delicately in accordance with the color scheme of the rooms, and there is a beautifully stenciled frieze which completes the decoration, if one accepts the sconces and gas fixtures which are of old bronze made for the room and the glass globes of a green shade also made for the room.[9]

One of the more interesting features of the room was its "artistic summer furniture," called driftwood furniture. It was described as exceedingly simple and useful, "made in the most dull, lifeless gray which everyone who is familiar with driftwood knows, and made on the simplest of lines, after the style of the California mission furniture."[10] It was, however, distinguished by its fine craftsmanship and finish, the ash wood "given the peculiar shade by a secret process which brings out the grain. . . . The result is one which has been a great delight to artists and people of artistic tastes. The furniture is made by hand: every piece is carefully selected. . . . It will not be inexpensive, as a piece of handwork, designed by an artist, and patterned, may be expected to be, and a set will cost perhaps $800."[11] Such simplicity of line and atten-

tion to finish were to be seen again in the furnishings Tiffany was later to design for Laurelton Hall.

LAURELTON HALL

Tiffany had been working on additions and renovations to the Briars when his father died.[12] The sizable inheritance he was left— roughly three million dollars—was in effect an invitation for him to give free rein to his vision of a dream house and gardens.

By the late nineteenth century, Long Island's North Shore, with its proximity to the city and its unspoilt lands, was beginning to be recognized by the affluent as a desirable site for a country estate.[13] A reporter for the *Brooklyn Daily Eagle*, writing in April 1899 of the grand new estates of August Heckscher, Walter Jennings, and Robert W. de Forest, noted that "the high hills and bold bluffs and promontories fronting the harbor and sound at Glen Cove, Locust Valley, Cold Spring Harbor, Huntington . . . afford surpassingly fine locations for large and stately residences."[14]

Tiffany had already been adding to his land holdings by 1901,[15] and in August 1902 he acquired an old resort hotel about fifteen minutes by automobile from the town of Oyster Bay (fig. 67). He was to adapt its name, Hotel Laurelton, for his future estate. Situated on a bluff overlooking Cold Spring Harbor and Long Island Sound, the site was just a mile south of Sagamore Hill, the Theodore Roosevelt estate. Tiffany added several parcels of adjacent acreage, and by the time he was finished the property totaled some 580 acres (fig. 68).[16]

In addition to the magnificent setting, Tiffany was drawn to that particular location by the presence in nearby Cold Spring Harbor of his closest friend, Robert W. de Forest, and his wife, Emily. Their house, Wawapek, designed by Grosvenor Atterbury and completed in 1900, would be just visible from across the harbor when Laurelton Hall was finished. Tiffany might also have been able to see Burrwood, the grand residence of Walter Jennings, designed by Carrère and Hastings and under construction at the same time as the de Forest estate.[17] Jennings, who had made his fortune in the oil and gas industry, not only socialized with the Tiffany family but also commissioned Tiffany to design what was to be one of his most important windows, an allegorical figural composition of the Four Seasons surrounded by an elaborate border of twelve floral panels, the latter by Tiffany designer Agnes F. Northrop (1857–1953). Only the two figural panels survive; the border is known through a design drawing in the Metropolitan Museum.[18]

The house site had been owned by one Dr. Oliver L. Jones, who built the four-story hotel, which opened with one hundred rooms in June 1873. Tiffany demolished the picturesque structure, replacing it with his masterpiece, once described as combining "the perfume of the Orient and the horse sense of America, with its revitalizing influence seen everywhere."[19]

The amount of time and effort that Tiffany expended in the designing of Laurelton Hall sets it apart from his other houses. It took more than two years to complete and reportedly cost two

million dollars. Once he owned the property, Tiffany set out to survey the land. He also had a model made of it in clay, and he prepared "portfolios of strange and interesting sketches, added to and worked over as the spirit moved."[20] The point of departure was the site itself (figs. 68, 69). As Samuel Howe (1854–?1928), an architect and associate of Tiffany's, remembered, "The place literally grew from the ground up, not from the drawing office down."[21]

The design of the house was conceived entirely by Tiffany himself. He was described as "[taking] a lump of modeling wax and, at the same scale, form[ing] his conception of the central court, the living room, the dining room, the little den, and the conservatory."[22] He worked out the requirements and proportions of each room, before putting the plan all together. In other words, as Henry Saylor wrote, "Tiffany's method was to determine the desirable proportions of each room first, and independently of all the others, and then arrange these in the best relation to each other, keeping in mind always the need for light, air, intercommuni-

cation, and a pleasing conformity to the natural lay of the land."[23]

While clearly the architect of Laurelton, Tiffany had the plans for the eight-level, eighty-four-room house drawn up by a young architect, Robert L. Pryor (1879–1964), then in the employ of Tiffany Studios (see figs. 97–101). Little is known of Pryor or his career. Although he designed a number of houses in the Oranges, New Jersey, where he moved after he married in 1905, it appears that Laurelton Hall was the most notable building of his career.[24]

For the construction of this large and complicated structure, Tiffany turned to Charles T. Wills, an experienced builder based in New York City with credits to his name that included city residences, clubhouses, schools, commercial buildings, and churches for such noted architects as Carrère and Hastings, Ernest Flagg, Peabody and Stearns, and McKim, Mead and White.[25] Tiffany had established professional relationships with two of the firms: McKim, Mead and White had implemented Tiffany's design for his family's house at Madison Avenue and Seventy-second Street in 1883, and

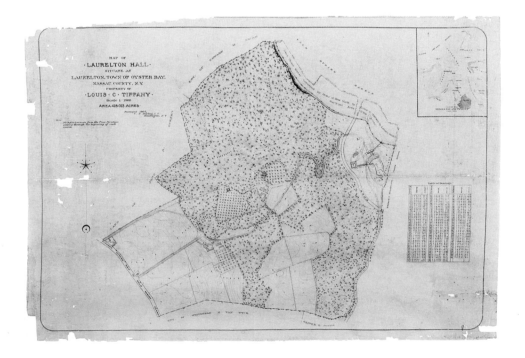

Fig. 68. *Map of Laurelton Hall*,
1907–8. Starched cloth, 50 x 72 in.
(127 x 182.9 cm). Society for the
Preservation of Long Island
Antiquities, Cold Spring Harbor,
New York

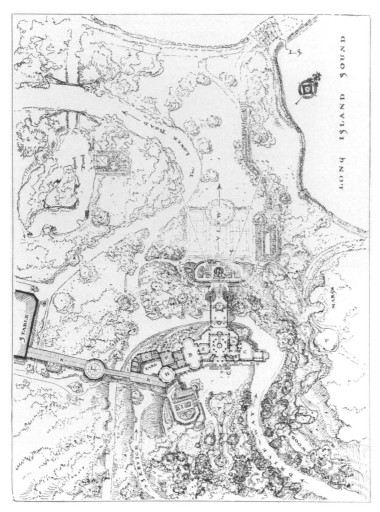

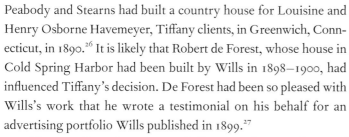

Fig. 69. Sketch of plan, Laurelton Hall. Drawn by Samuel Howe, from Howe "The Picturesque Fountain Scheme in the Long Island Home of Mr. Louis C. Tiffany," *American Country Houses of To-Day* (New York, 1915), p. 384

Fig. 70. Farm tower with peacock weather vane, originally on property of Laurelton Hall

Peabody and Stearns had built a country house for Louisine and Henry Osborne Havemeyer, Tiffany clients, in Greenwich, Connecticut, in 1890.[26] It is likely that Robert de Forest, whose house in Cold Spring Harbor had been built by Wills in 1898–1900, had influenced Tiffany's decision. De Forest had been so pleased with Wills's work that he wrote a testimonial on his behalf for an advertising portfolio Wills published in 1899.[27]

Tiffany confronted numerous challenges in his completion of the house. One of the most critical was his decision to bring electricity from the town of Oyster Bay, a costly undertaking but one essential to the achievement of his ambitious lighting scheme. In the *New York Times* of May 22, 1904, it was reported that despite strong opposition from his neighbors, Tiffany had erected poles along several miles of highway, some on property he did not own.[28]

In addition to the house, the estate included a series of outbuildings, among them stables, tennis courts, barns, silos (see figs. 69, 70, 316, 317), greenhouses (see fig. 318), and a gatehouse, and later the Tiffany chapel from the 1893 World's Columbian Exposition in Chicago (see fig. 112), a studio, and an art gallery (see figs. 133, 335–337).

Whereas in the interior decoration and architectural details of the house Tiffany referenced motifs from China, Japan, and the

Islamic world, for his gardens he responded to the naturalism of English garden design at the turn of the century. His reverence for nature, which found lasting expression in his artistic vision, was also evident in the care he lavished on the landscape surrounding Laurelton Hall. Native plants, trees, shrubs, and field flowers—all of which he was to incorporate into his art—were a vital and integral part of Laurelton Hall. But Tiffany did not use nature merely to serve his own purposes. He also became a devoted advocate of plant conservation. Describing Laurelton, he wrote: "This is the natural home of the birch, both black and yellow; of the chestnut and of the oak. Occasionally an evergreen pine or hemlock darkens or a dogwood brightens things. We have also maple and silver beech. When the old chestnuts get disturbed,—blown over and uprooted, or die out, we plant others of the same kind, and so restore the woods."[29]

Laurelton Hall was built at a time when landscape architecture was coming into its own as a professional discipline. Tiffany was not a professional landscape designer or a horticulturalist, but his lack of training did not deter him from immersing himself in the details of his gardens' creation.[30] Following the principles of the British horticulturalist William Robinson (1838–1935), Tiffany adapted his own vision to the existing site rather than imposing a particular style on it. He would likely have been familiar with

Fig. 71. Gardens with house in distance, Laurelton Hall. From Henry H. Saylor, "The Country Home of Mr. Louis C. Tiffany," *Country Life in America* 15 (December 1908), p. 157

Fig. 72. Lily pool behind Laurelton Hall. From Henry H. Saylor, "The Country Home of Mr. Louis C. Tiffany," *Country Life in America* 15 (December 1908), p. 158

Robinson's seminal book *The English Flower Garden*, first published in 1883, which advocated plantings using native species and naturalizing spring bulbs by planting them in large informal drifts, and set forth an approach to landscaping—evident in the surviving

Fig. 73. Rock crystal from terrace fountain, Laurelton Hall. Largest crystal: 19½ x 17½ x 11½ in. (49.5 x 44.5 x 29.2 cm). The Charles Hosmer Morse Museum of American Art, Winter Park, Florida

images of the grounds at Laurelton—in which plantings of trees, shrubs, perennials, and bulbs were massed in layers (figs. 71, 72).

Like Robinson, Tiffany rejected the Victorian practice of creating beds with annuals that would be changed as flowers faded. Similarly, for plant material he preferred old-fashioned varieties, or "naturalized emigrants," rather than "the highly cultivated darlings of fashionable society—prisoners of the greenhouse."[31] This meant he would select single flowers rather than double ones, or, as in his circular rose garden, old-fashioned varieties rather than new cultivars. In one section of the garden, the so-called Grandmothers' Garden, Tiffany incorporated jack-in-the-pulpits, bird's-eye violets, ferns, and other wild plants, which he, his children, and his thirty-five gardeners transplanted from their natural habitat.

Tiffany planned the grounds with an artist's eye, paying careful attention to color harmonies. He selected, for example, a cooler palette of flowers in one area to blend with the fog that rose from the arbor. The mile-long main entrance drive that led to the house was vibrant with rhododendrons, honeysuckle, laurel, fields of daffodils ablaze in yellow, dark masses of red cedar, and lighter deciduous trees. Each bend revealed a different view of the approaching house. Like an artist working with different hues, Tiffany "painted" the grounds with color—broad sweeps of pale

Fig. 74. Design drawing of a lotus blossom, ca. 1900–1915. Watercolor, graphite, and ink on paper, 18⅜ x 14 in. (46.7 x 35.6 cm). The Metropolitan Museum of Art, New York, Gift of Lenox, Inc.

Fig. 75. Design drawing of a peony blossom, ca. 1900–1915. Watercolor, graphite, and ink on paper, 18⅜ x 14 in. (46.7 x 35.6 cm). The Metropolitan Museum of Art, New York, Gift of Lenox, Inc.

pink mountain laurel, purple Japanese irises, yellow bearded irises, and tawny marsh marigolds edging and reflected in the ponds (see fig. 71), beds of tulips, azalea, and phlox.

Fountain terraces that descended in tiers toward the sound ended in a twenty-foot hanging garden supported on black locust trunks. Fountains abounded, both in the gardens (figs. 73, 116–118) and in the house (see figs. 110, 120, 130, 133, 134), evidence of Tiffany's fascination with water. His careful study of its sources, its routes, and its possibilities gave rise to various experiments: "Water from the hillside is caught, carefully treasured in a land basin in one of the high points. It is also pumped by steam and by electricity from driven wells into tanks which hold some forty thousand gallons."[32] Water sparkling in sunlight, shooting skyward in fountains, encircling large rock crystals (fig. 73,) cascading through terraced gardens, and creating reflections in still ponds spread a lustrous vitality overall.

Flowers on the outside of the house became an extension of the house: for instance, Tiffany designed heavy canopies of blue and white wisteria supported on great webs of wire outside, and in the dining room installed a frieze of leaded-glass windows whose floral motifs echoed the drooping wisteria vines (see figs. 149–152, 156). The entrance loggia (see figs. 105, 278), installed today in The Metropolitan Museum of Art (figs. 82, 107), in many ways epitomizes Tiffany's artistic mission in its combination of nature and architecture. The loggia derives directly from the eastern facade of a palace in the Red Fort at Agra, in India (see fig. 106). The origi-

nal was built of a distinctive uniform red sandstone, but Tiffany brightened his version of the facade, incorporating glass and pottery in its fanciful capitals. The stems supporting the glazed pottery blossoms are composed of many individual pieces of glass in shades of green. Each capital is a botanically accurate depiction of a different flower. From left to right are the East Indian lotus, the Greek peony, the opium poppy, and the saucer magnolia, all depicted in three stages of growth, from the bud at the bottom to the flower in full bloom to the seedpod crowning the very top of the capital.

The glass for the stems would have been made at Tiffany Furnaces in Corona, Queens, in New York City. The fabrication of the blossoms, however, raises questions. A group of five drawings discovered in the archives at Lenox, Inc., the New Jersey manufacturer of fine china, may provide a clue. These beautiful watercolor renderings depict blossoms, buds, and seedpods identical to those replicated in three dimensions on the capitals (figs. 65, 74–77). Since the materials from which the blossoms were made—ceramic with fired enamel colors—are not ones that Tiffany was yet producing, the flowers were most probably fabricated somewhere other than Tiffany Studios. Lenox is the most likely source. Tiffany and Lenox already had business affiliations through the Tiffany and Company store, and some of Lenox's fine art porcelains were for sale at Tiffany and Company in an exclusive arrangement.[33] To achieve his vision of naturalistically colored floral motifs, Tiffany may have instructed Lenox to mold the designs and then paint them with enamels in the broad color palette they had developed.

Fig. 76. Design drawing of a poppy blossom, ca. 1900–1915. Watercolor, graphite, and ink on paper, 18⅜ x 14 in. (46.7 x 35.6 cm). The Metropolitan Museum of Art, New York, Gift of Lenox, Inc.

Fig. 77. Design drawing of a magnolia blossom, ca. 1900–1915. Watercolor, graphite, and ink on paper, 18⅜ x 14 in. (46.7 x 35.6 cm). The Metropolitan Museum of Art, New York, Gift of Lenox, Inc.

The loggia brings together in one work many of Tiffany's important influences. The overall concept is drawn from Indian architecture, the stems on the capitals are bound to resemble Roman fasces, and the glass-mosaic panels in the spandrels and the iridescent blue glass-tile frieze evoke Byzantine mosaics (fig. 78). Three paneled lanterns in iridescent gold and opalescent blue glass, hanging from iron chains, recall Celtic ornament. Tiffany combined all these exotic sources and infused them with an original artistic sensibility to give a novel and fantastic quality to Laurelton Hall.

Tiffany's attention to plant life in all its variety and stages of evolution reflects the interests of several English and European designers of the late nineteenth century. The inclusion of ten plates of "leaves and flowers from nature" (one of them by Christopher Dresser) in Owen Jones's *Grammar of Ornament* (London, 1856) inspired a host of studies that examined the decorative possibilities of the natural world. Those by Maurice Pillard Verneuil (1869–1942), Eugène Grasset (*La Plante et ses applications ornementales*, 1896), A. E. V. Lilley and W. Midgley (*Plant Form and Design*, 1896), and Dresser himself were surely known to Tiffany.[34]

The Daffodil Terrace and porch were situated on the south side of the dining room, to the west of the loggia, providing a transition area between the house and the gardens (fig. 79). The supporting columns, of which there were originally twelve— eight for the terrace pavilion and four for the porch extending from the pavilion outside the dining room—were, like the loggia

Fig. 78. Louis Comfort Tiffany, Tiffany Furnaces, Four tiles from loggia, Laurelton Hall, ca. 1905. Favrile glass, each 4 x 4 x ⁷⁄₁₆ in. (10.2 x 10.2 x 1.1 cm). The Metropolitan Museum of Art, New York, Gift of Robert Koch

Fig. 79. Daffodil Terrace, Laurelton Hall, ca. 1920s. Gelatin silver print, 8⅛ x 10 in. (20.5 x 25.4 cm). Photograph by David Aronow. The Metropolitan Museum of Art, New York, Gift of Robert Koch, 1978 (1978.646.17)

Fig. 81. Sketch of a daffodil capital, ca. 1908–15. From notebook of Leslie H. Nash. Collection of the Juliette K. and Leonard S. Rakow Research Library of The Corning Museum of Glass, Corning, New York, Nash Archives

Left: Fig. 80. Louis Comfort Tiffany, Tiffany Studios, Capital from Daffodil Terrace, ca. 1914–15. Glass and cement, 22 x 21 in. (55.9 x 53.3 cm). The Charles Hosmer Morse Museum of American Art, Winter Park, Florida

columns, crowned by a floral motif, in this case, daffodils (fig. 80). Samuel Howe might have been describing these capitals in the article he wrote on Tiffany in 1906: "For years a Painter has given himself up to the peculiar study of transmitting beauties of Nature to elements of decoration. . . . The garden his school, the flower his companion, his friend and his inspirer."[35]

The stems of the daffodils, like those of the flowers decorating the loggia capitals, consisted of slivers of green glass. But the blossoms, rather than being made of glazed pottery, were fabricated of glass cast in molds, utilizing the skills of the Tiffany Studios glassmakers to create the evocative bouquets. According to Leslie H. Nash (1884–1958), production manager at Tiffany Furnaces, twelve different molds were required for each capital. The glass was, of course, to be "daffodil yellow"[36] (fig. 81), though it was actually of several different shades of yellow and varying degrees of opacity. The annealing of the thick glass blossoms provided an additional challenge to the glassmakers. The estimate for the capitals alone came to $5,280.00.[37] The fact that the Daffodil Terrace does not appear on Pryor's original floor plans, and that details of its fabrication are described by Nash, who was not in Tiffany's employ until 1908, suggest that it was added after the 1905 completion date, probably as late as 1914.

The country house, and Laurelton Hall in particular, was for Tiffany the culminating vision of a complete aesthetic environment, one imbued with a profound appreciation of nature. Laurelton was a testament to the ideals of the Arts and Crafts movement, which dictated that house and garden be designed as an integrated whole. Nature would serve to inspire art, and art would in turn be a reflection and an expression of the natural world. And thus would the sensibilities and ambitions of the artist be revealed.

1. Henry Tiffany to Annie Oliver Tiffany Mitchell, 1863, Mitchell-Tiffany Family Papers, Manuscripts and Archives, Yale University Library, group 701, box 7, folder 117.
2. The Irvington community feared that an alleged proprietor of a New York City gambling house was to buy the property. In the end, it was sold on April 24, 1902, to A. Lawrence Phillips, the treasurer and general manager of the Valentine Varnish Company at 57 Broadway, New York, acting as the buyer's agent, but to be used as a private residence. See "Canfeld" 1902.
3. De Forest's house was part of a complex of houses designed by McKim, Mead and White in 1882–1883 for the Montauk Point Association. See White 1998, pp. 85–93. The window, completed at the end of 1884 for Robert and Emily de Forest, featured thick brown seaweed in a background of deep blue glass and was the first of several early undersea windows. See Emily Johnston de Forest, "Inventory of Wawapek Farm," undated typescript (1920s?), collection of Priscilla de Forest Williams.
4. The first documentation of Tiffany's foothold on Long Island dates from October 20, 1888, when the following notice appeared in *The Long Islander*: "We are pleased to learn that Louis Comfort Tiffany, son of the great New York jeweler, is to build a very fine and large house on the Laurelton Road, not far from the Dr. Wood place. H[ewlett]. J. Long, of Huntington, has the contract for the new building."
5. On August 31, 1889, *The Long Islander* reported that "L. C. Tiffany and his wife are expected at their Summer residence during the early part of next week. They sailed from Europe on the 26th and will come direct to Cold Spring upon their arrival in the city."
6. Hugh G. Johnson, Laurel Hollow, to Mr. McCain [sic], Orlando, Florida, August 1, 1977, Charles Hosmer Morse Museum of American Art, Winter Park, Florida (hereafter Morse Museum). Johnson was handling the estate for his family, who owned the Briars in 1977, and was offering the clock tower to Hugh McKean as a possible purchase; nothing came of the deal, and the tower remains in its now ivy-covered state in situ today.
7. *The Long Islander*, January 22, 1904.
8. Ibid.
9. "Summer Furniture" 1901.
10. Ibid.
11. Ibid.
12. An article in *The Long Islander* (February 27, 1897) mentioned "extensive improvements" being made on the property, and several months later, the same journal noted that a new house was being built (April 17 and June 12, 1897). In April 1902, it reported that "L. C. Tiffany has had a large number of men employed for nearly a month, remodeling and redecorating his country residence on the west side."
13. For a thorough discussion of Long Island as a country retreat, see MacKay et al. 1997.
14. "Palatial" 1899.
15. Tiffany purchased a tract of land from Susan D. Brightson for $15,077. *The Long Islander*, July 12, 1901.
16. Like those of many who were trying to buy up parcels of land, Tiffany's name was kept anonymous, and all transactions were handled through his New York law firm. It was reported on August 8, 1902, that Charles A. Peabody of the law firm Baker and Peabody had purchased "Laurelton Hotel and grove and the residence of Dr. James R. Wood of Manhattan, both located on the west side of Cold Spring Harbor. . . . The purchase price is private, but it is said to be not far from $125,000 for the two properties." In 1903, Tiffany also purchased the "Heywood place at Laurelton formerly owned by L. C. Bell." *The Long Islander*, August 8, 1902, and March 20, 1903.
17. MacKay et al. 1997, pp. 101–2.
18. For an illustration of the figural panels, see Frelinghuysen 2000, p. 405. The Metropolitan drawing (67.654.317) has not been published.
19. Howe 1907, p. 156.
20. Howe 1915, p. 386.
21. Ibid. For Howe's career, see note 13 of the essay by Richard Guy Wilson in this volume.
22. Saylor 1908a, p. 157.
23. Ibid., p. 159.
24. "Robert L. Pryor—Architect, 1879–1964," typescript by Ethel Yule Pryor, n.d., Archives, Morse Museum.
25. *Illustrations of Buildings Erected by Charles T. Wills, 156 Fifth Avenue, New York* (New York, 1899). This portfolio includes testimonial letters along with large half-tone images of buildings Wills helped to construct. Such portfolios were undoubtedly intended as promotional vehicles to aid in securing new commissions. Collection of Chicago Art Institute Library, courtesy of Steve Finer, Bookseller, Greenfield, Massachusetts, cat. 159, no. 20.
26. For a discussion and illustrations of the Havemeyer country house, see Alice Cooney Frelinghuysen, "The Havemeyer House," in Frelinghuysen et al. 1993, pp. 173–98.
27. See note 25 above.
28. "Tiffany Wins" 1904.
29. Howe 1906, p. 108
30. His library contained seventy-five volumes devoted to different aspects of garden design, plants and trees; see Parke-Bernet 1946, pp. 101–11, lots 622, 623, 630–637, 667, 669, 706.
31. Howe 1906, p. 109.
32. Howe 1907, p. 158.
33. See Frelinghuysen 1989, pp. 250–51; and Denker 1989, pp. 29–37.
34. For a thorough discussion of contemporary European and British design theorists and their responses to nature, see Martin P. Eidelberg, "Nature Is Always Beautiful," in Eidelberg et al. 2005, pp. 45–51.
35. Howe 1906, p. 105.
36. Nash Notebooks, Rakow Library, Corning Museum of Glass, and courtesy of Christie's, New York. I thank Martin Eidelberg for bringing this to my attention.
37. Ibid.

Mysticism, Alchemy, and Architecture: Designing Laurelton Hall

Richard Guy Wilson

Nestled along a ridge with the wide blue panorama of Cold Spring Harbor in the background, Laurelton Hall appeared to float amid a sea of green trees and lawns speckled with flowers of all hues. To some viewers, the cream-colored house and tower, with blue-green roofs and colorful ornamental ceramic blossoms, resembled an apparition come to life. Twilight transformed the house into a glowing jewel box as the stucco took on a gray cast and set off the glittering leaded-glass windows. For Louis Comfort Tiffany, Laurelton Hall represented his consummate statement on the transformative power of art, on how the integration of architecture, decoration, landscape, and setting can create a metamorphic experience of intense beauty and with deep symbolic resonances. He intended it to be a demonstration of a new direction in American art and architecture in contrast to the historical styles of the many large houses and mansions of the period, whether in Chicago, San Francisco, or Newport, or along Long Island's so-called Gold Coast.

One approached the house by passing through a carefully controlled landscape, designed so that its plants and flowers would be in bloom from early spring to fall (fig. 83). A service road led in from the west, but the guest entered the estate of 580 acres from the southeast. This was the highest point on the grounds, with the land falling off toward the north. A gatehouse with a vaguely Moorish tower guarded the entrance, and a split in the road allowed the visitor to choose the path to the house. The road to the left, bordered by maple trees and day lilies, passed by Tiffany's chapel from the 1893 World's Columbian Exposition, fields filled with flowers, and a pond before swooping under the conservatory bridge at the service end of the house. The road to the right, bordered with red cedars—which ultimately grew to a height of seventy to eighty feet—and an undergrowth of mountain laurel, overlooked the water. Black and yellow birch trees native to the site stood beyond the russet-brown and green cedars, providing contrasts of color and texture. Fields appeared, planted with blooming wildflowers. Both roads had straight stretches and curves, following the contours of the land, and periodically the trees opened for vistas of fields or the blue harbor beyond. The contrast between sunlight and dark shade evoked suspense and mystery, according to one writer, and from time to time smaller roads or bridle paths intersected the main drives.[1] An apple orchard came into view, and if the time of year was right, pink blossoms consumed the trees. Ponds, rivulets, and fountains appeared (fig. 84), and the house and its tower could be glimpsed through breaks in the trees (fig. 85). One passed fountains along with cultivated flower beds filled with lilies, daffodils, and an increasing amount of pink and white phlox, which Tiffany, through a commentator, explained had "an ancient history": "The Greeks termed [phlox] a 'flame,' and the all-encompassing Romans assigned to it a noble place." Offsetting the phlox were large masses of alyssum, saxifrage, and arabies whose yellow, white, and silver colors were described as "nymph-like" and "pagan in [their] purity."[2]

Finally, one heard the chimes of the tower, and the entire house came into view, appearing to float on a green mat in front of the intense blue harbor (fig. 86). Molded into the hillside, the house was a long horizontal mass, and its color seemed to change with the light, from a textured cream to gray. The counterpoised tower marked the entrance loggia and the great interior court. The molded blue-green copper roofs and the dashes of bright ceramic colors on the capitals of the loggia provided a spectrum of color. Following the road, one's vehicle descended to a lower level and the porte cochere (fig. 87), and one either entered the house or continued on around to its north side under another terrace and a hanging garden. A profusion of plants, flowers, and gardens could be glimpsed as one turned to the left, passed under the conservatory (fig. 88), and headed back toward the chapel and the gatehouse, or instead went to the right and down the hill. After a few hundred feet a road branched off leading to the stables and farm buildings, and another continued past more ponds down to the tennis courts and the beach. Rising from the beach was a sixty-foot-tall Moorish-style telescoping minaret, covered with bands of iridescent glass and topped by a copper finial (figs. 89–91). This was the stack for the heating and pumping plant and stood near a bathing pavilion and a boathouse.

Fig. 83. Drive looking toward Long Island Sound, Laurelton Hall, ca. 1920s. Gelatin silver print, 8⅛ x 10 in. (20.5 x 25.4 cm). Photograph by David Aronow. The Metropolitan Museum of Art, New York, Gift of Robert Koch, 1978 (1978.646.40)

To visit Laurelton Hall was an unforgettable experience, and the residence became one of the most published grand houses in the years between 1900 and 1920. The visitor to Laurelton Hall actually stepped into and inhabited a work of art and through the experience, Tiffany contended, reached a new awareness or consciousness. This transformative journey was difficult, if not impossible, to put into words. Visitors struggled to describe Laurelton Hall; they employed terms such as "Oriental" and "[an] *Arabian Nights'* dream."[3] The estate was "unlike . . . any heretofore built on Long Island," observed one newspaper writer.[4] Another commentator, who came to Laurelton Hall many times, felt that in the creation of his estate Tiffany had refused "to be controlled by the harsh rule and iron despotism of classic precedent." The spirit of "mysticism" emanated from the house and gardens and, he continued, "The perfume of the Orient and the horse sense of America" had come together.[5] Laurelton Hall was an "experiment" in direct conflict with the usual American tendency to "follow the history and spirit of other nations," concluded another

Fig. 84. Garden waterfall, Laurelton Hall. Photograph by A. Radclyffe Dugmore, from Henry H. Saylor, "The Country Home of Mr. Louis C. Tiffany," *Country Life in America* 15 (December 1908), p. 160

Fig. 85. View of Laurelton Hall, ca. 1920s. Gelatin silver print, 8⅛ x 10 in. (20.5 x 25.4 cm). Photograph by David Aronow. The Metropolitan Museum of Art, New York, Gift of Robert Koch, 1978 (1978.646.2)

guest, who discerned the touch of an "alchemist"—a description Tiffany himself probably suggested, as it was his habit to do while escorting visitors about the grounds.[6] One of Tiffany's confidants hypothesized that "stars of wonder" must have danced in the eyes of Long Island locals brought up in prim traditional buildings.[7] "Americanism" dominated the exterior, claimed another visitor, whereas the great interior court was Persian-influenced.[8]

Interpretation of Laurelton Hall today is beset by problems, for the house was destroyed by fire in 1957. Although photographs, plans, descriptions, and many fragments of the estate remain, the primary object is absent, and one can no longer experience its size, scale, spaces, colors, decoration, and extensive gardens and landscape. Of Tiffany's sizable library only a portion is

known. The titles show his interest in oriental art and architecture and in gardens.[9] Tiffany himself was never a writer. His few writings can be sophistic: "Simplicity, and not the amount of money spent, is the foundation of all really effective decoration."[10] They can be saccharine: "'Nature is always right'—that is a saying we often hear from the past; and here is another, 'Nature is always beautiful.'" However, they can also be revealing: color, he claimed, is a "primal natural instinct," and human beings should never "forget or neglect what will always prove in after life a source of pure enjoyment such as we may imagine to be one of the delights of those beings of another world—who mayhap shall surpass the measure of human kind!"[11] He observed that the color yellow signifies brightness and mirth; the "primitive color red"

Fig. 87. Porte cochere, viewed from drive, Laurelton Hall, ca. 1920s. Gelatin silver print, 8⅛ x 10 in. (20.5 x 25.4 cm). Photograph by David Aronow. The Metropolitan Museum of Art, New York, Gift of Robert Koch, 1978 (1978.646.13)

Fig. 88. Drive leading under conservatory, Laurelton Hall, ca. 1920s. Gelatin silver print, 8⅛ x 10 in. (20.5 x 25.4 cm). Photograph by David Aronow. The Metropolitan Museum of Art, New York, Gift of Robert Koch, 1978 (1978.646.14)

Fig. 89. Terrace looking toward Long Island Sound, Laurelton Hall, ca. 1920s. Gelatin silver print, 8⅛ x 10 in. (20.5 x 25.4 cm). Photograph by David Aronow. The Metropolitan Museum of Art, New York, Gift of Robert Koch, 1978 (1978.646.25)

Fig. 90. Model of minaret, ca. 1903. Wood, 59¾ x 12 in. (151.8 x 30.5 cm). The Charles Hosmer Morse Museum of American Art, Winter Park, Florida

Oppostite: Fig. 91. Minaret, originally stack for heating and pumping plant (on property of Laurelton Hall). Concrete, wood, glass, and copper, 60 ft. (18.3 m). This recent photograph shows the most visible architectural element surviving from Tiffany's estate.

signifies the desire for warmth; and blue "appeals to the more developed intellectual faculty of refined thought and delicate sensation."[12] Only a few letters that deal with Laurelton Hall survive, and although they illuminate Tiffany's involvement, they say nothing about the meaning of his project.

What does survive, and is crucial to understanding Tiffany's intention at Laurelton Hall, is a series of articles authored by close friends, associates, and the occasional freelance writer. Tiffany controlled access to Laurelton Hall and always accompanied visiting writers, offering extended commentary that they frequently quoted in their publications. Tiffany loved to talk, and the repetition of certain themes in these articles can be taken as an indication that the ideas expressed are Tiffany's. At least seven articles were written between 1906 and 1914 by Samuel Howe (1854–?1928), who had been a superintendent and designer with Tiffany.[13] Henry H. Saylor (1880–1967), an important writer on architecture, produced several articles, and others were composed by individuals connected with the Tiffany Foundation.[14] These articles followed many of the themes enunciated by Howe and were likewise full of quotes from Tiffany. In *The Art Work of Louis C. Tiffany*, privately published in 1914, with text and many photographs (including of Laurelton Hall), Tiffany employed a ghost author, Charles de Kay (1848–1935), a well-known literary figure in New York and a relative through mar-

riage of Tiffany's, to explain his work (see fig. 169).[15] Tiffany's voice can be discerned in the volume's praise for the arts of the Orient and in statements such as the assertion that artists, "who can see below the surface, must give a wrench to the many prejudices imbibed from art schools and academies in which the majority of men are blind followers of those whose eyes never see." The theme of art's mysterious or unknowable elements was constantly evoked; the artist's realm of symbolism and meaning approached that of the priesthood. Alchemists and glassmakers, according to Tiffany and de Kay, bore a close resemblance.[16]

Tiffany, though he never practiced as an architect, had become involved in architecture in the late 1870s, when he joined the textile designer Candace T. Wheeler (1827–1923), the artist Lockwood de Forest (1850–1932), and others to form an interior-design firm. The group—Louis C. Tiffany and Company, Associated Artists— worked on interiors for the Veterans Room of the Seventh Regiment Armory, in New York City, for the White House (then occupied by President Chester Alan Arthur), and for the Mark Twain house, in Hartford, Connecticut.[17] The partnership ended in 1883. Tiffany's various successor companies designed and installed interiors for residences, public and commercial buildings, and churches, along with producing windows, ceramics, glassware, lamps, furniture, and other items. The huge scale of some of these interiors—for

Fig. 92. Entrance hall staircase from Frederick and Ellen Ayer residence, Boston, designed by Louis Comfort Tiffany, 1899–1900. Photograph by Richard Cheek, courtesy of Bayridge Residence and Cultural Center

example, the Chicago Public Library, done in association with Shipley, Rutan and Coolidge, and the Madison Square Presbyterian Church, New York, executed in partnership with McKim, Mead and White—provided Tiffany with extensive architectural experience. In 1899 and 1900, shortly before he began his design of Laurelton Hall, Tiffany worked closely with the architect A. J. Manning on a house for Frederick Ayer, a successful investor and a dealer in patent medicines. Tiffany and his associates provided the exterior decoration and most of the interiors for this residence on Commonwealth Avenue in Boston's Back Bay (fig. 92). In addition to working with outside architects, Tiffany kept several of them, such as Samuel Howe and Robert L. Pryor, on his own payroll.

Tiffany's knowledge of architecture was the result of work on his family's residences as well. He designed his penthouse in the Bella Apartments, at 48 East Twenty-sixth Street in New York, in 1878 (fig. 10); photographs of the principal public rooms were extensively published (see figs. 11, 14, 17, 20). In the early 1880s he worked closely with Stanford White (1853–1906) on the design of a mansion commissioned by his father, Charles Lewis Tiffany, at Seventy-second Street and Madison Avenue in New York (fig. 24). An initial sketch by Tiffany (fig. 93) provided the basis for the McKim, Mead and White design, and Tiffany designed theatrical, exotic interiors for his family's fourth-floor apartment

in the mansion and his own fifth-floor studio. He had these rooms photographed and published and also made several paintings of the spaces (see the essay "'The Most Artistic House in New York City'" in this publication). In 1888, at Oyster Bay, on Long Island, Tiffany acquired some acreage and set about building his first county estate, which he called the Briars. Work on the estate occupied him for the next decade. He paid a great deal of attention to the landscape and gardens, creating a circular forecourt, with a fountain and pool, surrounded by a border of lilies and irises (fig. 94). A low semicircular stone terrace with extensive plantings bordered one side, and the house and water tower stood on the other. Tiffany modeled the house into a large boxy structure with a two-level pergola across the front that linked it to the tower (fig. 95). Portions of the pergola were enclosed, and the columnar supports were of a simplified Doric type. The water tower and sections of the house were covered in shingles, in contrast to the stucco of the rest of the exterior. Finally, in 1902, with an inheritance from his father, Tiffany acquired beachfront property adjacent to the Briars, where the decrepit Hotel Laurelton was located (figs. 67, 68). It had been built in the 1870s and named after the mountain laurel that spread over the site. Tiffany demolished the structure, acquired more acreage, and set about creating a country estate.

From the beginning Tiffany intended Laurelton Hall to serve as an antidote to the American obsession with historical styles, for, as he noted, people seemed "to expect . . . a French chateau or a Tudor Hall."[18] Long Island—especially its North Shore—was a playground where the very wealthy competed to erect palatial estates. Huge formal gardens surrounded giant Georgian and Italian Renaissance Revival mansions that contained large collections of European art. Not too far away from Laurelton Hall, in Roslyn, McKim, Mead and White had just completed, in 1902, a gigantic Louis XIV–style château, called Harbor Hill, for the silver-mining heir Clarence Mackay and his wife, Katharine, at a reputed cost of more than two million dollars. Modeled on the Maisons-Laffitte, built in 1642 outside Paris, the Mackay estate with its vast formal gardens and its mansion filled with "the spoils

Fig. 93. Louis Comfort Tiffany, *The 72nd Street House*, ca. 1883. Graphite and ink on paper, 4⁹⁄₁₆ x 7⁹⁄₁₆ in. (11.6 x 19.2 cm). The Charles Hosmer Morse Museum of American Art, Winter Park, Florida

Fig. 94. Court elevation, The Briars. From Samuel Howe, "One Source of Color Values—Illustrating Mr. Louis C. Tiffany's Significant Handling of Things Greater than Architecture and One Source of His Strength in Color," *House and Garden* 10 (September 1906), p. 111

Fig. 95. Tower and terrace, The Briars. From Samuel Howe, "One Source of Color Values—Illustrating Mr. Louis C. Tiffany's Significant Handling of Things Greater than Architecture and One Source of His Strength in Color," *House and Garden* 10 (September 1906), p. 111

of European palaces," in the words of one critic, was exactly what Tiffany wanted to avoid (fig. 96; the château was demolished in 1947).[19] In nearby Wheatley Hills the same firm had designed a huge Colonial Revival house for the wealthy investor E. D. Morgan, along with an extensive set of outbuildings. In this case a modest one-and-a-half-story wooden Long Island colonial cottage was reincarnated into a four-story structure with more than eight thousand square feet.[20] Tiffany had "no patience with the servile copying of the work of past ages, whose needs and methods of life were so widely different from our own." Tiffany blamed this fashion on Paris's École des Beaux-Arts, which emphasized classical design precedents and influenced many late-nineteenth-

century American architects, including the principals of McKim, Mead and White. (He did admire the rigorous training required by the École des Beaux-Arts, however, and acknowledged that some of the better architecture in the United States had been designed by its disciples.) But Tiffany wanted to keep clear of "the easy thing, and [not to] reproduce, line for line, detail for detail, a villa of old Rome or a Venetian palace." His house was to be not a warmed-over piece of Italy but "a distinctly American house."[21]

Assisting Tiffany on the Laurelton Hall project was the young architect Robert L. Pryor (1879–1964). Pryor had been trained through the apprentice system, and about 1900, at the age of twenty-one, he became associated with Tiffany, working on some

Fig. 96. Armor Room, Harbor Hill, Roslyn, New York, ca. 1930s. Photograph by Edward J. Milla. The Metropolitan Museum of Art, New York, Files of the Department of Arms and Armor

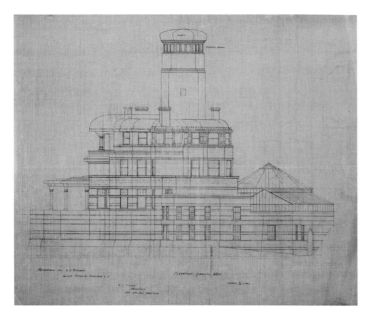

Fig. 97. Richard Pryor, Architectural drawing: Elevation of Laurelton Hall looking west, ca. 1902. Aniline dye on cloth, 23½ x 28½ in. (59.7 x 72.4 cm). The Charles Hosmer Morse Museum of American Art, Winter Park, Florida

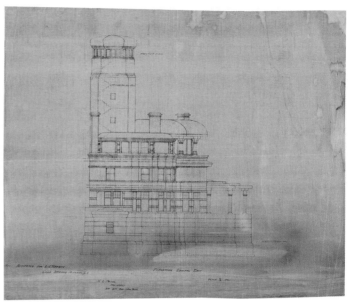

Fig. 98. Richard Pryor, Architectural drawing: Elevation of Laurelton Hall looking east, ca. 1902. Aniline dye on cloth, 24 x 27½ in. (61 x 69.9 cm). The Charles Hosmer Morse Museum of American Art, Winter Park, Florida

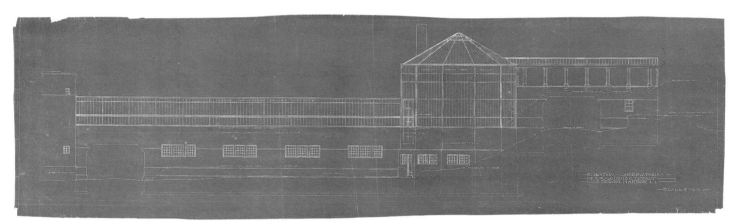

Fig. 99. Richard Pryor, Architectural drawing: Elevation of Laurelton Hall, conservatories, ca. 1903. Blueprint on wove paper, 18¼ x 60¾ in. (46.4 x 154.3 cm). The Charles Hosmer Morse Museum of American Art, Winter Park, Florida

of the interior designs for the churches that were a mainstay of Tiffany's business. According to Pryor's family, Tiffany paid for him to travel and study in Algiers (a drawing of a mosque survives from this trip).[22] Pryor maintained an office in Newark, New Jersey, and at the time of Laurelton Hall's design also worked out of Tiffany Studios' New York office. He signed the Laurelton Hall drawings with the Tiffany Studios' 341 Fourth Avenue address, and the few surviving letters about the planning of Laurelton Hall were addressed to him there. Pryor drafted the working drawings for the building (see figs. 97–101) and certainly had a hand in certain design decisions; Tiffany ordered him, for instance, to "have all the rooms of the second and third floor finished plain as contracted."[23] To judge by the surviving correspondence, Pryor's job was to put Tiffany's concepts on paper and to help supervise their realization. A timber-framed superstructure covered in stucco was placed over a concrete basement. Iron was employed in the tower and for some wide spans for the first floor. The builder for the ini-

tial house, constructed between 1903 and 1905, was Charles T. Wills, who billed Tiffany in 1906 for $214,079.64.[24]

Wanting to treat the site as a totality, Tiffany commissioned a clay model of the topography, showing all the small ridges, valleys, meadows, and the major trees. With modeling wax he then formed his structures and gardens in three dimensions, keeping in mind the various sight lines and the multiple exposures, to views and to light, of the major rooms. The long line of the house fit into the hillside (fig. 103), the entry road passed around it. Tiffany's approach came to be known as organic planning. As one commentator observed, "there is no cutting and filling on a wholesale plan . . . Nature has been met half-way, not antagonized and bullied."[25]

The house was a horizontal mass, more than 280 feet long, topped by a molded roof of acid-tinted blue-green or emerald copper that rolled back from the deep overhanging eves. The exterior was marked by horizontal striations—belt courses, moldings,

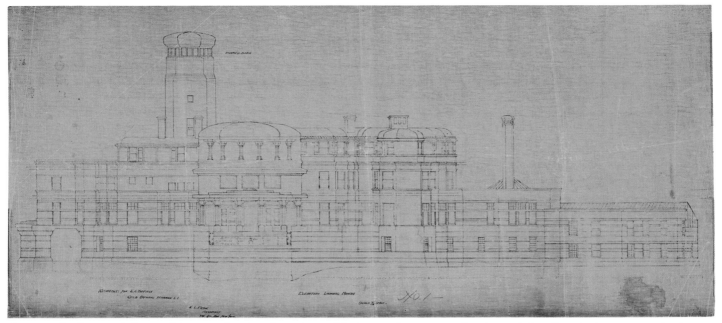

Fig. 100. Richard Pryor, Architectural drawing: Elevation of Laurelton Hall looking north, ca. 1903. Aniline dye on cloth, 23½ x 51 in. (59.7 x 129.5 cm). The Charles Hosmer Morse Museum of American Art, Winter Park, Florida

and setbacks—in shades of cream-colored stucco. The horizontality was highlighted by the fenestration; all the windows were placed between the exterior's long horizontal layers and were grouped in ribbons, forming both open loggias and rectangular voids. On the third floor, square wood panels between the windows helped to maintain the horizontal rhythm. Laurelton Hall's crisply delineated horizontal planes were further emphasized by a ledge between the house's concrete foundation, which was roughly textured with large stones, and the less coarse pebble dash of the floors above: the ledge formed a continuous base for the house, linking all the terraces and long rambling appendages. Moreover,

a copper trough was set into it, containing soil for plants. The effect, as an observer later noted, was that the house seemed alive: "Time has softened the daring masses. . . . Nature has filled the chinks with growing things, little and large."[26] This treatment of layers and vegetation was part of Tiffany's attempt to "symbolize Americanism" and create an "indigenous" American architecture; he claimed that the horizontality of Laurelton Hall had been inspired by the stratified cliffs at Yellowstone and the Grand Canyon, which he had seen during his travels in the American West.[27] A 1917 painting by Tiffany testifies to the impression made on him by the Yellowstone cliffs (fig. 102).

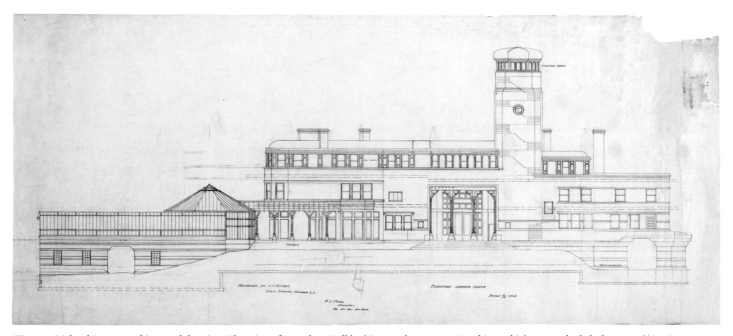

Fig. 101. Richard Pryor, Architectural drawing: Elevation of Laurelton Hall looking south, ca. 1903. Graphite and ink on starched cloth, 22 x 52¾ in. (55.9 x 134 cm). The Charles Hosmer Morse Museum of American Art, Winter Park, Florida

Fig. 102. Louis Comfort Tiffany, *Yellowstone Canyon*, 1917. Water-color and gouache on tinted paper, 17⅜ x 11⅛ in. (44.1 x 29.5 cm). Signed and dated at lower right: *Louis C. Tiffany/1917*. The Charles Hosmer Morse Museum of American Art, Winter Park, Florida

Fig. 103. Stone steps, Laurelton Hall. From Henry H. Saylor, "The Country Home of Mr. Louis C. Tiffany," *Country Life in America* 15 (December 1908), p. 157

The exterior of Laurelton Hall exhibited none of the usual Beaux-Arts symmetry and separation from the landscape. Instead, it opened on all sides, through windows and bays, to gardens, terraces, and pergolas, each treated as an extension of the interior space or as a separate room (fig. 104). On the north side, for instance, a large terrace opened off the central court and descended the hillside in stages. The Daffodil Terrace, added off the dining room on the south side about 1914, is another example (fig. 79). Marble columns topped with capitals set with glass daffodils supported a wood ceiling Tiffany had imported from Algiers (figs. 80, 81). The ceiling was open in the center so that an old pear tree need not be uprooted from the spot. This opening was surrounded by an attic of iridescent blue glass, in 5½-inch squares, that created a pattern of branches and leaves. At the end of the terrace, Tiffany installed a Renaissance-style open arch that resembled a shrine, thus bringing together the Orient and the Occident. Indeed, far from being isolated from nature, Laurelton Hall seemed to be consumed by it. Window boxes surrounded the house, filled with the ice plant *Mesembryanthemum*, a little plant with an endless variety of hues; in the 1920s it was replaced with "gay petunia[s]."[28] Fastened along the upper level of the south side of the house was a complex of wires on which a canopy of vines eventually grew. The wires, crisscrossed, were attached to tall vine-covered posts and dead trees. The trees were blighted chestnuts that Tiffany had refused to

remove and around which he planted wisteria. The series of gardens—some small and intimate, with fountains and statues; others broader, with sizable pools—that surrounded the house were in constant evolution and grew in complexity over the years.

Fig. 104. View of Laurelton Hall from formal gardens, ca. 1920s. Gelatin silver print, 8⅛ x 10 in. (20.5 x 25.4 cm). Photograph by David Aronow. The Metropolitan Museum of Art, New York, Gift of Robert Koch, 1978 (1978.646.5)

Fig. 105. View of loggia, Laurelton Hall. From Charles de Kay, *The Art Work of Louis C. Tiffany* (1914), opp. p. 70

Fig. 106. Eastern Court, Jahangiri Mahal, Agra Fort. From Syad Muhammad Latif, *Agra, Historical and Descriptive, with an Account of Akbar and His Court and of the Modern City of Agra* (Calcutta, 1896), p. 96

Fig. 107. Louis Comfort Tiffany, Loggia, Laurelton Hall, ca. 1905. Limestone, ceramic, and Favrile glass, 21 x 23 ft. (640 x 701 cm). The Metropolitan Museum of Art, New York, Gift of Jeannette Genius McKean and Hugh Ferguson McKean, in memory of Charles Hosmer Morse, 1978 (1978.10.1)

The sole counterpoint to Laurelton Hall's horizontality was the faceted tower that rose next to the loggia, on the south side (fig. 105). The loggia was based on the facade of the Jahangiri Mahal, in the Red Fort at Agra, India, which Tiffany may have known from a book or through photographs supplied by a friend such as Lockwood de Forest, his former business partner, who traveled extensively in India (fig. 106). Many elements of the loggia have survived, including mosaic panels composed of blue, white, and gold Favrile-glass tiles, in the spandrels, and four limestone columns with ceramic-and-Favrile-glass capitals (figs. 82, 107). Each capital represents, with botanical accuracy, a different flower. From left to right, these flowers are the East Indian lotus, the Greek peony, the opium poppy, and the saucer magnolia. Each of the capitals depicts the bud of the flower, the flower in full bloom, and the seedpod—the cycle, that is, of birth, decay, and rebirth.[29] Paneled glass lanterns with foursquare and labyrinthine patterns hung between the columns, and a pair of turquoise-and-yellow-glazed Kangxi-era Chinese ceramic lions stood guard in front (see figs. 265, 278, 279).

The house was a series of spaces—rooms, terraces, conservatories—each conceived so as to make the most advantageous use of the site's contours and vistas (fig. 108). There were eight levels, which included two basement stories, the three main living floors, and three more floors in the tower. The visitor normally entered the house at the east end, on the basement level under the porte cochère, and passed into the vestibule. A grilled window—Hindu in origin—illuminated by a deep light well gave the space an exotic air, which was enhanced by a large temple brazier, a Japanese temple gong, an altar, candles, and mosaic tiles (fig. 109). A staircase led to the first floor and the main public rooms. The floors of the entry hall and court were made of mosaic tiles, and the rest of maple and oak. The living room was a vast dim space, given warmth by a painted leaf pattern that covered the walls and ceiling; one end of the room was taken up by a huge inglenook and fireplace. In this and many other rooms Tiffany dispensed with traditional wood or plaster moldings for door and window surrounds or cornices. In an alcove of the living room (see fig. 242) he displayed several of his best windows, those depicting the four seasons (figs. 250–258) and *Feeding the Flamingoes* (figs. 245, 246). In the octagon-shaped library, Tiffany exhibited some of his collection of artifacts. The den (in the original plan, it had been the parlor) was hung with Japanese armor (fig. 273). The smoking room contained a large mural depicting an opium smoker's dream, featuring naked women and terrifying beasts (fig. 272). The dining room stretched fifty-eight feet through the house and provided views to the north and the south (figs. 155, 156). (A surviving plan shows a fireplace blocking the northern view; its position was eventually changed to the west wall.) In the center of the room hung an inverted dome made of thousands of pieces of blue Favrile glass, with bits of green, cream, gold, and orange, in a medallion pattern that was echoed in the pattern of the rugs below (see figs. 158, 159). Wisteria vines on an outside terrace climbed the window bays at the southwest, inspiring Tiffany after 1910 to create for the room leaded-glass panels depicting wisteria—these would remain in constant bloom (figs. 119, 149–154). Everywhere inside were large bouquets of flowers and pots of lilies, orchids, hydrangeas, and

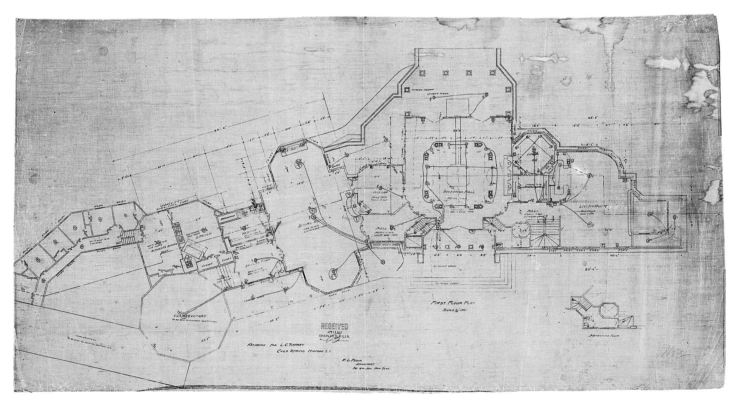

Fig. 108. Richard Pryor, Architectural drawing: First-floor plan, Laurelton Hall, ca. 1903. Aniline dye on cloth, 27 x 49 in. (68.6 x 124.5 cm). The Charles Hosmer Morse Museum of American Art, Winter Park, Florida

Fig. 109. Entrance vestibule, Laurelton Hall, ca. 1920s. Gelatin silver print, 8⅛ x 10 in. (20.5 x 25.4 cm). Photograph by David Aronow. The Metropolitan Museum of Art, New York, Gift of Robert Koch, 1978 (1978.646.21)

Fig. 110. Fountain Court, Laurelton Hall. From Samuel Howe, "The Dwelling Place as an Expression of Individuality: The House of Louis C. Tiffany," *Appleton's Magazine* 9 (February 1907), p. 163

other plants. Howe once claimed that Tiffany was a "florist"—which can be taken as an indication of the continuity between the gardens outside and inside.[30]

Behind the dining room, and in the basement, were service spaces, including the kitchen, pantry, scullery, servants' hall, servants' bedrooms and baths, and the laundry. The number of staff at Laurelton Hall remains unknown. At least thirteen servant bedrooms were drawn on the plans, but grounds staff lived in the stables and other buildings or came in as day service. A niece of Tiffany's recalled: "Heaven knows how many gardeners were employed, there must have been an army." By one estimate, during Laurelton Hall's heyday there were thirty-five of them.[31]

Visitors were allowed on the second floor of the central court to view Tiffany's extensive collection of icons, vases, and other items. His collections of Chinese and Japanese art were also located upstairs. Beyond them lay the private quarters of the family. The master-bedroom suite was located on the west side of the second floor and contained a studio with easels. Bedrooms and baths for other family members and for visitors were located on both the second and third floors.

The most memorable space in Laurelton Hall was the three-story reception hall, or Fountain Court, at its center (fig. 110). Measuring thirty-eight by thirty-nine by thirty-nine feet, the space was nearly a cube. Sixteen columns made of white marble (the original plans had called for cherrywood with white trim), vaguely Hindu in style, ringed the space at the lower level and supported the second- and third-floor balconies and columns, creating an octagonal inner space; the arrangement was remarkably similar to that of an Islamic bath (fig. 111). Covered by a translucent blue-purple glass dome from which hung a spherical glass lamp (see fig. 131)—it was said to resemble, at night, a moonstone—the space seemed made for mystical rites of some sort. The floor had

an inlay of black marble, which Tiffany, speaking through Samuel Howe, claimed was "oriental" in inspiration, "acknowledging [the] dark tones of mother earth."[32] At ground level the walls were covered in painted canvas stenciled with a cypress-tree pattern adapted from a tile mural in Istanbul's Topkapi Palace (see figs. 123–126). An organ stood along one wall (it also controlled the tower's chimes). Plants such as calla lilies, hydrangeas, chrysanthemums, and philodendrons (and, later on, *monstera deliciosas* and banana trees) stood in containers around the court, along with marble and wood benches, bear rugs, and rare objects, which included, after 1911, Joaquín

Fig. 111. *The Bath.* From *The Thousand and One Nights, Commonly Called, In England, the Arabian Nights' Entertainments*, vol. 3 (1840), p. 788

Fig. 112. Louis Comfort Tiffany, Tiffany Glass and Decorating Company, Tiffany Chapel, 1893, reassembled at Morse Museum of American Art, 1999. 37 x 24 ft. (11.3 x 7.3 m). The Charles Hosmer Morse Museum of American Art, Winter Park, Florida

Sorolla y Bastida's portrait of Tiffany (see figs. 129, 130). The middle of the court was occupied by a pool of water lighted from below. From its center emerged perhaps the most serene shape that ever issued from Tiffany's highly charged mind: a tall, simple pear- or pistil-shaped vase, similar to the long-necked flasks or *surahis* of Mughal India (see figs. 110, 132, 133).[33] Water emerged almost imperceptibly from its mouth and flowed down its sides. So subtly did the colors of the fountain change—depending upon the time of day, the multihued lighting from below (see fig. 135), reflections, the water itself, and the glass of the vase (over the years the vase turned from a creamy transparency to an orangey red)— that it seemed alive. As Tiffany himself said: "The Vase, it seems, has a term of life. . . . So ethereal, so exquisite is it that one seeks in vain for a simile."[34]

Located to the west of the house, and mostly hidden from view, were the farm and stable buildings, which looked out on Long Island Sound (figs. 316, 317). The extensive group of structures to house the horses, dairy herd, sheep, wagons, and farm tools as well as to provide lodgings for the superintendent and staff was designed by Alfred Hopkins (1870–1941), who specialized in "gentlemen's farms." Hopkins stated forthrightly: "The design of the buildings was carried out to meet the owner's very decided views." In style the stables followed the main house; they were vaguely Moorish, with arched openings and a stucco cladding. They were supposed to have been covered with vines, but none of the planting was done.[35] Eventually, the carriage house and stables were converted into studios and dormitories for the students of the educational foundation that Tiffany established.

Fig. 113. Louis Comfort Tiffany, Tiffany Glass Company, Window from art gallery, Laurelton Hall, ca. 1885–90. Leaded glass, 56½ x 116½ in. (143.5 x 295.9 cm). The Charles Hosmer Morse Museum of American Art, Winter Park, Florida

Another notable addition to Laurelton Hall was the chapel originally designed as the centerpiece of the Tiffany Glass and Decorating Company's exhibit at the 1893 World's Columbian Exposition in Chicago (fig. 112). It received fifty-four medals and 1.4 million visitors. In 1899 the chapel was installed in the crypt of the Cathedral Church of Saint John the Divine in New York City. However, by 1911 Saint John's closed the chapel when the decision was made to change the cathedral's initial Byzantine-Romanesque architectural style to a Gothic Revival one. Tiffany acquired it in 1916 and installed it in a new structure on the grounds at Laurelton Hall.[36]

In 1918 Tiffany converted an early-nineteenth-century house on the grounds into an art gallery to serve his educational foundation (see figs. 335–337). He added an octagonal tower with a curved copper roof, and he altered the fenestration pattern, to more closely follow that of the main house. About 1919 he added an elaborately carved three-story porch, Indian in origin and dating from an earlier century. Similar, though not identical, woodwork and columns were pictured in Lockwood de Forest's various publications on Indian architecture.[37] De Forest had been in a business partnership with Tiffany between 1880 and 1882, and they had worked together occasionally over the years since. In Ahmadabad, India, de Forest ran a workshop of craftsmen from the *mistri* subcast who produced intricate Indian woodwork for export. Tiffany used some of their woodwork as screens, wall paneling, trim, and doors in his Seventy-second Street house, and in 1908 de Forest sold his entire remaining stock to Tiffany Studios.[38] The third-floor columns of the art gallery supported a pierced

wood awning under a dome of blue glass, making for a mosaiclike effect. The exterior stairs had Tiffany colored glass on the risers, and a ceramic band framed the carved Indian doors, which had originally been in the Seventy-second Street house. Above them, in the wall of the second floor, Tiffany installed an early window (ca. 1885–90) with a central panel reminiscent of a peacock feather (fig. 113). A cast-lead chain of king-cobra heads and Celtic knots formed from the snakes' bodies surrounded the window.[39] On the interior Tiffany removed many of the walls and installed mosaics and more Indian carving.[40] Tiffany's own art and collections as well as the work of students from the Tiffany Foundation were put on exhibit in this space.

Tiffany had begun making alterations and additions at Laurelton Hall from the moment that the main house was constructed and the initial landscaping accomplished. He explained that he was an artist "'who does what he likes, when he likes, as he likes, but whose interest tires as his creation approaches completion!'" Hence "he must content himself with the pleasure of doing."[41] By the 1920s, however, Tiffany was in his seventies. Although he was still energetic, his focus was more on the school than on the estate. Financial problems also put a brake on his alterations to Laurelton Hall.

Interpreting Tiffany's design of Laurelton Hall or, indeed, any of his work is a complex task. Tiffany can be assigned to many schools. The influential collector and dealer Siegfried Bing (1838–1905), founder of the Parisian gallery L'Art Nouveau, admired, published, and exhibited Tiffany's work,[42] and similarities with European Art Nouveau can certainly be discerned in Tiffany's use of natural forms, blossoms, vines, and curves in his designs.

Fig. 114. Olana, home of Frederic Church, south facade, ca. 1900. Photograph by Granville Hills. Courtesy of Olana State Historic Site, New York State Office of Parks, Recreation and Historic Preservation

Other elements of Tiffany's work, however, can be identified as in the style of the Aesthetic, Arts and Crafts, or Orientalist movement. Occasional classical motifs and references suggest an American Renaissance approach. These diverse labels indicate that Tiffany, whose long and extremely productive career lasted from the 1870s into the 1920s, was stylistically a true eclectic; he had an exotic bent and drew upon multiple sources, ranging from Europe to the Orient to the natural world. Tiffany's eclecticism, however, was not the academic eclecticism of, say, the École des Beaux-Arts–trained Charles McKim (1847–1909) but one of emotion and synthesis.[43] Tiffany's eclecticism was usually reductive or abstract; he chose and combined, but seldom reproduced. Tiffany was explicit that the reproduction of historic styles was inappropriate; the age needed its own expression.[44]

When Tiffany began his career in the 1870s, the Aesthetic movement was making inroads in America from Britain. Much of his work in the 1870s and 1880s, and even later, had affinities with the Aesthetic style. Tiffany met the writer Oscar Wilde (1854–1900), a champion of the Aesthetic movement, during Wilde's 1882 lecture tour of America, and they discussed collaborating on a theater, but it never materialized.[45] Tiffany rejected Wilde's ultimately "decadent" route and explicitly dismissed the Aesthetic movement's celebration of "art for art's sake," yet he said repeatedly, even as late as 1916: "the expression of beauty; that has been my creed."[46] He followed Wilde and the English critic Walter Pater (1839–1894), whose writings had been central to the Aesthetic movement's assertion of the autonomy of art, when he rejected the Ruskinian attribution to art of moral values, arguing that "the search for beauty is in itself the most wholesome of all quests."[47]

A strong interest in Orientalism in architecture, painting, and the decorative arts had arisen in the United States about the time of the Civil War. Fueled, certainly, by contemporary English and French examples, such as the Orientalist decor in the London home of the Pre-Raphaelite painter Lord Leighton and the "Eastern" genre paintings of harems and snake charmers by Ingres and Gérôme, Oriental decorative details began to appear in American houses.[48] Oriental—more specifically, Turkish and Persian—elements were seen sporadically in buildings such as Olana, the home of the American painter Frederic Church (1826–1900) overlooking the Hudson River, designed in the early 1870s by Calvert Vaux and Frederick Withers (fig. 114). There various Turkish ornamental motifs were grafted onto an essentially Italianate house, without integration. Tiffany's paintings such as *Market Day outside the Walls of Tangiers, Morocco* (1873; Smithsonian American Art Museum, Washington, D.C.) and *Snake Charmer at Tangier, Africa* (fig. 115) show his interest in "Oriental" subjects. Later in life, recalling the 1870 visit he had made to "the East" (by which he meant Egypt and North Africa), Tiffany commented that the chance to travel there and to paint "where the people and also the buildings are clad in beautiful hues" had brought to his attention "the preeminence of color in the world." He observed: "The Orientals have been teaching the Occidentals how to use colors for the past 10,000 years or so."[49] (Though Tiffany traveled in Europe as well as the Middle East and North Africa, work and illness prevented him from fulfilling his desire to visit China, Japan, and India.)

The development of Orientalism in the United States was facilitated by two books first published in England: the *Rubáiyát of Omar Khayyám*, translated by Edward FitzGerald (1859), and *The Thousand and One Nights* (also known as *The Arabian Nights'*

Entertainments), translated by Edward William Lane (1839–41). Both became widely available about midcentury and proved extremely popular. FitzGerald's *Rubáiyát* had been admired by the English Aesthetic set as well; in 1884 the American artist Elihu Vedder (1836–1923), who styled himself an "old friend" of Tiffany's, produced the first illustrated version.[50] An edition of Lane's *Arabian Nights* with several hundred wood engravings by William Harvey (1796–1866) made a huge impact, as the appearance of Turkish-style smoking rooms and other decorative details in American interiors attests.[51] There is a strong kinship between many elements at Laurelton Hall and the fountains and gardens depicted by Harvey.

At the turn of the twentieth century many Americans, from the Harvard psychologist and philosopher William James (1842–1910) to popular writers, were also fascinated by mysticism, spiritualism, and various forms of the occult, along with exotic figures such as the Hindu monk Vivekananda.[52] Tiffany's parents were originally Congregationalists, and later Presbyterians, but in *The Art Work* Tiffany quoted approvingly the views of the Swedenborgian George Inness (1825–1894). Inness, with whom Tiffany had trained as a painter from 1863 to 1865, had passed on to him

the ideas of Emanuel Swedenborg, the Swedish philosopher and religious writer. "When in the presence of nature," Inness had said, the artist "is in process of his own spiritual development"; he had also asserted: "Rivers, streams, the rippling brook, the hillside, the sky, clouds—all things we see—will convey the sentiment of the highest art, if we are in the love of God and the desire of truth."[53] Inness argued that God existed in nature and that "the true artistic impulse is divine."[54]

In 1875 Helena Petrovna Blavatsky (1831–1891) and Henry Steel Olcott (1832–1907) founded the Theosophical Society in New York City. The American Theosophical movement attracted much public attention both through its concept of a "universal mind" or "universal traditions" that underlie all religions and ancient philosophies and also through its chief exponents' demonstrations of psychic phenomena, which were widely reported in the newspapers.[55] Through Blavatsky's books *Isis Unveiled* (1877) and *The Secret Doctrine* (1888), all who were interested could delve into occultism, mysticism, spiritualism, hermeticism, and the ancient mysteries, as well as Buddhism, Hinduism, and other religions. Alchemy figured prominently in Blavatsky's writings as one of the most ancient and universal practices; she defined

Fig. 115. Louis Comfort Tiffany, *Snake Charmer at Tangier, Africa*, 1872. Oil on canvas, 27½ x 38½ (69.9 x 97.8 cm). Signed at lower left: *Louis C. Tiffany* [illegible]. The Metropolitan Museum of Art, New York, Gift of Louis Comfort Tiffany Foundation, 1921 (21.170)

Fig. 116. Rock crystal fountain on terrace, Laurelton Hall, ca. 1920s. Gelatin silver print, 8⅛ x 10 in. (20.5 x 25.4 cm). Photograph by David Aronow. The Metropolitan Museum of Art, New York, Gift of Robert Koch, 1978 (1978.646.24)

Fig. 117. Fountain with bronze-and-mosaic dragon, Laurelton Hall. From Henry H. Saylor, "The Country Home of Mr. Louis C. Tiffany," *Country Life in America* 15 (December 1908), p. 162

alchemists as those "who sought for the *hidden spirit* in every inorganic matter."[56] By 1900 the *Theosophic Messenger,* the journal of the Theosophical Society in America, listed seventy-one branches of the society across the United States, in addition to its headquarters in New York City.[57] Theosophy's impact upon American architecture appeared in a variety of guises, including the architectural ornament of Louis Sullivan (1856–1924) and the writings of the architect Claude Bragdon (1866–1946), who was a contributor to the publication *Craftsman,* which popularized the Arts and Crafts style.[58]

Architectural symbolism, including the creation of a setting that would induce mystical contemplation, was the subject of

William R. Lethaby's book *Architecture, Mysticism and Myth* (1892). An English Arts and Crafts architect, Lethaby (1857–1931) argued that buildings enshrine ideas and symbols and that architecture's ultimate purpose is to explain the world. He claimed that universal symbols exist, and the book's twelve chapters treat forms such as the foursquare and the cube, domes and the sky, gates, labyrinths, jewel-bearing trees, candelabrums, planets, and emblems of creation such as the hanging ostrich egg. His wildly eclectic sources include the *Arabian Nights;* the Bible as well as Hindu, Islamic, and Buddhist texts; and studies of ancient Egyptian, Roman, and pre-Columbian art and architecture. Lethaby had a major impact on designers such as the Scottish architect Charles Rennie

Fig. 118. Pool with nymph statue, Laurelton Hall, ca. 1920s. Gelatin silver print, 8⅛ x 10 in. (20.5 x 25.4 cm). Photograph by David Aronow. The Metropolitan Museum of Art, New York, Gift of Robert Koch, 1978 (1978.646.30)

Mackintosh (1868–1928).[59] The American architect Bertram Goodhue (1869–1924) reviewed Lethaby's book in 1893 for the *Knight Errant,* a magazine of criticism on which he collaborated in Boston with the architect Ralph Adams Cram (1863–1942), and the volume influenced his and Cram's work together thereafter.[60] The early architectural signature of Frank Lloyd Wright (1867–1959) is a combination of Lethaby's two primary forms, the cube and the circle.

Because our knowledge of Tiffany's library is incomplete, it cannot be known if he read Lethaby or any Theosophical tracts or other books on symbolism. However, it can be posited that as an intelligent individual he certainly heard about Theosophy and some of the other mystical interests of the era; his writings and various quotations of him by other writers indicate an awareness of these currents. Many elements of Laurelton Hall, such as the patterned mosaic floor of the central hall, bear a strong resemblance to Lethaby's "Pavements of the Sea," which were floor patterns common in ancient religious buildings. (The same floor also echoes those described as being in the "City of Brass" in the *Arabian Nights.*) The Fountain Court at Laurelton Hall, nearly a cube, is evocative of Lethaby's "perfect temple," and the glass sphere suspended from its ceiling (see fig. 131) recalls the hanging ostrich egg that Lethaby defined as a symbol of creation.[61]

Tiffany claimed in *The Art Work* that the words *maisterie* (handicraft) and *mysterion* (a secret ritual of the Greeks) were very close and frequently confused. He went on to assert not only that "Art" was a mystery but that artists were similar to priests: artists in times past, he said, "ran a race with the priesthood." Artists also resembled "alchemists, whose methods and materials were very similar to those of painters, enamellers, glass-makers."

Artists had once been mystics, and the origin of the word *glass,* Tiffany averred, was "Teutonic . . . and . . . allied to glow and glare, as if it meant the 'shining thing.'"[62] Tiffany thus defined the artist as an individual allied with alchemy who through processes not understood by the layman created items of usefulness and beauty.

Tiffany's involvement in mysticism and alchemy can be most clearly seen in the water system of Laurelton Hall. Water was the element that drew together many of the different parts of Laurelton Hall and that dominated the central court. Tiffany began with two fountains, one inside the house and one outside. In time he added at least five more exterior fountains, several pools, and water tanks that held forty thousand gallons.[63] Steam and electricity generated by the minaret-towered plant pumped well water up a hill above the house. From there the water cascaded through a chain of fountains and pools and then disappeared, to emerge inside the house, in the fountain of the central court. An open marble rill allowed the water to pass outside, onto the north terrace and to an octagonal pool with a central fountain made of large rock-quartz crystals (fig. 116; see also fig. 73). From there the water fell to another terrace and emerged from the mouth of a large green mosaic-and-enamel dragon (fig. 117). The dragon spat the water into a rock-and-mosaic pool from the center of which a giant rock crystal emerged. Tiffany's confidant Samuel Howe noted that the mosaic pool and the giant crystal had a "magical transparency." Theirs was "an affinity that is chemical and esthetic. The mosaic is a product of industrial heat, the crystal a result of earth's primeval fires."[64] The water reemerged farther down the hillside in a hanging garden, where it flowed from a large shell guarded by a statue of a Venus-like nymph, sometimes called *The Spring* (fig. 118). From the hanging garden the water passed down the hill to twin lakes and finally emptied into the harbor. Water, Tiffany said, was an element of beauty, and "The Orientals worship water. To them it is a treasure rare, a guest they honor." Concerning his own use of water, Tiffany explained: "the vital liquid suggests hope, a message even to those living on the arid places of life."[65] Some contemporary commentators on Laurelton Hall noted that the decorative use of water in ancient Greece and Rome had fulfilled higher needs, and remarked that "to the Mohammedan water is the symbol for the principle of life."[66]

The specific meanings of water, or of the central court, or of Laurelton Hall as a totality are impossible to elucidate, and the effort is ultimately counterproductive. Great symbols defy exact definitions. Tiffany never intended precise meanings; his purpose, instead, was that beauty and mystery should lead to contemplation and transcendence. Great art contains elements of mystery, it is alchemical, its ultimate purpose is mystical. Art, like religion, must inspire wonder and awe; it is never transparent but opaque, for there are meanings, thoughts, and ultimate truths that cannot be spoken but only sensed and felt. Laurelton Hall was unique not just for its unusual Oriental stylistic touches. It was, rather, one of the very few houses in America that inspired among visitors a sense of transcendence, opening them to a larger world beyond.

1. Howe 1913a, p. 24. See also Martha Wren Briggs, "A Reconstruction of the Gardens of Louis Comfort Tiffany," in Van Wagner 1985, pp. 5–10. There are some conflicts between Briggs and visitors such as Howe regarding the location of various landscape features; in general I follow Howe's description.
2. Howe 1914b, pp. 41, 40.
3. Lyman 1914, p. 52.
4. "Notable Addition" 1904.
5. Howe 1907–8, p. 294; Howe 1907, pp. 165, 156.
6. Conway 1914.
7. J. Mumford 1921, p. 273.
8. Saylor 1908a, p. 160.
9. A portion of Tiffany's library was listed in Parke-Bernet 1946, lots 584–713.
10. L. Tiffany 1910.
11. L. Tiffany 1917a.
12. L. Tiffany 1911.
13. Koch 1964, pp. 80, 136, 142, touches on aspects of Howe's relationship with Tiffany. Howe was born in Leicester, England, and probably died in Camden, New Jersey. His training is unclear, but he worked as an architect and designer in England and the United States. He became involved with Tiffany following his immigration in 1883. In 1888 he displayed a window at the Architectural League of New York. A newspaper article ("Restoration" 1899) reports he "was for some years Superintendent of Tiffany Glass & Decoration Company" and was known as "Howe, the color man." Another article ("Art" 1900) states that he "was for a time the superintendent of the Tiffany Glass and Decorating Company in New York and . . . was in Chicago fifteen years ago to decorate the Farwell Mansion." Howe returned to England about 1897 and became a prominent art critic; he was also involved in the decoration of St. Paul's. He returned to the United States in 1900, made contact with Gustav Stickley, and wrote at least twelve articles for *Craftsman* magazine, including one on Stickley's Syracuse house (Howe 1902b) and two that praised Tiffany's work in glass and enamel (Howe 1902a, 1903). Howe exhibited photographs of Laurelton Hall at the 1907 Chicago Architectural Club exhibition (where Frank Lloyd Wright also had a major exhibit); his photos and watercolors of the house were shown at the Architectural League of New York's exhibits in 1906 and 1907. Howe wrote extensively on American and English architecture and design, with at least sixty articles and books to his credit, and after 1900 also practiced as an architect–landscape architect, designing numerous gardens and with a specialty in mosaic and terracotta-covered buildings. See *Who's Who in America* (Chicago, 1918–19), vol. 10, p. 1362; Freeman 1966, p. 82; and Cathers 2003, pp. 107, 212–13.
14. Saylor became prominent as the editor of numerous architectural journals and wrote extensively. He is best known for his book *Bungalows* (1911).
15. De Kay was an important literary figure in New York, a friend of James McNeill Whistler and many other artists, and an adherent of the Aesthetic movement. Koch 1964, p. 65, claims that Tiffany virtually dictated *The Art Work* to de Kay; see also pp. 142, 144, for the relationship between de Kay and Tiffany. De Kay's sister, Helena

de Kay, was also a writer and married Richard Watson Gilder, a very influential editor, writer, and Aesthete; their son Rodman de Kay Gilder married one of Tiffany's daughters, Comfort, on April 20, 1911. See also McKean 1980a, pp. 7, 149.
16. De Kay 1914, pp. xvii, xx.
17. Faude 1975; R. Mayer and Lane 2001.
18. L. Tiffany 1917b, p. 43.
19. Ferree 1903, p. 60.
20. Both houses, and many others, are illustrated in MacKay et al. 1997.
21. Saylor 1908a, p. 159.
22. Ethel Yule Pryor, "Robert L. Pryor—Architect, 1879–1964," typescript, Charles Hosmer Morse Museum of American Art, Winter Park, Florida (hereafter Morse Museum). After his work on Laurelton Hall, Pryor had an extensive architectural career in New Jersey. His family donated letters, drawings, and personal recollections of him to the Morse Museum.
23. Louis Comfort Tiffany to Robert L. Pryor, August 27, 1903, Morse Museum.
24. Charles T. Wills to Louis Comfort Tiffany, bill, January 16, 1906, Morse Museum.
25. Saylor 1908a, p. 159.
26. J. Mumford 1921, p. 273.
27. Saylor 1908a, pp. 159–60; Conway 1914, p. 27.
28. Howe 1914a, p. 6; L. Tiffany 1917b, p. 43; manuscript diary of Jean Gorely, quoted in Teller 1981, p. 233.
29. No descriptions of the capitals by Tiffany survive; my identification of the flowers follows e-mails from New York Botanical Garden to American Decorative Arts, The Metropolitan Museum of Art, November 10, 2005, and January 3, 2006. See also Briggs, "Reconstruction of the Gardens," in Van Wagner 1985, p. 6.
30. Howe 1914b, p. 40.
31. Dorothy Stewart Pierce, "Uncle Louis," typescript, 1979, Morse Museum, p. 3; Briggs, "Reconstruction of the Gardens," in Van Wagner 1985, pp. 5–10.
32. Howe 1915, p. 392.
33. Zebrowski 1997, ch. 13.
34. De Kay 1914, p. 62.
35. Hopkins 1916, pp. 127–30.
36. The chapel has been reerected at the Morse Museum. See Long 2002.
37. De Forest 1885, 1912.
38. Lockwood de Forest, "Diary of India/Indian Domestic Architecture," typescript, ca. 1921, pp. 3, 212, Morse Museum; R. Mayer and Lane 2001.
39. The window has been restored and installed in the Morse Museum.
40. Lothrop 1919, p. 50; Anne Love Hall, Building Structure Inventory Form, "Gatehouse/Art Gallery," December 9, 1976, Archives, Society for the Preservation of Long Island Antiquities. See also photographs in Frelinghuysen files, American Decorative Art, The Metropolitan Museum of Art, New York.
41. L. Tiffany 1917b, p. 43.
42. Articles by Bing are reprinted in Bing 1970; see also Weisberg 1986.
43. Meeks 1950, 1953.

44. De Kay 1914, p. xvii.

45. Martin Eidelberg, "Tiffany and the Cult of Nature," in Duncan et al. 1989, pp. 65–96; Burke et al. 1986; and Koch 1964, pp. 59–62.

46. On the notion of the autonomy of art, see De Kay 1914, p. xviii; and Louis C. Tiffany, quoted in LCT 1916.

47. L. Tiffany 1917b, p. 44.

48. The literature on Orientalism, especially that produced in the last twenty years, is vast, and the term "Orientalism" is now widely applied—in examinations of much earlier times as well as of the recent past and present day. My discussion is based upon Said 1978 and Edwards et al. 2000. On architecture, see Lancaster 1947, 1953a.

49. L. Tiffany 1917a.

50. Vedder 1910, p. 248. On the history of the *Rubáiyát of Omar Khayyám, the Astronomer-Poet of Persia*, see Arberry 1952 and Edwards et al. 2000, pp. 149–50.

51. There is a long history of Western translations of the book. Lane's appears to be the most popular translation into English; see the many editions of *The Thousand and One Nights: Commonly Called, in England, The Arabian Nights' Entertainments*, translated by Edward William Lane (London, 1840). See also Arberry 1952.

52. The literature is vast. Examples include Rhys 1900; "Revival" 1909; and S. Walker 1983.

53. Tiffany and Inness quoted in De Kay 1914, pp. 6–7. See also Burke 1987.

54. De Kay 1914, pp. 5, 7.

55. Blavatsky 1877 (1988 rpt.), vol. 1, pp. 289, xliv; Gomes 1987; and Godwin 1994.

56. Blavatsky 1877 (1988 rpt.), vol. 1, p. xxv.

57. Ellwood 1983, p. 110.

58. Sullivan 1924. Bragdon's articles are extensive; see Bragdon 1901, 1902 (six-part series), 1903. See also Ellis 2005.

59. Lethaby's impact on Mackintosh has been noted by many writers. Among the best is Neat 1994.

60. B.G.G. [Bertram Governor Goodhue], review, *Knight Errant* 1 (January 1893), p. 31.

61. Lethaby 1891 (1975 rpt.), pp. 206, 53, 256.

62. De Kay 1914, pp. xix, xx, 16.

63. Howe 1907, p. 158.

64. Howe 1914b, p. 42.

65. L. Tiffany 1917b, p. 44.

66. Saylor 1908b, p. 366.

An Expression of Individuality: The Interiors of Laurelton Hall

Alice Cooney Frelinghuysen

Laurelton Hall represented the evolution of Tiffany's interior-design aesthetic, building upon rooms he had created earlier in his Bella apartment and at the house on Madison Avenue and Seventy-second Street. Not only did he reapply in diverse ways individual motifs from the earlier homes; he also transported to the site architectural fragments, windows, light fixtures, and paintings and other artworks. While drawing from his own past, he was also looking to the future. The rooms at Laurelton Hall were sparer, more focused, and more modern than those that Tiffany had designed earlier.

In keeping with prevailing European and American design trends of the late nineteenth century, reinforced by Tiffany's travels and reading in his extensive art and design library, the three principal public rooms at Laurelton each had an identity of its own: one recalled Islamic architecture; another was inspired by the decorative arts of various Eastern cultures; and the third proclaimed the artist's deep appreciation for nature. The palette throughout the house, echoing that of its exterior and of the landscape and water beyond, consisted of cream-colored and silvery gray tones, with the many greens and blues of nature, enhanced by turquoise blue borrowed from Iznik ceramics.

Tiffany designed every detail of the rooms at Laurelton, from the flooring and floor coverings, the wall and ceiling treatments, and the furnishings and their upholstery to the lighting and accessories, and carefully integrated into the interiors his myriad art collections, which included Chinese, Japanese, and Native American objects as well as examples of his own work in many media. The harmony achieved in the different spaces resulted from his direction of every aspect of the design, from conception to fabrication and placement. Teams of workmen and women under Tiffany's supervision, in his workshops, produced the furnishings and decorative finishes to his meticulous specifications.

Laurelton's floor plan did not conform to the typical style of the day. Rather, it reflected Tiffany's desire to make the fullest possible use of the site, with its outstanding vistas and contours. Thus the principal ground-floor public rooms—the Fountain Court, the living hall, and the dining room—were virtually freestanding

pavilions. Each of these spaces, which were the largest in the house, had two exposures, one to the harbor and the other to the landscaped hillside. The knowledge of and preoccupation with color and light that dominated Tiffany's experience as a painter and as a maker of leaded glass and lighting fixtures were evident in these interiors.

The Fountain Court, also called the Oriental Court or central court, served as the entrance hall (figs. 120, 132). Tiffany called it "the soul of the house."[1] Its grandeur was due in part to its lofty three-story ceiling. Two upstairs balcony galleries surrounded this soaring space; pairs of fluted marble columns served to frame the ground floor, while more slender versions formed a colonnade around the second-floor balcony.

The court was considered the most "Oriental" room in the house, a term used loosely during the late nineteenth century to denote the spirit of the Near East and Far East. Although the fountain rooms

Fig. 120. Fountain Court, Laurelton Hall. From Henry H. Saylor, "Indoor Fountains," *Country Life in America* 14 (August 1908), p. 366

Opposite: Fig. 119. Detail of fig. 150

Fig. 121. Louis Comfort Tiffany, Hanging globe from Fountain Court, Laurelton Hall, 1904–10. Favrile glass, gilt-bronze collar, 13⅛ x 8½ in. (33.3 x 21.6 cm). The Charles Hosmer Morse Museum of American Art, Winter Park, Florida

Fig. 122. Louis Comfort Tiffany, Hanging globe, ca. 1904–10. Favrile glass, 11 x 8 x 8 in. (27.9 x 20.3 x 20.3 cm). Museum of Fine Arts, Boston, Anonymous gift in memory of John G. Pierce, Sr. (65.216)

Fig. 123. Fountain Court, Laurelton Hall. From Samuel Howe, "An American Country House," *International Studio* 33 (1907–8), p. 294

Fig. 124. Tile mural, Topkapi Palace, Istanbul. Photograph by Abdullah Frères, 1880–93. The Charles Hosmer Morse Museum of American Art, Winter Park, Florida. Photograph originally owned by Tiffany Studios

of Ottoman palaces come to mind, those of the Red Palace at the Alhambra, in Granada, are a more likely inspiration for Tiffany's court. In 1913 Howe, Laurelton Hall's most consistent chronicler, compared the room to the courts at the Alhambra, where "the Moors show their scholarly realization of the decorative value of water—a precious fluid."[2] The exoticism of the Alhambra was tremendously appealing to travelers and artists in the second half of the nineteenth century. Karl Baedecker, for example, devoted thirty-four pages of his guide to Spain and Portugal to this seat of Moorish aristocracy, which he praised as the "culminating point of a journey in Spain" for its strange and exotic culture and art.[3]

Tiffany's appetite for Moorish architecture was first whetted on a six-month trip abroad, from the end of July 1870 to the beginning of February 1871, when he and the American painter Robert Swain Gifford (1840–1905) traveled to Madrid, Malaga, Gibraltar, Tangier, Malta, Sicily, Egypt, Rome, and Florence.[4] Tiffany had hoped to go again to Spain, and perhaps to Granada, in the spring of 1875, but that trip was postponed. In the winter of 1875/76 he traveled with his first wife, May, to North Africa, where she wrote their friends Emily and Robert W. de Forest that her husband was working very hard, "painting, drawing, and photographing."[5] Although the precise date of their visit to the Alhambra cannot be documented, Tiffany's numerous paintings, watercolors, and pastels of its architecture certainly indicate a visit (see fig. 3).

Like the court at the Alhambra, the Fountain Court at Laurelton was essentially square in plan, but it was given an octagonal feeling by the angled, paired ornamental columns in the corners. In each archway between the columns hung illuminated, blown Favrile-glass globes in golden tones. Decorated with white-petaled flowers with yellow centers and abstract green stylized leaves and stems, the four on the ground floor were pear-shaped (fig. 121)

Right: Fig. 126. Stenciled wall fragment from Fountain Court, Laurelton Hall, ca. 1902. Painted textile, 124 x 20 in. (315 x 50.8 cm). The Mark Twain House and Museum, Hartford, Connecticut

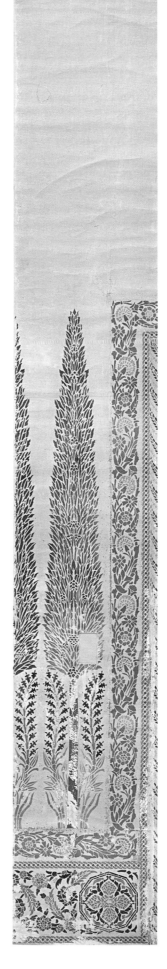

Below: Fig. 125. Detail of fig. 126

Fig. 157. Mantel in dining room, Laurelton Hall. From Gurdon S. Parker, "The Fireplace and Its Frame," *Country Life in America* 42 (August 1922), p. 78. The *Magnolia* leaded-glass panel in the door at the right was originally installed at the Tiffany house on Seventy-second Street (see fig. 38).

figs. 17, 18). It also appeared above the mantelpiece in the library of the Seventy-second Street house (see fig. 37). Tiffany's study of Owen Jones's *Grammar of Ornament* (London, 1856), a copy of which he had at Laurelton Hall, may have influenced his selection of the motif. The first plate of Jones's chapter devoted to "Leaves and Flowers from Nature" features horse chestnut leaves of varying sizes. Jones wrote that the "chestnut leaf contains the whole of the laws which are to be found in Nature; no art can rival the perfect grace of its form, the perfect proportional distribution of the areas."[32] Tiffany apparently agreed; at Laurelton the pattern was omnipresent, extending up the walls and ceiling seamlessly (no moldings were used). Even the blinds were eventually painted to match the wall pattern, which was enlivened by subtle shading of dark to light as it progressed up the wall.

Every aspect of the room was carefully conceived to achieve the essential harmony Tiffany desired. The color green was selected not only for its association with nature, but also because it was thought to be restful. As Lyman noted in 1914:

> The effects are all gained through the use of specially wrought glass, each fixture in the room having the same general tone, of dark green and opalescent glass combined, yet each one entirely

different in treatment. Over the long table and in front of the mammoth fireplace hangs suspended from the ceiling what may be called a wrought iron yoke, from either end of which are suspended glass spheres, each enclosing a light.[33]

The ornamental chains of the nearly thirteen-foot-long iron yoke were decorated with Japanese *tsuba*, or sword guards. Glass orbs hung from large iron rings at each end (fig. 141). The central band of the hanging globes was composed of large green turtleback tiles with a rainbow iridescent surface. Below were eight panels of a fish-scale pattern formed by leaded, green mottled glass. In the middle of the yoke, three semicircular hanging shades, each of the same deep green iridescent-glass turtleback tiles, shed light on the massive library tables and contributed to the consistency of tone (fig. 142). When the blinds were pulled and the room illuminated solely by the Favrile-glass-and-bronze fixtures, it must have seemed as though the visitor was surrounded by deep verdant foliage, with the glow of emeralds emanating from the shades above.

It is not known from which room a hanging shade with a pattern of black-eyed Susans came (fig. 143), but its nature theme would have suited many of the rooms at Laurelton. The black-eyed Susan (*Rudbeckia herta*) was a common meadow or roadside plant native to North America. In Tiffany's lamp, its vibrant flower heads shine like a blaze of gold amid the green foliage.

The other objects in the room all worked toward the chromatic harmony. The Tiffany green-metal-and-glass desk set, for example, was of the same coloration (fig. 145).[34] Here the grapevine in his "Etched Metal and Glass" line was backed with green marbleized glass relating to that of the shades above. The grapevine design was a popular stock item from Tiffany Studios' extensive line of desk accessories, but Tiffany must have thought it appropriate for this customized setting. It was complemented by an inkwell, also of patinated bronze, that featured green glass blown into the metal in a simulation of encrusted emerald green stones. The rest of the desk was covered by neatly stacked books and a variety of plants, which Tiffany would rotate frequently. Lyman noted in 1914 that "rare orchids of the lady slipper type were massed on the long carved table, while the farther end of the room, facing the door, was a veritable forest of hydrangeas."[35] Reinforcing the coloristic unity of the room was Tiffany's large pottery vase, described in the catalogue of the 1946 auction of the contents of Laurelton Hall as "[p]ear-shaped, with three rustic strap handles, and glazed a light apple green" (fig. 144).[36]

The fireplace was large, spanning nearly half the length of the long wall of the room, completely open, and devoid of architectural embellishment (fig. 146). Its effect was described by Howe in 1907–8: the "fire is literally on the hearth, without recess or jambs to bewilder the smoke from the logs burning upon it."[37] The roomy built-in settlelike seats provided a place where, according to Howe, "a score or more can sit round and listen to fireside stories."[38] At one time two large pottery vases anchored each end of the mantelpiece (figs. 147, 148).[39] The bold inverted-baluster

Fig. 158. Louis Comfort Tiffany, Tiffany Studios, Dome hanging shade from dining room, Laurelton Hall, ca. 1904–6. Leaded Favrile glass, 66 x 11 in. (167.6 x 27.9 cm). The Charles Hosmer Morse Museum of American Art, Winter Park, Florida

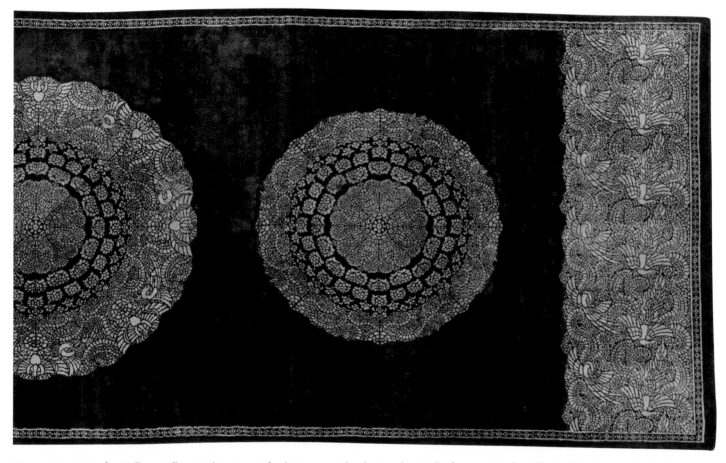

Fig. 159. Louis Comfort Tiffany, Tiffany Studios, Carpet for dining room (detail), Laurelton Hall, after 1913. Wool, 306¼ x 103⅜ in. (777.9 x 262.6 cm). The Charles Hosmer Morse Museum of American Art, Winter Park, Florida

Fig. 160. Louis Comfort Tiffany, Tiffany Studios, Dining table from dining room, Laurelton Hall, ca. 1905. Painted cherry (?), 29½ x 66 in. (74.9 x 167.6 cm). The Charles Hosmer Morse Museum of American Art, Winter Park, Florida

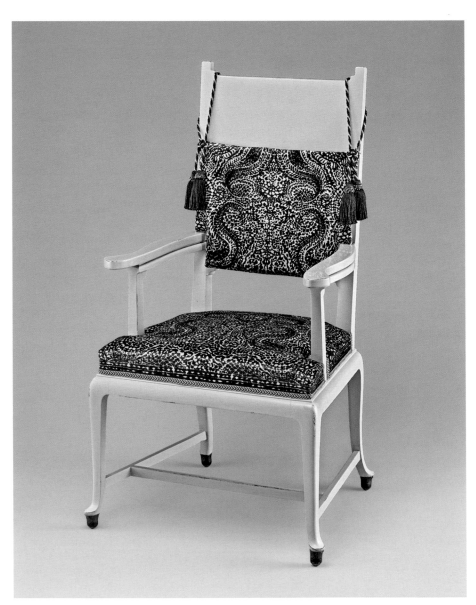

Fig. 161. Louis Comfort Tiffany, Tiffany Studios, Armchair from dining room, Laurelton Hall, ca. 1905. Painted cherry (?) (replicated upholstery), 45 x 19½ x 18½ in. (114.3 x 49.5 x 47 cm). The Charles Hosmer Morse Museum of American Art, Winter Park, Florida

Fig. 162. Dining room designed by Louis Comfort Tiffany, Milbank Residence, Greenwich, Connecticut. From A. W. Fred, "Interieurs von L. C. Tiffany," *Dekorative Kunst* 9 (1902), p. 113

Fig. 163. Alexander Koester (1864–1932), *Ducks*, ca. 1899. Oil on canvas, 43½ x 72 in. (110.5 x 182.9 cm). The Worrell Collection, Charlottesville, Virginia

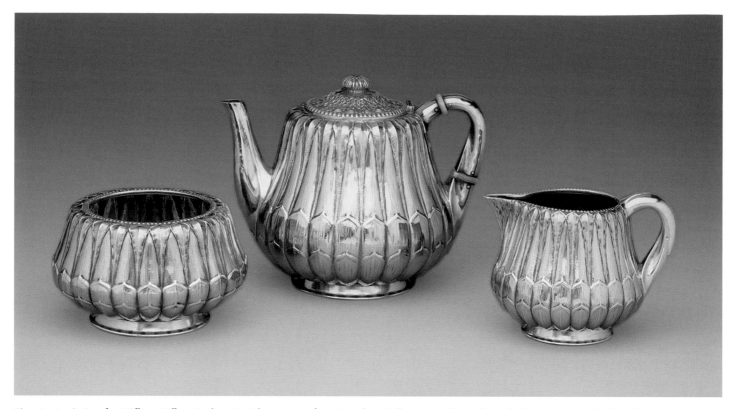

Fig. 164. Louis Comfort Tiffany, Tiffany Studios, Partial tea service from Laurelton Hall, 1902–4. Silver, silver gilt, ivory, waste bowl: 3¼ x 5⅜ in. (8.3 x 13.7 cm); teapot: 6¼ x 7⅞ x 5⅞ in. (15.9 x 20 x 14.9 cm); creamer: 4 x 5⅛ x 4⅛ in. (10.2 x 13 x 10.5 cm). Los Angeles County Museum of Art, Purchased with funds provided by the Director's Roundtable

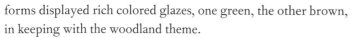

Fig. 165. Louis Comfort Tiffany, Tiffany Studios, Sugar bowl from Laurelton Hall tea service, 1902–4. Silver, silver gilt, 4⅞ x 6⅛ in. (12.4 x 15.6 cm). Collection of Eric Streiner

Fig. 166. Silver tea set with copper tray, shown in the auction catalogue for the 1946 sale of the contents of Laurelton Hall. From Parke-Bernet 1946, p. 199

forms displayed rich colored glazes, one green, the other brown, in keeping with the woodland theme.

The illumination was enhanced by an assortment of novel lamps. Lyman, who particularly admired Laurelton's originality, observed,

> The mantel over the fireplace bears four glass vases in iridescent golden and green tones. These are also illuminated. At one side of the room a vase with peacock feather design worked into the glass is also lighted, and gives an indefinable yet positive impression of bird life in this forest room. Back of the hydrangeas, on

the piano near the windows, there glows a cluster of lights, not a detail of whose beautiful color is lost.[40]

After 1918 the function of the living hall changed. It became the venue for Tiffany's collection of his leaded-glass windows. (See the essay "A Museum of His Own" in this publication.) His most notable windows—those shown to critical acclaim—he kept for himself. These were often first displayed in his New York showrooms, and also featured at international expositions, but after he had lived at Laurelton Hall for a decade, Tiffany transferred some of the very best to Long Island.

On the other side of the Fountain Court, across from the living hall, was the dining room (fig. 156), entered from a small hall with a mosaic floor. At either end were floor-to-ceiling clear, colorless glass windows that took advantage of the best light of the day. On the terrace side the windows were eventually crowned with leaded-glass wisteria vines, echoing the network of natural wisteria vines outside. Seven panels joined together to form a continuous transom (figs. 119, 149–154).[41] Author Gertrude Speenburgh recalled after several memorable visits to Laurelton Hall that the panicles of purple flowers were "so lifelike that when the garden vine mingles its blossoms with its replicas in glass one has to look closely to distinguish one from the other."[42]

The dining room was described by Howe as a "study in blue and rose,"[43] a clear reference to the works of James Abbott McNeill Whistler (1834–1903). That description is somewhat misleading because blue and creamy white actually dominated the palette. Its color scheme was reputed to have derived from a blue-and-white Chinese jacket that Tiffany had acquired on his travels.[44] Like the living hall, this room was carefully conceived as a complete work of art. As Speenburgh observed, its feeling of "modern simplicity" was "unmarred by any obstructive note. Line and color, restrained and dignified, make a perfect whole."[45] In contrast to the living hall's homage to nature, however, the dining room's theme was inspired by Tiffany's admiration for Asian design.

The tall marble chimney breast, which anchored one side of the large room, was modern in appearance, starkly simple and unexpectedly angular (fig. 157). The sides, rather than returning straight back to the wall, as was typical, were canted out, bringing more focus to the mantel. The cool gray-and-white marble rose unornamented straight to the ceiling, with only the simplest shallow shelf inset into it. A single recessed slot would have accommodated a plaque or a plate, although none of the period photographs indicate that one was in place.

In lieu of an overmantel, three blue-and-green glass mosaic medallions were inset into the marble. They were more than decorative: the three dials were illuminated from behind at night—one marked the time of the day, one the day of the week, and one the date of the month.[46] The room's walls were covered in "plain coloured canvas, relieved only by a frieze in white and silver grey."[47]

In each windowed bay hung a green leaded-glass lotus shade. The enormous central chandelier, a slightly domed disk of leaded glass in shades of blue, milky white, and pale celadon green, copied the design and palette of a Chinese embroidered medallion (fig. 158). Three long Mazarine-blue-and-cream wool carpets were designed and fabricated in Tiffany's studios (fig. 159). A border of stylized butterflies and paisleys lightened each end; the central medallions harmonized with the matching ceiling fixture above. For the upholstery, which was completed by the Studios in 1906,[48] Tiffany eschewed the traditional materials of dining furniture, notably horsehair or leather, in favor of a patterned silk velvet. The design took its cue from the carpet, and the seats and cushions, which hung on the backs from silk cords and tassels, were made of

hand-dyed silk velvet in a scaled-down version of the carpet pattern. A related upholstery scheme was found in the Tiffany-designed dining room for the Milbank House in Greenwich, Connecticut (fig. 162).[49]

The furniture designs reinforced the Chinese theme of the room. The three octagonal tables derived from Ming dynasty lobed stands, with their distinguishing features of high waists and shaped aprons (fig. 160). The Chinese versions were most often in black lacquer with mother-of-pearl inlay, an effect that Tiffany created in another version of the same shape that he made for his Chinese room at Laurelton Hall (see fig. 284). Tiffany earlier had adapted a Chinese form for several porch tables he designed for the Briars (see fig. 66). These tables had barrel-shaped bases modeled on Chinese garden seats or the common barrel-shaped stools of wood, metal, or porcelain that were popular from the Ming dynasty and throughout the nineteenth century in Europe and America.[50]

The dining chairs (fig. 161), with their simple backs and tall cabriole legs on raised pad feet, refer to the forms of Chinese furniture styles that were later interpreted by English and American cabinetmakers. The feet were extended by an ingenious castor similar to an oversized ball bearing that rolled within the casings, to continue the line of the foot. At Laurelton Hall a simple white-painted sideboard with a removable tray table in the center completed the furnishings.

Referencing such earlier styles, however, did not diminish the modern appearance of the chairs and tables. The surfaces Tiffany selected contributed to the new look. For their finish Tiffany departed from Chinese sources, reverting to cream enamel paint, with a soft sheen reminiscent of the table and chairs in his Seventy-second Street breakfast room or in the seating for the gallery in the Havemeyer house of 1892.[51] In both the Havemeyer house and Tiffany's own, the sober lines and stark finish of the furniture contrasted with the complexity of the patterned silk-velvet upholstery. By the time Tiffany incorporated such finishes into the interiors of Laurelton Hall, the sophisticated public would already have experienced their strikingly modern appearance in British contemporary furniture then in vogue, notably that of Charles Rennie McIntosh (1868–1928), as well as in examples of white-painted furniture shown in 1895 and 1896 at Siegfried Bing's exhibitions, where Tiffany's work was also displayed.

The walls were unadorned except for the mosaic dials and silver-stenciled frieze. By at least 1922, Tiffany added shelving at the height of the frieze for a collection of blue-and-white Chinese porcelain plates and jars whose palettes and designs complemented the scheme (see fig. 157). Over the sideboard he displayed a large painting from his collection. *Ducks*, by the German artist Alexander Koester (1864–1932), is a light-filled composition of the birds floating together on water in a vibrant palette of blues, greens, purples, and whites (fig. 163). Koester is little known outside Germany, but he exhibited three versions of duck subjects at the 1904 Louisiana Purchase Exposition in Saint Louis, where Tiffany had an acclaimed showing. As Speenburgh noted, the painting was a "study in the blues of the room—perfect."[52] The light-infused colors bring to mind the work of Sorolla (see fig. 129).

Contemporary photographs show that two closely related electrified candelabra were displayed on the sideboard and mantel (see figs. 156, 157). Tiffany alternated two designs, one nine-armed, the other eleven-armed. The latter relates to the turn-of-the-century designs of Bruno Paul (1874–1968) of the Vereinigte Werkstätten für Kunst im Handwerk, in Munich.[53] Tiffany probably would have seen Paul's work, if not abroad, at the 1904 Saint Louis fair. Paul's brass candelabra are similar to Tiffany's in their simple trumpet-shaped bases tapering to central candleholders, from which the slender, swiveling branches extend and form a triangle. Tiffany's other variation displays nine branches of unequal length, with the lower, or outer, arms growing progressively longer, so that they would all reach the same height at the top. This design, although modern, ultimately derives from plant forms, such as that of a corymb or other flat-topped cluster. The Tiffany Studios candelabra were of cool silver plate, with opalescent shades concealing the electric light source.

An exquisite sterling silver tea service in a repoussé design of stylized plant motifs resided on the sideboard (figs. 164, 165). Near the bases on the three pieces, overlapping lotuslike leaves suggest artichoke foliage, and the lids of the pot and covered sugar bowl feature delicate floral motifs, similar to those found on Tiffany's jewelry of the early decades of the twentieth century.[54] The shapes and relief pattern of all the pieces are adaptations of a similar form in bronze that Tiffany employed as a lamp base and that he later made use of in pottery.[55] A tray in a different pattern accompanied the service (fig. 166). A form generally associated with a related copper service, the tray was hand-hammered in a lozenge shape and bears an undulating border. Delicate sprays of trailing prunus blossoms were engraved on both ends.[56]

The expansive size of the dining room—twenty-eight by fifty-eight feet—made it especially suited for entertaining. Tiffany could accommodate as many as one hundred and fifty for dinner (see the essay "The Art of Magnificent Living" in this volume). After the meal, his male guests would retire to the small smoking room off the dining room (see fig. 272). Since the mid-nineteenth century smoking rooms had been variations on Moorish casbahs. In yet another nontraditional approach, however, Tiffany transferred the Moorish ornamentation to the Fountain Court and streamlined the decor of the smoking room. Simple, repeated squares of grass cloth covered the walls and ceiling. The room looked out through a broad set of glass doors onto the pear-tree terrace and opened toward a series of conservatories opposite the dining room door. Hung over an unadorned upholstered banquette was the focal point, a mural titled *The Opium Dream*, a subject deemed by some to be inappropriate in a house with Tiffany's children. (For a discussion of the painting, see the essay by Julia Meech in this volume.) A large fireplace embellished with Japanese sword guards brought from the Seventy-second Street library faced *Opium Dream*.

Little is known of the interior decoration of the rest of the house. Beyond the dining room a passageway led to a glass palm house, then via long greenhouses to another conservatory, and finally through additional greenhouses to the stables. The servants' quarters were off the kitchen to the west of the house. The family living quarters, on the second floor,[57] comprised six bedroom suites, including Tiffany's own. These were relatively large, each with a fireplace, and furnished with antiques from earlier family houses, as well as studio-made pieces. Adorning each room were objects from Tiffany's collections, from Oriental carpets to Native American baskets and Japanese textiles.

Tiffany's suite was the largest, but modest in its furnishings. The bed was described as a "massive rosewood 1st empire bedstead" and most of the other furniture was of rosewood.[58] One of Tiffany's granddaughters recalled that his suite was reached by a "black iron spiral staircase in the living room which led up to some very private sanctuary of Grandpa's."[59] The girls' rooms faced the pond. There was an additional family sitting room on the second floor as well. Sarah Hanley had a room near the rest of the family.

On the second floor near his bedroom Tiffany maintained a large private studio, which was filled with studio props moved there from the Seventy-second Street house. They included Oriental carpets, a large collection of textiles, and costumes. In addition there were several easels, stacks of frames, and numerous canvases and sketches.[60] A sleeping porch off the studio offered him an alternative bed during the warmer months. Two additional bedrooms, one facing the bay and the other the woods, were on the third floor.

It seems that Tiffany departed from the norm in the finishes of the more private spaces as well. For the bathrooms, it was recorded that he substituted cement for the more typical ceramic tiling or mosaics for floors and side walls.[61] Tiffany's use of cement for interior and exterior surfaces challenged traditional building materials. Considered at the time to be lacking the permanence of brick or stone, and questioned for its wood framework, cement appealed to him because of its flexibility and ability to be adapted for a multitude of textured surfaces, from smooth and clear to rough-cast or embedded with small stones or shells. Cement had a straightforward, honest simplicity about it. The premium Tiffany placed on the value of the craftsman was reflected in his use of the material, in which the workmanship could be seen in the marks the trowel left on the surface of wall or floor.

When he moved into Laurelton Hall in the autumn of 1905, still saddened, no doubt, by the passing of his wife, Tiffany regarded it more as a beginning. Laurelton was never "finished," or static. As he once said, the artist "tires as his creation approaches completion" and he must, therefore, "content himself with the pleasure of doing."[62] He was continually changing it, sometimes by merely altering the plantings and their placement in the Fountain Court. Such new placement of different flowering plants would substantially alter the character of the room. An accounting submitted in his Cold Spring Harbor Account in the spring of

1906 itemized such additional work as "making over library arm-chair," "recovering four divans," and "making drawings for additions."[63] This was only the beginning of significant changes Tiffany would make in ensuing years, the most significant being the integration of architectural elements and stained glasss from the Seventy-second Street house. This was followed by another major addition. In 1914 he even considered constructing a new terrace, into which he would incorporate fragments and objects he had acquired during his travels in North Africa.[64] This was the extension of the porch outside the dining room that resulted in the ambitious building of the Daffodil Terrace (see fig. 79).

The Laurelton Hall interiors drew upon those of the Bella apartment and of the Seventy-second Street house, each rooted in hallmarks of the Aesthetic movement in their eclectic mix of different non-Western sources in muted tonalities. And Tiffany's interest in surface treatments—for walls, floors, and ceilings—patterned with reflective gold or silver and variously painted, stenciled, or covered with textiles, never wavered. No one element dominated; Tiffany's careful control ensured that each contributed to the achievement of a harmonious artistic whole. He amalgamated the natural world and his own built environment. The principal rooms incorporated panoramic landscape views of extraordinary beauty, evinced an intriguing use of materials, and utilized a palette drawn from nature. Responding to new artistic trends as the nineteenth century drew to a close, and attentive to a multisensory experience, Tiffany developed a new aesthetic at Laurelton. As Edward Conway wrote in 1914, "As is everywhere manifest at Laurelton Hall, the motif, whatever it be, has first passed through the crucible of Mr. Tiffany's fancy. Emerging, it is something new, unique—a distinctive decorative entity."

1. L. Tiffany 1917b, p. 43.
2. Howe 1913b, p. 378.
3. Baedeker 1898, p. 334
4. R. Swain Gifford Letters, MSS 12, subgroup 1, series A, subseries 2, folders 11–16, New Bedford Whaling Museum, Massachusetts.
5. Tiffany had hoped to go to Algiers the preceding season, traveling with his first wife, May, and with Samuel Colman and his wife. While they were in Menton, in the south of France, the Tiffanys' newborn baby became sick and died, and the Colmans continued on to Algiers without them. Tiffany expressed interest in seeing not just Algiers but also India and Persia. Instead, he studied avidly the history of the Saracens and their culture, feeling that there "will be plenty of field for me which has never been touched before and yet which embraces the finest architecture and ornaments in existence." Louis C. Tiffany to Annie O. Mitchell, January 10, 1875, Mitchell-Tiffany Family Papers, Manuscripts and Archives, Yale University Library, box 7, folder 12.
6. "Panama-Pacific" 1915. Tiffany made for the 1915 Panama-Pacific Exposition a large silver covered jar with a miniature enamel frieze replicating *Flora* on one side and *Ceres* on the other. For an illustration of the jar, see Zapata 1993, p. 148.
7. Parke-Bernet 1946, lot 1073.
8. L. Tiffany 1917b, p. 43; Howe 1914a, p. 5.
9. Howe 1914a, p. 5.
10. Hugh F. McKean to his mother, n.d., Archives, Charles Hosmer Morse Museum of American Art, Winter Park, Florida (hereafter Morse Museum). Only a year or so earlier, Tiffany had hung a similar globe from the skylight of the central hall of Frederick Ayer's mansion in Boston. See fig. 92 in this volume.
11. Lyman 1914, p. 52.
12. Howe 1906, p. 107.
13. For a discussion of the Tiffany decorations of the Havemeyers' house, see Alice Cooney Frelinghuysen, "The Havemeyer House," in Frelinghuysen et al. 1993, pp. 173–98.
14. Havemeyer 1961 (1993 ed.), p. 13.
15. Howe 1915, p. 387.
16. Leslie Nash Papers, Christie's, New York.
17. Howe 1915, p. 388.
18. Hugh F. McKean to his mother, n.d. [193?], Archives, Morse Museum.
19. Howe 1915, p. 388.
20. Howe 1907, p. 159.
21. Nash Notebooks, Rakow Library, Corning Museum of Glass, and courtesy of Christie's, New York.
22. Ibid.
23. Ibid.
24. Saylor 1908a, p. 160.
25. Howe 1915, p. 388.
26. Tiffany 1917b, p. 43.
27. Saylor 1908a, p. 161.
28. L. Tiffany 1917b, p. 43.
29. Lyman 1914, p. 52.
30. Ibid.
31. Howe 1914, p. 6.
32. O. Jones 1856, p. 480, pl. XCI.
33. Lyman 1914, p. 52.
34. For a view of the desk set on Tiffany's desk in the living room at Laurelton, see Koch 2001, p. 124 (bottom).
35. Lyman 1914, p. 52.
36. Parke-Bernet 1946, lot 90.
37. Howe 1907–8, p. 296.
38. Howe 1914a, p. 6.
39. For a period photograph of the two vases on the living-room mantel at Laurelton, see Koch 2001, p. 125 (middle).
40. Lyman 1914, p. 52.
41. Six of the panels are in the collection of the Morse Museum. The seventh is in the Louis C. Tiffany Garden Museum, Matsue, Japan. See Duncan 2004, p. 153.
42. Speenburgh 1956, p. 100.
43. Howe 1907–8, p. 296.
44. Saylor 1908a, p. 161.
45. Speenburgh 1956, p. 99.
46. Tiffany also employed clock dials as decoration for dining-room mantelpieces at the Seventy-second Street house (see fig. 28) and at the Milbank house (see fig. 162).
47. Howe 1907–8, p. 296.
48. Order from Louis C. Tiffany, Esq., Cold Spring Harbor, with Tiffany Studios, New York, April 1, 1906, for "upholstery dining room chairs" and "making covers for dining room chairs," Archives, Morse Museum.
49. Robert Koch identified the house as that of the Millbank family. Koch 2001, p. 113.
50. One of these Chinese-style tables survives, unrestored, at the Mark Twain House and Museum, Hartford, Connecticut, to which it was given by one of Tiffany's descendants.
51. For an image of the gallery in the Havemeyer house, see Frelinghuysen et al. 1993, p. 189.
52. Speenburgh 1956, p. 99.
53. For an illustration of Paul's candelabra, see Greenhalgh 2000, p. 230, fig. 14.8.
54. The teapot, slop bowl (identified, incorrectly, as a sugar bowl), and creamer were featured in the 1946 auction catalogue of the contents of Laurelton Hall (see Parke-Bernet 1946, lot 1079). A hotwater kettle on a stand with its burner was also included in the lot, but its whereabouts is currently unknown. The covered sugar bowl was found independently, but is the missing form from the original set.
55. For the lamp base, see Eidelberg et al. 2005, p. 37; for the pottery version, see Eidelberg and McClelland 2001, p. 10. A pottery example is in the collection of the Morse Museum.
56. Parke-Bernet 1946, lot 1082. The tray was identified as being 32½ inches in length and with a "bright finish."
57. The original floor plans (figs. 97–101, 108) show five chambers on the second floor and five on the third, not including the maids' rooms. By the mid-1910s, however, several of these, including the Japanese room, were given different functions.
58. M. Frederick Savage, "Laurelton Hall Insurance Inventory," 1919, copy by John E. Terwilliger, January 1937, p. 420, Archives, Morse Museum.
59. Helena Gilder Miller to Hugh F. McKean, February 29, 1976, Archives, Morse Museum.
60. Howe 1907, p. 161.
61. See pp. 44–47 of the inventory named in note 58 above.
62. L. Tiffany 1917b, p. 43.
63. Order from Louis C. Tiffany, Esq. Cold Spring Harbor, with Tiffany Studios, New York, April 1, 1906, Archives, Morse Museum.
64. Conway 1914, p. 29.
65. Ibid.

Tiffany's Collections: Paintings, Glass, Ceramics, Enamelwork

Alice Cooney Frelinghuysen

Laurelton Hall was far more than a country house. It was a private gallery for Tiffany's diverse collections of objects and paintings. Perhaps more important, it presented the opportunity for this multifaceted artist to showcase his own exceptional accomplishments. Laurelton Hall was also an ever-evolving work of art in its own right. After moving there in 1905 Tiffany continued to make architectural and decorative changes, including the addition of the Daffodil Terrace (see fig. 79). His extensive collection of Chinese art was housed in a large "Chinese room" in which he installed a mock-period octagonal pavilion (see figs. 281, 282, 284). The second-floor balcony of the Fountain Court (fig. 168) was lined with cases exhibiting vases of his own making and related foreign examples, all against a backdrop of exotic imported patterned silks whose sheen complemented the luster of the iridescent glass. For paintings, in 1918 he created an art gallery in a separate building on the estate.

Tiffany was an inveterate collector. He began acquiring art at least by the early 1870s, on his travels in North America and abroad. An item's rarity or historical significance was of little interest to him. Rather, he sought objects exclusively for their aesthetic appeal, responding to their shapes, colors, and patterns, and he skillfully integrated them into the interiors he designed for himself. Every room held an abundance of objects, each carefully placed with an eye to its effect as part of a larger ensemble. His holdings ranged from Chinese and Japanese metalwork, ceramics, prints, textiles, and lacquerwork to Islamic tiles and ceramics, Oriental rugs, Syrian and Roman glass, Indian and Egyptian jewelry, Russian icons, and Dutch snuffboxes of mother-of-pearl and silver. (For Tiffany's collection of Asian art, see the essay by Julia Meech in this volume.) He was intrigued by handcrafted products and amassed a sizable collection of Native American baskets, textiles, and carved wooden objects (for these, see the essay by Elizabeth Hutchinson). And a good share of the objects at Laurelton Hall were examples of Tiffany's own work: paintings, watercolors, Favrile-glass vessels, pottery, enamelwork, and leaded-glass windows.

Tiffany's extensive collections are no longer intact, but several near-contemporary sources have proved invaluable in the challenging task of reconstructing them. One critical document is the typescript copy that John E. Terwilliger, superintendent of Laurelton Hall, prepared in 1937 of an inventory of the contents of the house made by M. Frederick Savage (1851–1934) in 1919.[1] (Savage presumably drew up the inventory in order to determine the value of the objects that Tiffany had given to the Louis Comfort Tiffany Foundation, which he had set up in 1918.) Further evidence is provided by period photographs of the rooms at Laurelton Hall and by the catalogue of the auction, at Parke-Bernet, New York, in 1946, at which the Tiffany Foundation sold most of the contents of Laurelton Hall. Forty-four Favrile-glass objects and pieces of enamelwork from his personal collection are today in The Metropolitan Museum of Art, having been lent to the

Fig. 168. Fountain Court, Laurelton Hall, with artworks displayed on second-floor balcony, ca. 1920s. Gelatin silver print, 8⅛ x 10 in. (20.5 x 25.4 cm). Photograph by David Aronow. The Metropolitan Museum of Art, New York, Gift of Robert Koch, 1981 (1981.1162.6)

Opposite: Fig. 167. Detail of fig. 206

Fig. 169. Charles de Kay, *The Art Work of Louis C. Tiffany*, 1914. Binding design by Louis Comfort Tiffany, 12¾ x 10¼ x 2⅞ in. (32.4 x 26 x 7.3 cm). The Charles Hosmer Morse Museum of American Art, Winter Park, Florida

Museum by Tiffany in 1925 and subsequently donated by the Tiffany Foundation. Still other works, most of them paintings, remain in the hands of his descendants. This essay examines Tiffany's collections of paintings, glass, ceramics, and enamelwork—both his own and others'. (Leaded-glass windows are discussed in the essay following.)

Published images show few paintings on the walls of the main public rooms during Laurelton Hall's first decade (see figs. 120, 155, 156, 242). It was probably about 1912, when Tiffany was first contemplating creating a kind of private museum, that he began systematically to move paintings from the Seventy-second Street house to Laurelton. The paintings, windows, and other objects he hung were large and their sites carefully selected, so that these artworks would advance the overall aesthetic mission of the rooms in which they were placed. He transferred his two large friezelike paintings, *Flora*, or *Spring* (fig. 173), and *Ceres*, or *Autumn*, from the dining room of the Seventy-second Street house to the third-floor balcony of the Fountain Court at Laurelton. He also purchased works by other artists specifically for Laurelton Hall. Most notable was the portrait by Joaquín Sorolla y Bastida (1863–1923), commissioned by Tiffany in 1911, which shows Tiffany painting in a garden at Laurelton Hall (see fig. 129). Sorolla depicted Tiffany in his habitual white suit, palette in hand, taking a minute to gaze

away from the canvas set on an easel amid a profusion of flowers. His border terrier, Funny, stands at his knee. Tiffany chose to sit for the portrait in May, when his gardens were at their peak.[2] The immense painting epitomizes what he had aimed to create at Laurelton Hall: an environment filled with the beauties of nature that would inspire artists forevermore. He paid Sorolla eight thousand dollars for the commission, an enormous fee at the time, and he gave the painting pride of place, above the divan in the Fountain Court (see fig. 130). The landscape just outside the court was like the one Sorolla had painted, with great heads of pink and blue hydrangea, masses of yellow and purple irises, and, in the distance, the sparkling blue water of Cold Spring Harbor. Tiffany also selected the portrait for the frontispiece of *The Art Work of Louis C. Tiffany*, the monograph he commissioned from Charles de Kay that was published in 1914 (fig. 169).[3]

Even before commissioning his own portrait, Tiffany was a great admirer of Sorolla's, undoubtedly drawn by the Spanish painter's attention to color and the extraordinary quality of light that he was able to capture in oil on canvas. He purchased four of Sorolla's paintings, including *On the Beach* (1908) and *Among the Oleanders* (1909), at an exhibition at the Hispanic Society of America, in New York, in 1909.[4] He may also have encountered his work at the World's Columbian Exposition in Chicago in 1893 and at the Exposition Universelle in Paris in 1900. The only other European painting Tiffany hung inside the main house at Laurelton was *Ducks* (ca. 1899), by the German artist Alexander Max Koester (1864–1932), which he acquired specifically for the wall above the sideboard in the spacious dining room (see figs. 156, 163). The white, gray, and pale lavender ducks swimming on a pond of shimmering blue-green water echoed the color scheme of the room.

The other European paintings at Laurelton Hall were displayed in the freestanding art gallery, which in 1918 was the last addition to the grounds (see figs. 335–337). For the gallery, Tiffany purchased and altered an early-nineteenth-century structure said to have been the James Wood house, stuccoing the exterior and adorning it with Indian architectural elements and Favrile-glass mosaic and tiles so that it complemented the main house. The octagonal central room of the gallery featured a ceiling of pierced wood suspended under a dome of deep cobalt blue glass that accentuated the foliate pattern of the piercing. On the upper balconies of the gallery Tiffany installed cases in which to display objects from his collections of glass, pottery, and enamelwork.

Tiffany was attracted to the qualities of light and color in the paintings of a number of other contemporary European artists whose work is relatively unknown today. One of the first such canvases he acquired at least by 1900 was the large *Winter Scene on a Waterfront*, by Luigi Loir (1845–1916).[5] The broad snow scene with men loading horse-drawn carts near a river hung in the dining room of the Seventy-second Street house (see fig. 27) before it was relocated to the Laurelton art gallery, where Tiffany placed it next to a far more carefree scene of a gray kitten in a field of clover and other wildflowers, *Cat among Dandelion Clocks* (1884), by the Swedish artist Bruno Liljefors (1860–1939).[6]

The early Loir purchase was something of an anomaly, for Tiffany had decorated his Seventy-second Street house and his Bella apartment mostly with his own works, and it was not until about 1910 that he began to increase his European holdings beyond the Sorollas and the Loir. Among the other European canvases in the art gallery at Laurelton were *Tales of War* (1915), by Sergei Vinogradov (Russian, 1869–1938), depicting a colorful grouping of people around a war veteran in a landscape of "bright green fields bordered by autumn woods," and *Nymph Satyr*, by Albert Kollar.[7]

Tiffany interspersed two of his own recent oils, *Daffodils and Magnolia* (1916) and *Dahlias* (1917), with the European paintings in the gallery. Two others, both still lifes of peonies painted in 1917, hung amid a cluster of paintings by American artists whom he admired, among them his mentor Samuel Colman (1832–1920) and R. Swain Gifford (1840–1905). Gifford may have painted *Near Naples*, one of the works in Tiffany's collection, during the extended trip he and Tiffany took together in 1870.[8] They spent a month in Tangier sketching people, buildings, and landscapes and then, in October, moved on to Malta, Sicily, and finally Naples, where, according to Gifford, the rainy and cold weather made it hard to work.[9]

Tiffany owned a large number of Colman's oils and watercolors. The two were extraordinarily close, sharing not only their artistic pursuits but also family gatherings, and throughout their long friendship Tiffany continued to seek advice from the older artist. Colman's watercolor *Near Algiers* would have been a poignant reminder of the trip Tiffany and his family took with Colman and his wife in 1874.[10] The group traveled to Paris in the spring of that year and then south to Menton, on the Côte d'Azur, planning to continue on to Algiers. But in Menton, on December 9, Tiffany's first wife, May, gave birth to a baby boy. When the baby died three weeks later, the heartbreak and May's health kept the Tiffanys from accompanying the Colmans to Algiers.[11]

On the Hudson at Dobbs Ferry (fig. 170) was one of the first of Colman's oils that Tiffany acquired. Colman painted this landscape from a location near his home in Irvington, New York. (Tiffany also spent time in Irvington at his father's home, especially during the summer months, so he and Colman were able to work together there.) In contrast to the larger, more dramatic views of the river painted by an earlier generation of American artists, Colman's interpretation depicts the Hudson as a placid body of water filled with working vessels. The long, narrow format and strong horizontality of the composition, with its broad expanse of sky, evokes the panoramic landscapes of seventeenth-century Dutch artists. Indeed, Colman had visited the Dutch countryside in the 1870s. This painting is one of only a few that can be identified as having been in Tiffany's Bella apartment, where it hung in the library, without a frame, held in place by the slats that divided the straw matting on the walls into sections (see fig. 19).

Tiffany also shared the aesthetic sensibility of his contemporary William Merritt Chase (1849–1916). He purchased two canvases at the sale of Chase's work following his death in 1916. One was an Italian garden scene; the other, called *The Music Lesson*, depicted a young girl in a white dress watching a woman dressed in a black kimono seated at a piano.[12] In all likelihood Tiffany acquired them, bearing in mind the needs of his educational foundation, as representative examples for his increasingly public collection.

The largest collection of paintings and watercolors displayed in the Laurelton art gallery were those Tiffany had made himself over the course of his long career, between 1869 and 1917. Identifying specific paintings in archival photographs of the Bella apartment, the house on Seventy-second Street, or Laurelton Hall is difficult. From the catalogue prepared in 1918 by the Tiffany Foundation, however, we know that nearly one hundred works by Tiffany, two-thirds of them watercolors and the rest oil paintings, were transferred to the art gallery at Laurelton Hall.[13] Tiffany obviously kept many of his own paintings and enjoyed living with them throughout his life. Even more than his artist friends, he used his art to chronicle his family life and his many travels.[14] He was seemingly never without a sketchbook or canvas, recording, often in intricate detail, the buildings, doorways, people, landscapes, and flora and fauna that caught his eye during his journeys. Just

Fig. 170. Samuel Colman (1832–1920), *On the Hudson at Dobbs Ferry*, ca. 1880. Oil on canvas, 16⅜ x 40 in. (41.6 x 101.6 cm). The Charles Hosmer Morse Museum of American Art, Winter Park, Florida

Fig. 171. Louis Comfort Tiffany, *Old Mill at Freiburg*, 1877. Watercolor and gouache on paper, 15¼ x 20⅜ in. (38.7 x 51.8 cm). Signed at lower right: *L. C. Tiffany*. The Charles Hosmer Morse Museum of American Art, Winter Park, Florida

as they had inspired his art in other media, Tiffany's homes and their grounds provided the setting and subject matter for many of his paintings, which celebrated the natural world he loved so much.

Tiffany not only worked in diverse media; he pushed them to new levels. Influenced, perhaps, by Samuel Colman, he was particularly enamored of watercolor. Colman was one of the eleven founders of the American Watercolor Society (then the American

Society of Painters in Water Colors) in 1866 and its first president; Tiffany was among its earliest members. Both artists were dissatisfied with the monochromatic, plain papers then commercially available to watercolorists. "We used to go rummaging about everywhere," Tiffany remarked, "buying all kinds of old wrapping to experiment with."[15] He also liked Japanese handmade papers for their smooth texture and handcrafted quality. The imperfections of the rough brown paper that forms the ground in *Old Mill at Freiburg* (fig. 171) add to the tone of the picture. In this 1877 watercolor, one of the earliest on display in the art gallery at Laurelton, Tiffany narrowed his focus to a single architectural vignette, the rustic paddle wheel, the rough awning overhead, and the windows and stonework of the building.

Louise Tiffany, Reading (see fig. 60) from 1888 is Tiffany's gentle and affectionate portrait of his second wife, whom he had married in 1886. Louise lies on a chaise in the corner of his studio at the Tiffany house at Madison Avenue and Seventy-second Street, resting because at the time she was perhaps pregnant with their third child, Annie Olivia, who was born on December 29, 1888 (their twins, Comfort and Julia, were born on September 24, 1887).[16] Tiffany exhibited an extraordinary facility with the highly unforgiving medium of pastel, especially in his rendering of textures, from the glossy sheen of the green-glazed vase filled with hydrangeas on the piano to the rich, soft luster of the velvet upholstery of the chaise.

Fig. 172. Louis Comfort Tiffany, *My Family at Somesville*, 1888. Oil on canvas, 23⅞ x 36 in. (60.6 x 91.4 cm). The Charles Hosmer Morse Museum of American Art, Winter Park, Florida

Fig. 173. Louis Comfort Tiffany, *Flora (Spring)*, 1887–98. Oil on canvas, 59½ x 94 in. (151.1 x 238.8 cm). Signed at lower left: *Louis C Tiffany*. The Charles Hosmer Morse Museum of American Art, Winter Park, Florida

Painted the same year and also set in the Seventy-second Street studio is a large watercolor of a young woman feeding flamingos (see fig. 62). When Tiffany showed *Taming the Flamingo* as part of his large display at the twenty-first annual exhibition of the American Watercolor Society in 1888, one critic described the work as "a scene in a glowing low-ceiled temple, probably in Nomansland, with a picturesque young priestess in very pale greenish-yellow draperies feeding some flamingos, who make an effective group with their rich color and their curving necks."[17] The watercolor served as the design for a leaded-glass window that was eventually installed in the living hall at Laurelton (see figs. 245, 246).

In the summer of 1888 the Tiffany family spent more than two months on Mount Desert Island, Maine, where the spectacular mountains and rough seas had been inspiring American artists since midcentury.[18] Although most of the artists who painted there focused on the dramatic water views and the changing sky, none of Tiffany's known paintings depict the sea at all, and they have high horizon lines, leaving little room for sky.[19] The broad Maine mountains appear in the distance in his oil painting *My Family at Somesville* (fig. 172), which shows Louise, a nanny, and the four Tiffany children with a large brown cow in a field awash in wildflowers.[20]

Tiffany brought to Laurelton his large painting of *Flora* (fig. 173) along with *Ceres*, its companion. Flora, with a daffodil wreath around her head, is seated in a bower of wisteria and hydrangea, while nymphs present offerings of wild flowers and bunches of violets. In the foreground are rows of pink, yellow,

Fig. 174. Louis Comfort Tiffany, *Peonies and Iris*, 1915. Oil on canvas, 37¾ x 24½ in. (95.9 x 62.2 cm). Signed at lower left: *Louis C. Tiffany*. The Charles Hosmer Morse Museum of American Art, Winter Park, Florida

Fig. 175. Second-floor balcony, Fountain Court, Laurelton Hall, ca. 1920s. Photograph possibly by David Aronow. Courtesy of Phillips-Hosking Collection

and white tulips; blossoming cherry branches frame the scene from above. Even the costumes are given the soft hues of spring-time, the flowing togas in pale tones of cream shading to soft yellows and greens to pale blue to deeper, more earthy hues on the older figures emerging from the woodland. Bathed in light shading from the aura around Flora on the right to a slightly darker shade moving across the canvas, the whole scintillates with light and color in opalescent tones. The faces of the young children are treated in great detail, as if portraits, while the landscape is more impressionistic. Although demonstrating Tiffany's great appreciation for nature and light in its glowing pastel colors, the painting includes a friezelike composition and Grecian-garbed subjects at odds with the exotic flavor of its new setting. Tiffany may have begun this picture in his studio, enlisting as models his young children, nephews, and nieces in costume and carrying props (see fig. 300).[6]

In a later canvas that hung in the art gallery, *Peonies and Iris* of 1915 (fig. 174), Tiffany depicted the flowers he incorporated into so many other compositions in different media, this time in a view so close that one has the sense of actually sitting among them.

Also exhibited in the art gallery at Laurelton Hall were eighty-three glass, pottery, and enamelwork objects, described in the 1919 inventory as "unique examples of form and color, consisting of solid color, blended, applied, etched, carved and engraved specimens, many being experimental and impossible of duplication."[22] Tiffany incorporated many other examples of his work in these media into the decor of the main house. But he made a special display in the Fountain Court, where three of the eight cases that lined the second-floor gallery were devoted to what he must have considered the best of his own production—by the time of the 1919 inventory, some four hundred examples of art glass alone (fig. 175). Of the other five cases, one housed Byzantine mosaic fragments, Russian icons, and polished agates; yet another, his collection of antique glass: Greek bottles, "Antique Tyrenian" glass, mounted fragments of "Tudor Glass dredged from the river

Thames," and small examples of Venetian glass flasks and perfume bottles.[23] Still others held Japanese lacquer, Chinese carved rhinoceros-horn cups, inlaid wood objects, metalwork, and Chinese and Persian porcelain and pottery. Two cases displayed Tiffany's extensive collection of jewelry, from Egyptian pottery necklaces and Babylonian amethyst-bead necklaces to a metal-and-turquoise African neckband and Indian filigree jewelry. Such works informed designs produced in his own studios. The museum-quality cases of steel and plate glass, with glass shelves and sliding doors, were lined with antique textiles: a fragment of a seventeenth-century church vestment of white silk adorned with colored embroidery, silver spangles, and paste gems; "blue hand stenciled Japanese cotton cloth, embellished with gold"; pieces of antique Japanese silks; and, to set off Tiffany's own works, "unusual examples of antique Cashimer camel-hair shawls, Oriental brocades, embroideries and hand stenciled Japanese cloths, enbelished [*sic*] with applied gold."[24]

By 1902, when he began construction of Laurelton Hall, Tiffany had already been producing the novel artistic glass he called "Favrile" (derived from the Old English *fabrile*, or "hand-wrought") for nearly a decade, and he had garnered considerable acclaim for his products from critics at home and, even more so, abroad. His Favrile glass won one of the Grand Prix awards at the 1900 Exposition Universelle in Paris, where "every known make of artistic glass ware was there on exhibition."[25] And at the 1901 Pan-American Exposition in Buffalo his work was again singled out; he presented an almost overwhelming display of more than three thousand pieces, "no two . . . similar in design or coloring."[26]

Fig. 176. Louis Comfort Tiffany, Tiffany Glass and Decorating Company or Tiffany Furnaces, Plaque, 1900–1915. Favrile glass, 1¹¹⁄₁₆ x 15½ in. (4.4 x 39.4 cm). The Charles Hosmer Morse Museum of American Art, Winter Park, Florida

Three full cases housed his blown Favrile-glass vases. The smaller examples were densely displayed on tiered shelving, the many types of glass mixed together. The larger vases were set on the top shelves, and plates and plaques (see fig. 176) were mounted on the walls above. The vessels that Tiffany kept for his own collection, many of them marked "A-coll" (for "Artist's collection"), exhibited the full range of techniques and color effects the scientists and gaffers at his glasshouse in Corona, Queens, New York, had mastered. They included "cabinet vases" large and small of almost every genre, some masterpieces of their kind, others more experimental in nature and among the sole surviving examples of a particular technique. The collection eventually represented nearly his entire oeuvre, from his earliest years of glassmaking through the first two decades of the twentieth century. Besides the twenty-seven glass objects Tiffany put on deposit at the Metropolitan Museum in 1925, only a few of the hundreds of pieces of Favrile glass from Laurelton have been identified. The catalogue of the auction of Laurelton's contents in 1946 illustrates only twenty-seven vases. The brief descriptions in the catalogue give only the height and a general idea of the shape and decoration of the objects, and although they mention whether pieces are signed they fail to catalogue individual numbers or markings or the "A-coll" mark. Even fewer pieces can be identified in period photographs of the interiors of Laurelton Hall.

From the international expositions in Paris, London, and Turin, Tiffany was aware of the innovative glass being produced in Europe at the time. The director of his glass operation, Arthur J. Nash (1849–1934), had learned his craft at the firm of Thomas Webb in Stourbridge, England (hence the name of Tiffany's glassworks between 1893 and 1902, the Stourbridge Glass Company). Tiffany owned a small group of contemporary vases by François-Eugène Rousseau (1827–1891) and Émile Gallé (1846–1904),[27] and he had visited Gallé's atelier in Nancy, France. He also owned a collection of Roman and Syrian glass, which he kept first in the ballroom of his Seventy-second Street house and later, in an identical arrangement, in one of the cases on the Fountain Court balcony in Laurelton Hall. Some of the glass vessels Tiffany produced were directly inspired by these centuries-old Roman or Syrian prototypes. His workmen did not attempt to mimic the shape or scale of the earlier versions; rather, they adapted and re-created decorative techniques or surface effects to their own forms. One of the simplest of those forms is an ovoid vase of pale green glass (the color of unrefined glass in its natural state) with threads of brown-red glass trailed on the surface, marvered into the glass, and then drawn up or down at the top and bottom of the vase to create a simple looped pattern (fig. 177). A slight iridescence on the surface of the nearly transparent glass also recalls its ancient models.

Trailed threading was used to create abstract designs of waves and other unusual effects on many of Tiffany's glass objects (see fig. 178). Around the base of a large early vase, close threading was drawn into tall peaks, creating a highly decorative pattern, and around its neck a more capricious arrangement of threads undulates

Fig. 177. Louis Comfort Tiffany, Tiffany Glass and Decorating Company, Vase, 1895–1900. Favrile glass, 12¾ x 11⅛ in. (32.4 x 28.3 cm). Collection of Eric Streiner

in wavelike patterns (fig. 179). The yellow designs stand out from the soft black, nearly opaque background. On a smaller vase, crisp silver threads applied to a brilliant red background in the same technique produces an entirely different effect (fig. 180). Such threaded designs could be equally effective in more subtle coloring, as seen in a vase with delicate long, vertical trailings of threads pulled in such a way that their outlines accentuate the vessel's slightly waisted shape (fig. 181). Threaded decoration also achieved a more controlled design that recalls stylized feathers or leaves (fig. 182).

Almost without exception the bowls and bottles in Tiffany's collection of ancient glass had iridescent surfaces. The effects varied from an "allover pearly" to "rainbow iridescence" to "silvery incrustation."[28] Similar variations occurred on the vessels made by the glassworkers at Tiffany's furnaces. The surfaces of three small vases (figs. 183, 185, 192), for instance, vary from a true rainbow iridescence to gold and purple tones to an almost moonscape surface in brilliant blue tinged with turquoise. Three cabinet vases described in the 1946 auction catalogue as "small . . . ovoid vases variously ornamented with simulated incrustations" may have resembled these.[29] The exuberant swirls of trailed golden luster (which turns to rainbow hues in reflected light) on one mold-blown vase with smooth fluted sides (fig. 186) were loosely based on ancient prototypes.

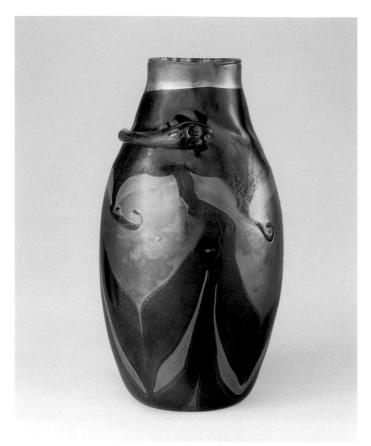

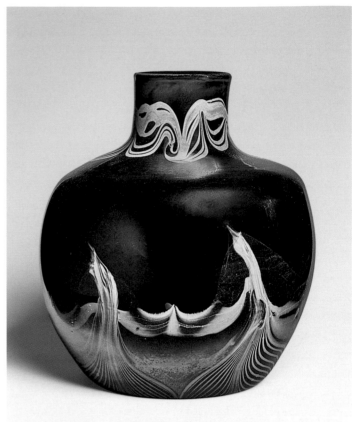

Fig. 178. Louis Comfort Tiffany, Tiffany Glass and Decorating Company, Vase, ca. 1897. Favrile glass, 13⅜ in. (34 cm). The Metropolitan Museum of Art, New York, Gift of Louis Comfort Tiffany Foundation, 1951 (51.121.25)

Fig. 179. Louis Comfort Tiffany, Tiffany Glass and Decorating Company, Vase, ca. 1897. Favrile glass, 11¼ in. (28.6 cm). The Metropolitan Museum of Art, New York, Gift of Louis Comfort Tiffany Foundation, 1951 (51.121.20)

Fig. 180. Louis Comfort Tiffany, Tiffany Furnaces, Vase, ca. 1910. Favrile glass, 5⁵⁄₁₆ in. (13.5 cm). The Metropolitan Museum of Art, New York, Gift of Louis Comfort Tiffany Foundation, 1951 (51.121.26)

Fig. 181. Louis Comfort Tiffany, Tiffany Glass and Decorating Company, Vase, 1895–1900. Favrile glass, 16½ x 8¼ in. (41.9 x 21 cm). Collection of Eric Streiner

Fig. 182. Louis Comfort Tiffany, Tiffany Furnaces, Vase, ca. 1906. Favrile glass, 4⅞ in. (12.4 cm). The Metropolitan Museum of Art, New York, Gift of Louis Comfort Tiffany Foundation, 1951 (51.121.1)

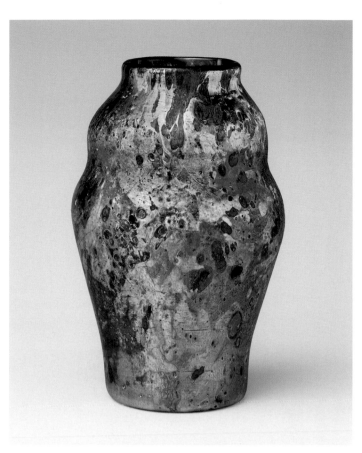

Fig. 183. Louis Comfort Tiffany, Tiffany Furnaces, Vase, ca. 1912. Favrile glass, 5³⁄₁₆ in. (13.2 cm). The Metropolitan Museum of Art, New York, Gift of Louis Comfort Tiffany Foundation, 1951 (51.121.4)

Fig. 184. Louis Comfort Tiffany, Tiffany Furnaces, Vase, ca. 1912. Favrile glass, 4¾ in. (12.1 cm). The Metropolitan Museum of Art, New York, Gift of Louis Comfort Tiffany Foundation, 1951 (51.121.7)

Fig. 185. Louis Comfort Tiffany, Tiffany Furnaces, Vase, ca. 1912. Favrile glass, 5⅞ in. (14.9 cm). The Metropolitan Museum of Art, New York, Gift of Louis Comfort Tiffany Foundation, 1951 (51.121.9)

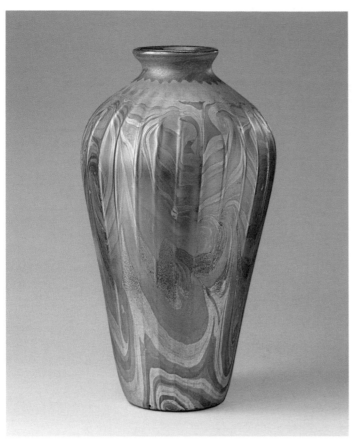

Fig. 186. Louis Comfort Tiffany, Tiffany Glass and Decorating Company, Vase, 1895–1902. Favrile glass, 17⅞ x 9½ in. (45.4 x 24.1 cm). Collection of Tony and Mary Ann Terranova

Fig. 187. Louis Comfort Tiffany, Tiffany Glass and Decorating Company, Vase, 1897–1900. Favrile glass, 5 x 2¼ in. (12.7 x 5.7 cm). The Charles Hosmer Morse Museum of American Art, Winter Park, Florida

Fig. 188. Louis Comfort Tiffany, Tiffany Glass and Decorating Company, Vase, 1895–1900. Favrile glass, 3¾ x 2³⁄₁₆ in. (9.5 x 5.6 cm). Collection of Eric Streiner

Fig. 189. Louis Comfort Tiffany, Tiffany Glass and Decorating Company, Vase, 1895–1905. Favrile glass, 6¾ x 2¼ in. (17.1 x 5.7 cm). The Charles Hosmer Morse Museum of American Art, Winter Park, Florida

Fig. 190. Louis Comfort Tiffany, Tiffany Furnaces, Vase, ca. 1905. Favrile glass, 3 13/16 in. (9.7 cm). The Metropolitan Museum of Art, New York, Gift of Louis Comfort Tiffany Foundation, 1951 (51.121.23)

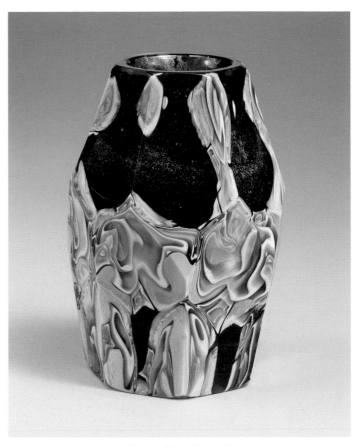

Fig. 191. Louis Comfort Tiffany, Tiffany Glass and Decorating Company or Tiffany Furnaces, Vase, 1895–1905. Favrile glass, 3 1/4 x 2 1/4 in. (8.3 x 5.7 cm). The Charles Hosmer Morse Museum of American Art, Winter Park, Florida

Historical glasses such as seventeenth-century Rhenish beakers with applied prunts and trailed and tooled threading around the foot may have inspired the form and decoration of the tumbler-shaped gold-glass vase that has a molded foot and two rows of circular ornaments in relief within a band at the base (fig. 187). Tiffany, experiementing continually with the glass scientists in his employ to achieve new effects, was particularly proud of those that involved a chemical reaction when different types and colors of glasses were manipulated or mixed together. Melding the different, often contrasting colors produced rich effects (figs. 188, 189).

Few examples of what the 1946 auction catalogue listed as Tiffany's "agateware" have survived. Tiffany owned several actual agate objects that may have inspired him, including four small polished agates and three small agate bowls.[32] Venetian glassmakers were the first, in the sixteenth century, to attempt to simulate agate, and their efforts were replicated by Bohemian glassmakers in the mid-nineteenth century. Tiffany was one of the few who successfully revived the technique in the late 1800s. Agate glass displayed most unusual color combinations. The finished vases, most of them quite small, were often faceted so as to further imitate the look of stone (figs. 190, 191).

A large open bowl that was among the objects Tiffany lent to the Metropolitan in 1925 (fig. 193) represents a variant of Favrile glass Tiffany called "Lava" or "volcanic" glass. Perhaps the most unusual example of the type, the bowl has an organic, irregular

Fig. 192. Louis Comfort Tiffany, Tiffany Furnaces, Vase, ca. 1915. Favrile glass, 3 7/8 in. (9.8 cm). The Metropolitan Museum of Art, New York, Gift of Louis Comfort Tiffany Foundation, 1951 (51.121.3)

Fig. 193. Louis Comfort Tiffany, Tiffany Furnaces, Bowl, ca. 1908. Favrile glass, 6⅜ in. (16 cm). The Metropolitan Museum of Art, New York, Gift of Louis Comfort Tiffany Foundation, 1951 (51.121.13)

Fig. 194. Louis Comfort Tiffany, Tiffany Glass and Decorating Company. Vase, ca. 1900. Favrile glass, 10¾ in. (27.3 cm). The Metropolitan Museum of Art, New York, Gift of Louis Comfort Tiffany Foundation, 1951 (51.121.2)

Fig. 195. Louis Comfort Tiffany, Tiffany Furnaces, Vase, ca. 1903. Favrile glass, 11 3/16 in. (28.4 cm). The Metropolitan Museum of Art, New York, Gift of Louis Comfort Tiffany Foundation, 1951 (51.121.8)

Fig. 196. Louis Comfort Tiffany, Tiffany Glass and Decorating Company or Tiffany Furnaces, Vase, 1900–1915. Favrile glass, 23 x 9⅜ in. (58.4 x 23.8 cm). Collection of Eric Streiner

Fig. 197. Louis Comfort Tiffany, Tiffany Glass and Decorating Company, Vase, ca. 1900. Favrile glass, 18½ x 9½ in. (47 x 24.1 cm). The Huntington Library, Art Collections, and Botanical Gardens, Gift of the Art Collectors Council

shape that looks as if it was dictated by the molten glass, and the broad areas of gold luster were meant to mimic hot molten rock spilling from the mouth of a volcano. The characteristic rough, black areas were made by introducing bits of basalt or talc into the molten glass. One small Lava vase is nearly encased in thick gold luster; only tiny areas of rough black show through the surface (fig. 192).

The shimmering, iridescent plumage of peacocks inspired another genre of Favrile glass. Tiffany adored peacocks and kept them at Laurelton; he often had the birds brought down from the barn complex to strut around the grounds. The most elaborate party he gave at Laurelton was his Peacock Feast of May 1914 (see the essay "The Art of Magnificent Living" in this volume). The 1946 auction catalogue describes ten vases, the smallest 3 inches tall and the largest 23½, as having "peacock-feather decoration" on an iridescent ground.[30] A vase with a peacock-feather design is known to have been part of the decoration of the living hall at Laurelton.[31] Presumably these vases resembled one Tiffany lent to the Metropolitan during his lifetime (fig. 194), a brilliantly colored example with simplified "eyes" glowing from the shaded turquoise iridescence of stylized peacock feathers. Some of Tiffany's most ambitious lamps also featured the peacock motif. The extraordinary table lamp, which went to Laurelton in 1931 in Charles W. Gould's bequest to the Tiffany Foundation, has an enameled cylindrical base with three peacocks whose heads support a golden iridescent blown Favrile-glass globe.[32]

Fig. 198. Three Favrile-glass vases, shown in the auction catalogue for the 1946 sale of the contents of Laurelton Hall. Fig. 196 is at the right, fig. 197 in the center. From Parke-Bernet 1946, p. 44

Tiffany translated his love for plants and flowers into many kinds of glass vessels. Among his favorite pieces, and one of the few he chose to illustrate in color in de Kay's book on his work,[33] is a tall, dark vase with wavy, sensuous decoration that he himself said suggested irises (fig. 195).[34] Like many Favrile-glass objects, the vase changes as light strikes it. In reflected light it appears to be a soft charcoal color with a mat, slightly iridescent surface

Fig. 199. Louis Comfort Tiffany, Tiffany Glass and Decorating Company, Three vases, 1900–1902. Favrile glass. Left: 16 x 6¼ in. (40.6 x 15.9 cm), Collection of Eric Streiner; center: 18¹¹⁄₁₆ in. (47.5 cm) and right: 15⅝ in. (39.7 cm), The Metropolitan Museum of Art, New York, Gift of Louis Comfort Tiffany Foundation, 1951 (51.121.17, .27)

Fig. 200. Louis Comfort Tiffany, Tiffany Furnaces, Vase, ca. 1903. Favrile glass, 18¼ x 5¼ in. (46.4 x 13.3 cm). Collection of Eric Streiner

Fig. 201. Detail of vase at left in fig. 199

and strong, metallic peacock blue decoration; in transmitted light the body metamorphoses into a very dark green, and the decoration into mottled earth tones. One of the largest from Tiffany's collection, 23 inches tall, is a vase with a brilliant allover iridescence on a blue ground and dark, lustrous leaves and stems trailing from its mouth (figs. 196, 198). Although the auction catalogue describes the vase as "decorated with trailing lily pads,"[35] the spearhead-shaped leaves look more like pear leaves, the motif Tiffany used in a similar fashion on iridescent tiles that ornamented the surround of a living pear tree in the middle of the Daffodil Terrace at Laurelton (see fig. 79). Appearing in the same auction-catalogue photograph as this vase (fig. 198) is one with delicate silvery vertical leaves on a rich green background (fig. 197). Before taking this vase to Laurelton, Tiffany had (by 1900) prominently displayed it on the mantel of his library in the Seventy-second Street house.[36]

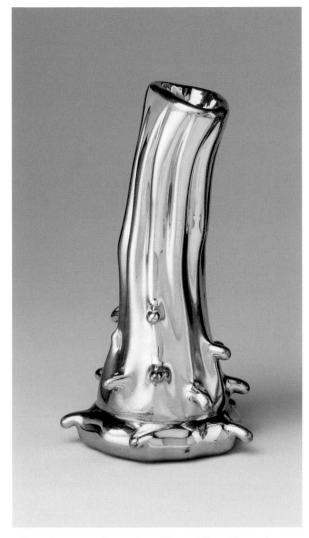

Above: Fig. 202. Louis Comfort Tiffany, Tiffany Glass and Decorating Company or Tiffany Furnaces, Vase, 1895–1910. Favrile glass, 5⅛ x 2½ in. (13 x 6.4 cm). Collection of Eric Streiner

Right: Fig. 203. Louis Comfort Tiffany, Tiffany Glass and Decorating Company or Tiffany Furnaces, Vase, 1895–1910. Favrile glass, 7½ x 3½ in. (19.1 x 8.9 cm). Collection of Eric Streiner

The forms of a group of delicate, goblet-shaped Tiffany vases (fig. 199) were meant to evoke actual blossoms on willowy stems. These vases varied not only in size but in shape and coloration, from more rounded and smooth bowls with iridescent leafy decoration to dynamic, irregularly ruffled bowls with delicate shading in pale green at the stem and gold or cream at the rim (fig. 201). Their bases were invariably adorned with abstract green leaf forms and threaded decoration. On an exceptional green-and-aqua example (fig. 200), broad leaves, their veins suggested by long, broken lines, extend from the bulb-shaped base to the rim, accentuating the piece's verticality.

That no other versions are known to survive suggests that two vases whose forms replicate tree trunks (figs. 202, 203) may have been experimental. The unusual shape and coloration of the largest of the two help to confirm this. The glassworker tooled the exterior of the thick cylinder to simulate the rough bark of a tree

and even wrapped a translucent gold iridescent glass vine around the trunk. The smaller vase, with a smooth silver surface, has a slightly swelled base covered with tiny prunts where "twigs" have been trimmed away. This could be the small glass vase "in the form of a tree trunk" described in the 1946 auction catalogue.[37]

One of the last techniques that Tiffany's glassworks perfected was an adaptation of a process developed in the mid-nineteenth century to make paperweights, whereby leaf- or blossom-shaped pieces of glass, often in combination with slices of millefiori canes, were encased in many layers of transparent glass. Only one "paperweight" vase is illustrated in the 1946 auction catalogue.[38] The catalogue describes it as "pear-shaped, decorated with pink and green floral stems," neglecting to mention the technique, but as the vase itself has survived (fig. 204) we know that the bright pinkish orange poppies and tall leaves are enclosed in a watery blue-tinted matrix of thick glass.

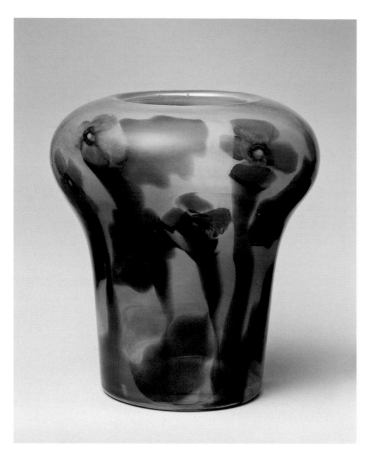

Fig. 204. Louis Comfort Tiffany, Tiffany Furnaces, Vase, 1905–15. Favrile glass, 7⅞ x 7⅞ in. (20 x 18.1 cm). Private collection

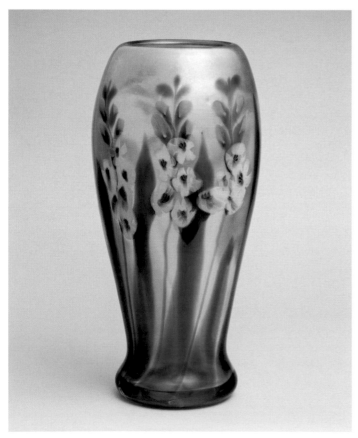

Fig. 205. Louis Comfort Tiffany, Tiffany Furnaces, Vase, ca. 1909. Favrile glass, 16⁷⁄₁₆ in. (41.8 cm). The Metropolitan Museum of Art, New York, Gift of Louis Comfort Tiffany Foundation, 1951 (51.121.22)

A similar juxtaposition of leaves and flowers occurs in a vase whose tall shape echoes the tall blossoms of white gladioli imprisoned within it (fig. 205). Tiffany thought very highly of this vase and displayed it on the top shelf in one of the middle bays of his balcony cases (see fig. 175). The regularly repeated forms were added to the glass while still molten, producing varying effects. The vase is so heavy that it must have taken more than one gaffer to manipulate it. Vases of this size have been lost in the making when they slumped on the end of the pontil while being finished. Like many of the so-called paperweight vases, this one is made of colorless glass, which Tiffany's workmen gave a golden luster by adding chemical iridescence not to the exterior surface, as was typical, but to the interior. Artistic license was also taken for decorative effect in another vase of roughly the same composition (fig. 206), where the thin leaves of the daffodil have been replaced with simple, tall, broad leaves suggestive of the plantain. Conveying in glass the deep, penetrating purple-black centers of the flowers and the subtle shading of the yellow petals with their slightly curled edges (see fig. 167) was not an easy feat.

The more complex network of stems, leaves, and flowers on other paperweight vases would also have been a challenge for the glassworker. One of the more abstract variations of these designs features bold, trilobed leaves and a web of stems punctuated with pale pink berries (fig. 207). As if submerged in moving water, the leaves developed a character of their own as they reacted with the many layers of molten glass. That effect may have prompted Tiffany to develop an entire series of vases of clear, colorless glass with blue morning-glory blossoms and leafy vines disposed over the bulbous upper portion of their inverted pear shapes. The results were achieved "by numerous glasses of various chemical constituents reacting one upon another."[39] A vase in the Musée d'Orsay, Paris, may be the earliest in the series; it was exhibited in 1900 at the Paris Exposition Universelle.[40] Tiffany kept at least one example for himself and later gave it to the Metropolitan Museum (fig. 208). That vase bears the "A-coll" designation; others in the series bear marks indicating that they were shown as late as 1914, at the Paris Salon, and 1915, at the Panama-Pacific Exposition in San Francisco.[41] One of the most unusual paperweight vases from Tiffany's collection is small and globular with a nearly abstract network of leaves and vines in shades that vary from deep orange red to pure crimson and change slightly in different light (fig. 209).

A group of objects that Tiffany called "Aquamarine" were created in a manner that is still not fully understood. Two large paperweights (a bit more than 5 inches in diameter) in his collection at Laurelton were described in the Parke-Bernet auction catalogue as glass spheres, "irregularly shaped, with *millefiori* marine decorations,"[42] the marine decoration being tiny goldfish magnified by the many layers of clear glass, just as if they were swimming in water. The fish motif was also used in Aquamarine vases.[43] Each of the Aquamarine vases in the collection at Laurelton, however, enclosed minute blossoms and stems composed of green

Fig. 207. Louis Comfort Tiffany, Tiffany Furnaces, Vase, ca. 1903. Favrile glass, 8⁷⁄₁₆ in. (21.4 cm). The Metropolitan Museum of Art, New York, Gift of Louis Comfort Tiffany Foundation, 1951 (51.121.28)

Fig. 206. Louis Comfort Tiffany, Tiffany Furnaces, Vase, ca. 1904. Favrile glass, 10⅜ in. (26.4 cm). The Metropolitan Museum of Art, New York, Gift of Louis Comfort Tiffany Foundation, 1951 (51.121.14)

Fig. 208. Louis Comfort Tiffany, Tiffany Furnaces, Vase, ca. 1913. Favrile glass, 6⅝ in. (16.8 cm). The Metropolitan Museum of Art, New York, Gift of Louis Comfort Tiffany Foundation, 1951 (51.121.15)

Fig. 209. Louis Comfort Tiffany, Tiffany Furnaces, Vase, ca. 1903. Favrile glass, 4½ in. (11.4 cm). The Metropolitan Museum of Art, New York, Gift of Louis Comfort Tiffany Foundation, 1951 (51.121.18)

Fig. 211. Detail of fig. 210

Fig. 210. Louis Comfort Tiffany, Tiffany Furnaces, Aquamarine water lily vase, ca. 1913. Glass, 15½ in. (39.4 cm). The Metropolitan Museum of Art, New York, Purchase, Friends of the American Wing Fund, 2006 (2006.246)

glass within the many layers of glass that formed the solid core of the vessel's extended base. One such "vase" is virtually solid glass, leaving only a shallow bowl at the top in which three small white blossoms surrounded by emerald green water lily leaves are floating as if in a pond, their long, thin green stems extending the entire length of the vase (figs. 210, 211). The design may have been inspired by Tiffany's own pools of water lilies on the grounds of Laurelton Hall.

Leslie H. Nash (1884–1958), Arthur Nash's son, whom Tiffany hired in 1908 and who eventually became production manager at Tiffany Furnaces, most likely played an important role in the development of the Aquamarine technique. In one of his notebooks Nash sketched the tall "water lilly" vase from Laurelton Hall (fig. 212).

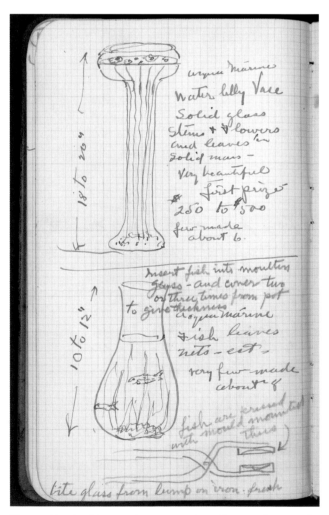

Fig. 212. Sketch of Aquamarine vases, 1908–15. From Leslie H. Nash, personal notebook. Collection of the Juliette K. and Leonard S. Rakow Research Library of The Corning Museum of Glass, Corning, New York, Nash Archives

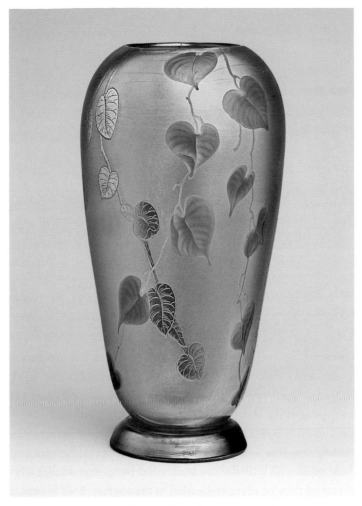

Fig. 213. Louis Comfort Tiffany, Tiffany Glass and Decorating Company, Vase, 1900–1915. Favrile glass, 12 in. (30.5 cm). Collection of Eric Streiner

Fig. 214. Louis Comfort Tiffany, Tiffany Glass and Decorating Company, Vase, 1895–1902. Favrile glass, 9⅞ x 5⅛ in. (25.1 x 13 cm). Collection of Tony and Mary Ann Terranova

Fig. 215. Detail of fig. 213

His notations indicate that the "very beautiful" vase won first prize at an exhibition, that only about six of them were made, and that they sold for between $250 and $500. At the bottom of the same page is a sketch of an Aquamarine vase enclosing fish, along with notes on how it was made. On another page in the same notebook, Nash wrote that such vases weighed fifteen to twenty-five pounds, making them extremely unwieldy.[44] In order to handle them the gaffers would have had to employ the thicker blowpipe rather than the standard pontil.

While most of Tiffany's Favrile-glass vases utilize strictly furnace techniques, a number incorporate cold decorative techniques such as acid etching and cutting more often than is generally recognized. A tall, ovoid footed vase (fig. 213) that was illustrated in the 1946 auction catalogue and described there as in "golden yellow iridescent glass, with ivy decoration" was more complex to execute than may be readily apparent.[45] The leaf and vine decoration on the simple, smooth form was achieved with intarsia, or applying small green glass forms while the bubble remained on the gaffer's blowpipe. A highly skilled craftsman carved the veins into the leaves after the vase had annealed and cooled, and the vines that crisscross behind the leaves were formed by lightly etching the surface iridescence with acid to reveal the golden layer below (fig. 215). Tiffany kept very few cut, carved, or engraved

Fig. 226. Louis Comfort Tiffany, Tiffany Glass and Decorating Company, Vase, ca. 1900. Porcelaneous earthenware, 4⅝ in. (11.7 cm). The Metropolitan Museum of Art, New York, Gift of Louis Comfort Tiffany Foundation, 1951 (51.121.21)

Fig. 227. Louis Comfort Tiffany, Tiffany Furnaces, Vase, 1904–14. Glazed earthenware, 10¾ x 9¾ in. (27.3 x 24.8 cm). The Charles Hosmer Morse Museum of American Art, Winter Park, Florida

Fig. 228. Louis Comfort Tiffany, Tiffany Furnaces, Vase, 1904–14. Glazed earthenware, 9⅝ x 11⅛ in. (24.4 x 29.5 cm). Collection of Eric Streiner

Fig. 229. Louis Comfort Tiffany, Tiffany Furnaces, Vase, 1904–14. Glazed earthenware, 14¾ x 7¼ in. (37.5 x 18.4 cm). The Charles Hosmer Morse Museum of American Art, Winter Park, Florida

appear on a number of the large, simple pottery forms that Tiffany displayed at Laurelton Hall, including a vase with relief decoration (fig. 228), a tall, melon-shaped vase in the Fountain Court balcony cases (see fig. 138), and the solid three-handled vase in the living hall (see fig. 144). A large, smooth vase with three small handles (fig. 227) has a more unusual mottled glaze in blues, blacks, and cream. The smooth, soft, deep brown glaze on a simple, nearly cylindrical vase (fig. 229) was pulled away in long, vertical fissures to reveal the creamy body below. Monochromatic allover glazes adorn other simple forms, including a vase in an unusual deep peacock blue (fig. 230). Three vases in variations on the bottle shape (figs. 231–233) display the soft, nearly matte green glaze Tiffany often used on his more naturalistic pottery.

That glazes preoccupied Tiffany can be seen in a rare vase that he must have retained in his possession (fig. 234). The nine long strokes of different colored glazes bear numbers that presumably coincided with notations in a glaze book. Although the vase gives a rare window into the manufacturing process and Tiffany's constant search for different effects, its naturalistic form is characteristic of Tiffany's pottery. Such forms were slip cast to give fine

Fig. 230. Louis Comfort Tiffany, Tiffany Furnaces, Vase, 1904–14. Glazed earthenware, 5 11/16 x 2 7/8 in. (14.4 x 7.3 cm). The Charles Hosmer Morse Museum of American Art, Winter Park, Florida

Fig. 231. Louis Comfort Tiffany, Tiffany Furnaces, Vase, 1904–14. Glazed earthenware, 10 15/16 x 5 in. (27.8 x 12.7 cm). Collection of Eric Streiner

Fig. 232. Louis Comfort Tiffany, Tiffany Furnaces, Vase, 1904–14. Glazed earthenware, 3¾ x 7¾ in. (9.5 x 19.7 cm). The Charles Hosmer Morse Museum of American Art, Winter Park, Florida

Fig. 233. Louis Comfort Tiffany, Tiffany Furnaces, Vase, 1904–14. Glazed earthenware, 4⅝ x 5¾ in. (11.7 x 14.6 cm). The Charles Hosmer Morse Museum of American Art, Winter Park, Florida

A Museum of His Own: Tiffany's Leaded-Glass Windows

Alice Cooney Frelinghuysen

Not long after his sixty-fifth birthday, in February 1913, Tiffany began to give thought to his artistic legacy. He may even then have been contemplating setting up a foundation, but it seems likely that his initial goal was to preserve for future generations not only the home he had created but also the very best of the art his studios had produced. A year or so earlier, he had commissioned his friend Charles de Kay to memorialize his career in the monograph *The Art Work of Louis C. Tiffany* (see fig. 169).[1] And his guests' glowing appraisal of his estate after the spectacular party he held at Laurelton Hall in May 1914—the Peacock Feast—may also have encouraged such inclinations. (For the Peacock Feast, see the essay "The Art of Magnificent Living" in this volume.)

In late 1914, shortly before the 1915 Panama-Pacific International Exposition was to open in San Francisco, Tiffany decided not to send the enormous ten-by-sixteen-foot leaded-glass window *The Bathers* that was to have been featured in the Tiffany Studios display. Because there was no window opening in the exhibition hall large enough to provide natural light, *The Bathers* would have had to be lit, unevenly, with electric light burners, which Tiffany thought would compromise the work.[2] Instead, he put the window on public view at his Madison Avenue showroom, where it attracted the attention of the art critics.[3] Then, in January 1915, he installed it at Laurelton Hall in the site for which it was made: the end wall of the raised piano alcove in his living hall (fig. 242). This positioning of *The Bathers* may have given him the idea to transform

Opposite: Fig. 241. Detail of fig. 260

Right: Fig. 242. Living hall, Laurelton Hall. Photograph by David Aronow, ca. 1920s. Private collection

Fig. 247. Design attributed to Frank Brangwyn (1867–1956), Tiffany Glass and Decorating Company, *Child with Gourd*, ca. 1898. Leaded Favrile glass, 53 x 45⅞ in. (134.6 x 116.5 cm). The Charles Hosmer Morse Museum of American Art, Winter Park, Florida

Fig. 248. Louis Comfort Tiffany, Tiffany Glass Company, *Flower, Fish, and Fruit* window, 1885. Leaded Favrile glass, 30½ x 41⅞ in. (77.5 x 106.4 cm). The Baltimore Museum of Art. This window was made for Mary Elizabeth Garrett. A similar one was installed at Laurelton Hall (see fig. 242).

Favrile-glass vases and his even more recent work in enamel were on view, but it was his windows that impressed the British public. Bing's selection of Brangwyn-designed Tiffany windows may have been part of his marketing strategy to sway the British public, for contemporary British window designers such as Morris and Company (the firm of the artist William Morris) and Heaton, Butler and Bayne were at the time still working in the Pre-Raphaelite style, on flat, colored glass with painted details. One critic highlighted Tiffany's technical ingenuity, especially the effects he achieved by "superimposition of different glass-plates [and] folds in drapery [that] are actually molded in the glass," though he found the display of the windows crowded and concluded, as did other commentators, that they seemed "somewhat heavy and meretricious in effect, for all their cleverness."[13]

The original cartoon for *Flower, Fish, and Fruit*, another window that Tiffany installed in the living hall at Laurelton Hall (just above *Feeding the Flamingoes*), was also exhibited at the Grafton in 1899.[14] The window at Laurelton, presumably destroyed in the fire, was a replica of one that formed the central section of a three-part transom in the dining room of the philanthropist Mary Elizabeth Garrett's house in Baltimore (fig. 248). The Garrett house also

Fig. 249. Detail of fig. 248

Fig. 250. Louis Comfort Tiffany, Tiffany Glass and Decorating Company, Upper border, with eagle, from *Four Seasons*, 1899–1900. Leaded glass, 17 x 80 in. (43.2 x 203.2 cm). The Charles Hosmer Morse Museum of American Art, Winter Park, Florida

Fig. 251. Louis Comfort Tiffany, Tiffany Glass and Decorating Company, One of four side border panels from *Four Seasons*, 1899–1900. Leaded Favrile glass, 56⅞ x 13⅜ in. (144.5 x 34 cm). The Charles Hosmer Morse Museum of American Art, Winter Park, Florida

Fig. 252. "The Seasons, Window Design [b]y Louis C. Tiffany." From Kirk D. Henry, "American Art Industries, III—Stained-Glass Work," *Brush and Pencil* 7 (December 1900), opp. p. 150

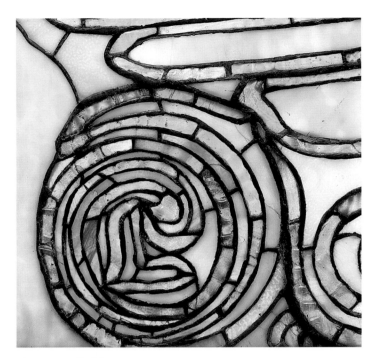

Fig. 253. Detail of fig. 250

making the left side of the window darker than the right. The motif offered him a perfect opportunity to plate one piece of glass over another for visual effect: the circle of glass closest to the viewer represents the fishbowl, and the separate pieces layered behind it convey the swirling water and the goldfish, whose expressions provide a touch of whimsy. The remarkable trompe l'oeil effect of the reflection of the mullioned windows onto the goldfish bowl on the left (fig. 249) was perhaps unique in window making of the era.

In the years following the 1893 Columbian Exposition, Tiffany had begun to look at nature in its more untamed state. For the Paris Exposition Universelle in 1900, he designed his most ambitious nature window to date.[17] *Four Seasons* was conceived as a single large window with a central jeweled ornament surrounded by four individual panels, each representing one of the seasons, joined by a highly decorative leaded-glass frame (fig. 252 shows the window as it was exhibited in Paris, before Tiffany altered it). At the sides of the frame stylized grape vines meandered through undulating scrolls of varying shades of gold and opalescent glass punctuated by rough-cut glass jewels in complementary colors (fig. 251). The calligraphic nature of the pattern was based on medieval border designs of illuminated manuscripts.[18] "Abundance and Peace and Prosperity" was inscribed at the top, beneath a spread-winged eagle (fig. 250), an expression of American national pride especially appropriate for an international exposition. Tiffany incorporated his monogram within a circle below the eagle's left wing (fig. 253) and the word *Favrile*, the trademark he gave to the glass produced at his Corona Furnaces, below its right. The date, 1900 given in roman numerals, appeared at the bottom of the composition, above a border of five classical-style vases ornamented with bands of various patterns and with golden scrolls and grapevines emanating from their mouths (fig. 254). The elaborate window was the most prominent object in the expansive Tiffany display at the Paris fair, where an international team of judges awarded Tiffany a gold medal and the French

featured decorations by Lockwood de Forest; she may have encountered de Forest's and Tiffany's work through her friendship with de Forest's sister Julia.[15] With its abundance of fruits and blossoms held in check by a flowing blue banderole, *Flower, Fish, and Fruit* recalls the garland-motif transom windows that Tiffany's rival John La Farge (1835–1910) executed for Cornelius Vanderbilt's Fifth Avenue mansion in 1880–83.[16] So dense and complex is the composition, with its myriad small, mosaiclike glass pieces, that it is difficult to read clearly. Identifying the six small blue birds hidden within the composition, for example, is a challenge.

The fishbowl motif that Tiffany introduced in *Feeding the Flamingoes* is repeated in the Garrett window. Almost like the pans of a scale, the two fishbowls anchor the ends of the banderole, balancing the composition. They are alike only in shape and size, for Tiffany played with the differing qualities of light by

Fig. 254. Louis Comfort Tiffany, Tiffany Glass and Decorating Company, Lower border, with urns, from *Four Seasons*, 1899–1900. Leaded glass, 28 15/16 x 83 3/8 in. (73.5 x 211.8 cm). The Charles Hosmer Morse Museum of American Art, Winter Park, Florida

Fig. 255. Louis Comfort Tiffany, Tiffany Glass and Decorating Company, *Spring* from *Four Seasons*, 1899–1900. Leaded Favrile glass, 40¼ x 39⅛ in. (102.2 x 100 cm). The Charles Hosmer Morse Museum of American Art, Winter Park, Florida

Fig. 256. Louis Comfort Tiffany, Tiffany Glass and Decorating Company, *Summer* from *Four Seasons*, 1899–1900. Leaded Favrile glass, 40½ x 36⅛ in. (102.9 x 93 cm). The Charles Hosmer Morse Museum of American Art, Winter Park, Florida

Fig. 257. Louis Comfort Tiffany, Tiffany Glass and Decorating Company, *Winter* from *Four Seasons*, 1899–1900. Leaded Favrile glass, 39¾ x 32⅞ in. (101 x 83.5 cm). The Charles Hosmer Morse Museum of American Art, Winter Park, Florida

Fig. 258. Louis Comfort Tiffany, Tiffany Glass and Decorating Company, *Autumn* from *Four Seasons*, 1899–1900. Leaded Favrile glass, 39⅛ x 36¼ in. (100.6 x 92.1 cm). The Charles Hosmer Morse Museum of American Art, Winter Park, Florida

Tiffany's Collection of Asian Art at Laurelton Hall

Julia Meech

L ouis Comfort Tiffany had a Chinese room, a Japanese room, and a houseful of Asian art at Laurelton Hall. It is well known that Tiffany's creations in glass, enamel, and even wood were often inspired by Asian art. However, the story of his personal collection and of the depth of his passion for Chinese and Japanese art has never been told.

The scanty documentation for the vast collection of Asian art that once graced Laurelton Hall consists of a handful of period photos approved for release by Tiffany himself; a 1919 insurance inventory running to ninety-nine pages; two cursory Louis Comfort Tiffany Foundation catalogues, each with only a few illustrations, commissioned in 1920 and 1921, the first listing Tiffany's Oriental and Chinese rugs, the second his Asian works of art; and the September 1946 Parke-Bernet auction catalogue of the contents of the house, with 1,147 lots but, again, with only the occasional black-and-white illustration.[1] There is not a single interior view of the Japanese room. Today, the only Asian objects whose whereabouts are still known are one Chinese wood box that found its way into the Tiffany and Company Archives (see fig. 290); a pair of large Chinese ceramic lions (see figs. 265, 279), a Chinese carpet and related fragments (see figs. 267, 268), and a pair of eighteenth-century red-lacquer Chinese side chairs inlaid with mother-of-pearl, all in private collections; and a group of objects purchased at the 1946 New York auction by Florence K. Sloane (1873–1953) for her Hermitage Foundation house museum in Norfolk, Virginia. She and her husband, William (1868–1940), founded the museum in 1937. This last group includes a few nineteenth-century Chinese jade and soapstone objects, two kingfisher-feather headdresses (see figs. 286, 287) as well as tiaras (see fig. 288) for Manchu court ladies, one nineteenth-century Japanese sword scabbard inlaid with rainbow-hued mother-of-pearl, and two framed Japanese prints.[2] Spurred on by the present exhibition, discoveries are under way. It can now be said, for example, that the design on a 1914 dinner menu was copied by Tiffany from a beloved Japanese lacquer panel (see below) and that an ornate glass-and-metal hanging panel in inverted-V shape

(see fig. 51), its significance heretofore a mystery, was modeled by Tiffany on an intricately carved Qing dynasty (1644–1912) spinach green jade musical chime acquired no later than 1882 and preserved at Laurelton Hall until 1946 (see fig. 53).[3]

Tiffany admired crafts, objects designed to be useful, especially small things he could hold in his hand, and he bought them in quantity. He transformed the vestibules and rooms on the upper floors of Laurelton Hall into his personal *Wunderkammer*. Conventional museum-style mahogany table cases lined with amber velvet or stenciled blue-and-white Japanese fabric served to show off his extensive holdings in late decorative arts. Japanese crafts were represented by at least 46 sets of leather tobacco pouches and pipe cases with metal and ivory fittings, 23 lacquer inro, 50 netsuke, 161 *ojime* beads, 37 ceramic tea caddies (fig. 266), 38 tea bowls, a dozen lacquer boxes, and some cloisonné vases. His Chinese acquisitions included many paintings and carved screens but also 14 rhinoceros-horn cups, 15 jade cups and ornaments, 16 red, blue, and green porcelain vases and bowls, 15 green and blue pottery jars and bowls, 13 hairpins with blue kingfisher

Fig. 266. Japanese pottery tea caddies in Tiffany's collection, illustrated in the sale catalogue of the 1946 auction of the contents of Laurelton Hall. From Parke-Bernet 1946, p. 126

Opposite: Fig. 265. Detail of fig. 279

Fig. 273. View of Japanese armor in den, Laurelton Hall, ca. 1920s. Gelatin silver print, 8⅛ x 10 in. (20.5 x 25.4 cm). Photograph by David Aronow. The Metropolitan Museum of Art, New York, Gift of Robert Koch, 1978 (1978.646.19)

Fig. 274. Four *tsuba* (sword guards). Japan, 19th century. Iron plate with gilt and soft-metal inlays, upper left: 2¾ x 2½ x ⁵⁄₁₆ in. (7 x 6.4 x 0.8 cm); upper right: 2⅝ x 2½ x ³⁄₁₆ in. (6.7 x 6.4 x 0.5 cm); lower left: 2¾ x 2½ x ⁵⁄₁₆ in. (7 x 6.4 x 0.8 cm); lower right: 3 x 2¾ x ³⁄₁₆ in. (7.6 x 7 x 0.5 cm). The Charles Hosmer Morse Museum of American Art, Winter Park, Florida. It is impossible to know whether Tiffany owned these four sword guards, but their carved and inlaid designs would have appealed to him.

Fig. 275. View of casks and fireplace, breakfast room, Tiffany house. From "The Arrangement of a Collection: A Note on the House of Louis C. Tiffany, Esq," *Arts and Decoration* 2 (June 1912), p. 295

wielding demonic figures, many of them composites of weird and terrifying beasts. Mara's three daughters, representing lust and sensual pleasures, disguise themselves as seductive beauties (the naked ladies at the left). But the supernatural powers of Prince Siddhartha protect him; even the poisonous breath of dragons becomes a fragrant breeze. The dragon in the painting echoes Tiffany's fanciful bronze-and-glass dragon fountain on the north porch of Laurelton Hall (see fig. 117).

As early as 1908 a visitor to Laurelton called attention to the dark Japanese armor hanging on the wall of the den.[17] An undated photo, probably from the 1920s, shows six suits of samurai armor complete with helmets and face masks hanging in a row on the wall abutting the conservatory (fig. 273).[18] Japanese armor, which featured colorful silk lacings and boldly sculptured helmets, was popular among American collectors at the turn of the century—a romantic evocation of the long-vanished Old Japan. Samurai were abolished as a class after the Meiji Restoration of 1868, and the wearing of swords was proscribed in 1876. Discarded by Japanese intent on Westernization and modernization, old armor was readily available at auction in New York. The same undated photo of the den shows a lampshade made of sword guards, or *tsuba*, suspended at the center of the room. At the upper right of the photo we see the bottom edge of one of three rectangular leaded-glass mosaic floral panels set within a frame of sword guards, another bizarre homage to Japan. We know from the 1946 Parke-Bernet catalogue that these hanging panels were fitted for electricity and suspended from five-foot-long chains also made of sword guards.[19]

Tiffany was probably collecting *tsuba* by the 1880s, long before he conceived Laurelton Hall (fig. 277). His partner Lockwood de Forest purchased a collection of 2,500 in Paris in 1882.[20] Discarded swords and mounts flooded the market and were eagerly snapped up by the Victorians. Sword guards were included in most of the Asian auctions in Manhattan in the 1890s; even Bing was selling them in New York in 1894. It is said that five million sword guards had been sent to Europe by the turn of the century (fig. 274).[21] Westerners often insisted on signed pieces, however, and craftsmen were kept busy at the wharf in Yokohama adding signatures to netsuke and sword guards. In 1911 William Sturgis Bigelow (1850–1926) gave 1,400 sword fittings (including 706 iron *tsuba*) that he had acquired while living in Japan in the 1880s to the Museum of Fine Arts, Boston, where he was a trustee. Dr. Hugo Halberstadt (1867–1945), who collected between 1895 and 1938, gave his collection of 1,500 sword fittings to the Danish Museum of Decorative Art, Copenhagen, in 1940.[22] Alexander Georg Moslé (1862–1949), a German businessman who lived in Japan in the late nineteenth century and sold armaments to the Japanese, accumulated some 1,600 sword fittings by 1909 with help from Japanese specialists. At the 1948 sale of his collection at Parke-Bernet Galleries, New York, a good price for one *tsuba* was $250. The *tsuba* in the 1946 Tiffany sale, by contrast, averaged about $2.50 each. Tiffany, of course, did not have examples of the highest quality, but as Sebastian Izzard observed, while "prices seem to have been ridiculously cheap, these were the immediate post-World War II years, and the market for Japanese art was severely

Fig. 276. Louis Comfort Tiffany, Tiffany Glass and Decorating Company, *Tsuba* window, 1892–1900. Leaded Favrile glass, 31½ x 43½ in. (80 x 110.5 cm). The Charles Hosmer Morse Museum of American Art, Winter Park, Florida

depressed."[23] Most of the Tiffany *tsuba* were iron with punched or uneven hammered surfaces and piercing (he responded to the openwork patterns), not the elaborately detailed and polished soft-metal examples of the later nineteenth century favored by most of his contemporaries. It is said that *tsuba* made of iron, because inexpensive, were sold in bulk on strings. One of Tiffany's publicists claimed he had purchased them by the barrel.[24]

From 1885 Tiffany and his family lived in a large house on the corner of Seventy-second Street and Madison Avenue. An 1897 photo of the fireplace in their library shows how much fun Tiffany had with these small, perforated iron disks (fig. 37). He mounted them in amusing decorative patterns on the wall to either side of the hearth and soldered them onto the iron smoke hood and the stack. He used them as well to fashion a pair of globular lampshades and chains suspended from beneath the mantel and for the shade hanging in the center of the library. Sword guards march right up the walls in paired rows on the divisions between the five-part bay windows, framing the glass panels of white magnolia blossoms (fig. 38). There must have been upward of two hundred *tsuba* around the windows alone. They even infiltrated the breakfast room, where the fireplace was flanked by two large wood casks

set into the wall as containers for table silver and wine bottles. The protruding ends had lead sheeting and were about thirty-four inches wide. One was decorated with glass mosaic, but the other featured circles of large iron rivets enclosing sword guards, each inelegantly attached with an iron rivet, a bizarre effect aptly described at the time as "barbaric magnificence" (fig. 275).[25] Tiffany later removed the end panels and stored them at Laurelton Hall. One of the twenty-some sword guards is still attached at the bottom of the vertical framing element at the left, a delicate design in silver of tiny pine needles and camellias, a winter theme.

The artist's dual interests, in decorative metalwork and in interior decoration, had clearly merged. By 1897 he had established a foundry and metal shop as part of his factory at Corona, Queens, which enabled him to expand the use of bronze and iron accessories in his interior decoration, especially for hanging lamps. At the same time he maintained a small metal workshop in his home, where he made handwrought items in metal.[26] Tiffany subsequently dismantled the curious, *tsuba*-encrusted smoke hood and the hanging lampshades and moved them to a corner of his smoking room at Laurelton Hall, just inside the door leading to the dining room.[27] Collectors like Tiffany at the end of the nineteenth century were just ignorant enough to be free to do whatever suited them with their exotic Asian things. The French critic and promoter of Japonisme Edmond de Goncourt (1822–1896), for example, arranged *tsuba* in decorative vertical rows on the wall of his study in 1886. The jeweler and creator of metal furniture Théodore Lambert made patterns with Noh masks on the wall of a French salon, and in Manhattan, William Hammond pasted a frieze of Japanese woodblock prints around the upper registers of his bedroom walls in 1879. Louisine Havemeyer was up-to-date when she took twelve Japanese knife handles (*kozuka*) and had them made into fish forks.[28]

Tiffany designed one leaded-glass window in the 1890s with a large circular motif floating off-center that definitely suggests a sword guard (fig. 276). A central bean-shaped element is the hole (usually wedge-shaped) pierced in the center of a *tsuba* that allows the guard to be fitted onto a sword blade, while a single curved opening to its left (often bean-shaped) represents the *hitsuana*, a hole (sometimes there are two) that allows the end of a skewerlike implement (*kōgai*) to be carried in the scabbard of the sword. The little red-and-black circular ornament floating to the right might be a *menuki*, a decorative metal ornament placed on each side of a sword hilt to enhance the grip.

Sword guards were Tiffany's personal obsession. He kept about two thousand examples, mostly iron and dating from the late eighteenth to early nineteenth centuries, in the Laurelton Hall smoking room. Twenty-four are illustrated in the 1946 Parke-Bernet Tiffany sale catalogue. A few are possibly from the seventeenth century, but none are great, as far as one can tell (fig. 277). He stored them in plain wood cabinets about three feet high with shallow tray drawers. Three were in the 1946 Parke-Bernet sale (unlisted lot 791A) and were purchased by Mrs. Sloane for her house museum, but without the sword guards, which were sold

Fig. 277. Japanese iron *tsuba* (sword guards) in Tiffany's collection, illustrated in the sale catalogue of the 1946 auction of the contents of Laurelton Hall. From Parke-Bernet 1946, p. 123

separately. (The empty cabinets must have been a bargain.) As Kristin C. Law, the curator of the Hermitage Foundation Museum and Gardens, notes, their story comes alive when the drawers are opened. The outline of each shape is visible above the impressed corresponding number (ending in 1424).[29] Tiffany also owned an olive green Japanese wood cabinet with two small and two long drawers mounted on the front with fourteen sword guards. It was thirty inches high and had two chamfered and drop leaves that opened to make a tabletop five feet long.[30] Clearly he enjoyed the tactile, kinetic sensation of holding a *tsuba* in the palm of his hand, the charm of the myriad designs (no two alike), and the fine workmanship. One of the artisans in his metalworking studio, Julia Munson Sherman, recalled that Tiffany always carried a sword guard in his waistcoat pocket. When he was unhappy with the sharp edges of an object crafted at Tiffany Studios, he would pull out the Japanese piece and praise its softly rounded edges.[31] His great appreciation of Japanese metalwork probably came to him through Edward C. Moore, who left his own collection of 93 *tsuba*, as well as large numbers of related sward fittings, to The Metropolitan Museum of Art in 1891.

The "exotic" setting of the Laurelton Hall den is enhanced by several Japanese architectural elements, notably a carved wood door and a *ranma* (carved horizontal panel on the upper registers of a building) decorated with chrysanthemums. Tiffany mounted the latter as a wall hanging. Between 1902 and 1906 doors and *ranma* from early Edo-period (1615–1868) shrines and temples that had been taken apart in the mid-nineteenth century were flooding the antiques market in New York. They were most aggressively marketed by Matsuki Bunkio (1867–1934), one of this country's first resident Japanese art dealers. From a family of art appraisers, he arrived in Salem, Massachusetts, at the age of twenty, learned English, took an American wife, and opened a gallery on Boylston Street in Boston. By 1898 he was sponsoring auctions of Japanese art in Boston, New York, and Philadelphia.[32] The original source of such carvings is unclear, but they captured the attention of most collectors at the time. One New York sale netted $31,000, mostly thanks to Bigelow's investment for the Museum of Fine Arts, Boston.[33] The fine craftsmanship and bright colors made these objects attractive to early collectors, though they soon fell out of favor.

In 1917 Tiffany was actively shopping for Asian art. He was sixty-nine, approaching retirement, and at the end of his artistic career. Anticipating the deeding of Laurelton Hall and its contents to his educational foundation the following year, he made a last big push to complete the decoration of his country estate. It was a final summing up of his career as he deliberately turned his home into a "museum."

It was about this time that he purchased the magnificent pair of large, glazed Kangxi-era Chinese ceramic lions for the loggia (figs. 265, 278, 279). He bought them from C. T. (Ching Tsai) Loo (1880–1957), who began selling Chinese art in New York about

Fig. 278. Loggia, Laurelton Hall, ca. 1920s. Gelatin silver print, 8⅛ x 10 in. (20.5 x 25.4 cm). Photograph by David Aronow. The Metropolitan Museum of Art, New York, Gift of Robert Koch, 1978 (1978.646.9)

Opposite: Fig. 279. Pair of lions. China, inscribed 1684. Glazed stoneware, H. 66 in. (167.6 cm) each. Private collection, Switzerland. Photograph © Christie's Images Ltd. 2004

March 1915. Despite the fact that Loo is acknowledged as one of the most important Asian art dealers of the first half of the twentieth century, little is known about him. An obituary written by the chief curator of the Musée Guimet, Paris, did not even mention his business venture in the United States.[34] Loo grew up in a merchant family in Shanghai and was sent to Paris as a young man to learn French and obtain a degree in international commerce. Instead, he started his own antiques business, Lai Yuan (Coming from Far Away), at 34 Rue Taitbout. In 1915, at the age of thirty-five, he opened a New York branch at 557 Fifth Avenue, dividing his time between France and the United States until at least 1921. In 1926 he bought an old hotel in Paris and had it transformed into the Chinese-style gallery that still stands today. Like Yamanaka and Company, his only close rival, his firm was responsible for looting China of some of its great stone sculptures and antiquities. Yamanaka and C. T. Loo were the two pipelines to this country and to Europe. The Tiffany lions once sat at the entrance to the great hall of some temple or grand house in Shanxi province, in northern China. They were listed at $3,000 in the 1919 insurance inventory, probably based on a now-lost Lai Yuan invoice, and brought $1,850 at the 1946 Parke-Bernet auction.[35] Their brilliant turquoise and yellow glazes were an ideal match for Tiffany's iridescent blue and yellow glass tiles on the lintel of the loggia at Laurelton Hall (see fig. 107).

Loo was aggressive in approaching wealthy local collectors of Chinese art from the moment he first set foot in the States. In 1915 he sold a painting attributed to Ma Yuan (later deaccessioned) to

Alfred Pillsbury in Minneapolis, and a group of thirteen Chinese paintings and some ceramics to Charles Freer in Detroit, and he negotiated deals with Eugene and Agnes Meyer in New York. He made his first gift to The Metropolitan Museum of Art in November 1915. Loo and his wife, who was French, visited Freer in Detroit in 1916. Between May 1915 and April 1921 his company held at least four auctions of Chinese antiquities in New York, and he himself was bidding at the major sales, sometimes side by side with Tiffany.

In January 1917 Tiffany spent two full days at two sales at the Anderson Galleries, on Madison Avenue at Fortieth Street, stocking up on ukiyo-e prints, paintings, and furniture for a Chinese room and a Japanese room he was completing on the third floor of Laurelton Hall. He was present at 2:30 P.M. on the afternoons of January 22 and 23 for the sale of the property of an anonymous Chinese art collector who had lived in Beijing before the revolution. At 8 P.M. he was back, bidding on the group of four hundred Japanese prints from the collection of the New York photographer Arnold Genthe (1869–1942). These sales were well publicized and attracted considerable interest. Tiffany was an amateur photographer and may have known and admired the German-born Genthe, who moved to New York from San Francisco in 1911. Genthe had traveled in Japan for six months in 1908 and his compositions often show the influence of Japanese prints. Print prices were rising dramatically about 1917, thanks in part to the new wealth and nascent nationalism in Japan in the early years of the Taisho period (1912–26), and Genthe was taking advantage of

Native American Art at Laurelton Hall

Elizabeth Hutchinson

On the approach to Laurelton Hall, visitors were treated to an unusual sight. Rounding a bend in the drive, they encountered a totem pole nestled in the shrubbery (fig. 294). The pole, carved with seated figures at the top and bottom and capped with a horizontal whale, is typical of the poles used in Kwak'wakw'wakw villages in British Columbia. Tiffany seems to have sited the pole in a way that would re-create the experience of a traveler in the Northwest, albeit here among East Coast flora. In the Northwest, one's first glimpse of a settlement was the silhouettes of poles against the sky. Tiffany had viewed these settlements during an inland passage cruise in 1916; he was reported to have purchased the Laurelton pole from a chief at Alert Bay during that trip. The visual effect he sought to reproduce had been captured by Edward S. Curtis (1868–1952), the photographer famous for his twenty-volume study of North American Indians, in his dramatically framed study *Nimkish Village at Alert Bay*, made just two years before Tiffany's cruise (fig. 295). The pole at the center of Curtis's image, with a plain central shaft topped by a human figure and a whale, is remarkably similar to Tiffany's.[1]

The totem pole was among more than five hundred Native North American objects, including baskets, implements, and articles of clothing from the Pacific Northwest, that were in the 1946 Parke-Bernet sale of the contents of Laurelton Hall.[2] Many of these objects were displayed in a special oblong room that had once been a bowling alley (fig. 296). Baskets, pottery, and textiles also served as decorative accents throughout the house. For example, the 1919 inventory notes the presence in the living hall of seven Alaskan and Californian baskets, a large "Cliff-dweller" pottery bowl, and a "Unique Hopi Olla . . . found in a cliff house of great antiquity" (fig. 297).[3]

Tiffany did not leave any written accounts of his interest in Native American art. Indeed, Native American design rarely influenced his own work, unlike the Asian and Islamic arts that he also collected. Nevertheless, the Kwak'wakw'wakw totem pole gives us some insight into Tiffany's interest and taste, for it is an unusual piece for a collector of the time. The most popular poles then were columns filled with figural carving up the entire shaft, frequently topped with a vertical figure with outstretched wings. Tourists bought large numbers of both full-size and miniature versions, made primarily by the Haida, Tsimshian, and Tlingit in southeastern Alaska. The relatively plainer style of the Kwak'wakw'wakw was in less demand, and beginning about the end of the nineteenth century the Kwak'wakw'wakw started to explore bolder carving and more vivid colors.[4] That Tiffany went for an old-fashioned style indicates the impact of his travels among Native North American communities on his taste. While his collection of Native American art was part of the "Indian Craze" that struck the United States at the beginning of the twentieth century, its display in Laurelton Hall reveals his sense of play and his love of texture, shape, and craftsmanship, as well as his characteristic boldness in mixing styles.

Spurred by the increased availability of Native American objects, urban consumers began filling their homes with "Indian corners"—small arrangements of baskets, pottery, textiles, and other implements. The Indian corner was a takeoff on the Turkish, or "Cozy," corners of the preceding generation. Both were designed as comfortable and luxurious spaces that encouraged more casual social interaction than formal parlors.[5]

The self-proclaimed Indian expert George Wharton James, who both wrote about and traded in Native American art, explained the appeal of Indian baskets:

> To the uninitiated a fine Indian basket may possess a few exterior attractions, such as shapely form, delicate color and harmonious design, but anything further he cannot see. On the other hand the initiated sees a work of love; a striving after the ideal; a reverent propitiation of supernatural powers, good or evil; a nation's art expression, a people's inner life of poetry, art, religion; and thus he comes to a closer knowledge of the people it represents, a deeper sympathy with them; a fuller recognition of the oneness of human life, though under so many and diverse manifestations.[6]

The display strategies used for the Indian corner reinforce the concept of making contact with the universal through interaction with Native objects. As a photograph of Joseph Keppler's collection

Opposite: Fig. 293. Detail of fig. 307

Fig. 294. Drive, with totem pole, Laurelton Hall, ca. 1920s. Gelatin silver print, 8⅛ x 10 in. (20.5 x 25.4 cm). Photograph by David Aronow. The Metropolitan Museum of Art, New York, Gift of Robert Koch, 1978 (1978.646.39)

Fig. 295. Edward S. Curtis (1868–1952), *Nimkish Village at Alert Bay*, 1915 (original photogravure by John Andrew and Son, ca. 1914, published in *The Kwakiutl*, pl. 350). Courtesy of Northwestern University Library, Evanston, Illinois

in Inwood, New York, demonstrates, Indian corners were dynamic, visually and physically stimulating spaces (see fig. 298). Leaning against the wall, draped jauntily over furniture, trailing fringe and feathers, stacked on shelves, or hanging in clusters, the objects in the Indian corner spark a desire to enter the space, touch them, and become absorbed in their complex construction, marvelous materials, and infinite variety.

Such idealism has been associated with "antimodernism," a term coined by cultural historian T. J. Jackson Lears to describe the cultural reaction to the spreading industrialism and commercialism of the late nineteenth century.[7] Antimodernists sought alternatives to their bureaucratic routines in physical activity and in encounters with preindustrial life symbolized by nature or so-called primitive cultures. Much of this activity was concentrated in the home, which, under the rubric of the international Arts and Crafts movement, was understood as an enclave in which to nourish the individuality and sentimentality that were threatened in larger society. Indian corners supported this idea by bringing together handmade objects in spaces associated with freedom and autonomy for the body and the imagination, the home, most importantly, but also rooms in the home such as dens, porches, and studies that are particularly associated with these qualities.

Although they have been seen as souvenirs of American travel, objects collected in Indian corners were broadly promoted to American consumers through mail-order catalogues and nationally circulating magazines.[8] Journals associated with country living and with the Arts and Crafts movement frequently carried

Fig. 296. Native American room, Laurelton Hall, illustrated in the sale catalogue of the 1946 auction of the contents of Laurelton Hall. From Parke-Bernet 1946, p. 53

Fig. 297. Living hall, Laurelton Hall. Photograph probably by David Aronow, ca. 1920s. Courtesy of Phillips-Hosking Collection

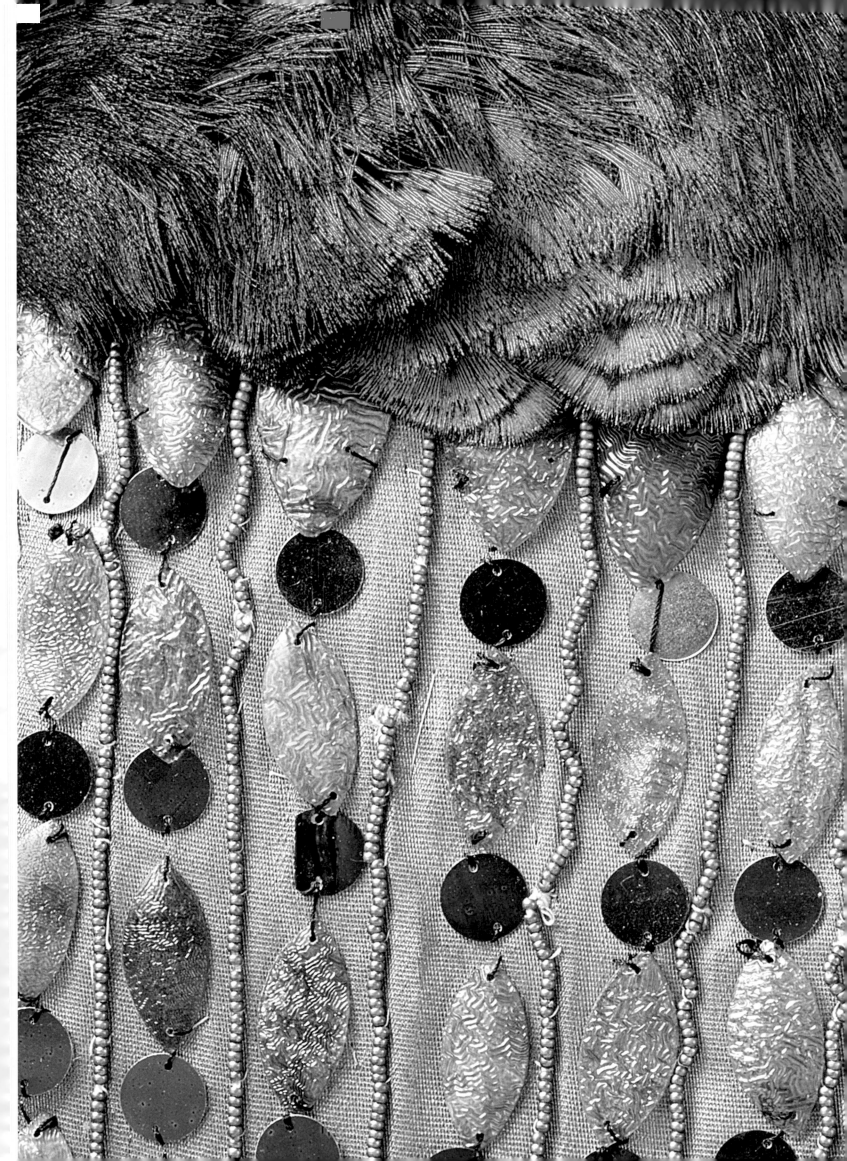

The Art of Magnificent Living: Life at Laurelton Hall

Alice Cooney Frelinghuysen

L aurelton Hall was a magical place of artistic exuberance, but it was also the site of both conventional and unconventional country-house activity. It was a place where Tiffany invited family members, friends, and artists to gather and enjoy the settings that he had so carefully designed and crafted.

In the manner of many affluent country estates, Laurelton Hall was, for the most part, a self-sufficient operation. Not only did it have its own railway station; it also had its own farm that raised horses, Hereford cows, chickens of several varieties, doves, pheasants, and apples. Vegetables and other fruits were grown in the hothouses. This part of the operation was managed from an extensive complex of farm buildings designed by Alfred Hopkins (1870–1941), the architect and innovator in farm buildings. The plan provides insight into the extent of the operation (fig. 316). One entered the complex into a walled courtyard with a trough in the center, off which were a wagon shed and storerooms for boots and feed. The dairy cattle had a separate yard, with calving pens, a milk room, washrooms, and a laundry. Similarly, the sheep had a penned winter yard adjoining the building, with a sheepfold and lambing pens. A fourteen-horse stable accommodated the Tiffanys' carriage horses, with the wagon room next door. The complex also included a room for machinery and an octagonal toolroom. A tall octagonal tower served as a dovecote. The flat-roofed, stucco-sheathed structures, with their unusual fenestration, were all connected to one another (fig. 317).

Such an extensive farming enterprise required numerous people to run it, in the hierarchy associated with the era. As the floor plan shows, the farm superintendent had his own room, though the notation "entrance to men's rooms" suggests far simpler quarters for the less-skilled hands. The staff accommodations included a communal sitting room, another dining room, and a kitchen.

The Tiffany family followed a routine which mirrored that of many of their friends and neighbors in Cold Spring Harbor, like the Robert W. de Forests, who lived across the bay from Laurelton Hall and with whom they socialized frequently. They began this routine in the late 1880s, when they would arrive from their city

home in early or mid-May at the Briars, their Long Island residence before Laurelton Hall. They would remain there during the first months of the summer, usually until the end of July or early August, by which time the heat, even on Long Island, must have seemed oppressive to Tiffany. During the relatively quiet month of August, the family customarily traveled, often to Europe.[1]

When the Tiffanys were in residence on Long Island, the maintenance of an elaborate house in addition to extensive gardens and greenhouses (fig. 318) required a large staff. At the Briars, Tiffany employed a household staff of four in addition to a nurse for the children and a cook,[2] but when he moved into the more extensive Laurelton Hall, the number of people needed to run the household swelled considerably. There, those who lived in—a housekeeper, a waitress, a parlor maid, a chambermaid, and nine additional female servants[3]—took care of the interior, and they stayed in a wing off the large dining room, in small rooms with their own dining room. An army of full-time gardeners and groundsmen tended the outdoors, supplemented by immigrant workers, who arrived daily by train. Tiffany constantly worked closely with the gardeners, directing their work to his satisfaction. He also employed a groom, a coachman, who lived with his family in his own house on the estate, and an estate superintendent, who also had his own house.[4] The staff soon included a night watchman as well as men to captain and maintain his boats.

Although Tiffany would officially move back to his New York City residence, usually at the beginning of November, he never closed his Long Island house entirely for the winter, unlike many of his neighbors.[5] The house was occasionally open over the Christmas holidays. More typically the Tiffanys would go to Long Island for several days at a time in January or February for house parties that included such midwinter activities as skating and sleighing, as well as social gatherings in the evenings.[6] While still at the Briars, Tiffany often took a group of friends and family to Long Island for a few days. The local newspaper reported that the Tiffanys had a weekend house party of some twenty-five over New Year's of 1902–3, "to enjoy sleighing, coasting and skating, carriage riding or whatever winter sports may come."[7] That same winter, at the end of February, he "and a number of friends enjoyed a sleigh ride here on Monday."[8] Those winter sports were

Opposite: Fig. 315. Detail of fig. 323

Fig. 320. Louis Comfort Tiffany in Egyptian costume. From "Contemporaries of Cleopatra at a Fête Given by Mr. Louis C. Tiffany of New York," *Town and Country* 67 (February 22, 1913), p. 28

Fig. 321. Julia Tiffany Parker in Egyptian costume. From "Contemporaries of Cleopatra at a Fête Given by Mr. Louis C. Tiffany of New York," *Town and Country* 67 (February 22, 1913), p. 29

Tiffany shared Laurelton Hall not only with his family and friends but also with those who worked for him, fostering a close relationship between him and his designers. Clara Driscoll, for example, one of Tiffany's foremost designers, was invited for Sunday dinner at Laurelton in March 1906. This was clearly a special treat, for Driscoll wrote in a letter in which she discussed the anticipated event that she would wear her "fine new dress."[19]

Music was always an important component for Tiffany, both in his New York City homes and in the country. Two years after he moved into Laurelton he hosted a Saturday afternoon recital by pianist Eleanor Altman for "a large number of society people" from Cold Spring Harbor and surrounding villages.[20] Each of his residences boasted superb pianos, and he installed organs both at the Seventy-second Street house and at Laurelton. In New York, the organ was in his top-floor studio, where it was said to rise forty feet up toward the forty-five-foot ceiling; the echo organ was shielded by a screen of Favrile glass. The music must have seemed to emanate mysteriously from the luminescence of the glass. The acoustics, too, were noted as being especially remarkable.[21] Tiffany engaged organist Harry Rowe Shelley, who also played for John

D. Rockefeller and William K. Vanderbilt, to give evening recitals and musicales both at Seventy-second Street and at Laurelton Hall. Shelley was the regular organist at the Fifth Avenue Baptist Church and also played for the Pilgrims Church in Brooklyn. The salary of a church organist was modest, but Shelley held the distinction of being the most financially successful organist in New York, perhaps due to his playing for these private clients.[22]

Tiffany had a flair for entertaining, and his homes became the setting for many dinners, small and large, as well as for a host of special events and, beginning in the mid-1880s, staged fetes. To celebrate the opening of his studio in the Seventy-second Street house in 1886, he gave "a series of entertainments to his Artist-friends—first was the Oyster roast, tonight is the Oriental."[23] For the "Oriental" evening, the monochrome printed invitation pictures a seated Asian man smoking a hookah; swirls of smoke emanating from the hookah frame the wording and at the upper left form Tiffany's conjoined initials (fig. 319). (Tiffany included the same monogram in the upper decorative border of his *Four Seasons* window, made for the Paris Exposition Universelle of 1900 [see figs. 250, 253].) This hearth warming, to which guests were requested to wear Oriental costumes, set the tone for future festivities both at Seventy-second Street and at Laurelton Hall.

Over the years, Tiffany became well known for his taste for the theatrical and his elaborate parties. On at least one occasion, mixing his fascination with color and light with his love of theatrics, he set off a display of fireworks to mark the Fourth of July.[24] The most famous of his parties was the elaborate costumed Egyptian Fête held on February 4, 1913, in the Tiffany Studios showrooms at 345 Madison Avenue, in honor of his sixty-fifth birthday. Theme parties and costume balls were in favor with the well-to-do during the last decade of the nineteenth and the first decade of the twentieth century, and they were assiduously chronicled by the local press. Some of the most flamboyant were given by members of the artistic set, such as Stanford White.[25] Tiffany's Egyptian extravaganza was the finale to the New York social season of 1913, which traditionally ended at the beginning of Lent, and it was considered by many the most important social entertainment of the year.[26]

The overall concept of the event was undoubtedly Tiffany's, but to give it authenticity he enlisted the help of Joseph Lindon Smith (1863–1950), a designer and Egyptology specialist from Boston whom Tiffany had met on his trip to Egypt with his daughters Comfort and Julia in the winter of 1908.[27] Smith provided many of the components that satisfied Tiffany's absorbing attention to detail, which involved months of preparation and about two weeks of work in the Tiffany Studios showroom, for which Tiffany paid him $1,000.[28] The invitation was written in hieroglyphics, and guests were instructed to come in costume.[29] Smith, who made several sketches to suggest specific types of costumes, himself arrived in shimmering patterned silks and a striped turban. The painter John White Alexander (1856–1915), then president of the National Academy of Design, and the sculptor François Tonetti (1863–1920) helped to supervise the guests' costumes, which were said to have been inspired by the collections of the Metropolitan Museum.[30] Tiffany came dressed as an "Oriental potentate," in a turban headdress, silk robes, and jewels (fig. 320).[31] His daughter Julia Tiffany Parker was likewise exotically attired (fig. 321).

For the event Tiffany brought together some three hundred distinguished guests from New York society and American arts and letters, including family members, friends, neighbors, and clients. Among them were his devoted patron Mrs. H. O. Havemeyer; Mr. and Mrs. Edward S. Harkness, he as a Persian and she as Zuleika; Mrs. Charles L. Tiffany as Cleopatra; Mr. and Mrs. Cleveland Dodge as Egyptian water carriers; Mr. and Mrs. Robert W. de Forest as the Maharajah and Maharanee of Punjab; Mr. and Mrs. Johnston de Forest as the Rajah and Ranee of Surat; Henry L. de Forest as a fan bearer; Mr. and Mrs. Walter B. Jennings, clients and Long Island neighbors, as Persians; Mrs. George Seligman; Mr. and Mrs. John D. Rockefeller Jr., she as Minerva and he as a Persian; the architect Cass Gilbert and his wife; and John White Alexander as an Egyptian mummy, who stood motionless for

nearly an hour.[32] As was his custom, Tiffany included younger members of his family and those of close friends, costumed to perform some role.[33] The Stewart children (de Forest grandchildren) were dressed as youthful slaves and "preceded the entrance of Cleopatra."[34] So sought after were the invitations to this party that engraved "cards of admission" were issued to those who accepted.[35] It would go down in history as "the most perfect costume party ever given in New York."[36]

The large gallery of the Tiffany Studios showroom, also called the rug room, was transformed to give it an Eastern flavor, with Tiffany wares as props. Walls were hung with Oriental carpets, and piles of rugs and divans were set around the floor for the guests to recline or sit on. For the entertainment, professional actors took the parts of the Ethiopians, the porters, the juggler, the fortune teller, Cleopatra, and Caesar. Hedwig Reicher was Cleopatra, and her Mark Anthony was played by Pedro De Cordoba; the Greek dancer and portrait painter Paul Swan danced for Cleopatra in a leopard-skin costume;[37] and Ruth St. Denis was the slave dancer. At Tiffany's insistence, the other parts were "to be taken by the family and such intimate friends as they feel they can control!"[38] Smith agreed that there were advantages to incorporating amateurs into the spectacle because it immediately put the audience into a sympathetic frame of mind.[39] Music was provided by members of the New York Philharmonic Orchestra. Theodore Steinway composed dance music especially for the event, and his firm supplied more than one piano for the evening. Vocal music performed by Greta Torpadie included the "Bell Song" from Delibes's *Lakmé*, and strains from Verdi's *Aida* echoed through the rooms. The elaborately choreographed pageant carried a theme associated with Tiffany's business, and in a clever bit of advertising, a scene in the second act involved an assemblage of Egyptian merchants and porters carrying bales of Tiffany Studios textiles, rugs, and glass, which they unpacked onstage for Cleopatra.[40]

Following the theatrical enactment and Ruth St. Denis's dance, the guests paraded around the room, after which Tiffany, with a fanfare of trumpets, led them in to dinner for an elegant meal catered by Delmonico's. The repast included "Gumbo clair . . . / . . . Terrapine a la Baltimore / Chaufroix de pintadeaux au mousse de jambon," as well as salad, fruit, and petits fours.[41]

The fete was a success by all standards. Newspapers from around the world featured headlines, articles, and pictures of the costumed guests and the elaborate setting.[42] Indeed, Tiffany hired Smith for one more grand-pageant celebration, a luncheon in the Tiffany Studios showroom in 1916. The theme for this event was the "Quest of Beauty," and again it was to celebrate Tiffany's birthday. The pageant itself was a salute to beauty, art, and craftsmanship, invoking allegories of the arts as well as the natural materials Tiffany utilized in his varied arts, such as glass, clay, wood, metal, and the gemstones moonstones, opals, and amethysts.[43]

Prior to that, however, and following the success of the Egyptian Fête, in 1914 Tiffany put on perhaps an even more elaborate event,

Fig. 322. Phyllis de Kay in costume as Juno, Peacock Feast, Laurelton Hall. From "Roman Luxuries at Tiffany Feast for Men of Genius," *New York Times*, May 24, 1914, pt. 1, p. 5

Hassam, F. Luis Mora, and Irving R. Wiles; sculptor Daniel Chester French; and architects Donn Barber, Cass Gilbert, Francis L. V. Hoppin, Joseph Howland Hunt, Guy Lowell, and Lloyd Warren. Some involved in the cultural life of New York were author and art critic Charles de Kay, R. T. Haines Halsey, and Samuel T. Peters. Literary society was represented by publishers Charles Scribner, Frank N. Doubleday, and Frederick Bok. Family members and close friends on the guest list included Charles L. Tiffany, Francis Jones, Dr. Graham Lusk, William A. W. Stewart, Rodman de Kay Gilder, Walter Palmer, Gurdon S. Parker, William Sloane Coffin, Robert de Forest, and his son Johnston de Forest. Also invited was George Frederick Kunz, the eminent mineralogist who was a gemologist at Tiffany and Company.

The gardens were the important feature, the guests being invited early enough in the evening that they might enjoy all the spring bulbs, shrubs, and fruit trees then in bloom. In anticipation of the event, Tiffany kept forty gardeners busy for two weeks. The resulting panoply of color began with white and pink laurel and other flowering shrubs as well as masses of white and purple phlox lining the banks of the drive immediately inside the gates. Tulips, pansies, and other early flowers in blues and yellows filled the beds and borders, "while the plentiful wisteria, which Mr. Tiffany so loved, festooned its graceful panicles from pergolas and trellises and even from trees in unexpected places. It was truly a feast of flowers."[45]

The characteristic pageantry began when, once the 150 guests were seated in the large dining room, Phyllis de Kay, a young family friend, entered from the garden that was now bathed in twilight (fig. 322). Leading a peacock and dressed as Juno, she wore a pale Grecian gown and a headdress composed of the head and feathers of a peacock with lappets of gold cloth appliquéd with shimmering blue sequins and iridescent paillettes, and with strings of gold beads at the back (figs. 315, 323), patterned after the vulture headdress of the Egyptian goddess Nekhbet. This may have been the same headdress worn at the Egyptian Fête by Tiffany's daughter Julia Tiffany Parker (see fig. 321). There followed a procession of Tiffany's daughters and their friends—Comfort Tiffany Gilder, Mary Woodbridge Tiffany Lusk, Dorothy Tiffany, and Francesca Gilder, as well as Phyllis de Kay—dressed similarly in long gauzy Grecian costumes ornamented with gold and green medallions, and sashes. The first three held aloft on large silver salvers stuffed peacocks resplendent in their plumage, followed by the other two carrying voluminous "bouquets" of peacock feathers (fig. 324). The brilliant blue and green coloration of the peacock's plumage and its oily iridescence had long since captured Tiffany's imagination, and he interpreted it in myriad ways and in varying media during his career (see fig. 194). He kept peacocks at Laurelton and had them brought from the farm buildings so he could watch them walk around the grounds.[46] One of the farm structures on the estate bore a weathervane in the shape of a peacock (see fig. 70).

this time at Laurelton Hall. He sent simple engraved invitations for an "Artists' Reception and to view the spring flowers at his country home," with supper following.[44] He was secretive about the details of the entertainment, leaving that as a surprise upon his guests' arrival. The reception and dinner, or Peacock Feast, were held on May 15, 1914, in honor of some 150 "men of genius." Guests left New York at four o'clock by special train, and automobiles met them at the Oyster Bay station to transport them the short distance to the estate.

The guest list comprised noted artists and architects, as well as family and some of Tiffany's male friends, many of whom had attended the Egyptian Fête the year before. Joseph Lindon Smith was one, but there is no evidence that his role was anything other than as a guest, for the party did not include a theatrical presentation. The artist invitees included painters John White Alexander, Carroll Beckwith, Edwin H. Blashfield, Childe

Fig. 323. *Peacock Headdress*, ca. 1913. Peacock feathers and head, cloth, metal, sequins, celluloid paillettes, 10 x 6½ x 8½ in. (25.4 x 16.5 x 21.6 cm). Museum of the City of New York, Gift of Julia Tiffany Weld (75.21.1)

Fig. 324. Women serving peacock at Peacock Feast, Laurelton Hall. From "Roman Luxuries at Tiffany Feast for Men of Genius," *New York Times*, May 24, 1914, pt. 1, p. 5

Fig. 325. Torchbearers at Peacock Feast, Laurelton Hall. From "Roman Luxuries at Tiffany Feast for Men of Genius," *New York Times*, May 24, 1914, pt. 1, p. 5

Fig. 326. Children serving suckling pig at Peacock Feast, Laurelton Hall. From "Roman Luxuries at Tiffany Feast for Men of Genius," *New York Times*, May 24, 1914, pt. 1, p. 5

Following the peacock parade were some of the younger members of the group—Ethel, Dorothy, and William Stewart, children of Robert de Forest's daughter, Frances de Forest Stewart; and Louis, Louise, and William Lusk Jr., children of Tiffany's daughter Mary Woodbridge Tiffany Lusk, also in pale gowns with gauzelike headscarves, each carrying a torch and a basket of rose petals (fig. 325). They were followed, finally, by more Tiffany and de Forest grandchildren dressed as chefs, complete with padded stomachs, long aprons, and chef's hats, carrying platters of suckling pig (fig. 326). In keeping with their roles, the peacock- and torchbearers wore sandals or were barefoot and the chefs wore dark shoes and socks. As the procession moved from table to table, Harry Rowe Shelley played the organ in the central court of the house.[42]

The guests sat at three large tables, each for sixteen, in the center of the large dining room, and at smaller tables placed around them. The dinner was again prepared by Delmonico's of New York and was made using only products from the Tiffany estate. There was a menu on heavy paper decorated with a motif taken from one of Tiffany's Japanese wood-and-lacquer Ritsuō panels (see figs. 270, 271): "Bouillon de Lucines Bellevue / Radis Onions nouveaux / Olives mûres Carciofini / Paupiettes de truite en gelée au Chablis / Cochon de lait farci à l'Americaine / Pommes Reinettes pochées / Epinards à la crème / Aiguillettes de caneton à l'orange / Petits pois nouveaux à l'Etuvée / Asperge sauce Hollandaise / Sorbet Frasia / Paons en Volière Salade coeur de laitue / Crêpes flambées au Bar le Duc blanc/ Fromage."[48] In the fashion of the day, the guests were served an aperitif of dry sherry, and the meal was accompanied by French wines, white, then Burgundy, followed by champagne.

After the meal, the men retired to Tiffany's Moorish room for cigars.[49] Coffee was served oriental-style in the central court and on the terrace outside, and each space provided a suitably dramatic sensory environment to finish off the evening. Strains of Beethoven, Bach, and Brahms wafted from the organ, while the flower-framed central pool shone with rainbow hues from the rotating color wheel lit below the Favrile-glass vase and basin. Masses of yellow orchids of a "rare variety" were banked around the fountain, and a moonlit glow emanated from the Favrile glass dome three stories above. In the large living hall, the fireplace was flanked by two apple trees in full bloom.

The terrace was equally magical, described evocatively as "where the spray of the rock crystal fountain was lighted like dancing rainbows just outside the door with the twinkling lights on Long Island Sound in the distance." The experience was further enhanced by children, three of whom scattered handfuls of rose petals from large baskets, while another group in togas carried lit braziers. "When the guests departed at eleven o'clock to board the special train, which awaited them at the station, vari-colored lights were played upon the gardens and out-door fountains, revealing them in a new and impressive beauty."[50] The local paper described the event as "a unique and interesting entertainment," saying that the "garden fete was most odd and unusual, while the dinner was a marvel."[51]

Tiffany's Peacock Feast was perhaps one of the last of the great country-house parties of its era. A month and a half after the party's lights were dimmed, the assassination of Archduke Franz Ferdinand of Austria precipitated World War I, and although the United States would not enter the war for three more years, the precarious world balance spread a sobering effect over the country in general. Subsequent events at Laurelton centered on special family occasions such as birthdays and weddings, notably that of Tiffany's youngest daughter, Dorothy, to Robert Burlingham later that same year.

On September 24, 1914, at noon, Dorothy Trimble Tiffany married Dr. Robert Burlingham in Saint John's Episcopal Church in Cold Spring Harbor. Tiffany walked down the aisle with his daughter for the ceremony, which was performed by the Reverend W. E. McCord, rector of Saint John's, "which the Tiffanys attend while occupying their Summer home."[52] It was "the bride's desire to have a small and simple country wedding instead of a large affair."[53] Only about fifty guests attended the wedding and the breakfast that followed, which was served in the Laurelton Hall dining room overlooking the harbor.[54] According to the wedding notice in the *New York Times*, "Autumnal flowers and foliage were used for the decoration of the little church and at Laurelton Hall. . . . White asters and purple clematis entered largely into the color scheme of the interior decoration, and in the large court of Laurelton Hall, a bower of clematis had been erected, under which the couple received the congratulations of their relatives and friends. A fountain playing in the centre of the court added to the effect of the background. Pink asters and orchids covered the walls of the court."[55] The guest list was made up primarily of family members, including Tiffany's sister Annie Olivia Tiffany Mitchell; his daughters and their husbands—Mr. and Mrs. Rodman de Kay Gilder, Dr. and Mrs. Graham Lusk, for example—as well as close friends and neighbors, Mrs. Richard Watson Gilder, Mr. and Mrs. Robert W. de Forest, Mr. and Mrs. Henry W. de Forest, Mr. and Mrs. Charles de Kay among them.[56]

Dorothy was the last of Tiffany's daughters to marry, and now all had homes of their own (he would build or give some of them houses on or near the Laurelton Hall estate). He had the company, however, of Sarah (Patsy) Hanley (d. 1958), an Irish nurse who had been hired in 1910 when Tiffany became ill. However the relationship may have developed after his recovery, Tiffany clearly enjoyed her companionship now that his offspring were occupied with their own lives and growing families. Hanley painted, played duplicate whist with Tiffany in the evenings, accompanied him on trips, and, as his daughters had, served as his hostess at Laurelton Hall (fig. 327). As one of his granddaughters would recall, "She kept him gay and happy."[57] Hanley remained at Laurelton well after Tiffany's death, residing in a modest house that he built for her on the estate.[58]

Over the years, numerous guests visited Laurelton Hall, both individually and in groups. The only guest book that survives

Fig. 327. Sarah Hanley in the Fountain Court, Laurelton Hall, ca. 1920s. Photograph by David Aronow. Courtesy of David Petrovsky

begins in 1916, with most of the entries dating from June 1918, the year Tiffany established the Louis Comfort Tiffany Foundation (fig. 328). It is evident that he welcomed visitors from across the country, including artists and museum curators and directors, as guests to what had become more than a home, a personal museum.[59]

Laurelton remained a place where Tiffany basked in the beauty he had created. His daughter Comfort Tiffany Gilder remembered of times spent as a family there an almost ritualistic end to the day:

> After dinner we would follow Papa in his white suit into the great court in the center of the house. He would climb the three velvet steps to the top of the dais, which was covered in stenciled green velvet. There he would sit in the middle of his "throne," as we called it, lean back on the cushions, cross his legs, and survey his beautiful creation. . . . Old Agnes would come with his coffee. She walked up the steps of the dais to him. He took a cup from her, lit a long cigar, and leaned back on the cushions again. Often, one of us would play his favorite pieces of music on the organ off in the corner, and sometimes we would also sing to it his favorite songs. When nine o'clock chimed in the tower, he would get up, kiss us goodnight in a perfunctory way, and walk up to bed.[60]

By the mid-1910s, Tiffany, perhaps thinking of Laurelton in terms of the foundation he wanted to set up, seemed to consider it something of a public property. In 1916, for instance, he invited

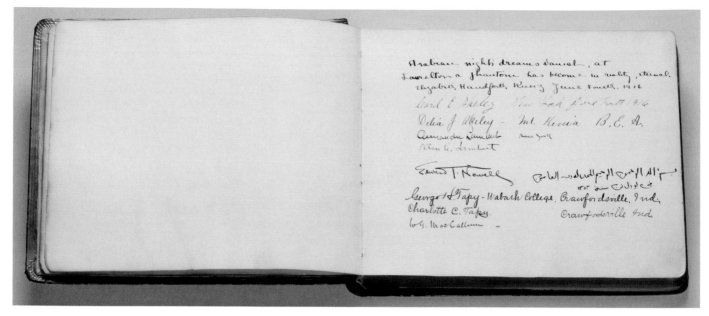

Fig. 328. Guest book, Laurelton Hall, ca. 1916–51. Leather, paper, gold leaf, 8½ x 10½ x 2 in. (21.6 x 26.7 x 5.1 cm). The Charles Hosmer Morse Museum of American Art, Winter Park, Florida

the public to look at his beautiful spring flowers.[61] When he gave the estate to the Tiffany Foundation, it came to be used for events that benefited the community in different ways. In fact, after 1919 Tiffany himself seems to have been more active in that role, for example, joining Mrs. William K. Vanderbilt, Mrs. Stephen C. Clark, Mrs. Walter B. Jennings, Robert de Forest, and others at a pageant in nearby Huntington to benefit a war effort, the Free Milk for France Organization.[62] In early May 1928, the School Nature League Flower Show, at Eighty-first Street and Avenue A in New York City, was embellished with cut flowers from Tiffany's greenhouses and gardens as well as from other estates, including those of Mrs. Marshall Field and Daniel Guggenheim, and from the New York Botanical Garden.[63]

In 1930 Tiffany held his final celebration, his eighty-third birthday, at Laurelton Hall. This event brought together artists and executives from Tiffany Studios to honor their mentor and employer at "his last birthday celebration before failing health and diminishing vigor took him to the milder climate of Florida for the few remaining winters of his life."[64] For Tiffany, the years that followed were marked by deafness and the consequences of age, making his tours of his beloved Laurelton Hall rooms and gardens exceedingly difficult. Three years later he died in his house at Seventy-second Street, bringing to a close a life that epitomized the "art of magnificent living."[65]

1. It was reported, for example, on July 29, 1910, that "Louis C. Tiffany and family are to spend some time abroad, sailing this week" (*The Long Islander*, July 29, 1910). The following year he sailed for Europe in the first week of July (*The Long Islander*, July 7, 1911).

2. The 1900 U.S. Census, in which Tiffany is listed as "Merchant (Decorator)," itemizes a parlor maid, chambermaid, one other maid, a waitress, and a cook, all from Ireland, as the live-in household staff.

3. The 1910 U.S. Census, in which Tiffany is listed as "Artist."

4. Ibid.

5. Tiffany made frequent visits to Laurelton during the winter season (*The Long Islander*, November 2, 1909). The exception to his moving back to the city in November was in 1910, when he was recovering from a severe illness and stayed at Laurelton to recuperate (*The Long Islander*, November 4, 1910).

6. *The Long Islander*, January 5, 1900.

7. *The Long Islander*, January 2, 1903. At the end of February, Tiffany and "a number of friends enjoyed a sleigh ride" at his country house (*The Long Islander*, February 27, 1903). In January 1910, the local paper reported that Tiffany would be at his estate over New Year's, along with neighbors Walter Jennings and Robert de Forest (*The Long Islander*, January 13, 1911). The following year, it was reported that "Louis C. Tiffany occupied his country mansion over the recent holiday, entertaining a house party" (*The Long Islander*, January 5, 1912). And in 1915, Tiffany, as well as the Walter Jenningses and the Robert de Forests, "entertained large house parties over New Year's Day and Sunday" (*The Long Islander*, January 8, 1915).

8. *The Long Islander*, February 27, 1903.

9. *The Long Islander*, January 5, 1906.

10. Julia Piatt (Saranac Lake) to Annie Olivia Tiffany Mitchell, January 5, 1907 or 1908. Mitchell-Tiffany Family Papers, Manuscripts and Archives, Yale University Library, group 701, box 6, folder 106. Hilda was not able to overcome her illness, however, and she died at the Saranac Lake sanatorium in September 1908.

11. *The Long Islander*, June 23, 1905. The private beach at Laurelton Hall was a bone of contention with the townspeople of Cold Spring Harbor.

12. *The Long Islander*, July 23, 1898. Edwin S. Marston, who had a house in nearby Bellport, was president of the Farmers' Loan and Trust Company.

13. *The Long Islander*, December 13, 1901.

14. *The Long Islander*, May 31, 1912.

15. *The Long Islander*, May 30, 1913.

16. *The Long Islander*, May 16, 1902. Tiffany was taking another "valuable horse" from the city via steamer in the summer of 1904, an event that was noted in the local paper. When the horse arrived at Eagle Dock in Cold Spring Harbor, no one was there to take it to Laurelton Hall, so a Captain Bingham led the horse. A near collision with an automobile caused the horse to jump, damaging Bingham's buggy but leaving all unharmed. See *The Long Islander*, August 19, 1904.

17. *The Long Islander*, April 24, 1903.

18. Helena Gilder Miller to Hugh F. McKean, February 29, 1978, Archives, Charles Hosmer Morse Museum of American Art, Winter Park, Florida (hereafter Morse Museum).

19. Clara Driscoll, family Round Robin letter, March 8, 1906, collection of Kent State University, Kent, Ohio. I thank Martin Eidelberg and Nina Gray, whose publication on the Driscoll correspondence will be published by the New-York Historical Society in spring 2007, for bringing this reference to my attention.

20. *The Long Islander*, October 18, 1907.

21. "Rich Men" 1911.

22. Ibid.

23. Charles L. Tiffany (New York) to his elder daughter, Annie Olivia Tiffany Mitchell (Sandwich Islands), February 19, 1886, Mitchell-Tiffany Family Papers, Manuscripts and Archives, Yale University Library, group 701, box 7, folder 115.

24. Tiffany's father sent him a box of fireworks when he was ten years old, perhaps starting a lifelong attraction. See Charles L. Tiffany to Annie Olivia Tiffany, June 30, 1858, Mitchell-Tiffany Family Papers, Manuscripts and Archives, Yale University Library, group 701.

25. For an account of some of Stanford White's flamboyant parties, see Baker 1989, pp. 247–51.

26. "Cleopatra" 1913a, p. 1.

27. Tiffany invited Smith to dine on his *dahabeyah* (boat) on his trip up the Nile in 1908. See Smith to his family, February 20, 1908, Joseph Lindon Smith and Smith Family Papers, Letters, Smithsonian Institution Archives of American Art, reels 5114–5124. Smith made extensive trips to Egypt, and later in his life he would become involved in archaeological excavations there with Harvard University and the Museum of Fine Arts, Boston. He was also an artist and a theatrical designer, staging numerous plays and fetes from the late 1890s through the late 1940s.

28. Joseph Lindon Smith to his wife, February 7, 1913, Joseph Lindon Smith and Smith Family Papers, Project file 35, Smithsonian Institution Archives of American Art, reels 5114–5124.

29. Manuscript notes and hieroglyphics by Smith written "to give an idea of the hieroglyphics I shall use" if Tiffany approved. Joseph Lindon Smith and Smith Family Papers, Project file 35, Smithsonian Institution Archives of American Art, reels 5114–5124 (and translated as: "Hail to the—great ones—happy friends [both] men and women . . . saith the lord [mistress] of the throne of the World. Come thou to me and make glad thyself at the sight of my beauty").

30. Ibid. Guests were directed to a Mrs. Sperry, from whom they could procure appropriate costumes and have them fitted. See Katrina E. to Joseph Lindon Smith, January 6, 1913, Joseph Lindon Smith and Smith Family Papers, Letters, Smithsonian Institution Archives of American Art, reels 5114–5124.

31. "Egyptian Fete" 1913.

32. Ibid.

33. At one of Tiffany's earliest parties, a celebration of his father's seventy-fourth birthday in 1886, Tiffany dressed his three children in costume and had them recite a dialogue in German to entertain his guests. See Charles Lewis Tiffany to his daughter Annie Olivia Tiffany Mitchell, February 16, 1886, Mitchell-Tiffany Family Papers, Manuscripts and Archives, Yale University Library, group 701, box 7, folder 115.

34. "Cleopatra" 1913b, p. 29.

35. See engraved admission card for "Mr. & Mrs. J. L. Smith" and engraved notice of the card in Joseph Lindon Smith's pageant files, Joseph Lindon Smith and Smith Family Papers, Project file 35, Smithsonian Institution Archives of American Art, reels 5114–5124.

36. "Cleopatra" 1913a, p. 1.

37. "Egyptian Scenes" 1913.

38. See Katrina E. to Joseph Lindon Smith, January 6, 1913, Joseph Lindon Smith and Smith Family Papers, Letters, Smithsonian Institution Archives of American Art, reels 5114–5124.

39. Joseph Lindon Smith and Smith Family Papers, Project file 35, Smithsonian Institution Archives of American Art, reels 5114–5124.

40. See staging notes for act 2 of the Egyptian Fête, Joseph Lindon Smith and Smith Family Papers, Project file 35, Smithsonian Institution Archives of American Art, reels 5114–5124. These papers contain a detailed account of the entire pageant, including the roles of all the actors and guests.

41. *New York Herald*, January 4, 1913.

42. Many of these press notices were clipped and kept in albums by Tiffany. Among the American papers that carried articles were the *New York American* (February 9, 1913), *The Sun* (New York) (February 9, 1913), *New York Herald* (February 19, 1913), *New York Tribune* (February 5, 9, 1913), *Town and Country* 67 (February 22, 1913), pp. 28–29. In Europe, press coverage appeared in *Sketch Supplement* (London) (February 26, 1913), *Paris Select* (March 2, 1913), *Breslauer Morgan Zeitung* (March 30, 1913), *Femina* (Paris) (April 15, 1913), *Wienese Mode* (June 1, 1913). Tiffany scrapbook, Smithsonian Institution Archives of American Art, lent by Henry Platt.

43. See Joseph Lindon Smith and Smith Family Papers, Project file 35, Smithsonian Institution Archives of American Art, reels 5114–5124. These papers contain details and newspaper clippings related to the Quest of Beauty pageant.

44. Invitation in Tiffany scrapbook, Smithsonian Institution Archives of American Art, lent by Henry Platt.

45. Speenburgh 1956, p. 106.

46. Helena Gilder Miller to Hugh F. McKean, Archives, Morse Museum.

47. "Peacock" 1914b.

48. Transcribed from the menu. The dinner started with soup; the fish course was trout fillet in white wine jelly; then came stuffed suckling pig, poached russet apples, and creamed spinach; sliced duck with orange sauce, steamed new peas, and asparagus with hollandaise sauce; strawberry sorbet; roast peacock; salad of hearts of lettuce; and a dessert of flaming crepes with white currant sauce, followed by cheese.

49. Knickerbocker 1914.

50. Speenburgh 1956, p. 106.

51. *The Long Islander*, May 15, 1914.

52. "Bride" 1914.

53. Ibid.

54. Ibid.

55. Ibid.

56. Ibid.

57. Louise Platt to Hugh F. McKean, May 5, 1966, Archives, Morse Museum.

58. In 1985 the contents of Sarah Hanley's house were auctioned. See Hanley 1985.

59. According to entries in the guest book, people from twenty-nine states and abroad were among those who visited Laurelton Hall from 1918 through 1931. Guest Book, Morse Museum.

60. Comfort T. Gilder, "Evenings at Tower Hall," typescript, n.d., Archives, Morse Museum.

61. *The Long Islander*, June 6, 1916.

62. "Milk Fund" 1919.

63. "Nature League" 1928.

64. Speenburgh 1956, p. 8.

65. Ibid., p. 93.

For the Advancement of Art: The Louis Comfort Tiffany Foundation

Jennifer Perry Thalheimer

When Louis Comfort Tiffany set out to build Laurelton Hall in 1902, he conceived it as a magnificent country estate. But in the final period of his creative evolution, Laurelton was invested with an important new role and purpose. In 1918, at the age of seventy, Tiffany organized the Louis Comfort Tiffany Foundation as both a school that would inspire generations of artists and a museum to preserve his artistic vision. Over the next decade, he modified Laurelton Hall from a private residence to an organization that reflected his interests and his career: "The nature of the institution is an art institute, the objects and purposes of which are art education directed toward both art appreciation and production, within the scope of the industrial as well as the fine arts, and as one means toward those education purposes, the establishment and maintenance of a museum to contain objects of art."[1] Impetus may have come partly from a slowing of his businesses and a general lessening of the appeal of his art. The students and the museum were intended to preserve for posterity his artistic vision and ideals.

Influenced undoubtedly by the late-nineteenth-century migration of artists to the outdoors, to work *en plein air*, Tiffany aimed to create a school for students who might not otherwise leave the city to experience nature on a grand scale (fig. 330). Schools, or colonies, were being established by artists inspired by their studies abroad, particularly in France, and soon spread throughout the northeastern United States. In 1877 William Morris Hunt (1824–1879) started one of the first American art colonies in the village of Magnolia, Massachusetts. Long Island, especially popular because of its quaint fishing villages and natural beauty, became home to many schools, such as the Shinnecock Summer School of Art, opened in 1891 by William Merritt Chase (1849–1916). Artists such as Charles Hawthorne (1872–1930; fig. 331) and Childe Hassam (1859–1935) were experienced participants in these schools and became art advisers to the Tiffany Foundation, during 1923–30 and 1922–33, respectively. Laurelton Hall stood apart

from the other institutions, however, because Tiffany specifically designed—rather than selected—the setting to encourage creativity.

Tiffany's plan for his foundation was "a place where students could . . . find a stimulus in the atmosphere and surroundings of Laurelton, and by the contact with other students and artists."[2] Students, called fellows, were expected to work at their art but not to learn any specific approach. Unlike other guilds and colonies, fellows were not pupils under Tiffany or any other artist. Their experience did not come through intellectual debate, as it did with protégés of William Morris (1834–1896). Nor was Tiffany promoting an ideal such as self-realization through creation. There were no stylistic or formulaic guidelines for the fellows to imitate, as was standard in the Arts and Crafts movement guilds such as Gustav Stickley's (1858–1942) Craftsman Farms and eventually Frank Lloyd Wright's (1867–1959) Taliesin. Instead, exposure to a model environment was the key. A contemporary writer colorfully conveyed the spirit of the foundation: "Greek women . . . lived in the presence of the most perfect marbles in order that they might bring forth offspring with beauty birthmarked in their souls

Fig. 330. Tiffany Foundation fellow Herbert Sanborn carrying an easel stand on the grounds of Laurelton Hall. Photograph, 1928. Courtesy of the Raymond Baxter and Anne Ophelia Todd Dowden papers, 1937–1996, Archives of American Art, Smithsonian Institution

Opposite: Fig. 329. Luigi Lucioni (1900–1988), Detail, *Laurelton Hall*, 1927. Oil on board, 24 x 20 in. (61 x 50.8 cm). The Long Island Museum of American Art, History and Carriages, Stony Brook, New York, Museum Purchase, 1994

Fig. 343. Film still from *The Beggar Maid*, with actor Reginald Denny in Daffodil Terrace, Laurelton Hall, 1921. Courtesy of Jay and Micki Doros and Milestone Film and Video

for the film. Although Tiffany had no part in the production or direction of *The Beggar Maid*, he may have influenced one of the scenes. Near the end of the film, as the nobleman played by Reginald Denny courts the servant girl, he is pictured on the grounds of Laurelton Hall. One can clearly identify the Daffodil Terrace, where he pauses to rest, and Tiffany's ponds and gardens behind him (fig. 343). Laurelton proved to be a setting well suited to cinematographic art.

After Tiffany's death in 1933 the trustees of the foundation continued to operate the artists' residency program at Laurelton. In 1935 they decided to expand the foundation's outreach and opened Laurelton for public viewing, fulfilling Tiffany's dream that his house would serve as a museum. The residence was open two days a week, on Wednesdays and Saturdays, throughout September, with admittance by a ticket obtainable at the foundation offices at Laurelton or from the superintendent of the estate, John E. Terwilliger.[6] Visitors toured the main house, where one of the primary attractions was Tiffany's studio, located on the third floor. The space was reported to be frozen in time, having been left exactly as it was upon Tiffany's death, complete with canvases still on the easels and a collection of portraits, all of which was said to provide an "intimate picture of the man himself."[7] Visitors also toured the art gallery and the Tiffany chapel from the 1893 World's Columbian Exposition, installed at Laurelton after 1916.

Nineteen forty-one was the last year in which artists came to work at Laurelton Hall. The trustees were increasingly concerned that the escalating taxes and maintenance costs for the estate were eroding the endowment's principal and jeopardizing the aims of the foundation.[8] The advent of the Second World War caused

them to postpone a decision on Laurelton's fate, and in 1942, to support the war effort (as well as receive certain monetary benefits), they offered the estate to the Research Committee of the Council of National Defense. The federal government used Laurelton for, among other work, camouflage testing, until 1945.[9] After Laurelton was returned to the foundation at the end of that year, the trustees made the decision—and received permission from the courts—to sell the estate, its furnishings, and its collections and to add the proceeds to the capital funds and distribute the income, in cash grants, to art students for travel and study. The trustees felt that this new approach to "the encouragement and education of art students" would "fulfill Mr. Tiffany's desire to help the student in a much broader and practical way."[10]

The contents of Laurelton Hall were sold at auction at the Parke-Bernet Galleries in New York City, then located at 30 East Fifty-seventh Street. The five-day auction was held from September 24 through September 28, 1946 (fig. 344). The lots included many of Laurelton's furnishings as well as Tiffany's myriad collections, not only of his own work but also of "objects of art of three continents": Native American art, Japanese and Chinese works of art, Near Eastern pottery and tiles, Syrian and Roman glass, Egyptian necklaces, and other antiquities. The auction also featured Tiffany's extensive rug collection, notably sixty-one Oriental rugs, as well as six bearskin and two lion-skin rugs (all mounted with mask and claws) and twenty-two carpets designed and woven by Tiffany Studios.[11] Although only one of the three large blue-and-white medallion carpets made for the dining room at Laurelton survives today (see fig. 159), the descriptions in the Parke-Bernet sale catalogue of the other rugs offer insight into the kind of carpets the Studios were able to make: every technique, from hand-tufted to hooked to broadloom, was represented, and the designs were primarily in the Chinese taste.

The five sessions of the auction yielded a little more than $103,000 in proceeds. Most of the lots were dispersed among a number of individual buyers, dealers, and collectors, and for the most part, the objects' whereabouts today is unknown. Some 1,300 Japanese sword guards from Tiffany's collection of Asian art were sold to a certain J. E. Richards of New York. "The Chinese carved red and gold lacquer octagonal room removed from the residence," the *New York Times* reported, "brought $1,000 from C. R. Gracie, Ltd., New York. . . . A New York collector bought a Ch'ing carved lacquer twelve-fold palace screen for $1,000. A Chinese sculptured stone haut relief with figures of the Buddhistic Trinity went to an agent for $600."[12] (This relief is now thought to be a forgery. See the essay by Julia Meech in this volume.) Higher prices were paid for the paintings in Tiffany's collection. Some of the most costly canvases were by Joaquín Sorolla y Bastida, one of which *(Idilio)* sold for $3,700 and another *(Pabellón de Carlos V, Sevilla)* for $2,400 in the final session of the auction.[13] A pair of Chinese turquoise- and yellow-glazed pottery lions (see figs. 265, 279, 344) went to an agent for $1,850, and an "Ispahan rug of Eastern Persian sixteenth century design" for $2,500 to another.[14] Such prices reveal that in some areas of collecting Tiffany's taste withstood the test of time. Other objects, including the work of Tiffany's studios, had declined in popularity, however, and sold for less even than the studios' asking price. Tiffany's Favrile glass, which by the 1940s had lost its wide appeal, found buyers among the first of the next generation of collectors and dealers. One of these buyers was James A.

Stewart (d. 1967), who worked as a master gaffer at Tiffany's glass furnaces for more than thirty years (see fig. 213).[15] Members of Tiffany's family purchased a variety of works, perhaps for sentimental reasons.

The recent identification of two buyers at the auction, both of whom founded museums, has led to the discovery of works that originally belonged to Tiffany. Florence K. Sloane (1873–1953) purchased a variety of Asian art at the auction for the Hermitage Foundation house museum, in Norfolk, Virginia, which she and her husband, William (1868–1940), founded in 1937 (see figs. 286–288 and the essay by Julia Meech in this volume).[16] Electra Havemeyer Webb (1888–1960) acquired numerous Native American baskets and three beaded miniature baby carriers with dolls, all now in the collection of the Shelburne Museum, in Shelburne, Vermont, which Webb founded in 1947.[17] Unfortunately, these came to light too late to be included in this catalogue.

Although Tiffany's collections were sent to the auction block, the fittings and fixtures remained at the house. All of the specially made lighting fixtures, including the enormous leaded-glass shade in the dining room and the series of emerald green turtleback hanging fixtures in the living hall, stayed at Laurelton Hall. There had been some discussion among the Tiffany Foundation trustees about donating some of Tiffany's extraordinary windows to The Metropolitan Museum of Art and retaining others as the property of the foundation. In the end, however, the windows were deemed to be part of the house, and consequently they, too, were kept from the auction.

When the trustees had voted to sell the contents of the house, they had also approved the liquidation of the property. In 1946

Fig. 344. Viewing of Louis Comfort Tiffany Foundation auction items, Parke-Bernet Galleries showroom, New York, 1946. Courtesy of Getty Images. A Chinese carpet owned by Tiffany (see fig. 267) and the two Chinese ceramic lions (see figs. 265, 279) that stood before the loggia of Laurelton Hall can be identified in the photograph.

they were seeking a buyer for the house, along with most of the acreage, and they even suggested that if a buyer could not be found, the building might be razed.[18] Hobart Nichols (1869–1962), the foundation's director for student affairs, noted that in any case the art gallery and Tiffany's chapel would be retained by the foundation, to form a "nucleus for a permanent memorial to Mr. Tiffany."[19] Ultimately, however, no physical structure at Laurelton was saved to memorialize Tiffany.

The foundation thought it had a potential buyer for the estate in Mary E. Smith, who proposed to use it as a hundred-bed nursing home. The sale made it to contract, but a zoning variance was required to permit its use as a rest home.[20] The village of Laurel Hollow, Laurelton Hall's township at that time, was scheduled to hold a public hearing on the zoning, but it was anticipated that estate owners in the area would protest it, and therefore Mrs. Smith withdrew her offer. Had that sale been successful, Laurelton Hall might still stand today.

In 1948 the foundation finally located a buyer, and in January 1949 the deed to Laurelton Hall was transferred to Thomas J. Hilton, a consulting aviation engineer from La Jolla, California, and his wife, Edith, for ten thousand dollars. The Hiltons spent little time at the house, although they visited during the summers. Another piece of the estate, the carriage house and eleven and a half acres with water frontage, servants' quarters, and a pond with

Old Tiffany Mansion Burns on L. I. North Shore

Firemen pour water on ruins of mansion in Laurel Hollow. Tall structure was a bell tower.

The New York Times

Special to The New York Times.
LAUREL HOLLOW, L. I., March 7—The former Tiffany mansion, one of the palatial landmarks on the Long Island North Shore, was destroyed by a fire that started last night and burned until this afternoon.

It was believed that the turreted fifty-one-year-old show place had been set ablaze by a fire left by vandals in one of the fireplaces.

Two hundred volunteer fire-

men from eight communities fought the fire, which left only smoking ruins of the great house, its stained-glass windows and an organ.

An eight-level structure consisting of eighty-two rooms and twenty-five baths, the house was owned originally by the late Louis Comfort Tiffany of the jewelry firm that bears his name. At one time there were 1,500 acres of woodland and waterfront in the estate. The cost of the

mansion, cobbled courtyard, stables, chapel, art gallery and landscaping was said to have been about $13,000,000.

The structure later housed the Tiffany Art Foundation, which operated a summer school for landscape artists. After the death of Mr. Tiffany in 1933, the estate became a tax liability and the grounds were cut up into plots for smaller homes. The mansion was sold to Mr. and Mrs. Thomas J. Hilton, who are now on the West Coast.

Fig. 346. "Old Tiffany Mansion Burns on L. I. North Shore," *New York Times*, March 8, 1957, p. 27

Fig. 345. Fashion model photographed in living hall, Laurelton Hall, October 1, 1948. Photograph by Horst P. Horst (1906–1999). Courtesy of Horst/ *Vogue.* Copyright ©1948 Condé Nast Publications. Reprinted by permission. All Rights Reserved.

an island and a footbridge, had been sold in 1948 to Estelle and Erwine Laverne, tenants of whom Tiffany would undoubtedly have approved.[21] The Lavernes were a design team who produced sleek and award-winning furniture and other house furnishings, including fabrics and wallpapers, during the middle of the twentieth century. Their attention to all aspects of the design of an interior would have been applauded by Tiffany. In their ample living room in the carriage house, Alexander Calder installed a large mobile in front of the fireplace. Not unlike Tiffany creating his artist-in-residence program, the Lavernes set up what they deemed an "artistic utopia": they converted many of the spaces that had adjoined the original house, including the bowling alley, into studios where they hand-screened their exuberant fabrics, and they invited artists to visit and work there.[22] A reporter reminisced that Erwine Laverne "could paint in a room overlooking the same wisteria-rimmed pond that had inspired Tiffany's most beautiful glass."[23] As artists, the Lavernes were inspired by the beauty that surrounded them, in much the same way that Tiffany had hoped the Tiffany Foundation fellows would be.

Even in its somewhat abandoned state, the main house at Laurelton continued to exert an artistic influence. In 1948 the fashion photographer Horst (1906–1999), then at the beginning of his illustrious career, was intrigued by the house (he lived in the area)

Fig. 347. Hugh F. McKean amid the ruins of Laurelton Hall, 1957. Photograph probably by Jeannette Genius McKean. The Charles Hosmer Morse Museum of American Art, Winter Park, Florida

and selected the living hall, with light entering only from the stained-glass windows, as the romantic setting of a fashion shoot for Condé Nast's *Vogue* magazine, with models adorned in green or blue satin ball gowns (fig. 345).[24] The gowns harmonized with the decor of the room, and the Chinese carpet underfoot (in one of the photographs) and the richly colored windows made for a sumptuous atmosphere.

On March 6, 1957, an enormous conflagration devoured the house (fig. 346). The fire that destroyed this majestic structure burned for nearly twenty-four hours, beginning at 5:00 P.M. and continuing through 4:00 P.M. the next day. The fire was so big that firefighters from eight communities were called to combat the blaze. Rather ironically, given the many wells and fountains that Tiffany had constructed on the property, the firemen were handicapped by a lack of water near the house. They had to extend hose lines some twelve hundred feet, from Long Island Sound to the house. The main house was virtually gutted, but the servants' quarters and the conservatory attached to the house received relatively little damage.[25] Newspaper photographs showed large sections of walls caved in, with "bordering minarets tilting crazily."[26] A reporter wrote: "The huge bells near the top of its eight levels had crashed through the floor of the ballroom."[27] Although the

cause of the fire remains unknown, it was the subject of much speculation. One theory was that Laurelton was set ablaze by a fire left by vandals in one of the fireplaces.[28] At the time of the fire, the Hiltons estimated that the damage totaled half a million dollars.[29]

Tiffany's daughter Comfort Tiffany Gilder, distraught over the destruction, sent a letter on March 16, 1957, to Hugh F. McKean (1908–1995) in Winter Park, Florida, that was to set in motion the salvaging and preservation of almost everything that remained to be saved at Laurelton. In 1930, when he was twenty-two, McKean had been accepted as a Tiffany Foundation fellow at Laurelton Hall (see the essay by Jennifer Perry Thalheimer in this volume). Forever afterward, McKean was a passionate admirer of Tiffany's art, in which he was initially at odds with popular taste. McKean and his wife, Jeannette Genius McKean (1909–1989), met and became friends with members of Tiffany's family, and he maintained a correspondence and friendship with several of them, notably Comfort Gilder.

Comfort wrote disconsolately to McKean of the effects of the fire, saying, "I suppose you saw in the paper that Laurelton Hall burned down."[30] She expressed a guarded hope that all was not lost, however, writing, "I understand that the wisteria, the magnolia and the snow ball windows are still intact," though no one

Fig. 348. Ruins of drive leading under conservatory, originally on property of Laurelton Hall (see fig. 88), in 2006

was allowed into the building at the time.[31] "It's all a sad business to have so much beauty destroyed," she lamented, suggesting that if McKean were interested in acquiring the windows, the owner, Thomas Hilton, might be willing to donate or sell them.[32] During the next few months, McKean tried to contact Hilton, without success, and by the end of May, Comfort despaired, writing, "I'm afraid there is little hope. There's been a cordon around the place. No one is allowed in. The police know nothing. The debris is being carted out by trucks."[33] By mid-September, however, McKean had apparently negotiated the acquisition of a number of salvageable items from Laurelton.[34] The visit that he and his wife made to the site must have been heartbreaking for McKean (fig. 347). Bits and pieces of stained-glass windows (see fig. 341), floral capitals, and other furnishings were strewn about. McKean discovered a muddied border panel of the *Four Seasons* window leaning against a tree.[35]

That window and many others, as well as various architectural elements, were saved by the McKeans and added to the collection of the Charles Hosmer Morse Museum of American Art, in Winter Park, Florida, which Jeannette McKean had founded in 1942, with Hugh McKean as its first director. The couple had begun collecting the work of Tiffany for public display when Hugh McKean was director of the art gallery at Rollins College, in Winter Park,

where he began his career as a professor of art. Their collection continued to grow and was exhibited at the art gallery when McKean was president of the college, from 1951 to 1969. This collection was ultimately the basis of the Morse Museum. The McKeans displayed many of the windows, vases, and architectural fragments from Laurelton Hall there, while other items remained in crates until such time as conservation could be undertaken. Tiffany's chapel from the World's Columbian Exposition of 1893, which was once on the Laurelton property (see fig. 112), has been completely reconstructed by the Morse Museum. The most recent work undertaken by the Morse Museum, prompted by this exhibition, addresses the restoration of the complete Daffodil Terrace (see fig. 79) and the marble-and-mosaic chimneybreast from the dining room (see fig. 155).

Perhaps the most impressive surviving element of Laurelton Hall is its four-column loggia (see figs. 82, 107). In 1978 Hugh and Jeannette McKean donated the loggia to the Metropolitan Museum, recognizing that in New York the loggia would be seen by a large public. Conservators spent more than a year assembling the surviving pieces and readying the loggia for installation in a new wing then under construction. The loggia has graced the southern end of The Charles Engelhard Court in The American Wing since 1980.

Today, Laurelton Hall's Moorish-style minaret, the only intact structure, with its shimmering iridescent blue glass ornamentation (see fig. 91), stands overlooking Cold Spring Harbor. The few fragmentary remains on the site of Laurelton Hall (fig. 348) poignantly evoke what was. The house and grounds of Laurelton Hall were an expression of Tiffany's artistic beliefs and aspirations. The estate encapsulated his concept of unified interiors as works of art; demonstrated his love of color, light, and glass in its many forms; represented, through his lamps, vases, pottery, enamels, and windows, the many media in which he worked. In its extravagance Laurelton Hall captured the essence of Tiffany the artist. Elizabeth Kunz, the young daughter of the Tiffany and Company gemologist George Kunz, described the lasting magic of the estate when she wrote in the Laurelton Hall guest book (see fig. 328), in 1916, "Arabian nights' dreams vanish, at Laurelton a phantom has become in reality, eternal."[36] Though destroyed, Laurelton Hall remains a testament to Louis Comfort Tiffany's originality and creative genius.

1. "Lorenzo" 1931, p. 27.
2. See the essay by Jennifer Perry Thalheimer in this volume.
3. De Kay 1920, p. LXXX.
4. Francis C. Jones, quoted in "Movies" 1921. A number of other films were completed, including *The Young Painter* (1922), based on a painting by Rembrandt, and *Hope* (1922), based on a painting by the Pre-Raphaelite painter George F. Watts.
5. See "Screen" 1921. The film was a Triart Picture Company production, distributed by Paramount Pictures Corporation, produced by Lejaran A. (Lajeren à) Hiller and Isaac Wolpe, with scenario by Reginald Denny, who also played the part of the earl. It was directed by Herbert Blaché. Art direction and cinematography were by Lejaran A. (Lajeren à) Hiller. It was released on September 25, 1921. See "Progressive Silent Film List," www.silentera.com/PSFL/data/B/BeggarMaid1921.html. I thank Dennis Doros for generously lending his copy of *The Beggar Maid* and for his insights on it.
6. "Home Opened" 1935. Tiffany had agreed in 1918 to allow visitors at Laurelton.
7. Ibid.
8. Just a few years earlier, in 1936, what was left of the Tiffany Studios was sold at auction, and the building demolished. In 1939 the Seventy-second Street house was razed.
9. Hobart Nichols, "Prefatory Note," in Parke-Bernet 1946, n.p. Nichols was also an artist and vice president of the National Academy of Design in New York.
10. Ibid.
11. Parke-Bernet 1946, lots 204–223.
12. "Art Sale" 1946. The C. R. Gracie firm was founded in 1898 by Charles R. Gracie and remains active today, specializing in hand-painted wallpaper. During the 1920s its business included Asian antiques.
13. "Painting" 1946.
14. Ibid.
15. Stewart, who had worked as a gaffer from February 11, 1895, until 1928 (see Koch 2001, p. 188), purchased five lots at the 1946 auction. See Parke-Bernet 1946, Results. I thank William J. Stahl Jr., Vice Chairman, Sotheby's North and South America, and his assistant, Catherine Torrey Stroud, for their generous assistance in determining a number of the buyers at the 1946 sale.
16. I am grateful to Julia Meech for bringing the Hermitage Foundation objects to our attention, and I thank Kristin C. Law, Curator of the Hermitage Foundation, for generously sharing with us the objects and her knowledge of them.
17. I am grateful to many on the staff of the Shelburne Museum for help in identifying and making available these objects and related documentation. In particular, I thank Jean Burks, Senior Curator, and Barbara Rathburn, Associate Registrar.
18. "Tiffany Home" 1946.
19. Ibid.
20. "Rest Home" 1947.
21. Salkaln 2004, p. 50.
22. Ibid.
23. Ibid.
24. I am grateful to Lou Gartner, Palm Beach, Florida, who was an assistant on this shoot, for bringing this to my attention and for an unpublished image of a model in a green gown standing behind a Chinese carpet.
25. The servants' wing was destroyed by another fire at Laurelton, in the summer of 1957. See Mrs. Rodman Gilder (Comfort Tiffany Gilder), Oyster Bay, to Hugh F. McKean, Winter Park, Florida, August 18, 1957, Archives, Charles Hosmer Morse Museum of American Art (hereafter Morse Museum).
26. "Fire" 1957c.
27. Ibid.
28. "Tiffany Mansion" 1957.
29. "Fire" 1957c.
30. Mrs. Rodman Gilder (Comfort Tiffany Gilder), New York, to Hugh F. McKean, Winter Park, Florida, March 16, 1957, Archives, Morse Museum.
31. Ibid.
32. Ibid.
33. Mrs. Rodman Gilder to Hugh F. McKean, May 28, 1957, Archives, Morse Museum.
34. Comfort Gilder wrote to Hugh McKean saying that it was "thrilling you've got those things at Laurelton, especially the daffodil columns and the wisteria window." Mrs. Rodman Gilder to Hugh F. McKean, September 15, 1957, Archives, Morse Museum.
35. See "Four Seasons," pamphlet, fall 2001, Archives, Morse Museum.
36. Guest book, Laurelton Hall, June 4, 1916, Morse Museum.

Chronology

Barbara Veith

1837

September 18 Charles Lewis Tiffany (hereafter CLT; 1812–1902) and John B. Young establish a fancy dry goods firm, Tiffany and Young, 259 Broadway, New York

1841

November 30 CLT marries Harriet Olivia Avery Young (1817–1897), sister of his partner John Young

Tiffany and Young's name is changed to Tiffany, Young, and Ellis, located at 259-260 Broadway

1848

February 18 Louis Comfort Tiffany (hereafter LCT; d. 1933) is born in New York to Harriet and CLT, their third child and second son; their other children are Charles Lewis Jr. (1842–1847), Annie Olivia (1844–1937), Louise Harriet (1856–1937), Henry Charles (1858–1859), Burnett Young (1860–?)

Tiffany, Young, and Ellis is now at 271 Broadway

1853

May 1 CLT assumes control of his business and renames it Tiffany and Company. By May 1, 1854, it has relocated to 550-552 Broadway

By 1860

Tiffany family moves to 255 Madison Avenue

1862–63

LCT attends Pennsylvania Military Academy, West Chester

1863–65

LCT attends Eagleswood Military Academy in Perth Amboy, N.J., until June 1865; there he studies under tonalist landscape painter George Inness (1825–1894)

Ca. 1865

CLT purchases a house and property in Irvington, New York

1865–66

November 1 LCT makes his first trip to Europe (financed by CLT), traveling to England, Ireland, France, and Italy, and sketches the places he visits, including Paris, Rome, Naples, Sorrento, and Florence; he returns to New York on March 21, 1866

1866

November 5 LCT is admitted to antique classes at the National Academy of Design for the 1866–67 academic year. He meets Samuel Colman (1832–1920), an instructor at the National Academy, a landscape painter, and a founder of the American Society of Painters in Water Colors (in 1878 the name changes to American Water Color Society), of which LCT becomes a member in 1870

1867

LCT first exhibits at the National Academy of Design; the work is *Afternoon*. He exhibits work at the National Academy annual exhibitions in 1867–75, 1877–81, 1883, 1888–92

1868–69

LCT travels to Paris to study with Léon-Charles Adrien Bailly (b. 1826); meets painter Léon-Adolphe-Auguste Belly (1827–1877), who specializes in Islamic genre scenes

1869

LCT lives in a studio in the Association Building (YMCA), 52 East 23rd Street at 4th Avenue, across from the National Academy of Design; also there are painters Edwin Austin Abbey (1852–1911), Robert Swain Gifford (1840–1905), and William Sartain (1843–1924). LCT retains a studio there until 1878

1870

July–February 1871 LCT and Gifford travel to London, Paris, Madrid, Málaga, Gibraltar, Tangier, Malta, Sicily, Naples, Amalfi, Sorrento, Alexandria, Cairo, Tunisia, Algeria, Rome, and Florence; they exhibit work from this trip in the YMCA building reception room in January 1872 and at the National Academy of Design in April 1872

Fall Tiffany and Company relocates to the corner of Union Square and 15th Street

LCT is elected to the Century Club, the youngest member to be admitted

1871

LCT is elected an Associate of the National Academy of Design

Oyster Bay, Long Island, property that will be the site of Laurelton Hall, owned by Oliver H. Jones, president of the New York Fire Insurance Company, is bequeathed to Dr. Oliver L. Jones, who will establish a summer resort called Laurelton

1872

May 15 LCT marries Mary (May) Woodbridge Goddard (1846–1884) in Norwich, Conn.; they live in CLT's home at 255 Madison Avenue

November Oliver L. Jones breaks ground for the hundred-room Hotel Laurelton

1873

April 3 Mary (May-May) Woodbridge Tiffany [Lusk] (d. 1963) is born in New York to Mary and LCT

June Hotel Laurelton opens

1874

April–December LCT and family travel to France; in May they are in Paris with Samuel Colman and his wife. LCT and Mary travel south to Menton on the Côte d'Azur, where Charles Louis Tiffany is born on December 9; he dies on December 29

1875–76

Winter LCT and Mary travel to North Africa

1875–77

LCT works at Thill's Empire State Flint Glass Works, Brooklyn; he develops drapery glass

1876

May–November LCT exhibits three oil paintings and six watercolors at the Centennial Exhibition in Philadelphia

1877

May Samuel Colman persuades LCT to participate in the Society of Decorative Art, along with textile artist Candace Wheeler (1827–1923), founder and corresponding secretary, and Lockwood de Forest (1850–1932); Colman, LCT, and de Forest are on the committee on design and teach classes at the society

LCT is elected a member of the Society of American Artists and serves as its first treasurer

1878

January 7 Charles Lewis Tiffany II (d. 1947) is born in New York to Mary and LCT

May–November LCT exhibits an oil painting and two watercolors at the Paris Exposition Universelle

After May LCT moves into the newly completed Bella apartment building at 48 East 26th Street; he relinquishes the studio at the YMCA

June 18 Louis C. Tiffany and Company is formed; its address is listed as Bella Apartments, 48 East 26th Street

Louis C. Tiffany and Company opens its first glasshouse under the supervision of Andrea Boldini of Venice; it burns, as will the second attempt a short time later

1879

August 24 Hilda Goddard Tiffany (d. 1908) is born to Mary and LCT

End of 1879 or beginning of 1880 LCT organizes with Candace Wheeler the interior decorating firm Tiffany and Wheeler, specializing in embroideries, underwritten by CLT, at 335 4th Avenue, adjacent to Colman's studio at 337 4th Avenue

1880

After November 11 Lockwood de Forest departs on a two-month honeymoon trip to India that extends to a year and a half, during which he establishes a woodworking shop in Ahmadabad and purchases carved teakwood panels and architectural elements for LCT

By the end of 1880 LCT directs three different firms from 373 4th Avenue: L. C. Tiffany and Company, Furniture; Tiffany and Wheeler, Embroideries; and, with Lockwood de Forest, Tiffany and de Forest, Decorators. Samuel Colman works with Tiffany and Wheeler as an independent artist in LCT's hire

LCT experiments at the Heidt Glass Furnace, Brooklyn, where John La Farge (1835–1910) is also working; LCT will continue there until 1893

1881

February 8 LCT is granted three patents: no. 237,416 for a new background surface for opalescent glass tiles to add brilliance and iridescence; no. 237,417 for a process of plating a mosaic of opalescent glass with colored glass, leaving an air space between; no. 237,418 for a process of improving the metallic luster as it is being given to one surface of a window or mosaic

March 26 LCT makes an agreement with Louis Heidt of the Heidt Glass Furnace, Brooklyn, to obtain opalescent glass for windows for the firm Louis C. Tiffany and Company, 333 4th Avenue, New York

May 8 LCT is made an Academician of the National Academy of Design

June 7 LCT is elected to the board of directors of Tiffany and Company

June 9–15 Tiffany and Wheeler and Louis C. Tiffany and Company merge to form Louis C. Tiffany and Company, Associated Artists, 333-335 4th Avenue; LCT is the head of the business and William Pringle Mitchell is a major partner and general manager. Candace Wheeler is in charge of the Embroidery Department, which moves to 115 East 23rd Street by November

1882

February 28 LCT applies for a patent for "useful improvements in colored-glass windows," which is granted as patent no. 254,409

By March Lockwood de Forest, still traveling in India, secures an entire house that was set for destruction in Ahmadabad; the facade goes to the Victoria and Albert Museum in London and the rest is intended for the CLT house being planned at 72nd Street. In June, de Forest purchases 2,500 Japanese sword guards in Paris

April CLT plans to build two houses on the northwest corner of Madison Avenue and 72nd Street, one to be occupied by three families and the other by one. CLT will occupy the first two floors of the larger house; his daughter, the third; and the top floor, under the peaked roof, will be used by LCT for his studio and other rooms. The architects will be McKim, Mead, and White

November 29 LCT terminates his partnership with Lockwood de Forest and acquires the sword guards de Forest purchased in Paris

December 12 Lockwood de Forest places an order with the Ahmadabad workshop on behalf of LCT for a teakwood door and mantel for an apartment he is planning in one of CLT's houses on 72nd Street

1883

April 28 Louis C. Tiffany and Company, Associated Artists, comes to an end, and LCT continues the business as Louis C. Tiffany and Company, 333-335 4th Avenue

1884

January 22 Mary (May) Woodbridge Goddard Tiffany (LCT's wife) dies

1885

October 1 The 72nd Street house is completed. It has a basement of large blocks of rough-faced bluestone; its exterior is faced with tawny brick made from Perth Amboy, N.J., clay; ornamentation is terracotta of the same clay; and the roof is covered with very dark corrugated tiles. CLT never lives in this house; his apartment is rented to financier Henry Villard in January 1887

December 1 Louis C. Tiffany and Company is dissolved, bankrupted by losses on the Lyceum Theatre in New York, a project commissioned in January 1885 by impresario Steele MacKaye, a former Eagleswood classmate of LCT. This is the first theater to utilize electricity for overhead fixtures and the stage. LCT incorporates his firm as the Tiffany Glass Company, 333-335 4th Avenue

LCT and family move from the Bella apartment to an apartment in the 72nd Street house

1886

November 9 LCT marries Louise Wakeman Knox (1851–1904), also a painter and a friend of Robert W. de Forest, older brother of Lockwood de Forest

1887

August Tiffany Glass Company, 333-335 4th Avenue, has facilities for designing and executing interior decorative works in a variety of media and techniques, including painting and fresco, papering, fabrics, relief ornament, leather, metal, interior woodwork, stained and leaded glass, glass tiles, and mosaic facings and floorings

September 24 Twins Louise Comfort Tiffany [Gilder] (d. 1974) and Julia de Forest Tiffany [Parker; Weld] (d. 1973) are born in New York to Louise and LCT

1888
October LCT plans to build a large house on Laurelton Road in Oyster Bay and hires Hewlett T. Long of Huntington as the builder. The house will be known as the Briars

December 29 Annie Olivia Tiffany (d. 1892) is born in New York to Louise and LCT

1889
September The Briars is ready for occupancy

LCT travels to Paris; visits Émile Gallé's glass factory in Nancy

LCT becomes a member of the Architectural League of New York

1891
October 11 Dorothy Trimble Tiffany [Burlingham] (d. 1979) is born to Louise and LCT

November 30 CLT and Harriet celebrate their fiftieth wedding anniversary at the 72nd Street house; LCT presents them with a *Cornucopia* window (Mark Twain House, Hartford, Conn.)

LCT designs and builds a six-story factory/studio building at 102 East 25th Street, next to the buildings he owns at 25th Street and 4th Avenue

1892
February 18 LCT reestablishes Tiffany Glass Company as Tiffany Glass and Decorating Company, 333 4th Avenue, incorporated in New Jersey; all directors of the old company transfer to the new company. The firm also has a studio at 110 East 23rd Street

April 24 Annie Olivia Tiffany (LCT and Louise's daughter) dies of scarlet fever at age three

By late 1892–early 1893 LCT acquires a three-story building at 43rd Avenue and 97th Place in Corona, Queens, and transforms it into his own glass furnace, where workers make blown Favrile-glass vases under superintendent Arthur J. Nash (1849–1934)

1893
April 7 LCT separates the glass production facility in Corona from Tiffany Glass and Decorating Company and calls it Stourbridge Glass Company, supervised by Arthur J. Nash

May 1–October 31 At the World's Columbian Exposition in Chicago, the Tiffany Glass and Decorating Company is awarded fifty-four medals; the firm's display includes a decorated light room, a decorated dark room, a chapel designed by LCT, and his first domestic windows including *Feeding the Flamingoes*

July LCT's essay "American Art Supreme in Colored Glass," discussing the history of stained-glass window making and its revival in America, is published in the *Forum* (15 [July 1893], pp. 621–28)

October 28 The Stourbridge Glass Company manufactory in Corona is destroyed by fire; the firm is uninsured and estimates its loss at about $20,000; loans from CLT help to rebuild it

1894
February The chapel, from the 1893 World's Columbian Exposition in Chicago, is displayed at Tiffany Glass and Decorating Company, 333 4th Avenue

February–April Siegfried Bing, owner of the gallery L'Art Nouveau, 22 rue de Provence, Paris, visits Tiffany Glass and Decorating Company in New York. Bing will become LCT's exclusive distributor in Europe

April 25 Opening of the Salon of the Société Nationale des Beaux-Arts, Paris; work by LCT is exhibited; in June he is elected an associate member of the Société Nationale des Beaux-Arts

July LCT displays Favrile glass in the Tiffany Glass and Decorating Company showroom

November 13 LCT registers "Favrile" as a trademark with the U.S. patent office, no. 25,512

1895
An apartment in the 72nd Street house is purchased by Louis Cass Ledyard (d. 1932), a lawyer

April LCT exhibits twenty examples of Favrile glass and a series of windows made from designs by Henri de Toulouse-Lautrec, Edouard Vuillard, Pierre Bonnard, Eugène Grasset, Henri-Gabriel Ibels, Paul-Elie Ranson, Ker-Xavier Roussel, Paul Sérusier, and Félix Vallotton at the Salon of the Société Nationale des Beaux Arts

May LCT has a well dug at the Briars; finds water at 150 feet

November LCT has a roof put on the tower of the windmill at the Briars

December 26 The inaugural exhibition at Siegfried Bing's gallery, entitled "Le Salon de l'Art Nouveau," includes LCT windows and twenty pieces of Favrile glass

1896
December 8 Henry Osborne and Louisine Havemeyer, LCT's most ardent patrons whose celebrated house he had redecorated by 1892, donate their collection of over forty pieces of Favrile glass to the Metropolitan Museum (96.17.4, .5, .9–.13, .15–.19, .21, .22, .24, .26–.39, .41–.46, .48–.56)

1897
February–June LCT extensively renovates the Briars, which is ready in time for his family to move in for the summer season

Summer Bing organizes an exhibition of LCT's Favrile glass at L'Art Nouveau in Paris

November 16 Harriet Olivia Avery Young Tiffany (LCT's mother) dies

LCT organizes foundry and metal shops at the factory in Corona; the first small metalwork objects are manufactured

1898
March 25 Tiffany Glass and Decorating Company, 333-335 4th Avenue, acquires Schmitt Brothers Furniture Company, for the "manufacture and sale of furniture, bric-a-brac, objects of art, interior woodwork, curtains, draperies, upholsteries and other articles and materials for interior furnishing and decorating."

The chapel is installed in the crypt of the Cathedral Church of Saint John the Divine in New York, which will open for services on January 8, 1899; it will remain there until September 1916. It is a gift to the cathedral from Mrs. Celia Hermoine Wallace as a memorial to her four-year-old son

LCT experiments with enamelware

1899
May–July LCT's work, including blown Favrile glass, windows, mosaics, cartoons and sketches, lamps, and metalwork, is in the exhibition organized by Siegfried Bing at Grafton Galleries, London

June 17 Telephone service is established for residents, including LCT and others, between the village of Laurel Hollow and the area of the Laurelton Hotel

December 20 Mary (May-May) Woodbridge Tiffany (LCT and Mary's daughter) marries Dr. Graham Lusk, professor of physiology at Bellevue Medical College

1900
April 2 Allied Arts Company, 333-335 4th Avenue, formerly Tiffany Glass and Decorating Company, is incorporated; until November 18, 1902, the firm markets objects under the name Tiffany Studios

April–November At the Exposition Universelle in Paris, LCT exhibits Favrile glass, windows, lamps, mosaics, and enamels in a gallery adjacent to the one occupied by Tiffany and Company; LCT and Arthur J. Nash are awarded grand prizes for applied arts; LCT is appointed a Chevalier of the Legion of Honor

November Stourbridge Glass Company factory in Corona is to be enlarged

LCT experiments with pottery production

1901
January Under LCT's direction, Allied Arts Company is to build a new plant for manufacturing decorative art metal in Corona, across the street from the Stourbridge Glass Company

May–November LCT wins a grand prize at the Pan-American Exposition in Buffalo, N.Y., where he exhibits an electric fountain in the grand court of the Manufacturers and Fine Arts Building. He also wins prizes at international expositions in Dresden and Saint Petersburg

June 4 Charles Lewis Tiffany (LCT and Mary's son) marries Katrina Ely

July LCT purchases a tract of land on the road from Cold Spring Harbor to Laurelton Hotel from Susan D. Brightson for $15,077. He constructs a private carriage road through the property to Oyster Bay Road

July 23 Eastern Arts Company, which is formed to buy, sell, import, export, and manufacture works of art and merchandise, is incorporated. It will merge with Tiffany Studios in 1909

LCT is elected third vice president of the Tiffany and Company board of directors

1902
January H. J. Dubois digs a well for LCT at the Briars on the high ground near the newly built road; by April the well is 186 feet deep and has reached water

February 18 CLT dies; he is buried in Greenwood Cemetery, Brooklyn; he leaves LCT about $3 million and a controlling interest in Tiffany and Company

February 25 Tiffany Studios, 333-341 4th Avenue, is incorporated (to April 16, 1932)

March 22 Tiffany and Company's board names Charles T. Cook as president and LCT as first vice president; LCT works in conjunction with Paulding Farnham as co-art director of Tiffany and Company

April LCT remodels and redecorates the Briars

April–November LCT receives a grand prize and special diploma from the art jury of the Esposizione Internazionale d'Arte Decorativa Moderna, Turin

August Charles A. Peabody, of the law firm Baker and Peabody in New York, acting as agent for LCT, purchases from Oliver L. Jones the resort Laurelton Hotel and forty acres plus a pier, and the residence of Dr. James R. Wood with seventeen acres in Oyster Bay, on the west side of Cold Spring Harbor

September LCT offers to buy the 72nd Street house from the executors of CLT's estate for $665,000

September 29 Stourbridge Glass Company is renamed Tiffany Furnaces

November 18 Allied Arts Company is consolidated with Tiffany Studios

Tiffany Jewelry Department is established in a small workshop at the 23rd Street studio of Tiffany Studios

1903
March LCT now owns Laurelton; the Iron Steamboat Company, which transports visitors from Manhattan and Brooklyn daily, has a lease on the Laurelton property for one more year; the proprietor is Skoien. LCT also owns the Haywood residence formerly owned by L. C. Bell

April Painters and decorators refurbish the Briars. At Laurelton, a cellar is being excavated for a large mansion that LCT has contracted architect Robert L. Pryor to design and C. T. Wills to build

June LCT is awarded an honorary Master of Arts degree by Yale University

July Proprietor Skoein sells LCT the lease for Laurelton and moves out

By October LCT has had a six-inch driven well put down in his new house and has two additional flowing wells, one six inches and one eight inches, to feed a pond from opposite sides

Electricity is extended to the Laurelton property from Lloyd's Neck; LCT already has electricity at the Briars

November LCT has another eight-inch well dug at Laurelton

November 21 LCT applies to the town board of Oyster Bay to close a public roadway through his Laurelton property so he can improve the part of his estate through which it passes; he will replace it with a wider road some distance away. He is opposed by Oliver L. Jones and a coalition of farmers, who say it will take longer to reach the shore and they will no longer have shore access. LCT will be granted this right

Winter Louise becomes ill while at the Briars, spends terminal illness there

LCT moves the enamel operations from Manhattan to Tiffany Furnaces in Corona

LCT introduces Favrile pottery

1904
January–February Work continues on LCT's mansion at Laurelton. It is nearly two hundred feet in length; it has a large clock tower with four bells for chimes and an elevator; and there is a subway to transport tradespeople from the gate to the house so that only LCT and his guests use the drives

April–December LCT wins a gold medal at the Louisiana Purchase International Exposition in Saint Louis; this is the first year he exhibits his own jewelry designs

May LCT has electricity at Laurelton Hall; in March, the Huntington Light and Power Company attempted more than once to erect poles to carry the wires; these were cut down, possibly by Oliver L. Jones, who resented the closing of the road on LCT's property the previous November

May 9 Louise Wakeman Knox Tiffany (LCT's second wife) dies of cancer at the 72nd Street house

June LCT begins work on a one-acre lake near Laurelton Hall

August Bell chimes at Laurelton can be heard in the village of Huntington

1905
January 26 LCT purchases three gold lacquer boxes, two Japanese and one Chinese, at auction at the American Art Galleries

February 6 LCT applies to the commissioners of the Land Office in Albany for a grant of twenty-two acres of land underwater in Cold Spring Harbor on which he intends to build docks and boat- and bathhouses. Residents of Oyster Bay object on the grounds that it will deprive them of their long-standing right to boat, fish, and swim

June LCT has an old schooner formerly owned by Oliver L. Jones dragged onshore at Laurelton and remodeled as a bathhouse

July LCT has a new driveway cut through his woods to connect with the Oyster Bay Cove Road, thus giving him a shorter route to the train station in Oyster Bay

October LCT and children have moved into Laurelton Hall

By October 21 Tiffany Studios showrooms have moved from 4th Avenue and 25th Street to the former Knickerbocker Building at 347 Madison Avenue at 45th Street

December The stables at Laurelton are enclosed so that workmen can continue to work on them through the winter. LCT has a car and a French chauffeur

LCT builds a ninety-foot tower topped by a twenty-four-foot windmill over an eight-inch well near Laurelton Hall

1906
February LCT entertains a large group of friends at Laurelton Hall over Lincoln's Birthday

March Work on LCT's barns progresses. LCT has two houses on his property stuccoed, the Wood house and the Daniel F. Young house at Oyster Bay Cove

July LCT posts "No Trespassing" signs on his property to discourage picnickers

August Stone walls belonging to LCT and piers belonging to Mrs. J. West Roosevelt, George C. Maxwell, and Frederic R. Coudert are destroyed by the highway commissioners of Oyster Bay because they are on a public road. On August 3, LCT is stopped by Constable MacQuade, who serves him restraining papers issued by the town board of Oyster Bay that forbid him to rebuild the walls on the beach. LCT hires security officers to keep trespassers off his beach. The question of who owns this shorefront is taken to the New York State Court of Appeals

LCT's Laurelton Hall property is assessed at $199,500 by the town of Oyster Bay

December 20 LCT hosts a tea and sale in the studio of his 72nd Street house to benefit the New York Infirmary for Women and Children, a charity on whose board his deceased wife Louise had served. During the same week LCT holds another benefit for the New York Infirmary in the studio, to which he invites the Calvary Church choir to sing Christmas carols

1907
February 15 The board of directors of Tiffany and Company elects John C. Moore II (grandson and son of Tiffany silversmiths John C. Moore and Edward C. Moore) as president and LCT as first vice president and assistant treasurer

February 19 Schmitt Brothers Furniture Company address changes to 40 East 23rd Street

Between April 1 and May 3 LCT assumes the role of Tiffany and Company's chief jewelry designer and moves his art jewelry production from Tiffany Studios to Tiffany and Company, 5th Avenue and 37th Street

April–December LCT exhibits at the Jamestown Exposition in Virginia; he is awarded a gold medal

May 29 Schmitt Brothers Furniture Company name changes to Tiffany Studios and then changes back to Schmitt Brothers on August 29

August Laurelton Hall sewer system is installed by Warren, Chapman and Farquahar

Fall LCT serves as patron and gives technical training in design, jewelry making, and art metalwork at the New York Evening High School for Men, 59th Street and 10th Avenue. He creates bronze and gold Louis C. Tiffany medals for the advancement of arts and crafts

1908
January–February LCT and his daughters go to Egypt; they travel up the Nile in a private *dahabeyah*; between Luxor and Aswan, Joseph Lindon Smith (1863–1950) is a dinner guest on the boat

Easter LCT, accompanied by his daughter Dorothy, is at Saranac Lake to be with his sick daughter Hilda

April 25–28 The Oyster Bay town board orders the concrete jetties on LCT's beach removed; LCT secures a temporary injunction from Nassau Supreme Court Justice Townsend Scudder restraining the highway commissioners from doing this

May Lockwood de Forest transfers his contract with the Ahmadabad workshop to Tiffany Studios and sells his stock of Indian carving

September 14 Hilda Goddard Tiffany (LCT and Mary's daughter) dies at Saranac Lake sanatorium

December LCT secures a permanent injunction from Judge Marean of the Supreme Court of the County of Nassau in Mineola barring the town of Oyster Bay from removing the stone wall, dock, and jetties from his beach

Tiffany Studios introduces bronze pottery

LCT hires Leslie H. Nash (1884–1958), Arthur Nash's son, to work at Tiffany Furnaces, where he will become production manager

1908–9
Laurelton Hall's farm buildings, designed by Alfred Hopkins (1870–1941), include a dairy, yards for cattle and sheep, workmen's rooms, machinery and tool rooms, and a dovecote

1909
March LCT hires Janes and Leo, architects, to remodel 898 Madison Avenue, adjoining the 72nd Street house, enlarging it from a five-story residence to an eight-story apartment building, installing new windows, and fireproofing it, but retaining its facade

June–October LCT exhibits work in the Alaska-Yukon-Pacific Exposition in Seattle; he is awarded a grand prize

December 1 Tiffany Studios and Eastern Arts Company consolidate

1910
LCT is ill; Sarah Eileen (Patsy) Hanley and two other nurses are employed

July 4 LCT, Walter Jennings, former president Theodore Roosevelt, and others put on a fireworks display at Oyster Bay

October LCT gives a lecture, "The Decorative Aspects of Illuminating Engineering," at the fourth annual convention of the Illuminating Engineering Society in Baltimore

November LCT's article "The Gospel of Good Taste" is published in *Country Life in America*; in it he extols the virtues of simplicity and beauty and states that beauty in the home has nothing to do with wealth or extravagance

December 10 Julia de Forest Tiffany (LCT and Louise's daughter) marries Gurdon S. Parker, an architect and son of Mr. and Mrs. Henry W. Parker of Boston, at the 72nd Street house; LCT had announced Julia's engagement in May

December 30 Appellate Division of the Supreme Court of Nassau County rules against 17th-century colonial patents that ensured Oyster Bay town rights to land under Cold Spring Harbor and in favor of LCT's right to build a stone wall, bathhouse, and boathouse on his property

LCT travels to Seattle

1911
January 20 LCT hosts a small, informal dance in honor of his daughter Dorothy, a debutante, at the 72nd Street house

April LCT's article "The Tasteful Use of Light: Color in Artificial Illumination" is published in *Scientific American* (104 [April 15, 1911], p. 373)

April 20 Louise Comfort Tiffany (LCT and Louise's daughter) marries Rodman de Kay Gilder, Harvard graduate employed in the electrical business and son of the late Richard Watson Gilder, at the 72nd Street house; LCT had announced Comfort's engagement in March

May Portrait of LCT is painted by Spanish artist Joaquín Sorolla y Bastida (1863–1923) in the gardens of Laurelton Hall

1912
May LCT's fleet of yachts is prepared for Seawanhaka Corinthian Yacht Club Decoration Day races by Capt. Frank Charleston

1913
February 4 (Shrove Tuesday) LCT hosts his Egyptian Fête of the time of Cleopatra for some three hundred guests at the Tiffany Studios showroom (rug room), 345 Madison Avenue

May LCT has the harbor in front of Laurelton Hall dredged to make it deep enough for large yachts to anchor near the shore

June The New York State Court of Appeals in Albany unanimously reverses the December 30, 1910, decision of the Appellate Division of the Supreme Court of Nassau County in favor of LCT in his case against Oyster Bay, disputing ownership of a half-mile stretch of beachfront property

1914
Friday, May 15 LCT hosts his Artist's Reception, the "Peacock Feast," to view the spring flowers at Laurelton Hall

September 24 Dorothy Trimble Tiffany (LCT and Louise's daughter) marries Dr. Robert Burlingham, Harvard graduate and house surgeon at Roosevelt Hospital, and son of Mr. and Mrs. Charles C. Burlingham; the wedding breakfast is held at Laurelton Hall. LCT had announced Dorothy's engagement in July

November The completed *Bathers* window is displayed at Tiffany Studios before it is to be sent to the Panama Pacific International Exposition in San Francisco in 1915 and its eventual installation at Laurelton Hall

December LCT decides that *The Bathers* window will not be exhibited at the exposition in San Francisco because the lighting there will not be satisfactory

The Art Work of Louis C. Tiffany, commissioned in 1912 and ghostwritten by Charles de Kay, is published by Doubleday, Page and Company in an edition of 492, with an additional ten printed on vellum and bound in a bronze cover designed by LCT; it is distributed to family, friends, Tiffany Studios employees, museums, and libraries

Tiffany Granite Quarries, Cohasset, Mass., opens

Ca. 1914
Daffodil Terrace is added to Laurelton Hall

1915
January The Bathers window is installed at Laurelton Hall

March–May LCT travels on his private railroad car, Columbia, with George F. Heydt (1861–1953) to Chicago, then transfers to the Atchison, Topeka and Santa Fe Railway. They make stops in Kansas, Colorado, New Mexico, Arizona, including the Grand Canyon, and California; they visit the Panama-California Exposition in San Diego and the Panama-Pacific International Exposition in San Francisco, where thirteen works by LCT are on exhibition and he is awarded a gold medal. They return east through Colorado

April A fire of unknown origin at LCT's boathouse causes considerable damage

1916
Saturday, February 19 LCT hosts a sixty-eighth birthday luncheon party for himself, a masque called "The Quest of Beauty," and a retrospective exhibition of his works in oil paint and watercolor, glass, iron, and textiles, for 300 guests at the Tiffany Studios showroom, 347 Madison Avenue at 45th Street; entertainment includes LCT's speech, "What is the Quest of Beauty?"

May LCT lends moving pictures to the local Men's Club, where they are shown in the library

June In LCT's ongoing dispute with the town of Oyster Bay over ownership of beachfront and underwater property, he is enjoined by the town because it claims he has damaged public property by torpedoing the bathhouse he converted from a beached schooner and destroying the breakwaters

June 28 LCT is denied his injunction against the town of Oyster Bay, in which he sought to prevent it from building public bathhouses on a strip of beach fronting his land

July 31–September 8 LCT travels via private railroad car, Ideal, and private yacht, *Princess Alice*, to Chicago, Saint Paul and Minneapolis, the Canadian Rockies, the Pacific Northwest, and Alaska with, among others, Sarah Hanley, George F. Heydt, and Jane Peterson

September The chapel is removed from the Cathedral Church of Saint John the Divine and taken to Tiffany Studios for repair; it is then installed at Laurelton Hall

1917
January LCT purchases twelve lots of Asian art—ukiyo-e prints, paintings, porcelain, a screen, scrolls, and furniture—at Anderson Galleries sales (January 22–23) and eight lots of Chinese art at a Yamanaka and Company auction at American Art Galleries (January 26–27), including jardinières, lacquered armchairs, a throne chair, and textiles

May LCT allocates eighty-five acres of his Laurelton estate for growing vegetables

LCT delivers a speech, "Color and Its Kinship to Sound," at the Rembrandt Club in Brooklyn

June LCT acquires a two-panel 18th-century Japanese screen of peacocks with pink and white peonies from the estate of William Merritt Chase

Ca. 1917
LCT purchases from the dealer C. D. McGrath a stone stele with the Buddhist triad that is later placed over the fireplace in the Chinese room of Laurelton Hall

LCT sells the building at 345 Madison Avenue and moves the Tiffany Studios operations that are there to 361 Madison Avenue

1918
January 5 LCT acquires Chinese throne mats and rugs at an Anderson Galleries auction

February LCT seeks a restraining order against the town of Oyster Bay to prevent it from building public bathhouses on the beach fronting his property

June 18 LCT resigns as art director of Tiffany and Company; he remains assistant treasurer and an unsalaried member of the board until his death

September LCT loses his battle with the town of Oyster Bay to prevent its building public bathhouses on the beach at his property

September 12 First meeting of the Louis Comfort Tiffany Foundation; the constitution is drafted; LCT-owned securities totaling over $1 million are donated

December The Tiffany Foundation permits visitors' days at Laurelton Hall once a week

LCT remodels an early 19th-century house, Oak Openings, on the grounds of Laurelton Hall, as an art gallery and installs on the facade carved Indian elements acquired through Lockwood de Forest

1918–19
LCT converts the Laurelton Hall carriage house and stables to art studios and dormitories for Tiffany Foundation fellows

1919
May Establishment of the Louis Comfort Tiffany Foundation as an art school is announced. First annual meeting of the Tiffany Foundation board is held on May 24; LCT adds to his original gift of Laurelton Hall and its contents some artwork and furniture from the 72nd Street house

October Stanley Lothrop is appointed art director of the Tiffany Foundation, a position he will hold until 1931. Contents of Laurelton Hall are inventoried for insurance purposes by M. Frederick Savage; in 1937 the typescript will be copied by John E. Terwilliger, who will become superintendent of the property

Early 1920s
LCT builds Comfort Lodge at 1865 Brickell Avenue, Miami, Fla.; it is an octagonal shape

1920
January 6 Tiffany Furnaces is reorganized and called Louis C. Tiffany Furnaces, run by A. Douglas Nash (1881–1940), funded by LCT

May 1 The Tiffany Foundation art school at Laurelton Hall opens for it first summer session with nine fellows, all male

Tiffany Studios is at 361 Madison Avenue (between 45th and 46th Streets) and 46 West 23rd Street

1921
October 31 The first annual exhibition of work of members of the Tiffany Foundation opens in a space leased in the Art Center Building on East 56th Street

Tiffany Foundation publishes a prospectus about Laurelton Hall—fellows' activities there, key people at the foundation, and LCT's collections

Tiffany Foundation donates to the Metropolitan Museum LCT's 1872 oil painting *Snake Charmer at Tangier, Africa* (21.170)

1922–23
December–January Heavy snow causes significant damage to a hanging-garden stanchion and a terrace at Laurelton Hall. LCT considers it so important a feature of Laurelton Hall that he pays to have it restored

1923
October Sarah Hanley is appointed assistant director of the Tiffany Foundation by the board, a position she will hold until 1933

1924
April Louis C. Tiffany Furnaces is dissolved; commissions completed after this date are made from remaining glass; after April 2 the company is called the A. Douglas Nash Company and LCT retains interest

May 25 Louise Harriet Tiffany (LCT's sister) donates $20,000 to the Tiffany Foundation so that women can enroll in the Laurelton Hall study program

1925
November 20 Tiffany Foundation and LCT lend to the Metropolitan Museum a representative collection of artworks by LCT dating from 1897 to 1913: twenty-seven pieces of Favrile glass, fifteen enamels, a small pottery vase, and a carved wood box; in 1951 they will be donated to the Museum (51.121.1–44)

1926
June–November The Sesquicentennial International Exposition opens in Philadelphia; LCT is awarded a gold medal

1927
November 23 Tiffany Foundation awards its first Art Guild Medal, which will be given annually for the most promising work of foundation fellows in the fields of painting, sculpture, and crafts; this year the medal is presented to LCT "for his work on behalf of young artists"

Ca. 1929–30
A. Douglas Nash Company closes

1930
February LCT celebrates his eighty-third birthday at Laurelton Hall

August 17 Julia de Forest Tiffany Parker (LCT and Louise's daughter) marries second husband, Francis M. Weld

September–October Hugh F. McKean is a Tiffany Foundation fellow at Laurelton Hall

1931
January The fiftieth anniversary of LCT's involvement with the National Academy of Design is acknowledged with the presentation of an illuminated parchment by the architect Cass Gilbert

March 18 LCT's friend Charles Winthrop Gould (lawyer, art collector, trustee of the Metropolitan Museum) dies and leaves the Tiffany Foundation $10,000 and his collection of LCT's paintings in oil and watercolor, Favrile glass, enamels, and other artworks

May 8 Charles Lewis Tiffany (LCT and Mary's son) marries second wife, Emilia de Apezteguia Howell

LCT participates in an unemployment relief project: more than thirty cords of firewood are cut and stacked by unemployed men in the woods surrounding Laurelton Hall

1932
April 17 Tiffany Studios, 391 Madison Avenue, files for bankruptcy

May 29 *Tree of Life* window is unveiled in the large studio room of the fellows' area at Laurelton Hall

June LCT announces the formation of the Louis C. Tiffany Studios Corporation, 46 West 23rd Street, with himself as president and art director, to continue the activities of the bankrupt Tiffany Studios

LCT donates his paintings at Laurelton Hall and the 72nd Street house to the Tiffany Foundation

1933
January 17 LCT, now eighty-four, dies of pneumonia at the 72nd Street house; he is buried with his family at Greenwood Cemetery in Brooklyn. His estate is valued at $880,701

January 29 LCT's will is filed for probate

April Louis C. Tiffany Granite Quarries, Cohasset, Mass., is closed

July 1 Tiffany and Company closes LCT's jewelry department

December 28 Tiffany Foundation executive committee requests the resignations of Stanley Lothrop, director of the foundation, and Sarah Hanley, assistant director

1934
Tiffany Foundation is granted tax-exempt status

1935
February George Kunz family donates two LCT paintings to the Tiffany Foundation picture gallery

June Comfort Lodge, LCT's Miami home, is sold for $20,000 to benefit the Tiffany Foundation. The foundation uses the proceeds to acquire work from the Louis C. Tiffany Studios Corporation

September Louis C. Tiffany Studios Corporation offers to sell to the Tiffany Foundation its LCT windows

September 2 Laurelton Hall is opened to the public with ticketed admission on Wednesdays and Saturdays for one month

November Comfort Lodge is destroyed in a hurricane

1936
March Contents of Louis C. Tiffany Studios Corporation, 46 West 23rd Street, are sold to auctioneer Percy A. Joseph for $65,000 (not including the corporation itself, which will continue to produce ecclesiastical art and memorials in glass and stone)

August 72nd Street house is demolished

November 4 Remaining inventory of the Louis C. Tiffany Studios Corporation (LCT art objects and Favrile glass) is sold to Percy A. Joseph

1937
February 10 Louise Harriet Tiffany (LCT's sister) dies

October 1 Seventeen-story apartment building designed by Rosario Candela and Mott B. Schmidt, 19 East 72nd Street, is completed on the site of the 72nd Street house

December LCT's industrial arts library is sold by Percy A. Joseph to the New York City Board of Education; the library will be housed at the School of Industrial Arts, 257 West 40th Street

1938
March 14–19 Liquidation of Louis C. Tiffany Studios Corporation by Lester Dutt and Associates, Washington, D.C.; studio's contents auctioned prior to demolition of the building

Ca. 1938
Westminster Memorial Studios is formed by former employees of Tiffany Studios at 148 West 23rd Street to finish outstanding stained-glass commissions

1942–45
Laurelton Hall is used by the U.S. Navy Office of Scientific Research and Development / Research Committee of the Council of National Defense for "secret war work," including camouflage testing

1944
January 25 Cathedral Church of Saint John the Divine transfers title of the Tiffany chapel to the Tiffany Foundation

1946
July 31 Tiffany Foundation applies to the New York State Courts for permission to deviate from the founder's original deed of trust in order to sell Laurelton Hall and its contents. Property is later divided into parcels and sold by real estate agent Russel F. Sammis

September 24–28 Contents of Laurelton Hall are auctioned at Parke-Bernet Galleries, New York, with lesser objects sold through Coleman Galleries, New York, and private sales

1947
April 3 Charles Lewis Tiffany (LCT and Mary's son) dies

May 15 Tiffany Foundation is again granting fellowships

June 17 Tiffany Foundation officially moves to the National Academy of Art building, 1083 5th Avenue

August Laurelton Hall and ten acres, including the chapel and the art gallery, are contracted for sale for use as a nursing home; the contract is signed as of August 28, but a zoning variance for this use is denied by the village of Laurel Hollow and the sale falls through

1948
May 17 Supreme Court of the County of Nassau in Mineola authorizes Tiffany Foundation trustees to sell foundation property

1949
January 9 Laurelton Hall is sold for $10,000 to Thomas Hilton, who uses it as a summer home during 1949–55

1957
March 6 Laurelton Hall is destroyed by fire

March 16 Comfort Tiffany Gilder requests Hugh F. McKean to rescue art at Laurelton Hall

May 11 McKean and his wife, Jeannette Genius McKean, purchase Laurelton Hall remains from salvagers

1958
Sarah Hanley dies

1963
Mary Woodbridge Tiffany Lusk (LCT and Mary's daughter) dies

1973
Julia de Forest Tiffany Weld (LCT and Louise's daughter) dies

1974
Louise Comfort Tiffany Gilder (LCT and Louise's daughter) dies

1978
McKeans donate the Laurelton Hall loggia to the Metropolitan Museum for the American Wing

1979
Dorothy Trimble Tiffany Burlingham (LCT and Louise's daughter) dies

Works Cited

American Art Association 1894a. *Antique Chinese and Japanese Porcelains, Pottery, Enamels, and Bronzes . . . To Be Sold at Public Sale by Order of S. Bing.* Sale cat., New York, American Art Association, February 23–March 2, 1894. New York, 1894.

American Art Association 1894b. *Catalogue of Japanese Engravings: An Important Collection of Old Prints in Color Belonging to Mr. S. Bing, Paris.* Sale cat., New York, American Art Association, March 12–24, 1894. New York, 1894.

American Art Association 1905. *Catalogue of the Art Treasures Collected by Thomas E. Waggaman, Washington, D.C.* Sale cat., New York, American Art Association, January 25–February 3, 1905. New York, 1905.

American Art Association 1909. *Beautiful Antique Chinese Rugs of the Imperial Ch'ien-Lung and Earlier Periods.* Sale cat., New York, American Art Association, January 7–8, 1909. New York, 1909.

American Art Association 1916a. *Ancient Oriental Imperial Treasures of Rare Artistic Distinction Recently Procured in China and Japan.* Sale cat., New York, American Art Association, February 7–8, 1916. New York, 1916.

American Art Association 1916b. *Beautiful Old Chinese Rugs and Carpets.* Sale cat. New York, American Art Association, April 28–29, 1916. New York, 1916.

American Art Association 1917. *Oriental Art Treasures from the Chinese Imperial Palace.* Sale cat., New York, American Art Association, January 26–27, 1917. New York, 1917.

Anderson Galleries 1916. *Old Chinese Rugs and a Few Other Rare Works of Chinese Art.* Sale cat., New York, Anderson Galleries, March 2–4, 1916. New York, 1916.

Anderson Galleries 1917a. *Brilliant Old Robes from the Late Court of the Manchus.* Sale cat., New York, Anderson Galleries, March 2–3, 1917. New York, 1917.

Anderson Galleries 1917b. *400 Japanese Color Prints Collected by Arnold Genthe.* Sale cat., New York, Anderson Galleries, January 22–23, 1917. New York, 1917.

Anderson Galleries 1917c. *Old Chinese Porcelain, Single Color Porcelain Ming, Sung, Yuan, and Tang Pottery, Decorated Chinese Porcelain, Old Chinese Bronzes, Jade, Ivory and Crystal, Old Chinese Kakemono, Makimono and Albums.* Sale cat., New York, Anderson Galleries, January 22–23, 1917. New York, 1917.

Anderson Galleries 1918. *Catalogue of Rare Chinese Rugs, Old Specimens, and Reproductions.* Sale cat., New York, Anderson Galleries, January 5, 1918. New York, 1918.

Arberry 1952. Arthur J. Arberry, ed. and trans. *Omar Khayyám: A New Version Based Upon Recent Discoveries.* London, 1952.

"Arrangement" 1912. "The Arrangement of a Collection: A Note on the House of Louis C. Tiffany, Esq." *Arts and Decoration* 2 (June 1912), p. 295.

"Art" 1900. "Art." *Chicago Daily Tribune*, March 25, 1900, p. 38.

"Art Sale" 1946. "Art Sale Yields $20,335: Oriental Items from Tiffany Foundation Go on Block." *New York Times*, September 28, 1946, p. 22.

"Artistic Homes" 1894. "Artistic American Homes." *Decorator and Furnisher* 23, no. 4 (January 1894), pp. 128–29.

"Artistic House" 1900. "The Most Artistic House in New York City: A Series of Views of the Home of Mr. Louis C. Tiffany." *Ladies' Home Journal* 17 (November 1900), pp. 12–13.

Artistic Houses 1883–84. *Artistic Houses: Being a Series of Interior Views of a Number of the Most Beautiful and Celebrated Homes in the United States.* 2 vols. in 4. New York: D. Appleton, 1883–84. Reprint, New York, 1971.

Auboyer 1957. Jeannine Auboyer. "C.-T. Loo (1880–1957)." *Arts Asiatiques* 4, no. 4 (1957), pp. 308–10.

Baedeker 1898. Karl Baedeker. *Spain and Portugal: Handbook for Travellers.* New York, 1898.

Baedeker 1907. Karl Baedeker. *Baedeker's Canada: The Dominion of Canada, with Newfoundland and an Excursion to Alaska.* 3d rev. ed. Leipzig, 1907.

Baker 1989. Paul R. Baker. *Stanny: The Gilded Life of Stanford White.* New York, 1989.

Bales 1908. L. L. Bales. "Totem Poles." *Outdoor Life* 21, no. 5 (1908), pp. 423–41.

Barnes 1903. Thomas F. Barnes. "The Washoe Baskets." *The Papoose* 1, no. 4 (March 1903).

"Bathers" 1914. "'The Bathers' Will Stay: Tiffany Window Will Not Be Shown at Panama Exposition." *New York Times*, December 13, 1914, p. 11.

Batkin 1999. Jonathan Batkin. "Tourism Is Overrated: Pueblo Pottery and the Early Curio Trade, 1880–1910." In *Unpacking Culture: Art and Commodity in Colonial and Postcolonial Worlds*, edited by Ruth B. Phillips and Christopher B. Steiner, pp. 282–97. Berkeley, 1999.

"Bella" 1878. "The 'Bella' Apartment House." *Real Estate Record and Builders' Guide* 21 (March 23, 1878), pp. 243–44.

Berlo 1992. Janet Catherine Berlo. "Introduction: The Formative Years of Native American Art History." In *The Early Years of Native American Art History: The Politics of Scholarship and Collecting*, edited by Janet Catherine Berlo. Seattle, 1992.

Beurdeley and Maubeuge 1991. Michel Beurdeley and Michèle Maubeuge. *Edmond de Goncourt chez lui.* Nancy, 1991.

Bing 1970. Siegfried Bing. *Artistic America, Tiffany Glass, and Art Nouveau.* Edited by Robert Koch. Cambridge, Mass., 1970.

Blanchan 1901. Neltje Blanchan. "Two Ways to Help the Indians." *The Indian's Friend* (January 1901), pp. 7–8.

Blaugrund 1987. Annette Blaugrund. "The Tenth Street Studio Building." Ph.D. diss., Columbia University, 1987.

Blaugrund 1997. Annette Blaugrund. *The Tenth Street Studio Building: Artist-Entrepreneurs from the Hudson River School to the American Impressionists.* Southampton, N.Y., 1997.

Blavatsky 1877. Helena P. Blavatsky. *Isis Unveiled: A Master-Key to the Mysteries of Ancient and Modern Science and Theology.* 2 vols. 6th ed. New York, 1877. Reprint, Pasadena, 1988.

Bragdon 1901. Claude Bragdon. "Mysticism and Architecture." *Interstate Architect and Builder* (July 13, 1901), pp. 13–14.

Bragdon 1902. Claude Bragdon. "Beautiful Necessity" (six-part series). *House and Garden* 2 (January–June 1902), pp. 10–14, 57–61, 91–95, 141–44, 193–96, 262–65.

Bragdon 1903. Claude Bragdon. "The Sleeping Beauty." *The Craftsman* (August 1903), pp. 338–47.

Brandimarte 1988. Cynthia Brandimarte. "Darling Dabblers: American China Painters and Their Work, 1870–1920." *American Ceramic Circle Journal* 6 (1988), pp. 7–27.

"Bride" 1914. "Miss Tiffany, Bride of Dr. Burlingham." *New York Times,* September 25, 1914, p. 11.

Bruschke-Johnson 1991. Lee Bruschke-Johnson. "Studies in Provenance: Japanese Wood Carvings and Sculpture from the Matsuki Sale of 1906." *Orientations* 22 (April 1991).

"Building Items" 1882. "New York City Building Items." *Manufacturer and Builder* 14, no. 5 (May 1882), p. 104.

Burke 1987. Doreen Bolger Burke. "Louis Comfort Tiffany and His Early Training at Eagleswood, 1862–1865." *American Art Journal* 19, no. 3 (1987), pp. 29–39.

Burke et al. 1986. Doreen Bolger Burke et al. *In Pursuit of Beauty: Americans and the Aesthetic Movement.* Exh. cat. New York, Metropolitan Museum of Art, October 23, 1986–January 11, 1987. New York, 1986.

Burns 1993. Sarah Burns. "The Price of Beauty: Art, Commerce, and the Late Nineteenth-Century American Studio Interior." In *American Iconology: New Approaches to Nineteenth-Century Art and Literature,* edited by David C. Miller, pp. 209–38. New Haven, 1993.

Burns 1996. Sarah Burns. *Inventing the Modern Artist: Art and Culture in Gilded Age America.* New Haven, 1996.

Cai 1991. Cai Zejun. *Shanxi liu li / Glazed Works in Shanxi Province.* Beijing, 1991.

"Canfield" 1902. "Not Bought by Canfield." *New York Times,* May 2, 1902, p. 16.

Carroll 1923. Dana H. Carroll. *The Freer Collection for the Nation.* New York: privately printed, 1923.

Cathers 2003. David M. Cathers. *Gustav Stickley.* New York, 2003.

Chalcraft 2004. Edwin L. Chalcraft. *Assimilation's Agent: My Life as a Superintendent in the Indian Boarding School System.* Edited by Cary C. Collins. Lincoln, Neb., 2004.

Christie's 1999. *Important 20th Century Decorative Arts.* Sale cat., New York, Christie's, November 29, 1999. New York, 1999.

Christie's 2004. *The C. Ruxton and Audrey B. Love Collection: Important European Furniture, Antiquities and Asian Works of Art.* Sale cat., New York, Christie's, October 20, 2004. New York, 2004.

Christie's 2005. *Important 20th Century Decorative Art and Design.* Sale cat., New York, Christie's, December 7, 2005. New York, 2005.

"Cleopatra" 1913a. "Cleopatra's Glories Revived in New York." *The Sun* (New York), February 9, 1913, sec. 8, pp. 1–2.

"Cleopatra" 1913b. "Contemporaries of Cleopatra at a Fête Given by Mr. Louis C. Tiffany of New York." *Town and Country* 67 (February 22, 1913), pp. 28–29.

"Cleopatra" 1913c. "One of Cleopatra's Nights." *Vogue* 41 (March 15, 1913), pp. 56–57.

"Cleopatra" 1913d. "Queen Cleopatra, Worshipped for Her Beauty by the Caesars, Leads in Picturesque Fete." *New York Tribune,* February 5, 1913, p. 9.

Cohodas 1992. Marvin Cohodas. "Louisa Keyser and the Cohns: Mythmaking and Basket Making in the American West." In *The Early Years of Native American Art History: The Politics of Scholarship and Collecting,* edited by Janet Catherine Berlo, pp. 88–113. Seattle, 1992.

Conway 1914. Edward Harold Conway. "Mr. Louis C. Tiffany's Laurelton Hall at Cold Spring, Long Island." *The Spur* 14, no. 4 (August 15, 1914), pp. 25–29.

De Forest 1885. Lockwood de Forest. *Indian Domestic Architecture.* Boston, 1885.

De Forest 1912. Lockwood de Forest. *Illustrations of Design: Based on Notes of Line as Used by the Craftsmen of India.* Boston, 1912.

De Kay 1911. Charles de Kay. "A Western Setting for the Beauty of the Orient." *Arts and Decoration* 1 (October 1911), pp. 469–72.

De Kay 1914. Charles de Kay. *The Art Work of Louis C. Tiffany.* Garden City, N.Y., 1914.

De Kay 1920. Charles de Kay. "Laurelton Studios: A New Idea." *International Studio* 71, no. 283 (October 1920), pp. LXXVIII–LXXXI.

De Quélin 1922. René de Quélin. "A Many-Sided Creator of the Beautiful: The Work of Louis Comfort Tiffany by an Associate." *Arts and Decoration* 17 (July 1922), pp. 176–77.

Deloria 1998. Philip J. Deloria. *Playing Indian.* New Haven, 1998.

Denker 1989. Ellen Paul Denker. *Lenox China: Celebrating a Century of Quality, 1889–1989.* Exh. cat. Trenton, New Jersey State Museum, October 21, 1989–January 7, 1990. Trenton, 1989.

Duncan 2004. Alastair Duncan. *Louis C. Tiffany: The Garden Museum Collection.* Woodbridge, 2004.

Duncan et al. 1989. Alastair Duncan, Martin Eidelberg, and Neil Harris. *Masterworks of Louis Comfort Tiffany.* Exh. cat. Washington, D.C., Renwick Gallery, September 29, 1989–March 4, 1990; New York, Metropolitan Museum of Art, April 12–September 9, 1990. New York, 1989.

Earle 2004. Joe Earle. *Lethal Elegance: The Art of Samurai Sword Fittings.* Exh. cat. Boston, Museum of Fine Arts, October 13, 2004–September 26, 2005. Boston, 2004.

Edwards et al. 2000. Holly Edwards et al. *Noble Dreams, Wicked Pleasures: Orientalism in America, 1870–1930.* Exh. cat. Williamstown, Mass., Sterling and Francine Clark Art Institute, June 6–September 4, 2000; Baltimore,

Walters Art Gallery, October 1–December 10, 2000; and Charlotte, N.C., Mint Museum of Art, February 3–April 23, 2001. Princeton, 2000.

"Egyptian Fete" 1913. "Egyptian Fete a Fine Spectacle." *New York Times*, February 5, 1913, p. 8.

"Egyptian Scenes" 1913. "Ancient Egyptian Scenes Grace Tiffany Ball." *New York Tribune*, February 5, 1913.

Eidelberg 1983. Martin P. Eidelberg. *E. Colonna*. Exh. cat. Dayton Art Institute, October 29, 1983–January 2, 1984; Montréal, Musée des Arts Décoratifs, January 20–March 26, 1984; Washington, D.C., Renwick Gallery, April 27–August 19, 1984. Dayton, Ohio, 1983.

Eidelberg 2005. Martin P. Eidelberg. "S. Bing and L. C. Tiffany: Entrepreneurs of Style." *Nineteenth-Century Art Worldwide* 4, no. 2 (Summer 2005), at http://www.19thc-artworldwide.org/summer_05/articles/eide.html.

Eidelberg and McClelland 2001. Martin P. Eidelberg and Nancy A. McClelland, eds. *Behind the Scenes of Tiffany Glassmaking: The Nash Notebooks*. New York, 2001.

Eidelberg et al. 2005. Martin P. Eidelberg et al. *The Lamps of Louis Comfort Tiffany*. New York, 2005.

Ellenius 1996. Allan Ellenius. *Bruno Liljefors: Naturen som livsrum*. Exh. cat. Stockholm, Prins Eugens Waldemarsudde, September 20, 1996–January 6, 1997; Göteborgs Konstmuseum, January 25–May 25, 1997. Stockholm, 1996.

Elliott 2005. Jeannette Shambaugh Elliott. *The Odyssey of China's Imperial Art Treasures*. Seattle, 2005.

Ellis 2005. Eugenia Victoria Ellis. "Squaring the Circle: The Regulating Lines of Claude Bragdon's Theosophic Architecture." Ph.D. diss., Virginia Polytechnic Institute and State University, 2005.

Ellwood 1983. Robert S. Ellwood Jr. "The American Theosophical Synthesis." In *The Occult in America*, edited by Howard Kerr and Charles L. Crow, pp. 110–34. Urbana, 1983.

Faude 1975. Wilson H. Faude. "Associated Artists and the American Renaissance in the Decorative Arts." *Winterthur Portfolio* 10 (1975), pp. 101–30.

Ferree 1903. Barr Ferree. "Talks on Architecture: A Morning at Harbor Hill, the Mackay Estate at Roslyn, N.Y." *Scientific American Building Monthly* (September 1903).

"Fire" 1957a. "Fire Destroys Mansion." *New York World Telegram*, March 7, 1957.

"Fire" 1957b. "Mansion Destroyed by Fire." *Daily News* (New York), March 8, 1957, p. 32.

"Fire" 1957c. "Tiffany Home on L. I. Is Destroyed by Fire." *New York Herald Tribune*, March 8, 1957, sec. 2, p. 1.

Fred 1902. A. W. Fred. "Interieurs von L. C. Tiffany." *Dekorative Kunst* (Munich) 9 (1902), pp. 110–16.

Freeman 1966. John Crosby Freeman. *The Forgotten Rebel: Gustav Stickley and His Craftsman Mission Furniture*. Watkins Glen, N.Y., 1966.

Frelinghuysen 1989. Alice Cooney Frelinghuysen. *American Porcelain, 1770–1920*. Exh. cat. New York, Metropolitan Museum of Art, April 8–June 25, 1989. New York, 1989.

Frelinghuysen 1995. Alice Cooney Frelinghuysen. "The Aesthetic Movement in Newport." *The Magazine Antiques* 147, no. 4 (1995), pp. 575–76.

Frelinghuysen 1998. Alice Cooney Frelinghuysen. *Louis Comfort Tiffany at the Metropolitan Museum*. Exh. cat. New York, Metropolitan Museum of Art, July 23, 1998–January 31, 1999. New York, 1998.

Frelinghuysen 2000. Alice Cooney Frelinghuysen. "Louis Comfort Tiffany and New York." In *Art Nouveau, 1890–1914*, edited by Paul Greenhalgh, pp. 398–411. Exh. cat. London, Victoria and Albert Museum; Washington, D.C., National Gallery of Art. London, 2000.

Frelinghuysen et al. 1993. Alice Cooney Frelinghuysen et al. *Splendid Legacy: The Havemeyer Collection*. Exh. cat. New York, Metropolitan Museum of Art, March 27–June 20, 1993. New York, 1993.

Garrett 1999. Wendell Garrett. "Garrett's Attic." artnet.com Magazine Features, July 13, 1999, at http://www.artnet.com/magazine_pre2000/features/garrett/garrett7-13-99.asp.

"Gives a Million" 1919. "Gives a Million for Art Institute." *New York Times*, October 20, 1919, p. 1.

Godwin 1994. Joscelyn Godwin. *The Theosophical Enlightenment*. Albany, N.Y., 1994.

Gogol 1985. John M. Gogol. "Cowlitz Indian Basketry." *American Indian Basketry Magazine* 5, no. 4 (1985), pp. 4–20.

Gomes 1987. Michael Gomes. *The Dawning of the Theosophical Movement*. Wheaton, Ill., 1987.

Grant 1977. Marena Grant. "Treasures from Laurelton Hall." *The Magazine Antiques* 111, no. 4 (April 1977), pp. 752–59.

Greiff 1971. Constance M. Greiff. *Lost America: From the Atlantic to the Mississippi*. Princeton, 1971.

Gustafson 1977. Eleanor H. Gustafson. "Museum Accessions." *The Magazine Antiques* 111, no. 4 (April 1977), pp. 734–44.

Halttunen 1989. Karen Halttunen. "From Parlor to Living Room: Domestic Space, Interior Decoration, and the Culture of Personality." In *Consuming Visions: Accumulation and Display of Goods in America, 1880–1920*, edited by Simon J. Bronner, pp. 157–89. New York, 1989.

Haedeke 1959. Hanns-Ulrich Haedeke. "Glas." In *Jugendstil: Der Weg ins 20. Jahrhundert*, edited by Helmut Seling. Heidelberg, 1959.

Handler 1976. Frederick John Handler. "Louis Comfort Tiffany's Pursuit of Beauty." *Great Neck News Magazine, Ltd.* (April 1976), pp. 11–17.

Handlin 1979. David P. Handlin. *The American Home: Architecture and Society, 1815–1915*. Boston, 1979.

Hanley 1985. *The Sarah Hanley Collection of Tiffany and Related Items*. Sale cat., New York, Phillips, Son and Neale, Inc., February 1, 1985. New York, 1985.

Harrison 1980. Martin Harrison. *Victorian Stained Glass*. London, 1980.

Harvey 1901. James L. Harvey. "Source of Beauty in Favrile Glass." *Brush and Pencil* 9, no. 3 (December 1901), pp. 167–76.

Havemeyer 1961. Louisine W. Havemeyer. *Sixteen to Sixty: Memoirs of a Collector*. New York, 1961. New ed. Edited by Susan Alyson Stein. New York, 1993.

Hawley 1976. Henry H. Hawley. "Tiffany's Silver in the Japanese Taste." *Bulletin of the Cleveland Museum of Art* 63 (October 1976), pp. 236–45.

Head 1986. Raymond Head. *The Indian Style*. Chicago, 1986.

Higham 1970. John Higham. *Writing American History: Essays on Modern Scholarship*. Bloomington, 1970.

Hinman 2003. Catherine Hinman. "From the Collection: Butterfly Window Has Clear Japanese Sources." *Insider* (Morse Museum) (May–June 2003), pp. 1, 3.

"Home Opened" 1935. "L.C. Tiffany Home Opened to Public." *New York Times*, September 2, 1935, p. 19.

Hopkins 1913. Alfred Hopkins. *Modern Farm Buildings*. New York, 1913.

Hopkins 1916. Alfred Hopkins. *Modern Farm Buildings*. Rev. ed. New York, 1916.

Horiuchi 1994. Takeo Horiuchi. *The World of Louis Comfort Tiffany: A Selection from the Anchorman Collection*. Nagoya-shi, 1994.

Howe 1902a. Samuel Howe. "Enamel as a Decorative Agent." *The Craftsman* 2, no. 2 (May 1902), pp. 61–68.

Howe 1902b. Samuel Howe. "A Visit to the House of Mr. Stickley." *The Craftsman* 3, no. 3 (December 1902), pp. 161–69.

Howe 1903. Samuel Howe. "The Making of the Glass." *The Craftsman* 3, no. 6 (March 1903), pp. 361–68.

Howe 1906. Samuel Howe. "One Source of Color Values—Illustrating Mr. Louis C. Tiffany's Significant Handling of Things Greater than Architecture and One Source of His Strength in Color." *House and Garden* 10 (September 1906), pp. 104–13.

Howe 1907. Samuel Howe. "The Dwelling Place as an Expression of Individuality: The House of Louis C. Tiffany." *Appleton's Magazine* 9 (February 1907), pp. 156–65.

Howe 1907–8. Samuel Howe. "An American Country House." *International Studio* 33 (1907–8), pp. 294–96.

Howe 1913a. Samuel Howe. "The Long Island Home of Louis C. Tiffany." *Town and Country* 68 (September 6, 1913), pp. 24–26, 42.

Howe 1913b. Samuel Howe. "The Silent Fountains of Laurelton Hall, the Long Island Home of Mr. Louis C. Tiffany." *Arts and Decoration* 3 (September 1913), pp. 377–79.

Howe 1914a. Samuel Howe. "A Country House with Human Appeal." *Long Island Home Journal* (March 1914), pp. 4–6.

Howe 1914b. Samuel Howe. "The Garden of Mr. Louis C. Tiffany: A Significant Handling of Color." *House Beautiful* 35 (January 1914), pp. 40–42.

Howe 1915. Samuel Howe. "The Picturesque Fountain Scheme in the Long Island Home of Mr. Louis C. Tiffany." In *American Country Houses of To-Day*, edited by Samuel Howe, pp. 382–93. New York, 1915.

Humphreys 1887. Mary Gay Humphreys. "Decoration and Furniture: Bits in the Tiffany House." *Art Amateur* 16, no. 2 (January 1887), pp. 38–42.

Izzard 2004. Sebastian Izzard. *Japanese Sword Fittings from the Alexander G. Moslé Collection*. New York, 2004.

James 1902. George Wharton James. *Indian Basketry*. 2d ed. Pasadena, Calif., 1902.

Janes 1912. Elisha Harris Janes. "The Development of Duplex Apartment Houses—I. Early Type." *The Brickbuilder* 21 (June 1912), pp. 159–61.

D. Johnson 1979. Diane Chalmers Johnson. *American Art Nouveau*. New York, 1979.

M. Johnson 2005. Marilynn A. Johnson. *Louis Comfort Tiffany: Artist for the Ages*. London, 2005.

P. Johnson 2003. Paul Johnson. *Art: A New History*. New York, 2003.

Jonaitis 1999. Aldona Jonaitis. "Northwest Coast Totem Poles." In *Unpacking Culture: Art and Commodity in Colonial and Postcolonial Worlds*, edited by Ruth B. Phillips and Christopher B. Steiner, pp. 104–23. Berkeley, 1999.

O. Jones 1856. Owen Jones. *The Grammar of Ornament*. London, 1856.

R. Jones 1999. Robert O. Jones. *D. Maitland Armstrong: American Stained Glass Master*. Tallahassee, 1999.

Knickerbocker 1914. Cholly Knickerbocker. "Artists Eat L. Tiffany Peacocks." *New York American*, May 16, 1914, p. 8.

Koch 1964. Robert Koch. *Louis C. Tiffany, Rebel in Glass*. New York, 1964.

Koch 1974. Robert Koch. "Tiffany's Abstractions in Glass." *The Magazine Antiques* 105, no. 6 (June 1974), pp. 1290–94.

König and Franses 2005. Hans König and Michael Franses. *Glanz der Himmelssöhne: Kaiserliche Teppiche aus China 1400–1750*. Exh. cat. Cologne, Museum für Ostasiatische Kunst. Cologne, 2005.

Kropp 1996. Phoebe S. Kropp. "'There is a little sermon in that': Constructing the Native Southwest at the San Diego Panama–California Exposition of 1915." In *The Great Southwest of the Fred Harvey Company and the Santa Fe Railway*, edited by Marta Weigle and Barbara A. Babcock, pp. 36–46. Phoenix, 1996.

Lancaster 1947. Clay Lancaster. "Oriental Forms in American Architecture, 1800–1870." *Art Bulletin* 29 (September 1947), pp. 183–93.

Lancaster 1953a. Clay Lancaster. "Indian Influence on the American Architecture of the XIX Century." *Marg* 6, no. 2 (1953), pp. 6–21.

Lancaster 1953b. Clay Lancaster. "Japanese Buildings in the United States before 1900: Their Influence upon American Domestic Architecture." *Art Bulletin* 35 (1953), pp. 217–25.

Lawton 1995. Thomas Lawton. "Yamanaka Sadajirÿ: Advocate for Asian Art." *Orientations* 26 (January 1995), pp. 80–93.

Lawton and Merrill 1993. Thomas Lawton and Linda Merrill. *Freer: A Legacy of Art*. Washington, D.C., 1993.

LCT 1916. "Louis C. Tiffany." *International Studio* 58, no. 230 (April 1916), p. 63.

"Leaded Glass" 1915. "Mr. Louis Tiffany's Latest Achievement in Leaded Glass." *Country Life in America* 27 (January 1915), p. 25.

Lears 1981. T. J. Jackson Lears. *No Place of Grace: Antimodernism and the Transformation of American Culture, 1880–1920*. New York, 1981.

Leonard 1901. Anna B. Leonard. "Exhibition of French Pottery at the Tiffany Studios." *Keramic Studio* 3 (August 1901), pp. 82–83.

Lethaby 1891. William R. Lethaby. *Architecture, Mysticism and Myth*. London, 1891. Reprint, New York, 1975.

Lewis et al. 1987. Arnold Lewis, James Turner, and Steven McQuillin. *The Opulent Interiors of the Gilded Age: All 203 Photographs from "Artistic Houses."* New York, 1987.

London 1899. *Grafton Galleries Exhibition of l'Art Nouveau: S. Bing, Paris.* Exh. cat. London, Grafton Galleries, May–July 1899. London, 1899.

Long 2002. Nancy Long, ed. *The Tiffany Chapel at the Morse Museum.* Winter Park, Fla., 2002.

"Lorenzo" 1931. "Lorenzo Beckons." *Art Digest* 6 (November 1, 1931), pp. 27–28.

Lothrop 1919. Stanley Lothrop. "The Louis Comfort Tiffany Foundation." *American Magazine of Art* 11 (November 1919), pp. 49–53.

Lothrop 1923. Stanley Lothrop. "Louis Comfort Tiffany Foundation." *American Magazine of Art* 14 (November 1923), pp. 615–17.

"Lothrop" 1944. "Stanley B. Lothrop." *New York Times*, March 18, 1944, p. 13.

Lyman 1914. Clara Brown Lyman. "Recent Achievements in Decorative Lighting." *Country Life in America* 26 (October 1914), pp. 52–55.

MacKay et al. 1997. Robert B. MacKay, Anthony K. Baker, and Carol A. Traynor, eds. *Long Island Country Houses and Their Architects, 1860–1940.* New York, 1997.

"Madison Avenue" 1884. "Upper Madison Avenue." *Real Estate Record and Builders' Guide* 33 (May 24, 1884), p. 560.

Mahler 1969. Alma Mahler. *Gustav Mahler: Memories and Letters.* Rev. and enl. ed. Edited by Donald Mitchell. New York, 1969.

Mason 1904. Otis Tufton Mason. *Indian Basketry: Studies in a Textile Art without Machinery.* 2 vols. New York, 1904.

G. Mayer 1958. Grace M. Mayer. *Once Upon a City: New York 1890–1910.* New York, 1958.

R. Mayer 1996. Roberta A. Mayer. "The Aesthetics of Lockwood de Forest: India, Craft, and Preservation." *Winterthur Portfolio* 31, no. 1 (Spring 1996), pp. 1–22.

R. Mayer and Lane 2001. Roberta A. Mayer and Carolyn K. Lane. "Disassociating the 'Associated Artists': The Early Business Ventures of Louis C. Tiffany, Candace T. Wheeler, and Lockwood de Forest." *Studies in the Decorative Arts* 8, no. 2 (Spring–Summer 2001), pp. 2–36.

McKean 1980a. Hugh F. McKean. *The "Lost" Treasures of Louis Comfort Tiffany.* Garden City, N.Y., 1980.

McKean 1980b. Hugh F. McKean. "Tiffany Windows." *American Craft* 40, no. 5 (October–November 1980), pp. 28–33.

McWhorter 1913. Lucullus V. McWhorter. *The Crime Against the Yakimas.* North Yakima, Wash., 1913.

"Medal" 1927. "Medal Awarded to L.C. Tiffany." *New York Times*, November 24, 1927, p. 23.

Meech 2001. Julia Meech. *Frank Lloyd Wright and the Art of Japan: The Architect's Other Passion.* Exh. cat. New York, Japan Society Gallery, Spring 2001. New York, 2001.

Meech-Pekarik 1982. Julia Meech-Pekarik. "Early Collections of Japanese Prints and The Metropolitan Museum of Art." *Metropolitan Museum Journal* 17 (1982), pp. 93–118.

Meeks 1950. Carroll L. V. Meeks. "Picturesque Eclecticism." *Art Bulletin* 32 (September 1950), pp. 226–35.

Meeks 1953. Carroll L. V. Meeks. "Creative Eclecticism." *Journal of the Society of Architectural Historians* 12 (December 1953), pp. 15–18.

Mercer 2005. Bill Mercer. *People of the River: Native Arts of the Oregon Territory.* Exh. cat. Portland [Oregon] Art Museum, January 22–May 29, 2005. Portland, 2005.

"Milk Fund" 1919. "North Shore to Aid French Milk Fund." *New York Times*, July 21, 1919, p. 12.

Mitchell 1882a. Donald G. Mitchell. "From Lobby to Peak: On the Threshold." *Our Continent* 1 (February 15, 1882), p. 5.

Mitchell 1882b. Donald G. Mitchell. "From Lobby to Peak: A Lobby." *Our Continent* 1 (February 22, 1882), p. 21.

Mitchell 1882c. Donald G. Mitchell. "From Lobby to Peak: Halls." *Our Continent* 1 (March 1, 1882), p. 37.

Mitchell 1882d. Donald G. Mitchell. "From Lobby to Peak: An Early Breakfast." *Our Continent* 1 (March 15, 1882), p. 69.

Mitchell 1882e. Donald G. Mitchell. "From Lobby to Peak: Round About the Room." *Our Continent* 1 (March 22, 1882), p. 85.

Mitchell 1882f. Donald G. Mitchell. "From Lobby to Peak: Round About— Again." *Our Continent* 1 (March 29, 1882), p. 101.

Mitchell 1882g. Donald G. Mitchell. "From Lobby to Peak: Over the Mantel." *Our Continent* 1 (April 5, 1882), pp. 117–18.

Mitchell 1882h. Donald G. Mitchell. "From Lobby to Peak: In the Library." *Our Continent* 1 (April, 12, 1882), p. 132.

Mitchell 1882i. Donald G. Mitchell. "From Lobby to Peak: Between Rooms." *Our Continent* 1 (April 19, 1882), p. 148.

Mitchell 1882j. Donald G. Mitchell. "From Lobby to Peak: A Library Corner." *Our Continent* 1 (May 3, 1882), p. 185.

Mitchell 1882k. Donald G. Mitchell. "From Lobby to Peak: A Rolling Screen." *Our Continent* 1 (May 17, 1882), p. 217.

Moran 1880a. John Moran. "Artist-Life in New York." *Art Journal* (London) 6 (January 1880), pp. 57–60, 121–24.

Moran 1880b. John Moran. "New York Studios III." *Art Journal* (Appleton's) 6 (January 1880), pp. 1–4.

Morton 1999. *Pratt and Its Gallery: The Arts and Crafts Years: An Exhibition of Paintings, Drawings, Photographs and Decorative Arts Representative of Works Shown at the Pratt Gallery During Its Critical First Decade, 1894–1904.* Exh. cat. Brooklyn, Rubelle and Norman Schafler Gallery, Pratt Institute, November 13–December 19, 1998. Brooklyn, 1999.

"Movies" 1921. "Movies Based on Paintings." *New York Times*, October 9, 1921, p. 74.

J. Mumford 1900. John Kimberly Mumford. *Oriental Rugs.* New York, 1900.

J. Mumford 1921. John Kimberly Mumford. "A Year at the Tiffany Foundation: The Progress Made by This Unusual New Development." *Arts and Decoration* 14 (February 1921), pp. 272–73, 310.

L. Mumford 1931. Lewis Mumford. *The Brown Decades: A Study of the Arts in America, 1865–1895.* New York, 1931.

Murase 2000. Miyeko Murase. *Bridge of Dreams: The Mary Griggs Burke Collection of Japanese Art*. New York: Metropolitan Museum of Art, 2000.

Naeve 1996. Milo M. Naeve. "Louis Comfort Tiffany and the Reform Movement in Furniture Design: The J. Matthew Meier and Ernest Hagen Commission of 1882–1885." In *American Furniture 1996*, edited by Luke Beckerdite, pp. 3–16. Milwaukee: Chipstone Foundation, 1996.

"Nature League" 1928. "Flower Show by Pupils: Nature League to Open Exhibition." *New York Times*, May 8, 1928, p. 32.

Neat 1994. Timothy Neat. *Part Seen, Part Imagined: Meaning and Symbolism in the Work of Charles Rennie Mackintosh and Margaret Macdonald*. Edinburgh, 1994.

"New Houses" 1883. "Decoration and Furniture: New Houses—Indoors and Out." *Art Amateur* 8, no. 3 (February 1883), pp. 66–68.

New York 1979. *Louis Comfort Tiffany: The Paintings*. Exh. cat. New York University, Grey Art Gallery and Study Center, March 20–May 12, 1979. New York, 1979.

New York 1994–95. *Herter Brothers: Furniture and Interiors for a Gilded Age*. Exh. cat. by Katherine S. Howe et al. Houston, Museum of Fine Arts, August 21–October 23, 1994; Atlanta, High Museum of Art, December 13, 1994–February 12, 1995; New York, Metropolitan Museum of Art, March 15–July 19, 1995. New York, 1994.

Norris 1907. Frank Norris. "Showing Off Alaska: The Northern Tourist Trade, 1878–1941." *Alaska History: A Publication of the Alaska Historical Society* 2, no. 2 (Fall 1987), pp. 1–19.

"Notable Addition" 1904. "A Notable Addition to L.I. Country Homes." *Brooklyn Daily Eagle*, February 9, 1904, p. 8.

Oakey 1882. Alexander F. Oakey. "A Trial Balance of Decoration." *Harper's New Monthly Magazine* 64 (April 1882), pp. 734–40.

Oaklander 1992. Christine I. Oaklander. "Studios at the YMCA, 1869–1903." *Archives of American Art Journal* 32, no. 3 (1992), pp. 14–22.

Ogasawara 1983. Ogasawara Nobuo. *Sword Guards and Fittings from Japan: The Collection of the Museum of Decorative Art, Copenhagen: Bequest of Dr. Hugo Halberstadt*. Tokyo, 1983.

Owen 2001. Nancy E. Owen. *Rookwood and the Industry of Art: Women, Culture, and Commerce, 1880–1913*. Athens, Ohio, 2001.

"Painting" 1946. "Painting Brings $3,700." *New York Times*, September 29, 1946, p. 27.

"Palatial" 1899. "Palatial Island Homes." *Brooklyn Daily Eagle*, April 30, 1899, p. 27.

"Pan-American" 1901. "The Tiffany Glass at the Pan-American." *Keramic Studio* 3, no. 2 (June 1901), p. 2.

"Panama-Pacific" 1915. "Exhibit of Louis Tiffany at the Panama-Pacific Exposition." *Jewelers' Circular* 70, no. 16 (May 19, 1915), p. 1.

Pardue and Howard 1996. Diana F. Pardue and Kathleen L. Howard. "Making Art, Making Money: The Fred Harvey Company and the Indian Artisan." In *The Great Southwest of the Fred Harvey Company and the Santa Fe Railway*, edited by Marta Weigle and Barbara A. Babcock, pp. 168–75. Phoenix, 1996.

Parke-Bernet 1946. *Favrile Glass and Enamel, American Indian Basketry and Relics, Antique Oriental Rugs, Chinese and Japanese Furniture and Objects of Art, Paintings, Antiquities, Decorations, Belonging to the Louis Comfort Tiffany Foundation*. Sale cat., New York, Parke-Bernet Galleries, September 24–28, 1946. New York, 1946.

Parke-Bernet 1948. *Japanese Art: Part One of the Collection of Alexander G. Moslé, Washington D.C., by Direction of Donald A. McCormack, Committee, Assistant Vice-President, The Riggs National Bank of Washington, D.C.* Sale cat., New York, Parke-Bernet Galleries, April 22, 1948. New York, 1948.

Parrott 2006. Lindsy Riepma Parrott. "The Ceramics of Louis Comfort Tiffany." *Nineteenth Century* 26, no. 1 (Spring 2006), pp. 3–11.

"Peacock" 1914a. "Peacock Bearers Surprise Guests of Mr. Tiffany." *New York Herald*, May 16, 1914, p. 10.

"Peacock" 1914b. "Tiffany Peacocks Feature at Feast." *Brooklyn Daily Times*, May 16, 1914, p. 8.

Peck and Irish 2001. Amelia Peck and Carol Irish. *Candace Wheeler: The Art and Enterprise of American Design, 1875–1900*. Exh. cat. New York, Metropolitan Museum of Art, October 10, 2001–January 6, 2002. New York, 2001.

Phillips 2006. Clare Phillips, ed. *Bejewelled by Tiffany, 1837–1987*. Exh. cat. London, Gilbert Collection, June 24–November 26, 2006. New Haven, 2006.

Pisano 1999. Ronald G. Pisano. *The Tile Club and the Aesthetic Movement in America*. New York, 1999.

Pons-Sorolla 2006. Blanca Pons-Sorolla. *Joaquín Sorolla*. London, 2006.

Real Estate 1898. Real Estate Record Association. *A History of Real Estate, Building and Architecture in New York City During the Last Quarter of a Century*. New York, 1898.

"Recent Exhibitions" 1888. "Some Recent Exhibitions in New York." *Art Review* 3, no. 1 (1888), pp. 16–25.

"Rest Home" 1947. "Tiffany's Estate May Be Rest Home." *New York Times*, August 29, 1947, p. 15.

"Restoration" 1899. "Restoration of St. Paul's." *New York Times*, August 30, 1899, p. 12.

"Revival" 1909. "The Revival of Mysticism." *Current Literature* 47 (November 1909), pp. 532–33.

Rhys 1900. Ernest Rhys. "The New Mysticism." *Fortnightly Review* 73 (June 1, 1900), pp. 1045–56.

"Rich Men" 1911. "Rich Men Who Have Organs Built in Their Homes." *New York Times*, September 17, 1911, p. SM12.

Riordan 1881a. Roger Riordan. "American Stained Glass: First Article." *American Art Review* 2, 1st division (April 1881), pp. 229–34.

Riordan 1881b. Roger Riordan. "American Stained Glass: Second Article." *American Art Review* 2, 2d division (May 1881), pp. 59–64.

Riordan 1881c. Roger Riordan. "American Stained Glass: Third and Concluding Article." *American Art Review* 2, 2d division (June 1881), pp. 59–64.

Said 1978. Edward W. Said. *Orientalism*. New York, 1978.

Salem 1993. *"A Pleasing Novelty": Bunkio Matsuki and the Japan Craze in Victorian Salem*. Exh. cat. Salem, Mass., Peabody Essex Museum, 1993. Salem, Mass, 1993.

Salkaln 2004. Elaine Mayers Salkaln. "The Invisibles." *New York Times Magazine: Home Design*, April 18, 2004.

Saylor 1908a. Henry H. Saylor. "The Country Home of Mr. Louis C. Tiffany." *Country Life in America* 15 (December 1908), pp. 157–62.

Saylor 1908b. Henry H. Saylor. "Indoor Fountains." *Country Life in America* 14 (August 1908), pp. 366–68.

Saylor 1911. Henry H. Saylor. *Bungalows*. New York, 1911.

Schlick 1994. Mary Dodds Schlick. *Columbia River Basketry: Gift of the Ancestors, Gift of the Earth*. Seattle, 1994.

Schmutzler 1962. Robert Schmutzler. *Art Nouveau*. New York, 1962.

"Screen" 1921. "The Screen." *New York Times*, September 26, 1921, p. 22.

Sheldon 1881. George W. Sheldon. *American Painters*. Enl. ed. New York, 1881. Reprint, New York, 1972.

Sloan and Yarnall 1992. Julie L. Sloan and James L. Yarnall. "Art of an Opaline Mind: The Stained Glass of John La Farge." *American Art Journal* 24, nos. 1–2 (1992), pp. 5–19.

Sotheby's 2006. *Americana*. Sale cat., New York, Sotheby's, January 19, 2006. New York, 2006.

Speenburgh 1956. Gertrude Speenburgh. *The Arts of the Tiffanys*. Chicago, 1956.

"Stained Glass" 1897. "Stained Glass at the Tiffany Galleries." *New York Times*, February 27, 1897, p. BR5.

"Studio" 1882. "New York Studios." *Art Journal* (Appleton's) 6 (January 1, 1882), p. 3.

Sullivan 1924. Louis H. Sullivan. *A System of Architectural Ornament According with a Philosophy of Man's Powers*. New York, 1924.

"Summer Furniture" 1901. "Artistic Summer Furniture." *New York Times*, July 18, 1901, p. 7.

Teller 1981. Barbara Gorely Teller. "Tiffany's Laurelton Hall, 1923." *The Magazine Antiques* 119 (January 1981), pp. 233–34.

L. Tiffany 1910. Louis Comfort Tiffany. "The Gospel of Good Taste." *Country Life in America* 19, no. 2 (November 1910), p. 105.

L. Tiffany 1911. Louis Comfort Tiffany. "The Tasteful Use of Light: Color in Artificial Illumination." *Scientific American* 104 (April 15, 1911), p. 373.

L. Tiffany 1917a. Louis Comfort Tiffany. "Color and Its Kinship to Sound." *Art World* 2, no. 2 (May 1917), pp. 142–43.

L. Tiffany 1917b. Louis Comfort Tiffany. "The Quest of Beauty." *Harper's Bazaar* 52 (December 1917), pp. 43–44.

N. Tiffany 1903. Nelson Otis Tiffany. *The Tiffanys of America: History and Genealogy*. Buffalo, N.Y., 1903.

"Tiffany Company" 1893. "Tiffany Glass and Decorating Company's Exhibit at the Columbian Exposition." *Decorator and Furnisher* 23 (October 1893), pp. 9–12.

Tiffany Foundation 1920. Louis Comfort Tiffany Foundation. *Catalogue of Oriental and Chinese Rugs*. Prepared by John K. Mumford and Dana H. Carroll. [S.l.], 1920.

Tiffany Foundation 1921a. Louis Comfort Tiffany Foundation. *Catalogue of Chinese and Japanese Objects of Art*. Prepared by Dana H. Carroll and Bunkio Matsuki. [Baltimore], 1921.

Tiffany Foundation 1921b. *The Louis Comfort Tiffany Foundation, Oyster Bay, Long Island*. Oyster Bay, N.Y., 1921.

Tiffany Foundation 1922a. *Exhibition of Watercolors by Louis C. Tiffany at the Louis C. Tiffany Foundation Gallery 2/4–25/22*. New York, 1922.

Tiffany Foundation 1922b. *The Louis Comfort Tiffany Foundation, Oyster Bay, Long Island*. Oyster Bay, N.Y., 1922.

"Tiffany Home" 1946. "Tiffany Home and Art Works Will Go on Sale." *New York Herald Tribune*, September 8, 1946, p. 46.

"Tiffany House" 1884. "The Tiffany House." *Real Estate Record and Builders' Guide* 34 (July 26, 1884), pp. 785–86.

"Tiffany House" 1900. "The Tiffany House." *Architectural Record* 10, no. 2 (October 1900), pp. 191–202.

"Tiffany Mansion" 1957. "Old Tiffany Mansion Burns on L. I. North Shore." *New York Times*, March 8, 1957, p. 27.

"Tiffany Property" 1946. "Tiffany Property to Go at Auction." *New York Times*, September 8, 1946, p. 39.

Tiffany Studios 1906. *The Tiffany Studios Collection of Notable Antique Oriental Rugs*. Text by Mary Churchill Ripley. New York, 1906.

Tiffany Studios 1907. *The Tiffany Studios Collection of Notable Oriental Rugs*. Text by Mary Churchill Ripley. New York, 1907.

Tiffany Studios 1908. *The Tiffany Studios Collection of Antique Chinese Rugs*. Text by Mary Churchill Ripley. New York, 1908.

Tiffany Studios 1913. Tiffany Studios. *Character and Individuality in Decorations and Furnishings*. New York, 1913.

"Tiffany Wins" 1904. "Louis C. Tiffany Wins." *New York Times*, May 22, 1904, p. 2.

"Tiffany's Hall" 1894. "Mr. Louis Comfort Tiffany's Hall." *Decorator and Furnisher* 25, no. 3 (December 1894), p. 94.

Townsend 1899. Horace Townsend. "American and French Applied Art at the Grafton Galleries." *International Studio* 8 (1899), pp. 39–44.

Van Wagner 1985. Judy Collischan Van Wagner, ed. *Long Island Estate Gardens*. Exh. cat. Greenvale, N.Y., Hillwood Art Gallery, Long Island University, May 22–June 21, 1985. Greenvale, N.Y., 1985.

Vedder 1910. Elihu Vedder. *The Digressions of V*. Boston, 1910.

Waern 1897. Cecilia Waern. "The Industrial Arts of America: The Tiffany Glass and Decorative Co." *International Studio* 2 (September 1897), pp. 156–65.

D. Walker 1939. Dorothy Walker. "Louis Comfort Tiffany Made Laurelton Hall a World's Museum." *New York World-Telegram*, December 29, 1939, sec. 2, p. 11.

S. Walker 1983. Steven F. Walker. "Vivekananda and American Occultism." In *The Occult in America*, edited by Howard Kerr and Charles L. Crow, pp. 162–76. Urbana, 1983.

Washburn 1984. Dorothy K. Washburn. "Dealers and Collectors of Indian Baskets at the Turn of the Century in California." *Empirical Studies of the Arts* 2, no. 1 (1984), pp. 51–74.

"Water-Color Society" 1888. "The Gallery: Exhibitions of the Water-Color Society and the Etching Club." *Art Amateur* 18, no. 4 (March 1888), pp. 82–84.

Weisberg 1986. Gabriel P. Weisberg. *Art Nouveau Bing: Paris Style 1900*. New York, 1986.

Weisberg et al. 1975. Gabriel P. Weisberg et al. *Japonisme: Japanese Influence on French Art, 1854–1910*. Exh. cat. Cleveland Museum of Art, July 9–August 31, 1975; Rutgers University Art Gallery, October 4–November 16, 1975; Baltimore, Walters Art Gallery, December 10, 1975–January 26, 1976. Cleveland, 1975.

Weisberg et al. 2005. Gabriel P. Weisberg et al., eds. *The Origins of L'Art Nouveau: The Bing Empire*. Exh. cat. Amsterdam, La Maison Bing, Van Gogh Museum, November 26, 2004–February 27, 2005. Amsterdam, 2004.

White 1998. Samuel G. White. *The Houses of McKim, Mead and White*. New York, 1998.

Williams 1989. Lester L. Williams. *C. N. Cotton and His Navajo Blankets: A Biography of C. N. Cotton, Gallup, New Mexico Indian Trader*. Albuquerque, 1989.

Wilmerding 1994. John Wilmerding. *The Artist's Mount Desert: American Painters on the Maine Coast*. Princeton, 1994.

Wood 1993. John Wood. *The Art of the Autochrome: The Birth of Color Photography*. Iowa City, 1993.

"Woodland" 1931. "Art Colony Woodland Becomes Job Centre: L. C. Tiffany Gives 200 Cords of Standing Timber to Furnish Work at Laurelton, L.I." *New York Times*, November 19, 1931, p. 32.

"World's Fair" 1889. "The Tiffany Exhibit at the World's Fair." *Jewelers' Review* (1889), pp. 18–19.

Zapata 1993. Janet Zapata. *The Jewelry and Enamels of Louis Comfort Tiffany*. New York, 1993.

Zebrowski 1997. Mark Zebrowski. *Gold, Silver and Bronze from Mughal India*. London, 1997.

Zukowski 1999. Karen Zukowski. "Creating Art and Artists: Late Nineteenth-Century American Artists' Studios." Ph.D. diss., City University of New York, 1999.

Works in the Exhibition

Paintings

1. Louis Comfort Tiffany, *A Corner of the 72nd Street Studio*, 1896. Oil on canvas, 30¼ x 12⅛ in. (76.8 x 30.8 cm). Yale University Art Gallery, New Haven, Connecticut, Gift of Louise Tiffany Lusk, B.A. 1929 (1955.13.1) Fig. 56

2. Louis Comfort Tiffany, *Flora (Spring)*, 1887–98. Oil on canvas, 59½ x 94 in. (151.1 x 238.8 cm). Signed at lower left: *Louis C. Tiffany.* The Charles Hosmer Morse Museum of American Art, Winter Park, Florida (70-001) Fig. 173

3. Louis Comfort Tiffany, *Inside Studio on 72nd Street with Flamingos*, 1888. Oil on canvas, 23¼ x 29 in. (59.1 x 73.7 cm). Signed at lower right: *Louis C. Tiffany.* The Charles Hosmer Morse Museum of American Art, Winter Park, Florida (78-012) Fig. 63

4. Louis Comfort Tiffany, *My Family at Somesville*, 1888. Oil on canvas, 23⅞ x 36 in. (60.6 x 91.4 cm). The Charles Hosmer Morse Museum of American Art, Winter Park, Florida (73-001) Fig. 172

5. Louis Comfort Tiffany, *Peonies and Iris*, 1915. Oil on canvas, 37¾ x 24½ in. (95.9 x 62.2 cm). Signed at lower left: *Louis C. Tiffany.* The Charles Hosmer Morse Museum of American Art, Winter Park, Florida (62-027) Fig. 174

6. Louis Comfort Tiffany, *Snake Charmer at Tangier, Africa*, 1872. Oil on canvas, 27½ x 38½ in. (69.9 x 97.8 cm). Signed at lower left: *Louis C. Tiffany*—[illegible]. The Metropolitan Museum of Art, New York, Gift of Louis Comfort Tiffany Foundation, 1921 (21.170) Fig. 115

7. Joaquín Sorolla y Bastida (1863–1923), *Louis Comfort Tiffany*, 1911. Oil on canvas, 59¼ x 88¾ in. (150.5 x 225.5 cm). Signed and dated at lower left: *J. Sorolla y Bastida 1911.* The Hispanic Society of America, New York, Gift of Mrs. Francis M. Weld, 1950 (A3182) Fig. 129

8. Samuel Colman (1832–1920), *On the Hudson at Dobbs Ferry*, ca. 1880. Oil on canvas, 16⅜ x 40 in. (41.6 x 101.6 cm). The Charles Hosmer Morse Museum of American Art, Winter Park, Florida (P-011-81) Fig. 170

9. Alexander Koester (1864–1932), *Ducks*, ca. 1899. Oil on canvas, 43½ x 72 in. (110.5 x 182.9 cm). The Worrell Collection, Charlottesville, Virginia Fig. 163
Lot 999 (illustrated) in 1946 Louis Comfort Tiffany Foundation sale catalogue

Watercolors and Pastels

10. Louis Comfort Tiffany, *The Alhambra*, 1911. Watercolor, 14⅜ x 20½ in. (36.5 x 52.1 cm). Signed at lower left: *Louis C. Tiffany.* Collection of Eric Streiner Fig. 3

11. Louis Comfort Tiffany, *Louise Tiffany, Reading*, 1888. Pastel on buff-colored wove paper, 20½ x 30¼ in. (52.1 x 76.8 cm). Signed and dated at lower right: *Louis C. Tiffany / 88.* The Metropolitan Museum of Art, New York, Partial and Promised Gift of the family of Dorothy Tiffany Burlingham, 2003 (2003.606) Fig. 60

12. Louis Comfort Tiffany, *Old Mill at Freiburg*, 1877. Watercolor and gouache on paper, 15¼ x 20⅜ in. (38.7 x 51.8 cm). Signed at lower right: *L. C. Tiffany.* The Charles Hosmer Morse Museum of American Art, Winter Park, Florida (75-006) Fig. 171

13. Louis Comfort Tiffany, *Taming the Flamingo*, 1888. Watercolor on paper, 28½ x 23 in. (72.4 x 58.4 cm). Signed and dated at lower left: *Louis C. Tiffany 88.* The Charles Hosmer Morse Museum of American Art, Winter Park, Florida (85-011) Fig. 62

14. Louis Comfort Tiffany, *Yellowstone Canyon*, 1917. Watercolor and gouache on tinted paper, 17⅜ x 11⅝ in. (44.1 x 29.5 cm). Signed and dated at lower right: *Louis C. Tiffany / 1917.* The Charles Hosmer Morse Museum of American Art, Winter Park, Florida (77-035) Fig. 102

Architectural Drawings and Elements

15. Louis Comfort Tiffany, Panel from dining-room lunette, ca. 1885. Plaster, glass, paint, 23¾ x 23⅛ in. (60.3 x 58.7 cm). The Charles Hosmer Morse Museum of American Art, Winter Park, Florida (57-033:01) Fig. 29

16. Louis Comfort Tiffany, Panel from dining-room lunette, ca. 1885. Plaster, glass, paint, 23 x 22 in. (58.4 x 55.9 cm). The Charles Hosmer Morse Museum of American Art, Winter Park, Florida (57-021:D) Fig. 30

17. Louis Comfort Tiffany, Panel from dining-room lunette, ca. 1885. Plaster, glass, paint, 25 x 22⅞ in. (63.5 x 58.1 cm). The Charles Hosmer Morse Museum of American Art, Winter Park, Florida (57-021:G)

18. Louis Comfort Tiffany, Two fragments from dining-room lunette, ca. 1885. Leaded glass, each: 15 x 11 in. (38.1 x 27.9 cm). The Charles Hosmer Morse Museum of American Art, Winter Park, Florida (77-036:F; 77-036:A) Fig. 31 (one fragment)

19. Louis Comfort Tiffany, Fragment from dining-room lunette, ca. 1885. Leaded glass, 19¼ x 19½ in. (48.9 x 49.5 cm). The Charles Hosmer Morse Museum of American Art, Winter Park, Florida (78-0140:D) Fig. 32

20. Louis Comfort Tiffany, *The 72nd Street House*, ca. 1883. Graphite and ink on paper, 4⁹⁄₁₆ x 7⁹⁄₁₆ in. (11.6 x 19.2 cm). Signed on separate backing: *My first sketch for the 72 Street House—LCT.* The Charles Hosmer Morse Museum of American Art, Winter Park, Florida (80-014) Fig. 93

21. Richard Pryor (1879–1964), Architectural drawing: Elevation of Laurelton Hall, conservatories, ca. 1903. Blueprint on wove paper, 18¼ x 60¾ in. (46.4 x 154.3 cm). The Charles Hosmer Morse Museum of American Art, Winter Park, Florida (78-511:08) Fig. 99

22. Richard Pryor (1879–1964), Architectural drawing: Elevation of Laurelton Hall looking east, ca. 1902. Aniline dye on cloth, 24 x 27½ in. (61 x 69.9 cm). The Charles Hosmer Morse Museum of American Art, Winter Park, Florida (78-511:02) Fig. 98

23. Richard Pryor (1879–1964), Architectural drawing: Elevation of Laurelton Hall looking north, ca. 1903. Aniline dye on cloth, 23½ x 51 in. (59.7 x 129.5 cm). The Charles Hosmer Morse Museum of American Art, Winter Park, Florida (78-511:10) Fig. 100

24. Richard Pryor (1879–1964), Architectural drawing: Elevation of Laurelton Hall looking south, ca. 1903. Graphite and ink on starched cloth, 22 x 52¾ in. (55.9 x 134 cm). The Charles Hosmer Morse Museum of American Art, Winter Park, Florida (78-511:07) Fig. 101

25. Richard Pryor (1879–1964), Architectural drawing: Elevation of Laurelton Hall looking west, ca. 1902. Aniline dye on cloth, 23½ x 28½ in. (59.7 x 72.4 cm). The Charles Hosmer Morse Museum of American Art, Winter Park, Florida (78-511:03) Fig. 97

26. Richard Pryor (1879–1964), Architectural drawing: Elevation of Laurelton Hall, reception-room mantel, ca. 1903. Ink and graphite on linen, 15¾ x 14⅜ in. (40 x 36.5 cm). The Charles Hosmer Morse Museum of American Art, Winter Park, Florida (77-021)

27. Richard Pryor (1879–1964), Architectural drawing: First-floor plan, Laurelton Hall, ca. 1903. Aniline dye on cloth, 27 x 49 in. (68.6 x 124.5 cm). The Charles Hosmer Morse Museum of American Art, Winter Park, Florida (78-511:09) Fig. 108

28. Richard Pryor (1879–1964), Architectural drawing: Second-floor plan, Laurelton Hall, ca. 1903. Aniline dye on cloth, 27 x 48¾ in. (68.6 x 123.8 cm). The Charles Hosmer Morse Museum of American Art, Winter Park, Florida (78-511:06)

29. Daffodil Terrace, originally built ca. 1914 (conserved and reassembled, 2006). Marble, Favrile glass, stenciled wood, composite tiles; column (includes capital, shaft, and base): H. 131 in. (332.7 cm). The Charles Hosmer Morse Museum of American Art, Winter Park, Florida (57-023; 57-027; 57-028; 59-004; 59-005; 59-006; 59-007)

30. Mantel from dining room, Laurelton Hall, originally installed 1904–6 (conserved and reassembled, 2006). Marble, Favrile glass, H. 162 in. (411.5 cm). The Charles Hosmer Morse Museum of American Art, Winter Park, Florida (59-014)

31. *Map of Laurelton Hall*, 1907–8. Ink on starched cloth, 50 x 72 in. (127 x 182.9 cm). Society for the Preservation of Long Island Antiquities, Cold Spring Harbor, New York Fig. 68

32. Model of minaret, ca. 1903. Wood, 59¾ x 12 in. (151.8 x 30.5 cm). The Charles Hosmer Morse Museum of American Art, Winter Park, Florida (60.009) Fig. 90

33. Pair of doors with frame, originally from vestibule to studio, Tiffany House. Ahmadabad, India, 1882. Imported by Tiffany and de Forest Decorators. Teakwood, 95 x 107½ x 5 in. (241.3 x 273.1 x 12. 7 cm) (with frame). The Charles Hosmer Morse Museum of American Art, Winter Park, Florida (59-012:A, B) Fig. 45

34. Wall fragments from Fountain Court, Laurelton Hall, ca. 1903. Painted plaster, 14 x 28 in. (35.6 x 71.1 cm). The Mark Twain House and Museum, Hartford, Connecticut (70.23.7) Fig. 128

35. Rock crystal from terrace fountain, largest crystal: 19½ x 17½ x 11½ in. (49.5 x 44.5 x 29.2 cm). The Charles Hosmer Morse Museum of American Art, Winter Park, Florida (2004-022) Fig. 73

36. Stenciled wall fragment from Fountain Court, Laurelton Hall, ca. 1903. Painted textile, 124 x 20 in. (315 x 50.8 cm). The Mark Twain House and Museum, Hartford, Connecticut (70.23.1) Fig. 126

Furniture

37. Louis Comfort Tiffany (case), Steinway & Sons, Piano, 1888. Cherry (?), 58 x 61¼ x 28¼ in. (147.3 x 155.6 x 71.8 cm). Private collection Fig. 49

38. Louis Comfort Tiffany, designer, J. Matthew Meier (1830–1913) and Ernest Hagen (1822–1889), cabinetmakers (active 1858–88), Armchair from 72nd Street house, 1882–85. Maple, white enamel paint (replaced upholstery), 49 x 18 in. (124.5 x 45.7 cm). The Mark Twain House and Museum, Hartford, Connecticut (76.17.4.1)

39. Louis Comfort Tiffany, designer, J. Matthew Meier (1830–1913) and Ernest Hagen (1822–1889), cabinetmakers (active 1858–88), Side chair from 72nd Street house, 1882–85. Maple, white enamel paint (replaced upholstery), 40¼ x 19½ x 18 in. (102.2 x 49.5 x 45.7 cm). The Mark Twain House & Museum, Hartford, Connecticut (76.17.4.2) Fig. 34

40. Louis Comfort Tiffany, designer, J. Matthew Meier (1830–1913) and Ernest Hagen (1822–1889), cabinetmakers (active 1858–88), Table from 72nd Street house, 1882–85. Maple, white enamel paint, 28 x 60 x 48 in. (71.1 x 152.4 x 121.9 cm). The Mark Twain House & Museum, Hartford, Connecticut (76.17.3) Fig. 34

41. Louis Comfort Tiffany, Tiffany Studios, Dining table from dining room, Laurelton Hall, ca. 1905. Cherry (?), cream enamel paint, 29½ x 66 in. (74.9 x 167.6 cm). The Charles Hosmer Morse Museum of American Art, Winter Park, Florida (58-010:1) Fig. 160

42. Louis Comfort Tiffany, Tiffany Studios, Armchair and three side chairs from dining room, Laurelton Hall, ca. 1905. Cherry (?), cream enamel paint (replicated upholstery), armchair: 45 x 19½ x 18½ in. (114.3 x 49.5 x 47 cm); side chair: 43½ x 15 x 17 in. (110.5 x 38.1 x 43.2 cm). The Charles Hosmer Morse Museum of American Art, Winter Park, Florida (58-010:2; 58-010:3; 58-010:5; 58-010:6) Fig. 161 (armchair)

Leaded-Glass Windows

43. Louis Comfort Tiffany, Louis C. Tiffany and Company, *Eggplant* window, ca. 1879. Leaded glass, 32¼ x 42¼ in. (81.9 x 107.3 cm). The Charles Hosmer Morse Museum of American Art, Winter Park, Florida (71-003) Fig. 22

44. Louis Comfort Tiffany, Bella apartment window, ca. 1880. Leaded glass, 24¼ x 29½ in. (61.5 x 74.9 cm). The Metropolitan Museum of Art, New York, Gift of Robert Koch, 2002 (2002.474) Fig. 13

45. Louis Comfort Tiffany, Tiffany Glass and Decorating Company, *Butterfly* window, ca. 1885–92. Leaded glass, 63 x 61⅝ in. (160 x 156.5 cm). The Charles Hosmer Morse Museum of American Art, Winter Park, Florida (60-006) Fig. 43

46. Louis Comfort Tiffany, Tiffany Glass Company, *Flower, Fish, and Fruit* window, 1885. Leaded glass, 30½ x 41⅞ in. (77.5 x 106.4 cm). The Baltimore Museum of Art (1979.173) Fig. 248

47. Louis Comfort Tiffany, Tiffany Glass Company, Three *Magnolia* panels, ca. 1885. Leaded glass, 52⅞ x 18½ in. (134.3 x 47 cm), 52⅞ x 19½ in. (134.3 x 48.6 cm), 52⅞ x 19 in. (134.3 x 48.3 cm). The Charles Hosmer Morse Museum of American Art, Winter Park, Florida (58-013) Fig. 39

48. Louis Comfort Tiffany, Tiffany Glass and Decorating Company, *Medallion* window, ca. 1892. Leaded Favrile glass, 144½ x 48³⁄₁₆ in. (367 x 122.4 cm). The Charles Hosmer Morse Museum of American Art, Winter Park, Florida (U-073) Fig. 243

49. Design attributed to Frank Brangwyn (1867–1956), Tiffany Glass and Decorating Company, *Child with Gourd*, ca. 1898. Leaded Favrile glass, 53 x $45\frac{7}{8}$ in. (134.6 x 116.5 cm). The Charles Hosmer Morse Museum of American Art, Winter Park, Florida (U-070) Fig. 247

50. Louis Comfort Tiffany, Tiffany Glass and Decorating Company, *Feeding the Flamingoes*, ca. 1892. Leaded Favrile glass, $60\frac{3}{16}$ x $43\frac{3}{8}$ in. (152.9 x 110.2 cm). The Charles Hosmer Morse Museum of American Art, Winter Park, Florida (U-072) Fig. 246

51. Louis Comfort Tiffany, Tiffany Glass and Decorating Company, Top border with eagle from *Four Seasons*, 1899–1900. Leaded Favrile glass, $17\frac{3}{8}$ x $80\frac{3}{16}$ in. (44.1 x 203.7 cm). The Charles Hosmer Morse Museum of American Art, Winter Park, Florida (57-020) Fig. 250

52. Louis Comfort Tiffany, Tiffany Glass and Decorating Company, Four side border panels from *Four Seasons*, 1899–1900. Leaded Favrile glass, A and B: 45 x $13\frac{3}{8}$ in. (114.3 x 34 cm); C and D: $56\frac{13}{16}$ x $13\frac{3}{8}$ in. (144.3 x 34 cm). The Charles Hosmer Morse Museum of American Art, Winter Park, Florida (64-036:A; 64-036:B; 64-036:C; 64-036:D) Fig. 251 (64-036:D)

53. Louis Comfort Tiffany, Tiffany Glass and Decorating Company, Bottom border with urns from *Four Seasons*, 1899–1900. Leaded Favrile glass, $28\frac{15}{16}$ x $83\frac{3}{8}$ in. (73.5 x 211.8 cm). The Charles Hosmer Morse Museum of American Art, Winter Park, Florida (U-083) Fig. 254

54. Louis Comfort Tiffany, Tiffany Glass and Decorating Company, *Spring* from *Four Seasons*, 1899–1900. Leaded Favrile glass, $40\frac{1}{4}$ x $39\frac{3}{8}$ in. (102.2 x 100 cm). The Charles Hosmer Morse Museum of American Art, Winter Park, Florida (57-018) Fig. 255

55. Louis Comfort Tiffany, Tiffany Glass and Decorating Company, *Summer* from *Four Seasons*, 1899–1900. Leaded Favrile glass, $40\frac{1}{2}$ x $36\frac{5}{8}$ in. (102.9 x 93 cm). The Charles Hosmer Morse Museum of American Art, Winter Park, Florida (57-017) Fig. 256

56. Louis Comfort Tiffany, Tiffany Glass and Decorating Company, *Winter* from *Four Seasons*, 1899–1900. Leaded Favrile glass, $39\frac{3}{4}$ x $32\frac{7}{8}$ in. (101 x 83.5 cm). The Charles Hosmer Morse Museum of American Art, Winter Park, Florida (62-033) Fig. 257

57. Louis Comfort Tiffany, Tiffany Glass and Decorating Company, *Autumn* from *Four Seasons*, 1899–1900. Leaded Favrile glass, $39\frac{5}{8}$ x $36\frac{1}{4}$ in. (100.6 x 92.1 cm). The Charles Hosmer Morse Museum of American Art, Winter Park, Florida (57-019) Fig. 258

58. Louis Comfort Tiffany, Tiffany Glass and Decorating Company, *Pumpkin and Beets*, ca. 1899–1900. Leaded Favrile glass, $44\frac{7}{8}$ x $56\frac{1}{4}$ in. (114 x 142.9 cm). The Charles Hosmer Morse Museum of American Art, Winter Park, Florida (U-074) Fig. 259

59. Louis Comfort Tiffany, Tiffany Studios, *Snowball*, ca. 1904. Leaded Favrile glass, $26\frac{3}{16}$ x $32\frac{1}{4}$ in. (66.5 x 81.9 cm). The Charles Hosmer Morse Museum of American Art, Winter Park, Florida (58-015) Fig. 260

60. Louis Comfort Tiffany, Tiffany Studios, *Rose* window, 1906. Leaded Favrile glass, $70\frac{1}{2}$ x $58\frac{5}{8}$ in. (179.1 x 148.9 cm). The Charles Hosmer Morse Museum of American Art, Winter Park, Florida (62-034) Fig. 263

61. Louis Comfort Tiffany, Tiffany Studios, *Wisteria* panel, ca. 1910–20. Leaded Favrile glass, $37\frac{1}{8}$ x $96\frac{1}{4}$ in. (94.3 x 244.5 cm). The Charles Hosmer Morse Museum of American Art, Winter Park, Florida (59-010) Fig. 150

62. Louis Comfort Tiffany, Tiffany Studios, *Wisteria* panel, ca. 1910–20. Leaded Favrile glass, $36\frac{1}{2}$ x $47\frac{3}{4}$ in. (92.7 x 121.3 cm). The Charles Hosmer Morse Museum of American Art, Winter Park, Florida (59-009:A) Fig. 149

63. Louis Comfort Tiffany, Tiffany Studios, *Wisteria* panel, ca. 1910–20. Leaded Favrile glass, $36\frac{5}{16}$ x $47\frac{5}{16}$ in. (92.2 x 120.2 cm). The Charles Hosmer Morse Museum of American Art, Winter Park, Florida (59-009:C) Fig. 151

64. Louis Comfort Tiffany, Tiffany Studios, *Wisteria* panel, ca. 1910–20. Leaded Favrile glass, $36\frac{5}{8}$ x $69\frac{3}{4}$ in. (93 x 177.2 cm). The Charles Hosmer Morse Museum of American Art, Winter Park, Florida (58-014) Fig. 153

65. Louis Comfort Tiffany, Tiffany Studios, *Wisteria* panel, ca. 1910–20. Leaded Favrile glass, $36\frac{5}{8}$ x $47\frac{3}{4}$ in. (93 x 121.3 cm). The Charles Hosmer Morse Museum of American Art, Winter Park, Florida (59-009:B) Fig. 152

66. Louis Comfort Tiffany, Tiffany Studios, *Wisteria* panel, ca. 1910–20. Leaded Favrile glass, $36\frac{3}{4}$ x $69\frac{3}{4}$ in. (93.3 x 177.2 cm). The Charles Hosmer Morse Museum of American Art, Winter Park, Florida (59-011) Fig. 154

67. Louis Comfort Tiffany, Tiffany Studios, *Tree of Life* window, 1928–31. Leaded Favrile glass, 120 x 82 in. (304.8 x 208.3 cm). The Charles Hosmer Morse Museum of American Art, Winter Park, Florida (67-022:A–H) Fig. 338

68. Louis Comfort Tiffany, Window fragment. Leaded glass, $21\frac{1}{2}$ x $26\frac{1}{2}$ in. (54.6 x 67.3 cm). The Charles Hosmer Morse Museum of American Art, Winter Park, Florida (78-0140:B) Fig. 341

69. Louis Comfort Tiffany, Window fragment. Leaded glass, $12\frac{1}{2}$ x 14 in. (31.8 x 35.6 cm). The Charles Hosmer Morse Museum of American Art, Winter Park, Florida (78-0140:A)

Lighting

70. Louis Comfort Tiffany, Pendant, ca. 1885. Leaded glass, $21\frac{3}{4}$ x $25\frac{1}{4}$ in. (55.2 x 64.1 cm). Associated Artists, LLC, Southport, Connecticut Fig. 51

71. Louis Comfort Tiffany, Tiffany Studios, Black-eyed Susan hanging lamp, 1900–1906. Leaded Favrile glass, Diam. $25\frac{1}{2}$ in. (64.8 cm). The Charles Hosmer Morse Museum of American Art, Winter Park, Florida (67-018) Fig. 143

72. Louis Comfort Tiffany, Tiffany Studios, Dome hanging shade from dining room, Laurelton Hall, ca. 1904–6. Leaded Favrile glass, Diam. 66 in. (167.6 cm). The Charles Hosmer Morse Museum of American Art, Winter Park, Florida (70-021) Fig. 158

73. Louis Comfort Tiffany, Tiffany Furnaces, Hanging globe from Fountain Court, Laurelton Hall, ca. 1904–10. Favrile glass, 11 x 8 in. (27.9 x 20.3 cm). Museum of Fine Arts, Boston, Anonymous gift in memory of John G. Pierce, Sr. (65.216) Fig. 122

74. Louis Comfort Tiffany, Tiffany Furnaces, Hanging globe from Fountain Court, Laurelton Hall, ca. 1904–1910. Favrile glass, gilt-bronze collar, $13\frac{1}{8}$ x $8\frac{1}{2}$ in. (33.3 x 21.6 cm). The Charles Hosmer Morse Museum of American Art, Winter Park, Florida (2003-021) Fig. 121

75. Louis Comfort Tiffany, Tiffany Studios, Two hanging spherical turtleback globes from living hall, Laurelton Hall, ca. 1905. Leaded Favrile glass, each: $13\frac{1}{2}$ x $12\frac{1}{2}$ in. (34.3 x 31.8 cm). The Charles Hosmer Morse Museum of American Art, Winter Park, Florida (56-044:1; 56-044:2) Fig. 141

76. Louis Comfort Tiffany, Tiffany Studios, Three hanging turtleback lamps from living hall, Laurelton Hall, ca. 1905. Leaded Favrile glass, each: Diam. 18 in. (45.7 cm). The Charles Hosmer Morse Museum of American Art, Winter Park, Florida (56-045:1; 51-045:2; 64-009:1) Fig. 142

GLASS

77. Louis Comfort Tiffany, Tiffany Glass and Decorating Company, Vase, 1895–1900. Favrile glass, H. 3¾ in. (9.5 cm). Inscribed on underside: *174 A-coll. / L.C.T.* Collection of Eric Streiner   Fig. 188

78. Louis Comfort Tiffany, Tiffany Glass and Decorating Company, Vase, 1895–1900. Favrile glass, H. 12¾ in. (32.4 cm). Inscribed on underside: *X855.* Collection of Eric Streiner   Fig. 177

79. Louis Comfort Tiffany, Tiffany Glass and Decorating Company, Vase, 1895–1900. Favrile glass, H. 16½ in. (41.9 cm). Inscribed on underside: *X2930.* Collection of Eric Streiner   Fig. 181

80. Louis Comfort Tiffany, Tiffany Glass and Decorating Company, Vase, 1895–1902. Favrile glass, H. 17⅞ in. (45.4 cm). Inscribed on underside: *L.C.T. / F 692.* Oval paper sticker affixed to shoulder, stamped: *120.* Collection of Tony and Mary Ann Terranova   Fig. 186
Lot 62 (illustrated) in 1946 Louis Comfort Tiffany Foundation sale catalogue

81. Louis Comfort Tiffany, Tiffany Glass and Decorating Company, Vase, 1895–1902. Favrile glass, H. 9⅞ in. (25.1 cm). Inscribed on underside: *L. C. Tiffany / Favrile / 123 A-coll.* Original paper label: *Favrile glass / Tiffany / Registered.* Collection of Tony and Mary Ann Terranova   Fig. 214

82. Louis Comfort Tiffany, Tiffany Glass and Decorating Company, Vase, 1895–1902. Favrile glass, H. 6¾ in. (17.1 cm). Inscribed on underside: *L. C. Tiffany–Favrile / 111 A-coll.* The Charles Hosmer Morse Museum of American Art, Winter Park, Florida (66-053)   Fig. 189

83. Louis Comfort Tiffany, Tiffany Glass and Decorating Company, Vase, 1895–1902. Favrile glass, H. 3¼ in. (8.3 cm). Inscribed on underside: *L. C. Tiffany–Favrile / 104 A-coll.* The Charles Hosmer Morse Museum of American Art, Winter Park, Florida (66-051)   Fig. 191

84. Louis Comfort Tiffany, Tiffany Glass and Decorating Company or Tiffany Furnaces, Vase, 1895–1910. Favrile glass, H. 7½ in. (19.1 cm). Inscribed on underside: *L. C. Tiffany–Favrile / 120 A-coll.* Collection of Eric Streiner   Fig. 203

85. Louis Comfort Tiffany, Tiffany Glass and Decorating Company or Tiffany Furnaces, Vase, 1895–1910. Favrile glass, H. 5⅛ in. (13 cm). Inscribed on underside: *101 A-coll. / L. C. Tiffany–Favrile.* Collection of Eric Streiner   Fig. 202

86. Louis Comfort Tiffany, Tiffany Glass and Decorating Company, Vase, ca. 1897. Favrile glass, H. 11¼ in. (28.6 cm). Inscribed on underside: *Louis C. Tiffany / 02956.* The Metropolitan Museum of Art, New York, Gift of Louis Comfort Tiffany Foundation, 1951 (51.121.20)   Fig. 179

87. Louis Comfort Tiffany, Tiffany Glass and Decorating Company, Vase, ca. 1897. Favrile glass, H. 13⅜ in. (34 cm). Inscribed on underside: *03028 / Louis C. Tiffany.* The Metropolitan Museum of Art, New York, Gift of Louis Comfort Tiffany Foundation, 1951 (51.121.25)   Fig. 178

88. Louis Comfort Tiffany, Tiffany Glass and Decorating Company, Vase, 1897–1900. Favrile glass, H. 5 in. (12.7 cm). Inscribed on underside: *109 A-coll. / L. C. Tiffany–Favrile.* The Charles Hosmer Morse Museum of American Art, Winter Park, Florida (65-004)   Fig. 187

89. Louis Comfort Tiffany, Tiffany Glass and Decorating Company, Vase, ca. 1900. Favrile glass, H. 10¾ in. (27.3 cm). Inscribed on underside: *Louis C. Tiffany / 07281.* The Metropolitan Museum of Art, New York, Gift of Louis Comfort Tiffany Foundation, 1951 (51.121.2)   Fig. 194

90. Louis Comfort Tiffany, Tiffany Glass and Decorating Company, Vase, ca. 1900. Favrile glass, H. 18½ in. (47 cm). Inscribed on underside: *T / 03076.* Original paper label: *TG&D Co.* The Huntington Library, Art Collections,

and Botanical Gardens, San Marino, California, Gift of the Art Collectors Council (2004.7)   Fig. 197
Lot 271 (illustrated) in 1946 Louis Comfort Tiffany Foundation sale catalogue

91. Louis Comfort Tiffany, Tiffany Glass and Decorating Company, Vase, 1900–1902. Favrile glass, H. 16 in. (40.6 cm). Inscribed on underside: *L.C.T. / M 1468.* Collection of Eric Streiner   Fig. 199

92. Louis Comfort Tiffany, Tiffany Glass and Decorating Company, Vase, 1900–1902. Favrile glass, H. 18¹¹⁄₁₆ in. (47.5 cm). Inscribed on underside: *T 1269 / L.C.T.* The Metropolitan Museum of Art, New York, Gift of Louis Comfort Tiffany Foundation, 1951 (51.121.17)   Fig. 199

93. Louis Comfort Tiffany, Tiffany Glass and Decorating Company, Vase, 1900–1902. Favrile glass, H. 15⅝ in. (39.7 cm). Inscribed on underside: *L.C.T. / M 2914.* The Metropolitan Museum of Art, New York, Gift of Louis Comfort Tiffany Foundation, 1951 (51.121.27)   Fig. 199

94. Louis Comfort Tiffany, Tiffany Glass and Decorating Company or Tiffany Furnaces, Vase, 1900–1915. Favrile glass, H. 12 in. (30.5 cm). Inscribed on underside: *9686-G / L. C. Tiffany–Favrile.* Original paper label: *LCT* [conjoined]. Collection of Eric Streiner   Fig. 213
Lot 37 (illustrated) in 1946 Louis Comfort Tiffany Foundation sale catalogue

95. Louis Comfort Tiffany, Tiffany Glass and Decorating Company or Tiffany Furnaces, Vase, 1900–1915. Favrile glass, H. 23 in. (58.4 cm). Inscribed on underside: *Louis C. Tiffany 03950.* Original paper label: *TG&D Co.* Collection of Eric Streiner   Fig. 196
Lot 273 (illustrated) in 1946 Louis Comfort Tiffany Foundation sale catalogue

96. Louis Comfort Tiffany, Tiffany Glass and Decorating Company or Tiffany Furnaces, Plaque, 1900–1915. Favrile glass, Diam. 15½ in. (39.4 cm). Inscribed on underside: *206 A-coll. L . C. Tiffany–Favrile.* The Charles Hosmer Morse Museum of American Art, Winter Park, Florida (82-001)   Fig. 176

97. Louis Comfort Tiffany, Tiffany Furnaces, Vase, ca. 1903. Favrile glass, H. 18¼ in. (46.4 cm). Inscribed on underside: *L.C.T. 7833.* Collection of Eric Streiner   Fig. 200

98. Louis Comfort Tiffany, Tiffany Furnaces, Vase, ca. 1903. Favrile glass, H. 11³⁄₁₆ in. (28.4 cm). The Metropolitan Museum of Art, New York, Gift of Louis Comfort Tiffany Foundation, 1951 (51.121.8)   Fig. 195

99. Louis Comfort Tiffany, Tiffany Furnaces, Vase, ca. 1903. Favrile glass, H. 4½ in. (11.4 cm). Inscribed on underside: *113 A-coll. / L. C. Tiffany.* The Metropolitan Museum of Art, New York, Gift of Louis Comfort Tiffany Foundation, 1951 (51.121.18)   Fig. 209

100. Louis Comfort Tiffany, Tiffany Furnaces, Vase, ca. 1903. Favrile glass, H. 8⁷⁄₁₆ in. (21.4 cm). Inscribed on underside: *Louis C. Tiffany / R 2415.* The Metropolitan Museum of Art, New York, Gift of Louis Comfort Tiffany Foundation, 1951 (51.121.28)   Fig. 207

101. Louis Comfort Tiffany, Tiffany Furnaces, Vase, ca. 1904. Favrile glass, H. 10⅜ in. (26.4 cm). Inscribed on underside: *135 A-coll. / L. C. Tiffany–Favrile.* The Metropolitan Museum of Art, New York, Gift of Louis Comfort Tiffany Foundation, 1951 (51.121.14)   Fig. 206

102. Pair of color wheels for fountain illumination, ca. 1904–10. Glass, lead, brass, each: Diam. 14 in. (35.6 cm). The Charles Hosmer Morse Museum of American Art, Winter Park, Florida (U:102:1; U:102:2)   Fig. 135

103. Louis Comfort Tiffany, Tiffany Furnaces, Four tiles from loggia, Laurelton Hall, ca. 1905. Favrile glass, each: 4 x 4 in. (10.2 x 10.2 cm). The Metropolitan Museum of Art, New York, Gift of Robert Koch   Fig. 78

104. Louis Comfort Tiffany, Tiffany Furnaces, Vase, ca. 1905. Favrile glass, H. 3 13/16 in. (9.7 cm). Inscribed on underside: *L. C. Tiffany–Favrile / Salon-1906 / 105 A-coll.* The Metropolitan Museum of Art, New York, Gift of Louis Comfort Tiffany Foundation, 1951 (51.121.23)   Fig. 190

105. Louis Comfort Tiffany, Tiffany Furnaces, Vase, 1905–15. Favrile glass, H. 7 7/8 in. (20 cm). Inscribed on underside: *8526 K / L. C. Tiffany–Favrile.* Private collection   Fig. 204
Lot 261 (illustrated) in 1946 Louis Comfort Tiffany Foundation sale catalogue

106. Louis Comfort Tiffany, Tiffany Furnaces, Vase, ca. 1906. Favrile glass, H. 4 7/8 in. (12.4 cm). Inscribed on underside: *6673 M.* The Metropolitan Museum of Art, New York, Gift of Louis Comfort Tiffany Foundation, 1951 (51.121.1)   Fig. 182

107. Louis Comfort Tiffany, Tiffany Furnaces, Vase for central fountain, Fountain Court, ca. 1906–15. Glass, H. 49 in. (124.5 cm). The Charles Hosmer Morse Museum of American Art, Winter Park, Florida (56-046)   Fig. 133

108. Louis Comfort Tiffany, Tiffany Furnaces, Bowl, ca. 1908. Favrile glass, H. 6 5/16 in. (16.0 cm). Inscribed on underside: *21 A / L. C. Tiffany–Favrile.* The Metropolitan Museum of Art, New York, Gift of Louis Comfort Tiffany Foundation, 1951 (51.121.13)   Fig. 193

109. Louis Comfort Tiffany, Tiffany Furnaces, Vase, ca. 1909. Favrile glass, H. 16 7/16 in. (41.8 cm). Inscribed on underside: *176 A-coll. / L. C. Tiffany–Favrile.* The Metropolitan Museum of Art, New York, Gift of Louis Comfort Tiffany Foundation, 1951 (51.121.22)   Fig. 205

110. Louis Comfort Tiffany, Tiffany Furnaces, Vase, ca. 1910. Favrile glass, H. 6 1/8 in. (15.6 cm). Inscribed on underside: *46 A-coll. / L. C. Tiffany–Favrile.* The Metropolitan Museum of Art, New York, Gift of Louis Comfort Tiffany Foundation, 1951 (51.121.10)   Fig. 4

111. Louis Comfort Tiffany, Tiffany Furnaces, Vase, ca. 1910. Favrile glass, H. 5 5/16 in. (13.5 cm). Inscribed on underside: *138 A-coll. / L .C. Tiffany–Favrile.* The Metropolitan Museum of Art, New York, Gift of Louis Comfort Tiffany Foundation, 1951 (51.121.26)   Fig. 180

112. Louis Comfort Tiffany, Tiffany Furnaces, Vase, ca. 1912. Favrile glass, H. 5 3/16 in. (13.2 cm). Inscribed on underside: *8319 J / L. C. Tiffany–Favrile.* The Metropolitan Museum of Art, New York, Gift of Louis Comfort Tiffany Foundation, 1951 (51.121.4)   Fig. 183

113. Louis Comfort Tiffany, Tiffany Furnaces, Vase, ca. 1912. Favrile glass, H. 4 3/4 in. (12.1 cm). Inscribed on underside: *7247 J / L. C. Tiffany–Favrile.* The Metropolitan Museum of Art, New York, Gift of Louis Comfort Tiffany Foundation, 1951 (51.121.7)   Fig. 184

114. Louis Comfort Tiffany, Tiffany Furnaces, Vase, ca. 1912. Favrile glass, H. 5 7/8 in. (14.9 cm). Inscribed on underside: *7239 J / L. C. Tiffany–Favrile.* The Metropolitan Museum of Art, New York, Gift of Louis Comfort Tiffany Foundation, 1951 (51.121.9)   Fig. 185

115. Louis Comfort Tiffany, Tiffany Furnaces, Vase, ca. 1913. Favrile glass, H. 6 5/8 in. (16.8 cm). Inscribed on underside: *150 A-coll. / L. C. Tiffany–Favrile.* The Metropolitan Museum of Art, New York, Gift of Louis Comfort Tiffany Foundation, 1951 (51.121.15)   Fig. 208

116. Louis Comfort Tiffany, Tiffany Furnaces, Aquamarine vase, ca. 1913. Glass, H. 15 1/2 in. (39.4 cm). Inscribed on underside: *L. C. Tiffany–Favrile / 8524 K.* The Metropolitan Museum of Art, New York, Purchase, Friends of the American Wing Fund, 2006 (2006.246)   Fig. 210
Lot 282 in 1946 Louis Comfort Tiffany Foundation sale catalogue

117. Louis Comfort Tiffany, Tiffany Furnaces, Vase, ca. 1915. Favrile glass, H. 3 7/8 in. (9.8 cm). Inscribed on underside: *7252 J / L. C. Tiffany–Favrile.* The

Metropolitan Museum of Art, New York, Gift of Louis Comfort Tiffany Foundation, 1951 (51.121.3)   Fig. 192

CERAMICS

118. Louis Comfort Tiffany, Tiffany Glass and Decorating Company, Vase, ca. 1900. Glazed porcelaneous earthenware, H. 4 5/8 in. (11.7 cm). Inscribed on underside: *181 A-coll. L.C. Tiffany–Favrile Pottery / LCT* [conjoined] / *B.* Inscribed over the glaze: *21 n BL.* The Metropolitan Museum of Art, New York, Gift of Louis Comfort Tiffany Foundation, 1951 (51.121.21)   Fig. 226

119. Louis Comfort Tiffany, Tiffany Furnaces, Vase, 1904–14. Glazed porcelaneous earthenware, H. 12 3/4 in. (32.4 cm). Inscribed on underside: conjoined *LCT / 87-A coll. / L. C. Tiffany–Pottery / Favrile / 7.* Collection of Eric Streiner   Fig. 144

120. Louis Comfort Tiffany, Tiffany Furnaces, Vase, 1904–14. Glazed porcelaneous earthenware, H. 10 in. (25.4 cm). Inscribed on underside: *P428 L. C. Tiffany Pottery.* The Charles Hosmer Morse Museum of American Art, Winter Park, Florida (96-001)   Fig. 147

121. Louis Comfort Tiffany, Tiffany Furnaces, Vase, 1904–14. Glazed porcelaneous earthenware, H. 9 3/4 in. (24.8 cm). Inscribed on underside: *P.247 L. C. Tiffany Favrile Pottery / LCT* [conjoined]. The Charles Hosmer Morse Museum of American Art, Winter Park, Florida (96-002)   Fig. 148

122. Louis Comfort Tiffany, Tiffany Furnaces, Vase, 1904–14. Glazed porcelaneous earthenware, H. 16 3/8 in. (41.6 cm). Inscribed on underside: *82 A-coll. L. C. Tiffany / Favrile Pottery.* The Charles Hosmer Morse Museum of American Art, Winter Park, Florida (66-055)   Fig. 138

123. Louis Comfort Tiffany, Tiffany Furnaces, Vase, 1904–14. Glazed porcelaneous earthenware with bronze base, H. 16 1/2 in. (41.9 cm). Inscribed on underside: *Tiffany Studios.* Incised on underside: *LCT* [conjoined]. The Charles Hosmer Morse Museum of American Art, Winter Park, Florida (78-233)   Fig. 139

124. Louis Comfort Tiffany, Tiffany Furnaces, Vase, 1904–14. Glazed porcelaneous earthenware, H. 10 3/4 in. (27.3 cm). Inscribed on underside: *L. C. Tiffany / Favrile Pottery / 201 A-coll.* The Charles Hosmer Morse Museum of American Art, Winter Park, Florida (79-532)   Fig. 227

125. Louis Comfort Tiffany, Tiffany Furnaces, Vase, 1904–14. Glazed porcelaneous earthenware, H. 14 1/4 in. (37.5 cm). Inscribed on underside: *84 A-coll. / L. C. Tiffany Favrile Pottery / "7"* [conjoined]. The Charles Hosmer Morse Museum of American Art, Winter Park, Florida (77-042)   Fig. 229

126. Louis Comfort Tiffany, Tiffany Furnaces, Vase, 1904–14. Glazed porcelaneous earthenware, H. 5 11/16 in. (14.4 cm). Inscribed on underside: *183 A-coll. L. C. Tiffany / Favrile Pottery.* The Charles Hosmer Morse Museum of American Art, Winter Park, Florida (65-022)   Fig. 230

127. Louis Comfort Tiffany, Tiffany Furnaces, Vase, 1904–14. Glazed porcelaneous earthenware, H. 4 5/8 in. (11.7 cm). Inscribed on underside: *LCT* [conjoined]. The Charles Hosmer Morse Museum of American Art, Winter Park, Florida (80-017)   Fig. 233

128. Louis Comfort Tiffany, Tiffany Furnaces, Vase, 1904–14. White earthenware with nine test glazes, H. 9 in. (22.9 cm). Inscribed on underside: *LCT* [conjoined] / *P.* Notations on glaze tests: *55B / 4q / 23 G / 4H 21 MX / .59L / 59A.* Collection of Eric Streiner   Fig. 234

129. Louis Comfort Tiffany, Tiffany Furnaces, Vase, 1904–14. Glazed porcelaneous earthenware, H. 9 5/8 in. (24.4 cm). Inscribed on underside: *LCT* [conjoined] / *80 A-coll. / L. C. Tiffany / Favrile Pottery.* Collection of Eric Streiner   Fig. 228

130. Louis Comfort Tiffany, Tiffany Furnaces, Vase, 1904–14. Glazed porcelaneous earthenware, H. $5\frac{1}{8}$ in. (13 cm). Inscribed on underside: *LCT* [conjoined] / *P668 / L. C. Tiffany Favrile Pottery / 35 A-coll.* Collection of Eric Streiner Fig. 236

131. Louis Comfort Tiffany, Tiffany Furnaces, Vase, 1904–14. Glazed porcelaneous earthenware, H. $8\frac{3}{4}$ in. (22.2 cm). Inscribed on underside: *LCT* [conjoined]. The Charles Hosmer Morse Museum of American Art, Winter Park, Florida (76-003) Fig. 235

132. Louis Comfort Tiffany, Tiffany Furnaces, Vase, 1904–14. Glazed porcelaneous earthenware, H. $8\frac{3}{4}$ in. (22.2 cm). Inscribed on underside: *L.C.T. Favrile Pottery / P1249.* The Charles Hosmer Morse Museum of American Art, Winter Park, Florida (84-001) Fig. 235

133. Louis Comfort Tiffany, Tiffany Furnaces, Vase, 1904–14. Glazed porcelaneous earthenware, H. $8\frac{7}{8}$ in. (22.5 cm). Inscribed on underside: *LCT* [conjoined]. The Charles Hosmer Morse Museum of American Art, Winter Park, Florida (64-002) Fig. 235

134. Louis Comfort Tiffany, Tiffany Furnaces, Vase, 1904–14. Glazed porcelaneous earthenware, H. $7\frac{3}{4}$ in. (19.7 cm). Inscribed on underside: *L. C. Tiffany Favrile Pottery / 129 A-coll.* The Charles Hosmer Morse Museum of American Art, Winter Park, Florida (55-001) Fig. 232

135. Louis Comfort Tiffany, Tiffany Furnaces, Vase, 1904–14. Glazed porcelaneous earthenware, H. $10\frac{15}{16}$ in. (27.8 cm). Inscribed on underside: *LCT* [conjoined] / *L.C.T. Tiffany–Pottery / 31 A-coll. / P618 / 7.* Collection of Eric Streiner Fig. 231

136. Louis Comfort Tiffany, Tiffany Furnaces, Vase, 1910–14. Electroformed copper coating over white earthenware, H. $7\frac{1}{4}$ in. (18.4 cm). Incised on underside: *L. C. Tiffany–Favrile Bronze Pottery / B.P. 325 / 40 A-coll.* The Charles Hosmer Morse Museum of American Art, Winter Park, Florida (65-026) Fig. 237

137. Louis Comfort Tiffany, Tiffany Furnaces, Vase, 1910–14. Electroformed copper coating over white earthenware, H. $6\frac{7}{16}$ in. (16.4 cm). Incised on underside: *BP 229 / Favrile Bronze Pottery / 33 A-coll.* Collection of Eric Streiner Fig. 238

138. Four tiles. Iznik, Turkey, 1575–1650. Glazed earthenware, each: $7\frac{3}{4}$ x $7\frac{3}{4}$ x $\frac{3}{4}$ in. (19.7 x 19.7 x 1.9 cm). Ball State University Museum of Art, Muncie, Indiana, Gift of David T. Owsley (1991.068.242gg,jj,kk,ll) Fig. 48

139. Two tiles. Iznik, Turkey, 1575–1650. Glazed earthenware, each: $10\frac{1}{2}$ x $10\frac{1}{2}$ x 1 in. (26.7 x 26.7 x 2.5 cm). Ball State University Museum of Art, Muncie, Indiana, Gift of David T. Owsley (1991.068.244a-b) Fig. 127

Enamelware

140. Louis Comfort Tiffany, Tiffany Glass and Decorating Company, Vase, 1898–1902. Enamel on copper, H. $7\frac{1}{8}$ in. (18.1 cm). Inscribed on underside: *162 A-coll L. C. Tiffany / SG123.* The Charles Hosmer Morse Museum of American Art, Winter Park, Florida (66-001) Fig. 221

141. Louis Comfort Tiffany, Tiffany Glass and Decorating Company, Bowl, 1898–1902. Enamel on copper, H. $6\frac{1}{8}$ in. (15.6 cm). Inscribed on underside: *SG44 / Louis C. Tiffany.* The Metropolitan Museum of Art, New York, Gift of Louis Comfort Tiffany Foundation, 1951 (51.121.29) Fig. 220

142. Louis Comfort Tiffany, Tiffany Glass and Decorating Company, Covered box, 1898–1907. Enamel on copper, $2\frac{5}{8}$ x $5\frac{1}{2}$ in. (6.7 x 14 cm). Inscribed on underside: *Louis C. Tiffany / 9151 / 1.* The Metropolitan Museum of Art, New York, Gift of Louis Comfort Tiffany Foundation, 1951 (51.121.33a,b) Fig. 224

143. Louis Comfort Tiffany, Tiffany Glass and Decorating Company, Bowl, 1898–1907. Enamel on copper, H. $2\frac{1}{4}$ in. (5.7 cm). Inscribed on underside: *L.C.T. 109 EL 91.* The Metropolitan Museum of Art, New York, Gift of Louis Comfort Tiffany Foundation, 1951 (51.121.34). Fig. 5

144. Louis Comfort Tiffany, Tiffany Glass and Decorating Company, Covered box, 1898–1907. Enamel on copper, H. $3\frac{1}{16}$ in. (7.8 cm). Inscribed on underside: *EL / 113.* The Metropolitan Museum of Art, New York, Gift of Louis Comfort Tiffany Foundation, 1951 (51.121.35a,b) Fig. 222

145. Louis Comfort Tiffany, Tiffany Glass and Decorating Company, Vase, 1898–1907. Enamel on copper, H. $1\frac{11}{16}$ in. (4.3 cm). Inscribed on underside: *L.C.T. EL 261 90.* The Metropolitan Museum of Art, New York, Gift of Louis Comfort Tiffany Foundation, 1951 (51.121.36) Fig. 223

146. Louis Comfort Tiffany, Tiffany Glass and Decorating Company, Vase, 1898–1907. Enamel on copper, H. $2\frac{1}{8}$ in. (5.4 cm). Inscribed on underside: *EL 112 / XX.* The Metropolitan Museum of Art, New York, Gift of Louis Comfort Tiffany Foundation, 1951 (51.121.37) Fig. 218

147. Louis Comfort Tiffany, Tiffany Glass and Decorating Company, Bowl, 1898–1907. Enamel on copper, H. $1\frac{5}{8}$ in. (4.1 cm). Inscribed on underside: *L.C.T. 263 EL / 114.* The Metropolitan Museum of Art, New York, Gift of Louis Comfort Tiffany Foundation, 1951 (51.121.40) Fig. 5

148. Louis Comfort Tiffany, Tiffany Glass and Decorating Company, Covered box, 1898–1902. Enamel on copper, H. $1\frac{15}{16}$ in. (4.9 cm). Inscribed on underside: *111 / L.C.T. SG 198.* The Metropolitan Museum of Art, New York, Gift of Louis Comfort Tiffany Foundation, 1951 (51.121.41a,b) Fig. 222

149. Louis Comfort Tiffany, Tiffany Glass and Decorating Company, Covered box, 1898–1902. Favrile glass, enamel on copper, $3\frac{7}{8}$ x 6 x $4\frac{13}{16}$ in. (9.8 x 15.2 x 12.2 cm). Inscribed on underside: *Louis C. Tiffany / SG 300 9A.* The Metropolitan Museum of Art, New York, Gift of Louis Comfort Tiffany Foundation, 1951 (51.121.42a,b) Fig. 219

150. Louis Comfort Tiffany, Tiffany Glass and Decorating Company, Bowl, 1898–1907. Enamel on copper, H. $1\frac{1}{2}$ in. (3.8 cm). Inscribed on underside: *L.C.T. 22 469 / EL 230.* The Metropolitan Museum of Art, New York, Gift of Louis Comfort Tiffany Foundation, 1951 (51.121.43). Fig. 5

151. Louis Comfort Tiffany, Tiffany Glass and Decorating Company, "Gourd" tray, ca. 1900. Enamel on copper, $25\frac{1}{2}$ x 14 in. (64.8 x 35.6 cm). The Erving and Joyce Wolf Collection Fig. 225
Lot 316 (illustrated) in 1946 Louis Comfort Tiffany Foundation sale catalogue

152. Louis Comfort Tiffany, Tiffany Furnaces, Inkwell, 1898–1907. Enamel on copper, $1\frac{1}{2}$ x 6 x $11\frac{1}{4}$ in. (3.8 x 15.2 x 28.6 cm). Inscribed on underside: *Louis C. Tiffany / EL 169.* The Charles Hosmer Morse Museum of American Art, Winter Park, Florida (70-016) Fig. 216

153. Louis Comfort Tiffany, Tiffany Furnaces, Pin tray, 1907. Enamel on copper, 2 x 3 in. (5.1 x 7.6 cm). Inscribed on underside: *EL 246 B / m L.C.T.* The Charles Hosmer Morse Museum of American Art, Winter Park, Florida (69-010) Fig. 217

Silver and Other Metalwork

154. Louis Comfort Tiffany, Tiffany Studios, Partial tea service from Laurelton Hall, 1902–4. Silver, silver gilt, ivory, waste bowl: $3\frac{1}{4}$ x $5\frac{3}{8}$ in. (8.3 x 13.7 cm); teapot: $6\frac{1}{4}$ x $7\frac{7}{8}$ x $5\frac{7}{8}$ in. (15.9 x 20 x 14.9 cm); creamer: 4 x $5\frac{1}{8}$ x $4\frac{1}{8}$ in. (10.2 x 13 x 10.5 cm). Marked on underside: *TIFFANY STUDIOS / NEW YORK / STERLING / 925/1000 / 6646.* Los Angeles County Museum of Art, Purchased with funds provided by the Director's Roundtable (M.85.3a–c) Fig. 164
Lot 1079 (illustrated) in 1946 Louis Comfort Tiffany Foundation sale catalogue

155. Louis Comfort Tiffany, Tiffany Studios, Sugar bowl from Laurelton Hall tea service, 1902–4. Silver, silver gilt, $4\frac{7}{8}$ x $6\frac{1}{8}$ in. (12.4 x 15.6 cm). Marked on underside: *TIFFANY STUDIOS / NEW YORK / STERLING / 925/1000 / 6646.* Collection of Eric Streiner Fig. 165

156. Louis Comfort Tiffany, Tiffany Studios, Nine pieces from "Etched Metal and Glass" grapevine-pattern desk set, ca. 1910–20. Favrile glass, bronze, letter opener: H. $9\frac{1}{8}$ in. (23.2 cm); pen tray: $9\frac{3}{16}$ x $2\frac{13}{16}$ in. (23.3 x 7.1 cm); blotter: $1\frac{15}{16}$ x $5\frac{13}{16}$ x 3 in. (4.9 x 14.8 x 7.6 cm); bill holder: H. $7\frac{1}{8}$ in. (18.1 cm); paper rack: $8\frac{5}{8}$ x $12\frac{1}{2}$ x $3\frac{1}{2}$ in. (21.9 x 31.8 x 8.9 cm); stamp box: 4 x $2\frac{3}{16}$ in. (10.2 x 5.6 cm); blotter holders: L. $19\frac{1}{16}$ in. (48.4 cm). The Metropolitan Museum of Art, New York, Gift of Mrs. H. S. Mesick, 1962 (62.233.2, .3, .5, .7, .14, .18a,b, .19a,b). Paper holder: $3\frac{3}{4}$ x $2\frac{3}{8}$ in. (9.5 x 6 cm). The Metropolitan Museum of Art, New York, Gift of Estate of John F. Scharffenberger, 1990 (1990.314.7) Fig. 145

157. Four hanging chains from the Tiffany house. India, ca. 1882. Bronze, $76\frac{3}{4}$ x 5 in. (194.9 x 12.7 cm); $78\frac{3}{4}$ x 3 in. (200 x 7.6 cm); $39\frac{3}{4}$ x 5 in. (101 x 12.7 cm); 52 x 3 in. (132.1 x 7.6 cm). The Charles Hosmer Morse Museum of American Art, Winter Park, Florida (75-008:A; 75-009:B; 75-011; 75-012) Fig. 59

Wood Objects

158. Louis Comfort Tiffany, Tiffany Studios, Covered box, 1905–10. Maple, fruitwood, mother-of-pearl, $5\frac{1}{2}$ x $4\frac{1}{8}$ in. (14 x 10.5 cm). Marked on underside: *TIFFANY STUDIOS / NY / 177.* Collection of Eric Streiner Fig. 239

159. Louis Comfort Tiffany, Tiffany Studios, Covered box, 1905–13. European walnut (?), glass, H. $2\frac{5}{8}$ in. (6.7 cm). Marked on underside: *TIFFANY STUDIOS / NEW YORK.* The Metropolitan Museum of Art, New York, Gift of Louis Comfort Tiffany Foundation, 1951 (51.121.44a,b) Fig. 240

160. Textile printing block. Probably India, probably 19th century. Wood, 19 x $18\frac{1}{4}$ in. (48.3 x 46.4 cm). The Charles Hosmer Morse Museum of American Art, Winter Park, Florida (56-057:2) Fig. 15

161. Textile printing block. Probably India, probably 19th century. Wood, $19\frac{3}{8}$ x $19\frac{3}{8}$ in. (49.2 x 49.2 cm). The Charles Hosmer Morse Museum of American Art, Winter Park, Florida (56-057:11) Fig. 16

162. Textile printing block. Probably India, probably 19th century. Wood, $19\frac{1}{4}$ x $19\frac{1}{4}$ in. (48.9 x 48.9 cm). The Charles Hosmer Morse Museum of American Art, Winter Park, Florida (56-057:10)

163. Textile printing block. Probably India, probably 19th century. Wood, 18 x 17 in. (45.7 x 43.2 cm). The Charles Hosmer Morse Museum of American Art, Winter Park, Florida (56-057:14)

Carpet

164. Louis Comfort Tiffany, Tiffany Studios, Carpet for dining room, Laurelton Hall, after 1913. Wool, $306\frac{1}{4}$ x $103\frac{3}{8}$ in. (777.9 x 262.6 cm). The Charles Hosmer Morse Museum of American Art, Winter Park, Florida (67-012) Fig. 160
Lot 214 (illustrated) in 1946 Louis Comfort Tiffany Foundation sale catalogue

Costume

165. Peacock headdress, ca. 1913. Peacock head and feathers, cloth, metal, sequins, celluloid paillettes, 10 x $6\frac{1}{2}$ x $8\frac{1}{2}$ in. (25.4 x 16.5 x 21.6 cm). Museum of the City of New York, Gift of Julia Tiffany Weld (75.21.1) Fig. 323

Books, Drawings, and Ephemera

166. Louis Comfort Tiffany, *Invitation to a Hearthwarming*, ca. 1886. Sepia print and ink on paper, $2\frac{7}{8}$ x $9\frac{1}{2}$ in. (7.3 x 24.1 cm). The Charles Hosmer Morse Museum of American Art, Winter Park, Florida (67-037) Fig. 319

167. Louis Comfort Tiffany, Dinner menu for Peacock Feast at Laurelton Hall, May 15, 1914. Ink on papercard, 6 x 8 in. (15.2 x 20.3 cm). The Charles Hosmer Morse Museum of American Art, Winter Park, Florida (67-033) Fig. 270

168. Charles de Kay (1848–1935), *The Art Work of Louis Comfort Tiffany*, binding design by Louis Comfort Tiffany, 1914. $12\frac{3}{4}$ x $10\frac{1}{4}$ in. (32.4 x 26 cm). The Charles Hosmer Morse Museum of American Art, Winter Park, Florida (69-017) Fig. 169

169. Design drawing of magnolia blossom on floral capital from loggia, Laurelton Hall, ca. 1900–1915. Watercolor, graphite, and ink on paper, $18\frac{3}{8}$ x 14 in. (46.7 x 35.6 cm). The Metropolitan Museum of Art, New York, Gift of Lenox, Inc. Fig. 77

170. Design drawing of lotus blossom on floral capital from loggia, Laurelton Hall, ca. 1900–1915. Watercolor, graphite, and ink on paper, $18\frac{3}{8}$ x 14 in. (46.7 x 35.6 cm). The Metropolitan Museum of Art, New York, Gift of Lenox, Inc. Fig. 74

171. Design drawing of poppy blossom on floral capital from loggia, Laurelton Hall, ca. 1900–1915. Watercolor, graphite, and ink on paper, $18\frac{3}{8}$ x 14 in. (46.7 x 35.6 cm). The Metropolitan Museum of Art, New York, Gift of Lenox, Inc. Fig. 76

172. Design drawing of peony blossom on floral capital from loggia, Laurelton Hall, ca. 1900–1915. Watercolor, graphite, and ink on paper, $18\frac{3}{8}$ x 14 in. (46.7 x 35.6 cm). The Metropolitan Museum of Art, New York, Gift of Lenox, Inc. Fig. 75

173. Design drawing of flower buds and seedpods on floral capitals from loggia, Laurelton Hall, ca. 1900–1915. Watercolor, graphite, and ink on paper, $18\frac{3}{8}$ x 14 in. (46.7 x 35.6 cm). The Metropolitan Museum of Art, New York, Gift of Lenox, Inc. Fig. 65

174. Guest book of Laurelton Hall, 1916–51. Leather and gold leaf, paper, $8\frac{1}{2}$ x $10\frac{1}{2}$ in. (21.6 x 26.7 cm). The Charles Hosmer Morse Museum of American Art, Winter Park, Florida (1999-022) Fig. 328

175. *Prospectus for The Louis Comfort Tiffany Foundation*, 1920. Bound paper, $9\frac{1}{4}$ x $6\frac{1}{8}$ in. (23.5 x 15.6 cm). The Charles Hosmer Morse Museum of American Art, Winter Park, Florida (1999-083:2)

176. *Catalogue of Oriental and Chinese Rugs*, published by The Louis Comfort Tiffany Foundation, 1920. Bound paper, $8\frac{1}{2}$ x $6\frac{1}{4}$ in. (21.6 x 15.9 cm). The Charles Hosmer Morse Museum of American Art, Winter Park, Florida (77-030:B)

177. *Catalogue of Chinese and Japanese Objects of Art*, published by The Louis Comfort Tiffany Foundation, 1921. Bound paper, $8\frac{1}{2}$ x $6\frac{1}{4}$ in. (21.6 x 15.9 cm). The Charles Hosmer Morse Museum of American Art, Winter Park, Florida (164)

Asian Art

Chinese objects once owned by Louis Comfort Tiffany

178. Fragment of temple carpet. China, Ming (1368–1644) or Qing dynasty (1644–1911), 1600–1650. Wool pile on cotton foundation, $53\frac{1}{8}$ x $41\frac{3}{8}$ in. (135 x 105 cm). Private collection, Ticino, Switzerland Fig. 268
Lot 1043 (illustrated) in 1946 Louis Comfort Tiffany Foundation sale catalogue

179. Pair of lions. China, Qing dynasty (1644–1911), inscribed 1684. Glazed stoneware, H. 66 in (167.6 cm). Private collection, Switzerland Fig. 279
Lot 986 (illustrated) in 1946 Louis Comfort Tiffany Foundation sale catalogue

180. Ornament. China, Qing dynasty (1644–1911), 18th century. Jade, 3 x 3 x ¼ in. (7.6 x 7.6 x 0.6 cm). The Hermitage Foundation Museum and Gardens, Norfolk, Virginia (1946.0022.01)
Lot 929 in 1946 Louis Comfort Tiffany Foundation sale catalogue

181. Ornament. China, Qing dynasty (1644–1911), 18th century. Jade, 2¼ x 2¼ x ¼ in. (5.7 x 5.7 x 0.6 cm). The Hermitage Foundation Museum and Gardens, Norfolk, Virginia (1946.0023.01)
Lot 929 in 1946 Louis Comfort Tiffany Foundation sale catalogue

182. Ornament. China, Qing dynasty (1644–1911), 18th century. Jade, 1¾ x 3 x ¼ in. (4.4 x 7.6 x 0.6 cm). The Hermitage Foundation Museum and Gardens, Norfolk, Virginia (1946.0024.01)
Lot 929 in 1946 Louis Comfort Tiffany Foundation sale catalogue

183. Ornament, with cord. China, Qing dynasty (1644–1911), 18th century. Ornament: jade, silk, 3 x 1¾ x ¼ in. (7.6 x 4.4 x 0.6 cm), Cord: L. 21 in. (53.3 cm). The Hermitage Foundation Museum and Gardens, Norfolk, Virginia (1946.0025.01)
Lot 929 in 1946 Louis Comfort Tiffany Foundation sale catalogue

184. Pair of seals. China, Qing dynasty (1644–1911), 18th century. Soapstone, 12½ x 5 x 5 in. (31.8 x 12.7 x 12.7 cm). The Hermitage Foundation Museum and Gardens, Norfolk, Virginia (1946.0030.01)
Lot 955 in 1946 Louis Comfort Tiffany Foundation sale catalogue

185. Covered document box. China, Qing dynasty (1644–1911), 2nd half of 18th century. *Huang huali* wood, mother-of-pearl, stained ivory, lacquer, soapstone, various hard stones, 4 x 11½ x 18 11/16 in. (10.2 x 29.2 x 47.5 cm). [Old label affixed to underside, inscribed in ink script]: *#5961 - from Tiffany of New York - / Rare walnut Chinese box inlaid with 2/ -precious stones, carved and silver inlaid/ lower edge of box & cover 25075*; [in blue ink, later]: *B-51*; [painted inscription on interior of box]: *Collection / of / Louis Comfort Tiffany / Laurelton Hall.* Tiffany & Company Archives, Parsippany, New Jersey (1999.3) Fig. 290

186. Headdress. China, Qing dynasty (1644–1911), late 19th century. Gilded silver, kingfisher feathers, semiprecious stones, pearls, 9½ x 10½ in. (24.1 x 26.7 cm). The Hermitage Foundation Museum and Gardens, Norfolk, Virginia (1946.0028.01) Fig. 286
Lot 950 (illustrated) in 1946 Louis Comfort Tiffany Foundation sale catalogue

187. Headdress. China, Qing dynasty (1644–1911), late 19th century. Gilded silver, kingfisher feathers, cloth, fiber, 7 x 11½ in. (17.8 x 29.2 cm). The Hermitage Foundation Museum and Gardens, Norfolk, Virginia (1946.0029.01) Fig. 287
Lot 949 (illustrated) in 1946 Louis Comfort Tiffany Foundation sale catalogue

188. Tiara. China, Qing dynasty (1644–1911), late 19th century. Gilded silver, kingfisher feathers, 7 x 5½ x 1 in. (17.8 x 14 x 2.5 cm). The Hermitage Foundation Museum and Gardens, Norfolk, Virginia (1946.0026.01) Fig. 288
Lot 932 in 1946 Louis Comfort Tiffany Foundation sale catalogue

189. Tiara. China, Qing dynasty (1644–1911), late 19th century. Gilded silver, kingfisher feathers, tourmaline, 3¼ x 4 x 1 in. (8.3 x 10.2 x 2.5 cm). The Hermitage Foundation Museum and Gardens, Norfolk, Virginia (1946.0027.01) Fig. 288
Lot 932 in 1946 Louis Comfort Tiffany Foundation sale catalogue

Japanese objects once owned by Louis Comfort Tiffany

190. Katsukawa Shunchō (active 1780–95), *Women in the Bathhouse*. Japan, Edo period (1615–1868), ca. 1785–95. Color woodcut, pillar print, 25¼ x 4¾ in. (64.1 x 12.1 cm). The Hermitage Foundation Museum and Gardens, Norfolk, Virginia (1946.0042.002)
Lot 839 in 1946 Louis Comfort Tiffany Foundation sale catalogue

191. Katsukawa Shunsen (active ca. 1790s–1820s), *Woman Strolling in the Snow*. Japan, Edo period (1615–1868), ca. 1815. Color woodcut, 29¼ x 9¾ in. (74.3 x 24. 8 cm). The Hermitage Foundation Museum and Gardens, Norfolk, Virginia (1946.0042.001)
Lot 839 in 1946 Louis Comfort Tiffany Foundation sale catalogue

192. Set of sword fittings *(koshirae)*. Japan, Edo period (1615–1868), 18th–19th century. Sheath: mother-of-pearl; handle: sharkskin wrapped in silk; and soft-metal fittings, L. 38½ in. (97.8 cm). The Hermitage Foundation Museum and Gardens, Norfolk, Virginia (1946.0018.01)
Lot 759 in 1946 Louis Comfort Tiffany Foundation sale catalogue

Chinese objects that are similar to objects in Tiffany's collection

193. Vase. China, Qing dynasty (1644–1911), Kangxi period (1622–1722). Glazed porcelain, H. 4½ in. (11.4 cm). The Metropolitan Museum of Art, New York, Bequest of Benjamin Altman, 1913 (14.40.32)

194. Musical stone with theme of the "Hundred Antiques." China, Qing dynasty (1644–1911), Qianlong period (1736–95). Jade (nephrite), 13 7/16 x 9 7/16 x 1 15/16 in. (34.1 x 24 x 4.9 cm). The Metropolitan Museum of Art, New York, Gift of Herbert R. Bishop, 1902 (02.18.644)

195. Cup. China, Qing dynasty (1644–1911), 18th century. Rhinoceros horn, 10¼ x 7¾ x 4 in. (26 x 19.7 x 10.2 cm); base: 3½ x 6⅛ in. (8.9 x 15.6 cm). The Metropolitan Museum of Art, New York, Gift of J. Pierpont Morgan, 1908 (08.212.12)

196. Throne. China, Qing dynasty (1644–1911), 18th–19th century. Lacquered wood, 40 x 41½ x 29¼ in. (101.6 x 105.4 x 74.3 cm). The Metropolitan Museum of Art, New York, Bequest of Florence Waterbury, in memory of her father, John I. Waterbury, 1968 (68.149.3)

197. Bottle. China, Qing dynasty (1644–1911), Kangxi period (1662–1722). Glazed porcelain, H. 12½ in. (31.8 cm). The Metropolitan Museum of Art, New York, Bequest of Benjamin Altman, 1913 (14.40.173)

Japanese objects that are similar to objects in Tiffany's collection

198. Armor *(yoroi)*. Japan, Late Kamakura period, early 14th century. Lacquered iron and leather, silk, stenciled leather, gilt copper, 37½ x 22 in. (95.3 x 55.9 cm); helmet: 6 1/16 x 11 1/16 in. (15.4 x 28.1 cm). The Metropolitan Museum of Art, New York, Gift of Bashford Dean, 1914 (14.100.121)

199. Sanyū (1685–1739), Tea bowl. Japan, Edo period (1615–1868), ca. 1730. Clay with black glaze, 3⅜ x 4 in. (8.6 x 10.2 cm). The Metropolitan Museum of Art, New York, Rogers Fund, 1917 (17.118.67)

200. Gourd-shaped sake bottle with design of the Tokugawa Family Crest "Aoi," Cherry Blossoms, Cords, and Net. Japan, Edo period (1615–1868), 18th century. Black lacquer with gold *maki-e* and silver *togidashi;* silk cord, 12 x 7 in. (30.5 x 17.8 cm). The Florence and Herbert Irving Collection (L.2003.32a–c)

201. Inrō with design of Crab in Basket. Reverse: Crab in Bamboo Leaves. Japan, Edo period (1615–1868), 19th century. Lacquer with gold, ceramic, pewter and mother-of-pearl inlay, 3⅜ x 2 11/16 x 15/16 in. (8.5 x 6.8 x 2.4 cm). The Metropolitan Museum of Art, New York, H. O. Havemeyer Collection, Bequest of Mrs. H. O. Havemeyer, 1929 (29.100.738)

202. Inrō with design of Dragonflies. Japan, Edo period (1615–1868), 18th–19th century. Lacquer, *fundame*, gold, brown and red *hiramakie*, *takamakie*,

ceramic inlay; interior: *roiro* and *fundame*, 2 15/16 x 2 5/16 x 1 in. (7.4 x 5.9 x 2.5 cm). The Metropolitan Museum of Art, New York, H. O. Havemeyer Collection, Bequest of Mrs. H. O. Havemeyer, 1929 (29.100.904)

203. Writing box with design of Warbler in Plum Tree. Japan, Edo period (1615–1868), 18th century. Gold and silver *maki-e* on black lacquer, 2 3/8 x 9 3/8 x 10 1/4 in. (6 x 23.8 x 26 cm). The Metropolitan Museum of Art, New York, H. O. Havemeyer Collection, Bequest of Mrs. H. O. Havemeyer, 1929 (29.100.904)

204. Attributed to Tosa Mitsumachi (active 1525–59), inscribed by Ogata Korin (1658–1716), *Red and White Poppies*. Japan, Momoyama period (1573–1615) or Edo period (1615–1868), 17th century. Six-panel folding screen; ink, color, and gold on gilded paper, 65 3/4 x 147 1/2 in. (167.0 x 374.7 cm). The Metropolitan Museum of Art, New York, H. O. Havemeyer Collection, Gift of Mrs. Dunbar W. Bostwick, John C. Wilmerding, J. Watson Webb Jr., Harry H. Webb, and Samuel B. Webb, 1962 (62.36.1)

205. Tea caddy. Japan, Edo period (1615–1868), 18th century. Gray clay covered with a thin red-brown glaze, streaked with golden yellow (Seto ware), H. 3 1/2 in. (8.9 cm). The Metropolitan Museum of Art, New York, Edward C. Moore Collection, Bequest of Edward C. Moore, 1891 (91.1.151)

206. Tea caddy. Japan, Edo period (1615–1868), 18th century. Brown clay covered with brown and yellow glaze burnt away on one side (Seto ware), 2 5/8 x 3 3/8 in. (6.7 x 8.6 cm). The Metropolitan Museum of Art, New York, Edward C. Moore Collection, Bequest of Edward C. Moore, 1891 (91.1.336)

207. Tobacco pouch and pipe. Japan, Edo period (1615–1868), 18th century. Pouch with design of Cupid and flowers, Dutch embossed leather with silver foil, and color; clasp of design of a monk writing at a desk, gold, *shakudō*, and *shibuichi;* ojime in a shape of *Jurōjin*, gold; netsuke: pear framed with waves, freshwater pearl and gold; pipe with floral scrolling design, metal; pipe case with design of flowers, Dutch embossed leather with gold and silver foils, and color, pouch: H. 4 x 5 1/4 in (10.2 x 13.3 cm); pipe case: L. 9 in (22.9 cm). The Metropolitan Museum of Art, New York, Bequest of Benjamin Altman, 1913 (14.40.843a,b)

208. Four sword guards *(tsuba)*. Japan, Edo period (1615–1868), probably 19th century. Iron plate with gilt and soft-metal inlays, upper left: 2 3/4 x 2 1/2 x 5/16 in. (7 x 6.4 x 0.8 cm); upper right: 2 5/8 x 2 1/2 x 3/16 in. (6.7 x 6.4 x 0.5 cm); lower left: 2 3/4 x 2 1/2 x 5/16 in. (7 x 6.4 x 0.8 cm); lower right: 3 x 2 3/4 x 3/16 in. (7.6 x 7 x 0.5 cm). The Charles Hosmer Morse Museum of American Art, Winter Park, Florida (71-017:B; 71-017:C; 71-017:D; 71-017:A) Fig. 274

209. Style of Ogawa Haritsu, or Ritsuō (1663–1747), Panel with design of flatfish. Japan, Edo period (1615–1868), 1890s. Lacquer, mother-of-pearl, bone, and pottery on wood, 14 3/4 x 10 3/4 in. (37.5 x 27.3 cm). The Metropolitan Museum of Art, New York, The Howard Mansfield Collection, Purchase, Rogers Fund, 1936 (36.100.151) Fig. 271

Native American Art

Native American objects owned by Louis Comfort Tiffany

210. Miniature baby carrier with doll. Plateau, United States, probably Nez Perce, late 19th or early 20th century. Linen, wool, glass beads, wood, leather, human hair, 28 x 6 1/2 x 5 in. (71.1 x 16.5 x 12.7 cm). Collections of Shelburne Museum, Shelburne, Vermont (20.3-162)
Lot 513 (illustrated) in 1946 Louis Comfort Tiffany Foundation sale catalogue

211. Miniature baby carrier with doll. Plateau, United States, probably Yakima or Cascade, late 19th or early 20th century. Linen, wool, glass beads, wood, leather, human hair, 15 5/8 x 4 1/4 x 2 3/4 in. (39.7 x 10.8 x 7 cm). Collections of Shelburne Museum, Shelburne, Vermont (20-3-164)
Lot 532 in 1946 Louis Comfort Tiffany Foundation sale catalogue

212. Grain bag. Plateau, United States, Wasco or Wishram, late 19th or early 20th century. Rush (probably sedge), cornhusk, other plant fibers, 12 1/2 x 12 in. (31.8 x 30.5 cm) Collections of Shelburne Museum, Shelburne, Vermont (46.10-13)
Lot 498 in 1946 Louis Comfort Tiffany Foundation sale catalogue

213. Grain bag. Plateau, United States, Wasco or Wishram, late 19th or early 20th century. Rush (probably sedge), cornhusk, other plant fibers, leather, 13 1/2 x 10 in. (34.3 x 25.4 cm). Collections of Shelburne Museum, Shelburne, Vermont (46.10-14)
Lot 498 (illustrated) in 1946 Louis Comfort Tiffany Foundation sale catalogue

214. Woven bag. Columbia River, Washington, Nez Perce, late 19th or early 20th century. Grass, wool, 21 7/8 x 13 9/16 in. (55.5 x 34.5 cm). Brooklyn Museum, Charles Stewart Smith Memorial Fund (46.193.3) Fig. 309

215. Imbricated basket. Plateau, United States, Klikitat, late 19th or early 20th century. Cedar root, bear grass, horsetail root dye, rawhide, 15 x 15 x 15 in. (38.1 x 38.1 x 38.1 cm). Brooklyn Museum, Charles Stewart Smith Memorial Fund (46.193.1) Fig. 311

216. Cylindrical basket with bold zigzag patterns. Plateau, United States, Wasco or Klikitat, late 19th or early 20th century. Indian hemp, dogbane, cattail, dye from berry juices, 14 15/16 x 9 7/16 x 9 7/16 in. (37.9 x 24 x 24 cm). Brooklyn Museum, Charles Stewart Smith Memorial Fund (46.193.2) Fig. 312
Probably lot 433 in 1946 Louis Comfort Tiffany Foundation sale catalogue

217. Globular basket with star patterns. Columbia River, Washington, Wasco, late 19th or early 20th century. Corn husks, wool, 4 5/16 x 7 1/16 x 7 1/16 in. (11 x 17.9 x 17.9 cm). Brooklyn Museum, Charles Stewart Smith Memorial Fund (46.193.4) Fig. 310

218. Imbricated basket with stepped patterns. Unknown Native American artist, early 20th century. Cedar fibers, spruce root, grass, bleach, 11 1/2 x 12 x 10 15/16 in. (29.2 x 30.5 x 27.8 cm). Brooklyn Museum, Charles Stewart Smith Memorial Fund (46.193.5) Fig. 307

219. Imbricated basket with geometric figures. Northwest Coast, Washington, Klikitat, early 20th century. Cedar root, grass, dye, 11 1/2 x 8 1/2 x 9 in. (29.2 x 21.6 x 22.9 cm). Brooklyn Museum, Charles Stewart Smith Memorial Fund (46.193.6) Fig. 313

220. Basket. Northwest Coast, Washington, Skokomish, Coast Salish, late 19th or early 20th century. Bark, grass, 10 1/4 x 10 5/8 x 10 5/8 in. (26 x 27 x 27 cm). Brooklyn Museum, Charles Stewart Smith Memorial Fund (46.193.7) Fig. 308

221. Imbricated basket. Plateau, United States, Salish or Klikitat, late 19th or early 20th century. Plant fibers, 16 x 14 1/2 in. (40.6 x 36.8 cm). Collections of Shelburne Museum, Shelburne, Vermont (46.10-1)
Lot 365 in 1946 Louis Comfort Tiffany Foundation sale catalogue

222. Imbricated basket. Plateau, United States, probably Klikitat, late 19th or early 20th century. Cedar root, other plant fibers, 8 x 14 in. (20.3 x 35.6 cm). Collections of Shelburne Museum, Shelburne, Vermont (46.10-7)
Lot 467 in 1946 Louis Comfort Tiffany Foundation sale catalogue

223. Imbricated basket. Plateau, United States, probably Klikitat, late 19th or early 20th century. Plant fibers, 9 1/4 x 8 in. (23.5 x 20.3 cm). Lot tag: *464/3*. Collections of Shelburne Museum, Shelburne, Vermont (46.10-10)
Lot 464 in 1946 Louis Comfort Tiffany Foundation sale catalogue

224. Basket with cover. Northwest Coast, probably Tlingit, late 19th or early 20th century. Spruce root, other plant fibers, 7 x 6 in. (17.8 x 15.2 cm). Collections of Shelburne Museum, Shelburne, Vermont (46.10-12)
Lot 389 in 1946 Louis Comfort Tiffany Foundation sale catalogue

225. Imbricated basket. Plateau, United States, probably Klikitat, late 19th or early 20th century. Plant fibers, 8½ x 3 x 9 in. (21.6 x 7.6 x 22.9 cm). Lot tag: *465/3*. Collections of Shelburne Museum, Shelburne, Vermont (46.10-16)
Lot 465 in 1946 Louis Comfort Tiffany Foundation sale catalogue

226. Basket with imbrication. Plateau, United States, probably Klikitat, late 19th or early 20th century. Plant fibers, 4 x 7 in. (10.2 x 17.8 cm). Collections of Shelburne Museum, Shelburne, Vermont (46.10-20)
Lot 465 or 464 in 1946 Louis Comfort Tiffany Foundation sale catalogue

227. Imbricated basket cradle. Unknown Native American artist, late 19th or early 20th century. Plant fibers, 8 x 16 x 25¾ in. (20.3 x 40.6 x 65.4 cm). Collections of Shelburne Museum, Shelburne, Vermont (46.10-15)
Lot 485 in 1946 Louis Comfort Tiffany Foundation sale catalogue

228. Imbricated basket washtub. Unknown Native American artist, late 19th or early 20th century. Plant fibers, 15 x 20⁷⁄₁₆ x 35½ in. (38.1 x 51.9 x 90.2 cm). Collections of Shelburne Museum, Shelburne, Vermont (46.10-19)
Lot 409 in 1946 Louis Comfort Tiffany Foundation sale catalogue

229. Bowl. Probably Columbia River, Washington/Oregon border, Wasco or Wishram, 1800–1840. Bighorn-sheep horn, 5 x 6¼ x 7½ in. (12.7 x 15.9 x 19.1 cm). National Museum of the American Indian, Smithsonian Institution, Washington, D.C. (20/9391)   Fig. 305
Lot 375 in 1946 Louis Comfort Tiffany Foundation sale catalogue

230. Bowl. Probably Columbia River, Washington/Oregon border, Wasco or Wishram, 1825–60. Bighorn-sheep horn, 5 x 8 x 9 in. (12.7 x 20.3 x 22.9 cm). National Museum of the American Indian, Smithsonian Institution, Washington, D.C. (20/9390)   Fig. 306
Lot 375 in 1946 Louis Comfort Tiffany Foundation sale catalogue

231. Beaded dress. Plateau, Washington, Yakima, late 19th century. Buckskin, glass beads, metal coins, 46 x 45½ in. (116.8 x 115.6 cm). Brooklyn Museum,

Museum Collection Fund (46.181)   Fig. 314
Lot 503 (illustrated) in 1946 Louis Comfort Tiffany Foundation sale catalogue

232. Beaded dress. Plateau, United States, probably Yakima, ca. 1875. Mountain-sheep hide, glass pony beads, sinew, L. 52 in. (132.1 cm). Collection of Ken and Judy Siebel
Lot 505 in 1946 Louis Comfort Tiffany Foundation sale catalogue

233. Saddlebag. Probably Oregon or Washington, Plateau tribe, ca. 1900. Elkhide, wool cloth, glass beads, 1 x 13½ x 117½ in. (2.5 x 34.3 x 298.5 cm) (with fringe). National Museum of the American Indian, Smithsonian Institution, Washington, D.C. (20/9382)
Lot 518 in 1946 Louis Comfort Tiffany Foundation sale catalogue

Native American objects that are similar to objects in Tiffany's collection

234. Mush bowl. California, Pomo. Plant fiber, wood, 14⁹⁄₁₆ x 16⁹⁄₁₆ in. (37 x 42 cm). American Museum of Natural History, New York (50/767)

235. Dagger. Southeastern Alaska, Tlingit, 1850–60. Wood, steel, abalone-shell inlay, ivory, Native-tanned skin, 14¾ x 2¾ in. (37.5 x 7 cm). The Metropolitan Museum of Art, New York, Gift of Ralph T. Coe, 2002 (2002.602.4)

236. Female doll. Northern Montana or Alberta, Blackfoot, late 19th century. Native-tanned skin, glass beads, hair, wool trade cloth, commercial leather, metal, 10¼ x 6¾ in. (26 x 17.1 cm). Ralph T. Coe Collection

237. Kayak model with hunter. Aleutian or Pribilof Islands, Alaska, Aleut, 1840–50. Gutskin, fur, painted wood, sinew, 4 x 12 x 2 in. (10.2 x 30.5 x 5.1 cm). Ralph T. Coe Collection

238. Sheath. British Columbia, Tahltan, 1850–60. Wool and cotton trade cloth, glass, metal beads, 26½ x 3⅛ in. (66 x 7.9 cm). The Metropolitan Museum of Art, New York, Gift of Ralph T. Coe, 2002 (2002.602.5)

Index

Photograph Credits